Toni Morrison

D0219672

Toni Morrison's visionary explorations of freedom and identity, self and community, against the backdrop of African American history, have established her as one of the foremost novelists of her time; an artist whose seriousness of purpose and imaginative power have earned her both widespread critical acclaim and great popular success.

This guide to Morrison's work offers:

- an accessible introduction to Morrison's life and historical contexts
- a guide to her key works and the themes and concerns that run through them
- an overview of critical texts and perspectives on each of Morrison's works
- cross-references between sections of the guide, in order to suggest links between texts, contexts and criticism
- a chronology of Morrison's life and works.

Part of the *Routledge Guides to Literature* series, this volume is essential reading for all those beginning detailed study of Toni Morrison and seeking a guide to her work and a way into the wealth of contextual and critical material that surrounds it.

Pelagia Goulimari is Convenor of the M.St. in Women's Studies, and Lecturer in English at Wadham College, University of Oxford.

Routledge Guides To Literature

Editorial Advisory Board: Richard Bradford (University of Ulster at Coleraine), Shirley Chew (University of Leeds), Mick Gidley (University of Leeds), Jan Jędrzejewski (University of Ulster at Coleraine), Ed Larrissy (University of Leeds), Duncan Wu (St Catherine's College, University of Oxford)

Routledge Guides to Literature offer clear introductions to the most widely studied authors and texts. Each book engages with texts, contexts and criticism, highlighting the range of critical views and contextual factors that need to be taken into consideration in advanced studies of literary works. The series encourages informed but independent readings of texts by ranging as widely as possible across the contextual and critical issues relevant to the works examined, rather than presenting a single interpretation. Alongside general guides to texts and authors, the series includes "Sourcebooks", which allow access to reprinted contextual and critical materials as well as annotated extracts of primary text.

Already available:*

Geoffrey Chaucer by Gillian Rudd
Ben Jonson by James Loxley
William Shakespeare's The Merchant of Venice: A Sourcebook edited by S. P. Cerasano
William Shakespeare's King Lear: A Sourcebook edited by Grace Ioppolo
William Shakespeare's Othello: A Sourcebook edited by Andrew Hadfield
William Shakespeare's Macbeth: A Sourcebook edited by Alexander Leggatt
William Shakespeare's Hamlet: A Sourcebook edited by Sean McEvoy
William Shakespeare's Twelfth Night: A Sourcebook edited by Sonia Massai
John Milton by Richard Bradford
John Milton's Paradise Lost: A Sourcebook edited by Margaret Kean
Alexander Pope by Paul Baines
Jonathan Swift's Gulliver's Travels: A Sourcebook edited by Roger D. Lund
Mary Wollstonecraft's A Vindication of the Rights of Woman: A Sourcebook edited by Adriana Craciun
Jane Austen by Robert P. Irvine
Jane Austen's Emma: A Sourcebook edited by Paula Byrne
Jane Austen's Pride and Prejudice: A Sourcebook edited by Robert Morrison
Byron by Caroline Franklin
Mary Shelley's Frankenstein: A Sourcebook edited by Timothy Morton
The Poems of John Keats: A Sourcebook edited by John Strachan
The Poems of Gerard Manley Hopkins: A Sourcebook edited by Alice Jenkins
Charles Dickens's David Copperfield: A Sourcebook edited by Richard J. Dunn
Charles Dickens's Bleak House: A Sourcebook edited by Janice M. Allan

* Some titles in this series were first published in the Routledge Literary Sourcebooks series, edited by Duncan Wu, or the Complete Critical Guide to Literature series, edited by Jan Jędrzejewski and Richard Bradford.

Toni Morrison

Pelagia Goulimari

Routledge
Taylor & Francis Group

LONDON AND NEW YORK

First published 2011
by Routledge
2 Park Square, Milton Park, Abingdon, Oxon OX14 4RN

Simultaneously published in the USA and Canada
by Routledge
711 Third Avenue, New York, NY 10017

Routledge is an imprint of the Taylor & Francis Group, an informa business

British Library Cataloguing in Publication Data
A catalogue record for this book is available from the British Library

Library of Congress Cataloging in Publication Data
Goulimari, Pelagia.
  Toni Morrison / Pelagia Goulimari. – 1st ed.
    p. cm. – (Routledge guides to literature)
  Includes bibliographical references and index.
  1. Morrison, Toni – Criticism and interpretation. I. Title.
  PS3563.O8749Z654 2011
  813'.54 – dc22
                  2010052481

ISBN: 978-0-415-42073-0 (hbk)
ISBN: 978-0-415-42074-7 (pbk)
ISBN: 978-0-203-81324-9 (ebk)

Typeset in Perpetua
by Taylor & Francis Books

MIX
Paper from
responsible sources
FSC
www.fsc.org
FSC® C004839

Printed and bound in Great Britain by
TJ International Ltd, Padstow, Cornwall

For Roula and Fotis

Contents

2: Work   29

3: Criticism   157

Acknowledgements

I am very grateful to Gerard Greenway for his editorial work in the final stages of this book. Many thanks to Jan Jędrzejewski and Routledge's anonymous readers for their suggestions. At Routledge, my thanks to my commissioning editor, Polly Dodson, for her tremendous support and to Emma Nugent for all her work; my thanks also to Anna Callander in Production and my copy-editor, Paula Clarke. Thank you to Sue Usher, Librarian of the English Faculty Library at Oxford University.

How to use this book

This book will guide the reader through Toni Morrison's major texts and selected secondary criticism. Part 1, "Life and contexts", will introduce Morrison's life in its relation to African American history and culture, providing the literary, intellectual and political contexts immediately relevant to the elucidation of Morrison's texts. Part 2, "Work", is intended primarily to enhance the reader's understanding of the novels, and a basic familiarity with them is assumed. "Work" will discuss each one of the novels in separate sections and in chronological order; its last section will also cover a selection of Morrison's nonfiction. Part 3, "Criticism", is intended primarily to help the reader develop an argument and write an essay on Morrison, by providing them with frameworks and building blocks for their essay. It introduces selected criticism on each one of the novels and on Morrison's selected nonfiction in separate sections, grouping the material into theoretical/critical movements. Effort has been made to discuss a wide selection of critical texts, especially those in need of elucidation, and to explain difficult concepts and arguments clearly. Cross-references connecting the book's sections are in bold.

Introduction

Toni Morrison is one of the cultural icons of the contemporary world. She has defined our times, as Jean-Paul Sartre and Simone de Beauvoir defined the mid-twentieth century or as Euripides defined the second half of the fifth century BC. We have made Morrison a cultural icon, and future generations will use this collective act to understand us.

Morrison, a self-identified "black woman writer", has written in a variety of forms, but has made her outstanding contribution as a novelist. A thinker and a public intellectual, she has done most of her thinking and "theorizing" in her nine novels to date, to paraphrase Barbara Christian (Christian 1988, 2257). Morrison's international impact since the 1970s seems a contradiction in terms: she is "at once difficult and popular" (Gates 1993, x). Gates adds that Morrison has "a large and cosmopolitan readership of women" (x); but let us not forget Marlon Brando and Barack Obama among her enthusiastic male readers. Morrison has won numerous prestigious awards, including the 1993 Nobel Prize for Literature, but is also familiar to the audience of *The Oprah Show*, who bought millions of copies of her novels through "Oprah's Book Club".

Morrison's storytelling both thrills the casual reader and taxes the student and professional literary critic. Her novels, as Horace would say, both delight and instruct. She would hasten to add that she instructs by posing new questions. Morrison is good to think with but, in return, invites her serious reader on a long process of cross-cultural apprenticeship. Her work is intertextual – it interrogates a broad spectrum of discourses: Ancient Greek tragedy; West African cosmological ideas; the Bible; the Western canon; canonical literature in English, especially modernism; dominant cultural stereotypes; African American oral traditions; the African American written literary tradition; African American history; contemporary theory and criticism; contemporary aesthetics and politics, etc.

This openness and multiplicity of intertextual reference stems from Morrison's multicultural education – as well as her commitment to pluralism, multiperspectivism and an active role for the reader. She is paradoxically a figure of authority who questions authority, including her own. In response to her multifaceted texts, Morrison criticism is notable for its heterogeneity: a gathering of African Americanists, Africanists and classicists; feminists, psychoanalytic critics, deconstructionists, postcolonial critics, Marxists. Morrison has written about, for and to African American women, while also bringing about a "remarkable universalizing of the African-American experience" (Said 1993, 405).

1

Life and contexts

Introduction

This section will introduce the reader to Morrison's life, within the larger historical situation in which she found herself growing up as a working-class African American woman. While the lives of the privileged few might support the illusion that we are makers of our own life, "the best art is political" (Morrison 1984a, 345), in the sense that it investigates the reciprocal determination of the individual and larger social, political and historical forces. Morrison has always acknowledged the weight of the world on individual lives – the province of "naturalism" in literature – while also affirming personal responsibility, the effectiveness of social critique and the power of the imagination. In her nonfictional writings she has always situated her own life in the context of African American history, and her engagement with aspects of this history in all of her writings, often controversially and with revisionist intent, is a major feature of her work. A full outline of African American history is beyond the scope of this book; this section will sketch out topics and debates in African American history relevant to elucidating Morrison's work, including political and aesthetic movements. It will interweave this historical narrative and the narrative of Morrison's life.

Slavery (1619–1863)

For many historians African American history begins with slavery, in its modern form. The use of West African slaves in large-scale agricultural production in European colonies in the Americas – from Latin America to the West Indies to North America – began in 1517 and "[b]y 1540 the annual importation of African slaves into the

West Indies was estimated at 10,000" (Franklin and Moss 2000, 40). However, the first 20 Africans who landed in Jamestown, Virginia, in 1619 were not yet legally slaves; the statutory recognition of slavery in Virginia took place in 1661. Following the War of Independence (1775–83), the American republic was founded both on the idea of freedom and on slave labour, a contradiction Morrison explores in "Unspeakable Things Unspoken", *Playing in the Dark* and *A Mercy*. It was to be more than two hundred years after Virginia's institutionalization of slavery, in 1865, that the Thirteenth Amendment abolished slavery in the United States, following the end of the Civil War. Commentators call it the American Holocaust.

Both poor Europeans, as indentured servants, and Native Americans were also enslaved, until the African was adopted as the most viable and profitable. Native Americans' deracination by white settlers and vulnerability to European diseases, combined with attempts to enslave them, devastated whole populations. European indentured servants could escape and hide themselves among the free population, something that escaped Africans could not do. It was Africans in Africa who captured the people to be exported as slaves, receiving guns in exchange. Africans competed for control of the trade in capturing; just as there was European competition for control of the trade in transporting to and selling in the colonies.

Whilst a racist science developed that defined Africans as sharing a uniform and unchanging inferior character or essence that legitimated their enslavement in the eyes of some Westerners, contemporary historians stress that "Africans were ethnically, linguistically, religiously, and culturally varied peoples" (Horton and Horton 2001, 14), whose social organizations ranged from small tribes to large kingdoms. Diverse West African cultures mixed with each other and with European cultures to form the first African Americans; this is why Paul Gilroy, in *The Black Atlantic* (1993), argues that African Americans are modern in an exemplary way. Without denying this diversity, Morrison has singled out aspects of West African "collectivism" or "communitarianism" that she considers especially valuable:

- The "ancestor" is shared by the group and binds it together (Morrison 1984a). Ancestors may return as fully embodied living beings, a reanimation which does not recognize the dualism of body and soul.
- "Griots" or storytellers have an important communal role. Continuities between African and African American folktales point to the survival of griots among slaves and the griots' changing role: to preserve and transform their ancestral oral culture in the service of the slaves' survival and cultural resistance. Morrison has

consistently presented herself as a latter-day griot (Morrison 1981b, 120; Morrison 1984a, 344–45).

The transportation of slaves from West African ports across the Atlantic was known as the Middle Passage. Appalling overcrowding, poor hygiene and nutrition, and contagious diseases resulted in massive loss of life: historians estimate that between 33 per cent and 50 per cent of slaves died during the Middle Passage. The male slaves were chained together in the hold for six to eight weeks. Equiano wrote in his slave narrative, *The Interesting Narrative of the Life of Olaudah Equiano, or Gustavus Vassa, the African* (1789): "each had scarcely room to turn himself" (41). Female slaves and their children were usually unchained and above deck, largely in order to make the women sexually available to the crew, it has been speculated. Morrison's *Beloved* opens with the dedication "Sixty Million and more", referring to those who died *before* setting foot in the New World. Morrison remarked: "The smallest number I got from anybody was 60 million" (Morrison 1989b, 257).

Franklin and Moss (2000) stress that slaves resisted at every stage and by a variety of means. During transportation they jumped into the sea, and there were slave mutinies such as the mutiny aboard the *Amistad* in 1838. Once in the New World, groups of escaped slaves – or Maroons – would establish their own communities in inaccessible locations such as mountains and swamps. In "Rediscovering Black History", Morrison (1974a) stunned readers of the *New York Times* with graphic descriptions of the tortures invented to discipline slaves.

The Declaration of Independence (1776), while endorsing "unalienable Rights" for all, did not abolish slavery. Indeed the new American republic was extraordinarily resistant to abolition. In spite of anti-slavery voices, the Constitutional Convention of 1787 and the resulting federal Constitution entrenched the legality of slavery. The Haitian uprising of 1791, led by Toussaint Louverture, contributed to the prohibition of the slave trade first in England and then in America in 1807, but the prohibition was unenforced in America. Instead, the Haitian uprising led, in 1793, to the first American Fugitive Slave Law to facilitate the recapture of runaway slaves. It took the Civil War (1861–65) – after Lincoln's election on an anti-slavery platform – to bring an end to slavery. The Industrial Revolution had turned cotton into the pre-eminent textile material and led to a huge inflation in the number of slaves in the new cotton plantations of the South West, the "cotton kingdom", in the early nineteenth century. At the last census before the Civil War there were 3,953,760 slaves.

After the War of Independence, anti-slavery societies had emerged; the Northern states were abolishing slavery and becoming interested in black education; and independent black churches nurtured political and oratorical skills and provided an experience of autonomy and self-determination. Equiano's influential book was followed by a wave of slave narratives published between 1800 and 1850, demonstrating slave literacy (still illegal at this time) and, obviously, delivering a resonantly abolitionist message. The genre initiated the African American written literary tradition, to which Morrison has paid tribute: "I read slave narratives for sustenance" (Morrison 1976a, 29).

Militant abolitionism, both black and white, grew after the 1830s. The two leading black abolitionists were Frederick Douglass – runaway slave, author of *Narrative of the Life of Frederick Douglass, an American Slave Written by Himself* (Douglass 1845), orator, newspaper editor and journalist – and Sojourner Truth. She had been freed in 1827 when slavery was abolished in the state of New York; she was a preacher, abolitionist and advocate of women's suffrage, and dictated *Narrative of Sojourner Truth, A Northern Slave* (Truth 1850).

As slavery was being abolished in the Northern states, the organization known as the Underground Railroad developed as a very extensive network of both blacks and whites helping Southern runaway slaves to hide in the North or to escape to Canada. Legendary for her contribution to the Underground Railroad was Harriet Tubman. After the Fugitive Law of 1850 enabled the capture of Southern runaway slaves in the North, resistance became more fierce. Frederick Douglass declared that the streets "would be running red with blood" before the law was enforced in Boston (quoted in Turner-Sadler 2006, 152). Posters urged the black community to watch out for slave catchers, and runaway slaves were sometimes rescued even after capture by the authorities.

From Reconstruction to the Harlem Renaissance (1863–1930)

Reconstruction was initiated by Lincoln's 1863 Proclamation of Amnesty and Reconstruction. Morrison, in interviews, has told the story of an ancestor who was a young child at the time of the Proclamation. When the adults told him that the Emancipation Proclamation was coming, he hid under the bed. This amusing anecdote in fact gives us insight into the apprehensiveness of the time: it tells us that the antebellum period was not a time of rejoicing, but anxious and potentially life-threatening, for freed slaves. The Proclamation promised to be the true American Revolution and to give at least male African Americans full citizenship: the right to vote and stand for political office, access to education, economic opportunity. For a brief period, African American men were both voting and taking part in government in the South, but soon political emancipation was in reverse. W.E.B. Du Bois famously stated: "The slave went free; stood a brief moment in the sun; then moved back again toward slavery" (quoted in Franklin and Moss 2000, 288). The Compromise of 1877 between Republicans and Democrats formally ended Reconstruction; by the end of the nineteenth century it had been overthrown.

After the Civil War, numerous white-supremacist organizations, most infamously the Ku Klux Klan, emerged in the South. In response to the enfranchisement of black men, such organizations used terror in order to stop them from exercising their new rights. Gradually, effective disenfranchisement was legislated, mainly through property and educational requirements that the great majority of African Americans didn't meet. From the 1870s laws for racial segregation and against intermarriage were passed in the South, including the first "Jim Crow" or segregation law of 1875. In 1896 the Supreme Court upheld segregation in the infamous *Plessy v. Ferguson.*

From the late 1870s a black exodus began from the rural South to the urban North and to the West. Migrants West were called "Exodusters". Migration to Kansas was especially intense in 1879 and 1880 with the Governor of Kansas promising help and justice to 15,000 "poor people, dressed in patched, tattered clothes" (Horton and Horton 2001, 195). Many all-black towns were founded, but most of them failed to thrive.

After Reconstruction African Americans focused their energies on education. They were supported by churches and Northern industrialists' private philanthropic foundations, whose aim was the creation of a skilled workforce. However, educational funds were mainly spent on whites. The heated African American debate as to the nature and aims of black education crystallized in the antagonistic views of Du Bois and Booker T. Washington. Washington advocated vocational training rather than higher education for African Americans, in the context of the rural economy of the South. Du Bois saw these views as accommodationist, as too accepting of the inferior place of African Americans in American society. In *The Souls of Black Folk* (1903), particularly in "The Talented Tenth", he argued for liberal black education rather than mere money-making education; he also espoused political activism. Washington considered Du Bois's views elitist.

In the late nineteenth century, the African American written literary tradition initiated by the genre of slave narratives was consolidated, with novels such as Frances E.W. Harper's *Iola Leroy, or, Shadows*

Uplifted (1892). Hazel Carby and other critics have argued that Harper and other African American women writers of the 1890s are important predecessors for Morrison and her contemporary black women writers.

In 1905, the African American "Niagara Movement" was launched at the Niagara Conference, held near the Falls, in Canada. Led by Du Bois, it proposed radical reform, including black male suffrage. In 1910, the National Association for the Advancement of Colored People (NAACP) was founded. Initiated by whites, it included the radicals of the Niagara Movement. Such political activity addressed continuing discrimination and violence against blacks, both in the South and in the North. In the industrial North, white and black workers were played against each other by industrialists, and labour organizations didn't welcome black members. Between 1900 and the beginning of World War I there were more than 1,000 lynchings; white race riots occurred in both South and North. From 1912 onwards, laws for segregation of residence in cities were passed; these resulted in black slums.

During World War I (1914–18), the American army fought for freedom, while discriminating against its black soldiers. However, Horton and Horton (2001) argue that black soldiers were treated well by Europeans and had their first experience of racial equality in Europe. It was all the more difficult for black war veterans to return home in the midst of continuing discrimination and segregation and increasing racist violence.

During the War, due partly to employment opportunities in the Northern munitions factories, black migration North greatly intensified. The African American Great Migration North, understood narrowly, refers to the decade 1910–20. The Great Migration was not unopposed. On 2 July 1917, white riots erupted in East St. Louis, Illinois, because a factory working on government contracts was employing African Americans. Forty African Americans were killed and 6,000 African Americans were forced to leave their homes. In response the NAACP organized the Silent Protest in New York on 28 July 1917. Eight thousand African Americans of all ages marched silently on Fifth Avenue to the beat of muffled drums. The end of war and the return home of black veterans only intensified white race rioting. Historians have called the summer of 1919 "the Red Summer": there were 26 white riots against blacks, with blacks fighting back.

In the course of World War I a new black leader emerged: Marcus Garvey. A Jamaican, he set up the Universal Negro Improvement Association (UNIA) in Jamaica in 1914 and in America from 1916 onwards. Garvey was working class and dark skinned in the context of Jamaica's strict colour hierarchy, and his message was black pride. He was very popular, especially among poor blacks, who felt that the NAACP, led by the light-skinned and highly educated Du Bois, was elitist. In 1920, Garvey organized a parade of 50,000 African Americans through Harlem, followed by a convention in Madison Square Garden attended by 25,000. Garvey's populist message of black pride was an influence on the high-brow Harlem Renaissance.

The period after World War I is known as the Jazz Age, because of the defining role of jazz music – an African American art form. This is also the time of the Harlem Renaissance, otherwise known as the Black Renaissance or the Negro Movement (post-war to circa 1930). Prominent in the Harlem Renaissance are Du Bois (who now moves to New York), the philosopher Alain Locke, the writers James Weldon Johnson (perhaps the central figure), Jean Toomer, Countee Cullen, Langston Hughes, and the Jamaican Claude McKay; also the late-comer, Zora Neale Hurston, a writer and anthropologist trained at Columbia University, who collected folklore and, atypically, embraced rural black folk culture. Their milieu was that of a glamorous cosmopolitan elite – an elite satirized by Zora Neale Hurston as "the glitterati". Their leading hostess was A'Lelia Walker, heiress of Madame C.J. Walker, born Sarah Breedlove, who had established a highly successful cosmetics company making hair and skin beauty products for black Americans at the turn of the century.

Alain Locke's edited anthology, *The New Negro* (1925), and other Harlem Renaissance texts define the "New Negro" as urban, proud to be African American, defiant, self-inventing. However, texts such as Alain Locke's homonymous introduction to the 1925 anthology, James Weldon Johnson's *Black Manhattan* (1930) and Langston Hughes's *The Big Sea* (1940) (the last capturing the excitement of life in Harlem), were perhaps over-optimistic about the future for black people in the urban centres of the North. Barbara Christian, in *Black Feminist Criticism* (1985), singles out the atypical Zora Neale Hurston as the Harlem Renaissance figure who was the significant precursor for Morrison.

Lorain, Ohio, 1931

Toni Morrison was born Chloe Ardelia Wofford in Lorain, Ohio, on 18 February 1931. Chloe was the second of four siblings. Her parents, George and Ramah, after a short period in Pittsburgh when they were first married, moved to Lorain, a small mid-Western steel town on Lake Erie, 25 miles west of Cleveland. George was a skilled shipyard worker. He held three jobs simultaneously for almost 17 years (Morrison 1979, 49). However, after the Crash of 1929 and during the Depression, he was periodically unemployed and the family had to rely on help from the state to survive. Ramah, a housewife, fended off debt collectors and wrote to the President to complain about the poor quality of food rations.

In "A Slow Walk of Trees (as Grandmother Would Say), Hopeless (as Grandfather Would Say)" (Morrison 1976b), her most auto-biographical article to date, Morrison situates her family's history in the context of the African American Great Migration North. Morrison's maternal great-grandmother, who was a Native American, was given 88 acres of land during Reconstruction. This land was taken away from her grandfather, John Solomon Willis, by white legal sharks, who exploited his illiteracy. Solomon, pessimistic and cynical, and his wife Ardelia, a forceful optimist, fled from a life as poor sharecroppers in Alabama and migrated North in 1912, in search of economic opportunity and a good education for their seven children. Ardelia valued education so highly that she moved the family from a Kentucky town to Ohio in her search for a good school. Solomon worked as an itinerant violinist. The family struggled to survive. Their daughter, Ramah, responded to her situation with unfailing reasonableness. Her husband, George, recently migrated North from racist Georgia, responded with a strong work ethic, as a source of pride, and an aggressive black racism. He looked at the world critically and distrusted "every word and every gesture of every white man on earth" (Morrison 1976b, 6).

When Morrison was growing up, Lorain was a multiracial town, though she was the only black girl in her class. Morrison grew up in a multiracial neighbourhood: "I never lived in a Black neighbourhood in Lorain, Ohio, because there weren't any at the time" (Morrison 1985b, 172). This was an atypical situation, as most American schools and neighbourhoods were segregated. Ohio River is a line of demarcation between North and South; Ohio is just north of the river. As Morrison explained, Ohio is "an interesting state from the point of view of black people because it's right there by the Ohio river" that runaway slaves crossed on the way North, and "at its northern tip is Canada", final destination of many runaway slaves (Morrison 1976a, 12). As a borderline state, Ohio is a mixture of North and South: "there were these fantastic abolitionists there, and also the Ku Klux Klan lived there" (ibid.). This in-between or hybrid character of Ohio means that it "offers an escape from stereotyped black settings. It is neither plantation nor ghetto" (Morrison 1983a, 158). Long before defining Ohio's doubleness, Morrison was perhaps defined by it.

African American history 1930–50

The Depression of the 1930s was a time of hardship for many Americans, especially for working-class African American families like Morrison's. In 1932, Roosevelt is elected President and introduces the New Deal to alleviate hardship. He uses a large number of black advisors on African American issues and initially has strong black support. In 1935 Mary McLeod Bethune founds the National Council of Negro Women (NCNW); her inter-racial friendship with Eleanor Roosevelt has a lasting public significance. From the 1930s, black workers are allowed to join labour unions, and the antagonism and suspicion between black and white workers begins to be addressed.

When America entered the War in December 1941, the military was segregated and black soldiers experienced discrimination in the army and from civilians. However, progress was made during World War II (1939–45), on several fronts. In 1941 President Roosevelt issued the famous Executive Order 8802, against racial discrimination in the defence industries; and the Supreme Court ruled that separate facilities for white and black railroad passengers must be significantly equal. In 1942 the Congress of Racial Equality (CORE) was founded in Chicago. In 1944 the Supreme Court ruled that Southern white primaries, which barred black voters, were unconstitutional. Also in 1944 President Truman issued an executive order desegregating the military.

After the War, the national and international political climate was promising. The NAACP was very active. Truman conducted an investigation into the state of civil rights, and his Fair Deal policies supported equal rights and racial integration in all fields. Despite such advances, after the War education was still largely segregated. In the South by 1900 every Southern state had legislated separate schools for whites and blacks, with substantially lower expenditure for black schools. Northern states had both integrated and segregated schools. However, most Northern schools were effectively segregated, as many African Americans were confined to ghettos.

Morrison's early years (1931–49)

Toni Morrison did not grow up in a stereotypical middle-class nuclear family. She grew up in an extended working-class family that included her maternal grandparents, Ardelia and Solomon, and she helped to look after her grandparents when they became old and infirm. She would read from the Bible to her grandmother during her last illness. Solomon became senile, he "used to walk away and we had to go out and find him" (Morrison 1979, 58). Morrison returned to her family with her two young sons, Ford (Dino) and Slade, when her marriage broke down, and expected her sons to help to look after her parents.

Morrison's early family life revolved around a vibrant, largely African American, musical and storytelling culture. Her grandfather played the violin and her mother's singing spanned the genres from blues to opera. Her parents' supernatural and animal stories, her father's chilling ghost stories, and her grandmother's interpretations of dreams, familiarized her with African American folktales and oral culture. Her family's stories contributed an important element to Morrison's fiction: a supernatural element she calls "enchantment". Morrison explains:

> My own sense of enchantment simply comes because that's the way the world was for me and for the black people I knew ... I grew up in a house in which people talked about their dreams with the same authority that they talked about what "really" happened. They had visitations and didn't find that fact shocking.
>
> (Morrison 1986, 226)

Morrison has attributed a second important element of her fiction – its emphasis on the reader's active participation – to the participatory, call-and-response nature of African American oral culture. Morrison has never tired of stressing the importance of this participation: "[O]ne of the major characteristics of black literature as far as I'm concerned ... is the participation of the *other*, that is, the audience, the reader" (Morrison 1986, 231). She argues that, in keeping with the African American tradition of improvisation and audience participation, "the text ... cannot be the authority – it should be the map" (Morrison 1984b, 388–89). In an oft-quoted passage, she declares:

> [Literature] should try deliberately to make you stand up and make you feel something profoundly in the same way that a Black preacher requires his congregation to speak, to join him in the sermon, ... to stand up and to weep and to cry and to accede or to change and to modify – to expand on the sermon that is being delivered ... [T]o have the reader work *with* the author in the construction of the book – is what's important.
>
> (Morrison 1984a, 341)

Toni Morrison was precocious in her relation to language. She recalled that when she entered first grade at school, she was the only child in her class who could read. She was a voracious reader as an adolescent, but her favourites were Tolstoy, Dostoyevsky, Flaubert and Jane Austen. Morrison has said that they "spoke directly to [her] out of their own specificity" and inspired her to "capture that same specificity about the nature and feeling of the culture [she] grew up in" (Morrison 1981e). She listened to African American music and stories with her family, while she read European literature privately. Morrison was therefore bi-cultural: "I grew up with both cultures" (Morrison 1980, 71). In 1949 Morrison graduated with honours from Lorain High School and left home to go to university, the first member of her family to do so.

African American history 1950–65

In 1950 the Supreme Court ordered an end to segregation at universities, after vigorous court actions brought by black applicants. The 1954 Supreme Court decision in *Brown v. Board of Education* was the beginning of the end of segregation in primary and secondary schools. Desegregation in public places, such as hotels, restaurants, cinemas, bus terminals, railroad carriages and waiting rooms, was initiated in Washington in the late 1950s and slowly progressed through the 1960s. In interview Morrison has recalled her mother joining in the protesting by sitting in the whites-only section at the local cinema (Morrison 1981c).

Congress passed the Civil Rights Act of 1957, the first civil rights act since 1875. The end of colonialism and the emergence of the independent sub-Saharan states, beginning with Ghana in early 1957, put international pressure on the American government to address its civil rights deficit. Indicative of this deficit is the story of Emmett Till. In the summer of 1955 Emmett, a 14-year-old from Chicago, was visiting relatives in Money, Mississippi, when he was beaten to death and thrown into the Tallahatchie River for allegedly whistling at a white woman. Roy Blanton and his brother-in-law J.W. Milam, who had later bragged about the crime, were acquitted by a jury that deliberated for less than an hour.

In literature, following the Harlem Renaissance, the 1940s and 1950s saw many black newspapers and magazines begin to publish and a significant number of black writers to emerge. Perhaps the outstanding texts of this period are Richard Wright's *Native Son* (1940) and Ralph Ellison's *Invisible Man* (1952).

Independent black churches continued to be the pre-eminent African American institution, nurturing many activists, including the man who would go on to become perhaps the most revered African American of the twentieth century. In 1955, in Montgomery, Alabama, Rosa Parks refused to give her bus seat to a white male passenger and move to the back of the bus. After her arrest, African Americans boycotted Montgomery's bus lines for 381 days, supported by the local branch of the NAACP, until the city changed its bus laws. A new and initially reluctant leader emerged during the boycott: a 26-year-old minister, Martin Luther King. In 1957 the Southern Christian Leadership Conference (SCLC) was established by King and others to promote civil rights. Desegregation was resisted vigorously by Southern organizations, and black activists, especially, were threatened with violence.

In 1960 Kennedy was elected President with African American support. On 1 February 1960, the Sit-in Movement was launched in Greensboro, North Carolina, when four black students insisted on being served at a segregated lunch counter. The Sit-in Movement was a black and white peaceful protest movement against segregation staged in libraries, hotels, beaches and other public spaces. Related to the Sit-in Movement, in April 1960 the Student Nonviolent Coordinating Committee (SNCC) was founded by students in Raleigh, North Carolina, inspired by Gandhi's nonviolent tactics.

In 1961 so-called "Freedom Riders" travelled on public transport from the North to the South, in order to challenge segregated interstate transport. The NAACP launched its "Free by '63" campaign in view of the forthcoming centenary of the Emancipation Proclamation of 1863 abolishing slavery. The year 1963 was one of intense political activism. In a large demonstration in Birmingham, Alabama, led by Martin Luther King, the police used dogs and water hoses on demonstrators, an act which sparked a wave of further demonstrations. On 28 August 1963 the "March on Washington for Jobs and Freedom" takes place. Many organizations, black and white, and a total of 200,000 people take part. They witness King delivering his "I Have a Dream" speech. James Baldwin publishes his essay *The Fire Next Time* (1963), an important civil rights document. After the euphoria, the autumn of 1963 is bleak. In September, a bomb explodes in the black Sixteenth Street Baptist Church in Birmingham, Alabama, killing one 11-year-old and three 14-year-old girls. Of the four white suspects, one was convicted 14 years later, another 32, yet another 39 years later. In November 1963 President Kennedy is assassinated.

Congress passed Kennedy's Civil Rights Act in 1964: it prohibited discrimination in public places and called for equal opportunities in education and employment. In 1964 Martin Luther King won the Nobel Peace Prize for leading non-violent demonstrations for civil rights, and in 1965 he led 30,000 people on a march in Alabama. Also in 1965 Congress passed the Voting Rights Act, enfranchising thousands of Southern blacks who had never voted before. On 21 February 1965 Malcolm X, minister and spokesperson for The Nation of Islam, was assassinated. Along with Martin Luther King, Malcolm X was the outstanding black political leader of the 1960s. King believed that the fight for civil rights should be nonviolent; Malcolm X believed that racism was too entrenched to be fought by nonviolent means and espoused the political use of violence. In August 1965 black riots erupted in the Watts neighbourhood of Los Angeles. Thirty-four people were killed and more than 1,000 injured.

Morrison's student years and early academic career (1949–65)

In 1949 Morrison began attending Howard University, in Washington, DC. Howard, a black university established in 1867, was conventional in many ways. Morrison majored in English and minored in classics, obtaining a degree in English. Black writers were not part of the curriculum. As Morrison later recalled Howard, it was a middle-class environment where colour prejudice ruled. She has told the story of a female student who was unable to get a date because she was dark skinned and who then found instant popularity when it was discovered that her parents were rich. Morrison, a light-skinned but working-class girl, did not feel at home. Perhaps in an effort to fit in, she abandoned her name, Chloe, and adopted the name Toni. She claimed that her middle name was Anthony – hence the name Toni – until the critic John N. Duvall discovered in 2000 that the middle name on her birth certificate was Ardelia, the name of her grandmother. He commented that, while Morrison later proudly embraced her grandmother's heritage in public, in the 1950s "such identification was apparently not a comfort" (Duvall 2000, 39). Morrison's one source of enjoyment during the Howard years was her involvement with the acting troupe, the Howard University Players, especially their tours of the South during the summers. In 1953 Morrison graduated from Howard and started an MA at Cornell University, where black graduate students were a rarity at the time. Once again the curriculum excluded black writers. Morrison completed an MA thesis on Virginia Woolf and William Faulkner, neither of them canonical at the time; she wrote on mental alienation in Woolf's *Mrs Dalloway* and Faulkner's *Absalom, Absalom!* She graduated in 1955.

From 1955 and for two years Morrison was employed as an English instructor at Texas Southern University in Houston, a radical environment:

> I came to [the value of being black] as a clear statement very late in life … [T]he consciousness of being Black

happened when I left Cornell and went to teach at Texas
Southern University ... [I]t was as a novice teacher, and
that was in 1957 or 1958, that I began to think about Black
culture ...

(Morrison 1985b, 173)

In 1957 Morrison returned to Howard to teach English. Her students
included Stokeley Carmichael, Houston A. Baker, Jr. and Claude
Brown, who showed Morrison the manuscript of *Manchild in the
Promised Land*. Carmichael, who entered Howard in 1960, joined
the Freedom Riders in 1961. In 1966 he became chairman of the
SNCC and defined "Black Power" in a 1966 speech and a 1967 co-
authored book, *Black Power*. Richard Wright had used the term
"Black Power" to refer to African independence movements in his 1954
nonfiction book, *Black Power*. Carmichael redefined the term, giving
it its now familiar 1960s meaning: assertion of African American
pride and rejection of white values. Carmichael later joined the Black
Panther Party.

In 1958 Toni Wofford married Harold Morrison, a young architect
from Jamaica. In 1964 Morrison was travelling in Europe with her
husband and two young boys. She returned from Europe without her
husband, resigned her job at Howard, and lived at her parents' home in
Lorain for 18 months with her sons. She has commented that, rather
than being subservient to a husband, "I was a constant nuisance to
mine. He didn't need me making judgments about him, which I did.
A lot" (Morrison 1979, 51–52).

African American history 1965 to date

In 1966 the SNCC, in spite of its nonviolent Gandhian origins, came
under the posthumous influence of Malcolm X and began to advocate black separatism and Black Power. In September 1966, the Black
Panther Party was founded. It was inspired by various sources: the
postcolonial theorist Frantz Fanon, who was closely linked to the
national liberation struggle of Algeria against France in the early
1960s; Malcolm X; and socialist ideas. Black Panthers believed that
African Americans were "a colonized people within the United
States" (Horton and Horton 2001, 308); espoused extremist forms of
activism; and stressed the cultural significance of Africa for African
Americans. Black Panther Party spokesman, Eldridge Cleaver, wrote
the definitive Black Panther text, *Soul on Ice* (1968), whilst in prison.
In 1968 the mood among civil rights activists across the political
spectrum became more pessimistic; numerous civil rights activists

were murdered, but many of the criminals went unconvicted. On 4 April 1968 Martin Luther King was shot dead in Memphis and wide-scale violence erupted. A white man, James Earl Ray, was convicted.

In the meantime the Vietnam War (1961–75) was escalating. It started inconspicuously in 1961, developing to become one of the defining events of the decade and provoking a strong anti-war movement. African American war casualties were disproportionately high, and many African Americans, including Martin Luther King and Muhammad Ali, opposed the war.

By the 1970s white Americans were moving to the suburbs in large numbers and companies (and jobs) were relocating to business parks; African Americans remained in the inner cities. African American unemployment, especially among men, put black families under severe pressure. In the late 1970s the gap between middle-class blacks and poor blacks was widening. In January 1981 Ronald Reagan was elected President, and the situation for African Americans worsened. The Reagan years (1981–89) were years of reaction, and the reaction continued during the George H.W. Bush administration (1989–93). Morrison declared that African Americans were "being devoured" (Morrison 1981b, 121). Pointing to the fact that the rate of unemployment for black teenagers in New York was 60 per cent, she warned that important legislation was being dismantled by the Republican administration (Morrison 1989b). In March 1991 Rodney King was severely beaten up by LAPD policemen. The beating was caught on camera, but the men responsible were acquitted. Black riots erupted in Los Angeles.

Clinton's Presidency in 1993–2001 changed the political climate; there was a substantially increased presence of African Americans in the administration. However, while middle-class blacks were now leaving the inner cities for affluent suburbs, social and economic discrimination against African Americans continued. Franklin and Moss (2000) write that in 1995 two million black men were in prison, on probation, or on parole.

During the second and highly unpopular term of George W. Bush's presidency (2001–09) the world witnessed the emergence of Barack Obama. Toni Morrison in a Letter to Barack Obama of 28 January 2008, her first public endorsement of a presidential candidate, added: "Nor do I care very much for your race(s). I would not support you if that was all you had to offer" (Morrison 2008c). His election was a hopeful sign that we can collectively envisage a post-racist society to come.

Particular political and aesthetic aspects of the period will be discussed in subsequent sections.

Morrison's emergence as a novelist (1964–77): "Why write?"

In 1964 at the age of 33 and while she was teaching at Howard, Morrison joined a writers' group in Washington. Her marriage was coming to an end and, as she later said, she was lonely. For this group she wrote a story about a young black girl who wanted blue eyes – the first version of her first novel, *The Bluest Eye* (1970). Soon after Morrison was a single mother of two young children with a full-time job in publishing. It took her five years to write a relatively slim novel. Initially she would write from 5 a.m. until the children woke up or she would isolate herself in a room to write, perhaps heeding Virginia Woolf's famous advice that women writers need a room of their own. Later, she wrote in the "big room", surrounded by her sons, Dino and Slade, as they were more content and more likely to allow her to write when she was physically present (Morrison 1978, 32). She did a lot of thinking about her writing whilst driving.

The manuscript of *The Bluest Eye* was rejected by numerous publishing houses. It was finally accepted by "this young guy" at Holt, Rinehart, and Winston:

> A lot of black men were writing in 1968, 1969, and he bought it, thinking that there was a growing interest in what black people were writing and that this book of mine would also sell. He was wrong. What was selling was "Let me tell you how powerful I am and how horrible you are."

> (Morrison 1993b, 245)

White reviewers praised the quality of the writing but were less positive about the story – incest and the mental disintegration of a young black girl. Black critics like Ruby Dee praised both. *The Bluest Eye* was out of print by 1974 and was not a commercial success, but Morrison became a frequent reviewer and commentator for the *New York Times* on the strength of the novel. Her second novel, *Sula*, was published in 1973. It was a modest commercial and critical success. Reviewers, once again, were impressed by the quality of the writing but uncomfortable with the story. Some felt that her literary talent was wasted on the story of the friendship between two insignificant black women. Morrison's third novel, *Song of Solomon*, whose protagonist is a middle-class man, was published in 1977 to a "standing ovation" (Furman 2003b, 3), "catapult[ing] Morrison into the ranks of the most revered contemporary writers" (Smith 1995b, 10), and went on to become a bestselling paperback.

Morrison has said that she only identified herself as a writer *after* writing her first two novels, possibly after writing her third novel (Morrison 1983a, 167; Morrison 1985a, 204). Given that Morrison wrote for more than a decade without identifying herself as a writer, why did she write and persevere with her writing? Morrison's own answer is seemingly contradictory. On the one hand, she has always insisted that she writes *for herself*, as an existential affirmation of her self, her subjectivity:

> I used to live in this world ... And at some point I didn't belong here anymore. I was somebody's parent, somebody's this, somebody's that, but there was no me in this world ... And as I began to [write *The Bluest Eye*], I began to pick up scraps of things I had seen or felt, or didn't see or didn't feel, but imagined. And speculated about and wondered about. And I fell in love with myself. I reclaimed myself and the world – a real revelation.
>
> (Morrison 1985a, 198)

Morrison has described writing as: "the only thing I do for myself alone" (Morrison 1978, 31). On the other hand, she has equally stressed that she writes *for others*: "I am not interested in indulging myself in some private, closed exercise of my imagination" (Morrison 1984a, 344–45). "I write what I have recently begun to call village literature, fiction that is really for the village, for the tribe. Peasant literature for *my* people" (Morrison 1981b, 120).

Over the years Morrison has continued to elaborate on the question of why she writes and the purpose of her art. Writing, for her, is open and free thinking *for the writer and the reader alike*. In this sense, she writes both for herself and for others. She explains: "I write out of ignorance ... about the things I don't have any resolutions for" (Morrison 1983a, 169). She insists: "All the books are questions for me" (Morrison 1989c, 270). But writing does not provide answers; it defines questions: "It became ... possible for me to sort out the past, and the selection process, being disciplined and guided, was *genuine thinking as opposed to simple response or problem-solving*" (Morrison 1981b, 119–20; my emphasis). The novel "should have something in it that enlightens; ... Something in it that suggests what the conflicts are, what the problems are. But it need not solve those problems" (Morrison 1984a, 341).

Writing of this sort appeals to and elicits the reader's own capacity for open and free thinking, involving writer and reader in an interactive process. In *The Dancing Mind* Morrison describes reading as "the dance of an open mind when it engages another equally open one" (Morrison 1997a, 7). She claims for herself both the role of free and open writer and the role of free and open reader, without the "encroachment of private wealth, government control, or cultural expediency" (ibid., 16–17).

Morrison's editorial career and continuing academic career (1965–2006)

In 1965 Morrison reinvented herself professionally as an editor and, in the next 20 years, had a successful career in publishing. Initially she was employed as editor at L.W. Singer, textbook subsidiary of Random House, and moved to Syracuse. In 1968 she became textbook editor, then trade-book editor at Random House – editing mostly books by black writers – and moved to New York. Later, as senior editor at the headquarters of Random House in Manhattan, Morrison brought a number of black writers to the publisher's list: Muhammad Ali, Toni Cade Bambara, Claude Brown, Angela Davis, Henry Dumas, Leon Forrest, Gayl Jones, Andrew Young. In 1974 she took on in-house editorial responsibility for *The Black Book*, an innovative project looking like a giant scrapbook and documenting African American experience through nineteenth- and twentieth-century memorabilia and ephemera.

During this period Morrison continued to teach part-time at university level: she taught at a number of colleges and universities, including Bard College, Yale University, SUNY at Albany and SUNY at Purchase. In 1984 she left publishing for the Albert Schweitzer Professorship of the Humanities at SUNY-Albany. From 1988 and until her retirement in 2006, she held the Robert F. Goheen Professorship of the Humanities at Princeton University.

Morrison, the Black Aesthetic Movement and African American literature from 1965 to date

While Ralph Ellison and James Baldwin continued publishing into the 1980s, in the 1960s the Black Power movement interacted strongly with a new African American artistic movement, the Black Aesthetic Movement or Black Arts Movement (1965–75). LeRoi Jones (Amiri Baraka), Larry Neal and Addison Gayle, Jr. are some of the major figures of the movement. *Black Fire* (1968), edited by Baraka and Neal, and *The Black Aesthetic* (1971), edited by Gayle are important documents. Morrison emerged as a writer and published her first novels during the period of the Black Aesthetic

Movement and it is an important cultural context for understanding her work.

African American writers responded to the desegregation of the 1940s and 1950s with, in the words of Houston A. Baker, Jr., a "poetics of integration" (Andrews, Foster and Harris 1997, 68). In opposition to this integrationist generation, the 1960s Black Aesthetic Movement, one of the most politically militant aesthetic movements in African American cultural history, advocated resistance, autonomy and difference. In this, it revived and radicalized a tradition of African American writers claiming the right to speak for themselves and address not society at large – i.e. white society – but each other, stretching back to the early nineteenth century. The Black Aesthetic Movement rejected universalism and called for the representation of black experience by African Americans for African Americans. Following this it renewed the call for distinctively black art forms, emerging out of African American oral or folk traditions. Precedent for this can be seen in Du Bois's identification of spirituals as an example of a distinctively black art in *The Souls of Black Folk* (Du Bois 1903); nineteenth-century writers such as Frederick Douglass and Charles Waddell Chesnutt made use of black folklore in their work (see Harris 1991); and the 1920s writers of the Harlem Renaissance made extensive use of folkloric forms (focusing for the most part on Northern urban forms, though Zora Neal Hurston drew on Southern rural forms). The Movement further argued for specifically black criteria by which to judge black art forms. Du Bois, in "A Negro Theatre" (1926), had also argued that black art forms must be judged by black standards and black critics. In this way the Black Aesthetic Movement self-consciously formalized earlier black aesthetic traditions and debates into principles of a black art, and argued that black art is and must be political art. The Black Aesthetic Movement prioritized poetry, theatre and, more generally, performance. It also emphasized the need for an independent black press, including magazines and journals by African Americans for African Americans.

Perhaps what was novel and without obvious precedent in the 1960s Black Aesthetic Movement, at least in the context of African American thought, was a black essentialism: grounding positive black stereotypes in a black human nature and a unique black history emphasizing Africa as origin. Whereas white racism spread degrading black stereotypes, this movement polemically asserted the value, and the superiority, of blackness. In this, the Black Aesthetic Movement is close to the Francophone *négritude* movement, especially the ideas of Léopold Sédar Senghor (1906–2001), poet, politician and first president of Senegal. One of the limitations of black essentialism, in its use of positive black stereotypes, is that it is just as reductionist as white racism, transforming the complexity and heterogeneity of African American experience into a narrow repertoire of types. Some critics viewed the Black Aesthetic Movement as sexist and homophobic.

Morrison, at the beginning of her literary career, endorsed many of the tenets of the Black Aesthetic Movement. In 1971, reviewing Addison Gayle's *The Black Aesthetic* and two other anthologies of Black writing, she praised all three works and embraced the principle of Black art as a form of psychic liberation. In interview she has always insisted that she writes about African Americans for African Americans. In her novels she has made extensive use of African American folk traditions. She has also argued for the need for black criteria in the judgement of her own works, and for black critics of her work: "Black people must be the only people who set out our criteria for criticism" (Morrison 1974b, 6); "Critics of my work have often left something to be desired, in my mind, because they don't always evolve out of the culture, the world, the given quality out of which I write" (Morrison 1983b, 151). In 1984, she defined her own version of Black art (see **p. 145**).

Simultaneously, Morrison has distanced herself from aspects of the Black Aesthetic Movement. She has defined herself as a black *woman* writer, "placing black women center stage in the text" and *speaking to* black women (Morrison 1986, 231). She has claimed, perhaps unfairly, that Ralph Ellison and Richard Wright – the "classics" of African American literature – could not speak to her because they addressed white men (Morrison 1981d, 96). In her novels, she has avoided the use of unambiguously positive black stereotypes (against the use of positive black stereotypes by the Black Arts Movement). She has stressed the heterogeneity of black experience and acknowledged divisions: "the *enormous* differences are more interesting to me than the similarities because it's too easy to get into the trap of the monolithic black person" (Morrison 1986, 227–28). Against black essentialism, she has argued that "Being Black now is something you have to choose to be. Choose it no matter what your skin color" (Morrison 1985b, 186).

In the 1960s and early 1970s many significant African American women poets emerged: Nikki Giovanni and Sonia Sanchez, who were members of the Black Aesthetic Movement; the lesbian poet Audre Lorde; the poet, autobiographer and civil rights activist Maya Angelou, whose first volume of autobiography, *I Know Why the Caged Bird Sings*, was published in 1969. Morrison, however, championed the value of the novel, a genre neglected by the Black Aesthetic Movement, arguing that, whereas in the past African American music was the main art form that ensured African American cultural survival, the novel is now significantly contributing to – if not taking over – this role (Morrison 1981b, 121). In the 1970s, she emerged as a prominent member of a loose group of African American women writers concentrating on fiction and setting out to present African American women in their complexity and diversity. The group included Toni Cade Bambara, Gayl Jones, Gloria Naylor and Alice Walker. Paule Marshall, whose first novel was *Browngirl, Brownstones* (1959), is considered a harbinger/predecessor of the group. The popularity and critical acclaim of this group internationally – especially Morrison and Walker – were unprecedented in the history of African American literature. (While Morrison has not situated herself in relation to contemporary African American male fiction writers, a list of prominent figures would include: Leon Forrest, Ernest J. Gaines, Alex Haley, Charles Johnson, James A. McPherson and Albert Murray.)

Over the years Morrison has articulated her relation not just to the Black Aesthetic Movement but, more generally, to African American aesthetic traditions. In her essay "Memory, Creation, and Writing" she summarized what she considered valuable in these traditions: "antiphony, the group nature of art, its functionality, its improvisational nature, its relationship to audience performance, the critical voice which upholds tradition and communal values and which also provides occasion for an individual to transcend and/or defy group restriction" (Morrison 1984b, 388–89).

Morrison and Black Feminism

Black women took part in the Civil Rights Movement of the 1960s and the anti-war movement of the 1960s and 1970s in large numbers. Fannie Lou Hamer and Ella Jo Baker were prominent black civil rights activists, as was Angela Davis. Davis was born to middle-class civil-rights activist parents, was educated at Brandeis University and the University of California at San Diego, studied with the philosopher Herbert Marcuse, whose 1964 book, *One-Dimensional Man*, was a seminal text for the 1960s student movement, and became a philosophy instructor at UCLA. Davis initially joined the SNCC but found its political culture sexist and resigned. She then affiliated herself with the Black Panthers and became a national figure. She was arrested and was defended in the media by James Baldwin amongst others. Toni Morrison herself wrote in defence of Davis in a *New York Times* review (Morrison 1972).

Angela Davis worked to bring attention to the condescension towards women throughout the civil rights and anti-war movements. Women activists found themselves in a contradictory situation comparable to the situation of African American soldiers in the two

World Wars: fighting for "freedom" within an army that discriminated against them. In articles and interviews, Morrison has focused her criticisms on the Black Power movement and its rhetoric – particularly, the application of its "Black is beautiful" slogan to women and the oppressive fetishization of black female beauty. Morrison rejected Black Power female models such as the ancient Egyptian queen Nefertiti for their escapism and exoticism (Morrison 1974a). She commented: "I was not impressed with much of the rhetoric of Black men about Black women in the Sixties, I didn't believe it" (Morrison 1980, 72–73). She goes on to explain that traditionally black women both worked and raised a family. As a result, black women's relation to black men was potentially one of comradeship and equality. Black female resilience – and black women's real-life roles as breadwinners and heads of family – is a better political model than stereotypical beauty and eroticism.

In 1971, in an article for the *New York Times*, "What the Black Woman Thinks About Women's Lib", Morrison welcomed a new inter-racial women's organization, the National Women's Political Caucus (NWPC), formed in 1971 and including black activists such as Fannie Lou Hamer. Simultaneously, in the same article, Morrison voiced the unease of black women towards the traditionally white and upper-middle-class women's movement (Morrison 1971b). While the civil rights and anti-war movements silenced and marginalized women in general and black activism's portrayal of women was often stereotyped and oppressive, the women's movement itself silenced and marginalized black women. In 1973 the National Black Feminist Organization (NBFO) was founded by Eleanor Holmes Norton, Margaret Sloan-Hunter and others. In the 1970s and 1980s black feminist scholarship burgeoned as a new academic field across the humanities. Naturally, prominent critics in this new field, such as Barbara Christian, Barbara Smith and Hortense Spillers, wrote on Toni Morrison and their work will be discussed in this book.

Morrison the novelist, critic and public figure (1977 to the present)

After the publication of *Song of Solomon*, Morrison became famous, a media celebrity, nationally and internationally. Her reputation and stature have been growing ever since. She is now widely admired as one of the foremost writers of her time, a major literary artist who has also enjoyed great popular success.

In 1978 *Song of Solomon* won the National Book Critics' Circle Award and the American Academy and Institute of Arts and Letters

Award and was a Book-of-the-Month Club selection; the American Academy and Institute of Arts and Letters also named Morrison Distinguished Writer of the Year. In 1979 President Carter appointed her to the National Council of the Arts. In 1996 *Song of Solomon* received Oprah Winfrey's Book Club endorsement. Winfrey's continued support over the years and Morrison's appearances on her show have contributed to mass awareness and millions of sales.

Tar Baby (1981), Morrison's fourth novel, was also a bestseller. On publication, Morrison appeared on the cover of *Newsweek*, only the second black woman to do so, after Zora Neale Hurston in 1943. Though *Tar Baby* was not universally or unreservedly praised, *Newsweek*'s lengthy piece, "Toni Morrison's Black Magic", presented Morrison as a literary genius. In 1982 Morrison collaborated with Donald McKayle on the musical, *District Storyville*, for which she wrote the story and lyrics (unpublished to date). Her only published short story, "Recitatif", was published in 1983, in *Confirmation: An Anthology of African American Women*, edited by Amiri and Amina Baraka (her only other known short story is the first version of *The Bluest Eye*). Morrison's specially commissioned play, *Dreaming Emmett*, was produced in Albany, NY, on 4 January 1986. It remains unpublished.

Beloved (1987), Morrison's fifth novel, basked in the "immediacy of glowing public response" (McKay 1999, 4), made it into the *New York Times* Bestseller List in the week of its official publication date and was in its third printing within a month, after an initial run of 100,000. When Morrison failed to win the National Book Award for *Beloved*, 48 black writers signed a statement of protest published in *The New York Times Book Review*. The novel did however win the 1988 Pulitzer Prize for Fiction, the 1988 Robert F. Kennedy Award, and many others.

In the 1990s Morrison published a number of critical texts investigating the nature of racism in American literature and society. "Unspeakable Things Unspoken: The Afro-American Presence in American Literature" (1989) was an early version of *Playing in the Dark: Whiteness and the Literary Imagination* (1992) – the latter based on her three William E. Massey, Sr. Lectures in the History of American Civilization at Harvard in 1992. The book had a first print-run of 25,000, very high for an academic book and indicative of Morrison's high profile and selling power by this point. In 1992 she published the edited collection, *Race-ing Justice, En-Gendering Power: Essays on Anita Hill, Clarence Thomas, and the Construction of Social Reality*, which included her essay, "Friday on the Potomac", serving as Introduction. In 1997 she coedited, with Claudia Brodsky Lacour, *Birth of a Nation'hood: Gaze, Script, and Spectacle in the*

O.J. Simpson Case, which included her own introductory essay, "Dead Man Golfing".

In 1992 Morrison published her sixth novel, *Jazz*, at which point her career was transformed with the award of the highest honour available to a writer. In 1993 she was the recipient of the Nobel Prize for Literature; rarely awarded to Americans, but considered the ultimate accolade of the international literary establishment. She has since been the recipient of many other national and international honours. *The Nobel Lecture in Literature, 1993* was published in 1994 and *The Dancing Mind: Speech Upon Acceptance of the National Book Foundation Medal for Distinguished Contribution to American Letters* was published in 1997. A further three critically acclaimed novels have been published: *Paradise* (1998), *Love* (2003) and *A Mercy* (2008). *A Mercy*, an attempt to imagine a pre-racial and post-racial America, appeared in November 2008, the month Barack Obama was elected America's first black President. Since 1999 Morrison has published several books of children's fiction cowritten with her son, Slade Morrison. In 2004 she published the nonfiction book, *Remember: The Journey to School Integration*. She wrote the libretto for the opera *Margaret Garner*, which premiered in May 2005 (it remains unpublished).

2

Work

The Bluest Eye (1970)

The Bluest Eye takes place in Morrison's native Lorain, Ohio, between autumn 1940 and autumn 1941. Morrison was nine years old at this time. From the point of view of the history we learn at school, these are the years of the fight against fascism and World War II. America entered the War in the winter of 1941, on 7 December. However, the War is conspicuously and quite deliberately absent here: the novel's characters face a form of fascism that World War II will not defeat.

The novel tells the story of an 11-year-old black girl, Pecola Breedlove – "the first novel to give a black child centre stage" (Peach 2000, 7). In autumn 1940 Pecola has her first menstruation, symbolically entering the adult world. She is anxious to be part of that world, eager to learn how one becomes part of it, actively seeking answers. Her efforts centre upon love. "[H]ow do you get someone to love you?" she asks nine-year-old Claudia and ten-year-old Frieda (23; all page numbers in this chapter refer to *The Bluest Eye* [Morrison 1970] unless otherwise indicated). "How come [all your boyfriends] love you?" (40) she asks Miss Marie, "the whor[e] in whores' clothing" (43), together with a string of other questions. But by autumn 1941 Pecola has forever left the ordinary shared world. She has become mad, psychotic, a schizophrenic: she believes that her dark eyes have turned blue, that she has been granted blue eyes. She hallucinates a new friend, a friend who can see her blue eyes. They have long and frank conversations together. What could have happened to interrupt Pecola's *Bildungsroman* – her rites of passage into the adult world – so quickly and irrevocably?

We are told in brief, proleptically, that in the summer of 1941 Pecola was "having her father's baby" (4). Could this be the answer to Pecola's madness? The initial chapters of the novel allow us to focus on Pecola's dysfunctional family and to privatize Pecola's madness. What we are initially offered – in the context of a distinction between the public sphere and the domestic or private sphere, which this novel will go on to problematize – is the story of an atypical and very dysfunctional family culminating in a rape, a story therefore that is disturbing but that neither concerns us directly nor implicates us in any way. This is a "unique situation, not a representative one", as Morrison writes in the Afterword (168). However, the experience of reading this novel tests very severely any such interpretation. Morrison foregrounds, mobilizes and makes us aware of our assumptions and uses on-going narrative revision in order to subject them to critique. To show this strategy I will discuss *The Bluest Eye* following its own sequence.

The opening paragraph of the novel is a pastiche of the contemporary Dick and Jane series of primers for teaching American first-grade children how to read. It describes little Jane's "happy" family, "nice" mother, "smiling" father (1), cat, dog and Jane's visiting friend. The paragraph is repeated twice: a first time with punctuation and capital letters removed; a second time with all spaces between words removed. It is as though, from the point of view of the unacculturated young child or the alienated adult, the words about happy conventional middle-class families dissolve into noise, blur into meaninglessness. The suggestion is that the second and third versions are increasingly removed from the happy family. While the second version is still close enough to the original to be legible, the third version is painfully illegible.

The Dick and Jane primers were in use from 1930 to 1970 – they were in use both at the time when Pecola and Toni Morrison were learning to read and at the time the novel was written. They initially depicted a world of white suburban comfort. Jane is usually blonde. From 1965 onwards, there were illustrations of African American characters; and one of the books in the series, *Fun with the Family*, was published in two versions: either with white or with African American illustrations of the family. Because of the primers' status as classics, they were reissued in 2002. In Morrison's pastiche, Jane wears a red dress and the house has a red door. Jane obviously wears a variety of outfits in the primers, including a red dress on the cover of an early edition of *Fun with Dick and Jane*. Morrison's choice of red, with its connotations of sexuality and danger, lends a sinister air to the house and the dress and links them with Pecola's story, announced on page 4 and already précised on the back cover of the novel's first edition.

AUTUMN

The chapter comprising pages 5–23 (chapters and sections are not numbered) is the opening chapter of the novel's first section,

"Autumn". The book's four sections are named after the four seasons of the year and take place during those seasons. The book begins with autumn, when school (and the school year) starts, in keeping with a child's perspective. The chapter is set firmly within a family. It describes Claudia's and Frieda's African American family, the MacTeers, and tells the story of Pecola's brief stay with the MacTeers in the autumn of 1940, during which Pecola has her first menstruation.

The MacTeers, unlike the family of the primer, have to stuff broken windows with rugs and struggle to keep the "outdoors" (11) from invading their home. Mrs MacTeer is not "nice": her "fussing soliloquies … told everybody and everything off" (16). However, the MacTeers manage to preserve and insulate their family and to defend the borders of their home. "Love, thick and dark as Alaga syrup, eased up into that cracked window" (7). The MacTeers can be read as the second version of the repeated paragraph that is a pastiche of the Dick and Jane primer.

This chapter makes a distinction between this ordinary and good black family and the extraordinary and bad black family to which Pecola belongs, the Breedloves, allowing us, the readers, to settle into a position of false moral comfort. Mr and Mrs Breedlove are unable to fulfil even the most minimal duties as parents. Cholly Breedlove, the father, tries to burn down their rented house, damaging it sufficiently to render the family homeless. After the fire Pauline Breedlove, the mother, takes refuge in her wealthy white employers' house, abandoning Pecola and her unnamed brother. In circumstances rather less happy than the iconic visit of Jane's friend, the County authorities have to take action and a white official temporarily houses Pecola with the MacTeers. Mrs MacTeer and her female friends, gossiping in her kitchen, distinguish between good black people and "crazy nigger[s]" (8). The narrator of this chapter, adult Claudia, elucidates their perspective: "Cholly Breedlove … had joined the animals; was, indeed, an old dog, a snake, a ratty nigger" (12). Mrs Breedlove, absent during Pecola's stay with the MacTeers, is also less than human in Mrs MacTeer's eyes. "What kind of something is that?" she asks during one of her soliloquies (17).

The MacTeers are a bi-cultural family, mixing white middle-class values and cultural resources with African American ones, especially music. On the one hand, Mrs MacTeer sings blues songs in her kitchen and her father, Big Papa, plays the violin in Big Mama's kitchen. On the other hand, in the eyes of MacTeer adults, "[t]he big, the special, the loving gift was always a big, *blue-eyed* Baby Doll" (13; my emphasis). Young Claudia, too young to be fully socialized, or heretical already, dismembers such "yellow-haired, pink-skinned" dolls as are given to her (14) and feels the impulse to dismember their real-life originals and unlock "the secret of the magic they weaved on others" (15).

The Breedloves can be read as the third version of the paragraph that is a pastiche of the Dick and Jane primer. The following two chapters (24–44) describe the Breedlove's abandoned "storefront" home (28) and their family. These chapters are headed by relevant chunks from the third-version primer, further distorted. For example: "HEREISTHEHOUSEITISGREENANDWHITEITHASAREDDOOR ITISVERYPRETTYITISVERYPRETTYPRETTYPRETTYP" (24). The repetition of "It is very pretty, pretty, pretty, p" starkly announces with its echo the huge distance that separates the model home of the Dick and Jane books and the Breedloves' home. What does this huge distance consist in? The third-person unidentified and seemingly extradiegetic and omniscient narrator of these chapters questions and revises the earlier distinction between the good MacTeers and the bad Breedloves. The Breedloves are too powerless to defend their space and to keep out the world at large. The illusion of the family as a world unto itself – an illusion propagated by the primer – is rudely shattered. Their "home" has no picket fence and their "front room" (25) – the living room – is defined by a "large plate-glass window" (24) that puts them on abject display, and a sofa – centrepiece of the living room – delivered with a large split in the cover; so inconsequential are they, in the eyes of the world, that when they complain the shop refuses to replace it.

The chapter describing the Breedloves' family life shows that, unlike the MacTeers, there is no boundary between this family and its exposure to the world outside. The great white world fixes them in its gaze mercilessly, with blue eyes that see what they want to see. "It was as though some mysterious all-knowing master had given each one a cloak of ugliness to wear, and they had accepted it without question. The master had said, 'You are ugly people'" (28). Pecola tries to understand "the secret of the ugliness, the ugliness that made her ignored or despised at school, by schoolmates and teachers alike" (34). She reasons that, had she blue eyes, people would see her differently, and she prays for blue eyes. She also experimentally explores other kinds of response. She attempts to magically transform herself into a blonde and blue-eyed white girl by consuming blonde and blue-eyed icons: she consumes Mary Janes – candy with the picture of a blonde, blue-eyed girl on the wrapper – and drinks obsessively from a Shirley Temple cup. (Keith E. Byerman [1993], Donald D. Gibson [1993] and other critics discuss Pecola's attempts to transubstantiate herself.) Yet another response is a bold existential affirmation of herself, against the judgement of the world: "Why, she wonders, do people call [dandelions] weeds? She thought they were pretty" (35). But the white immigrant shop owner, Mr Yacobowski, stares at her with a "total absence of human recognition" (36). After this nullifying experience, her power of self-affirmation ebbs and she concludes that dandelions "*are* weeds" after all (37). Morrison has argued that racism was a "unifying" factor for white immigrants from Europe: "what one has in common with that other immigrant is contempt for *me* [the 'nigger']" (Morrison 1989b, 255).

The absence of a picket fence, a protective boundary, between Pecola and the world also represents her freedom to enter territories forbidden to Claudia and Frieda. Pecola befriends the three whores – Poland, China and especially Miss Marie, whom the world calls the Maginot Line and whose threshold Claudia and Frieda are strictly forbidden to cross. Mrs MacTeer "hated" the whores (60), especially the Maginot Line. Adult Claudia explains through the perspective of young Claudia: "That was the one church women never allowed their eyes to rest on. That was the one who had killed people, set them on fire, poisoned them, cooked them in lye" (60). Parents scare their little girls away from the Maginot Line with murderous stories.

The three whores are named Poland, China and the Maginot Line by the community as a bad joke. The names are those of, or associated with, countries recently invaded by Germany and its allies. China was attacked by Japan in 1937. World War II was initiated by Germany's "blitzkrieg" invasion of Poland. The Maginot Line, a French line of concrete fortifications on the borders with Germany and Italy, built after World War I, was ineffectual in preventing another German invasion in World War II. The names are obviously a crude comment on women who make their living by being sexually invaded. However, the description of the three whores by the third-person narrator through the perspective of – focalized by – young Pecola is a celebration of the whores as folk artists and simultaneously the only sustained affirmation of Pecola's own perspective on the world. China forever experimenting with different unlikely hairdos and styles of makeup; Poland singing blues songs; fat Miss Marie, whose "laughter came like the sound of many rivers ... heading for the room of an open sea" (40), improvising "breezy and rough" stories for Pecola (43). Pecola "loved them"; in return China and Poland "did not despise" her (38) and Miss Marie returned her gaze "lovingly" (44).

Comparing this atypical household, this "whorehousehold", with the nuclear family of the first version of the Dick and Jane primer, it is possible to argue that it is, in some sense, preferable to the nuclear family. In the Dick and Jane primer, neither the mother nor the father answers the question: "will you play with Jane?" – neither of them answers the call to play with Jane. Michael Awkward argues: the emotional "estrangement suggested by the family's inability to respond to the daughter Jane's desire for play ... implies that theirs is solely a surface contentment" (Awkward 1989, 179). By contrast, Mrs MacTeer's rough love and Miss Marie's rough stories suggest their real emotional involvement.

This is the closing chapter of the "Autumn" section of the novel. Up to this point in the novel, Pecola is devalued by the *white* world, and those branded "nigger" by good blacks – Cholly Breedlove and the Maginot Line – seem to have *done something* to deserve it. The reader can retain a sense of moral comfort by rejecting white racism and identifying with good blacks. However, the next chapters (47–72) – the chapters of the "Winter" section of the novel – undercut this comfortable position. The alarming development is that, in a series of violent incidents, black characters treat Pecola as the exemplary "nigger" simply because she is a dark-skinned, poor girl with "no people" (148), while they confer beauty *and* goodness on light-skinned and affluent black girls and white girls. For me, the reader, there is no morally superior position left to occupy, I am rendered homeless, and I am forced to consider my implicatedness in Pecola's victimization, demonization and scapegoating. The exceptions here are young Claudia and Frieda, and they present the reader's only hope.

WINTER

The grown-up Claudia returns as the narrator of the chapter covering pages 47–62, presenting us with a distinction between a "beautiful" black girl, Maureen, who "enchanted the entire school" (48), with the notable exception of Claudia and Frieda; and an "ugly" black girl, Pecola. Maureen is "high-yellow" (47) and affluent, Pecola is dark-skinned and poor. Pecola is used as a scapegoat: "[a] group of boys was circling and holding at bay a victim, Pecola Breedlove. Bay Boy, Woodrow Cain, Buddy Wilson, Junie Bug ... danced a macabre ballet around the victim, whom, for their own sake, they were prepared to sacrifice to the flaming pit" (50). Growing up in a racist society, the black boys attempt to magically or ritually cleanse themselves of the stigma of blackness by transferring it to Pecola. They chant: "Black e mo black e mo" (50) – in other words, Pecola is "black even more than they are", as Lucille P. Fultz explains (Fultz 2003, 18).

Claudia, Frieda and Maureen witness the incident, defend Pecola and a precarious alliance emerges among the girls. An alliance that is quickly undermined, for Maureen has already accepted that blackness is ugly – "this mulatto girl hates her mother 'cause she is black and ugly", she explains of a Hollywood film plot (52) – and soon throws the boys' chant at the other girls. Maureen is a "false spring day"

(49) in the middle of winter. Morrison later commented that she was "unfair to [Maureen]. I did not ... look at anything from her point of view" (Morrison 1985a, 203).

Claudia and Frieda, on the other hand, intuitively choose a pre-reflective affirmation of the value of blackness: "we were still in love with ourselves then. We felt comfortable in our skins" (56). This affirmation differs significantly from the "Black is beautiful" rhetoric of the Black Power movement that highlighted idealized models such as Nefertiti. Claudia and Frieda identify with Pecola – while "antagonized" by her inability to fight back (57) – and, more heretically, with the Maginot Line. When they find their lodger scandalously entertaining China and the Maginot Line in their mother's absence, Claudia looks at the Maginot Line, the woman her mother said she "wouldn't let eat out of one of her plates": "it may have been my own image that I saw ... in her eyes that reminded me of waterfalls", Claudia comments, echoing Pecola's earlier sense of Miss Marie (60). In a later encounter, Claudia again describes the Maginot Line's eyes as "clean as rain" and "rain-soaked" (80).

The third-person narrator takes over in the chapter covering pages 63–72. Geraldine, highly respectable black middle-class housewife and mother of Junior, is representative of a social group examined in this chapter: "brown" girls migrated to the North from respectable black homes in Southern urban centres (63). Junior, Pecola's classmate at school, sees her "standing alone, always alone, at recess" (69) and lures her into his house for a bit of gentle torment safely administered to an easy target. He throws his mother's cat at her face, knocking the cat unconscious. Geraldine – an admirable "pretty milk-brown lady" (72) in Pecola's eyes – walks in, assumes that Pecola has killed the animal, and violently expels her from the house. This expulsion is a symbolic expunging of Geraldine's own dreaded, ever-threatening blackness onto Pecola. Geraldine "had explained to [Junior] the difference between colored people and nigger ... He belonged to the former group" (67). But "[t]he line between colored and nigger was not always clear; subtle and telltale signs threatened to erode it, and the watch had to be constant" (68). Pecola's expulsion re-inscribes the line, the boundary, and turns Pecola into a terrifying, deathly figure: "They were everywhere ... Grass wouldn't grow where they lived" (72).

The third-person narrator, having adopted Geraldine's perspective, then reverses this perspective and confidently rejects Geraldine's paranoiac self-constitution as self-mutilating. In the process, Geraldine has herself become a deathly, Winter force because she has cut herself off from her own "Funk": "the funkiness of the wide range of human emotions" (64). Her respectability is blind "obedience" and only serves to do "the white man's work with refinement" (64).

SPRING

In the opening chapter (75–85) of this section, narrated by the adult Claudia, Pecola is expelled by her own mother, Pauline Breedlove. Pauline is an "ideal servant" (98) in one of the largest and most prosperous houses in Lorain, the house of the Fishers; she is a modern, Northern version of the "mammy" of the Southern mansion. In the midst of an accident with a burning berry pie in the Fishers' kitchen, Pauline expels her injured daughter while tenderly comforting the white girl in her care. Refusing to reveal and recognize her kinship with Pecola and therefore refusing her own inclusion in the category of "nigger" to which she has consigned Pecola, she allies herself with the white girl. As a counterpoint – the full significance of which will emerge later – Claudia's and Frieda's parents expel their lodger, Mr Henry, when Frieda tells them that he touched her breasts.

Pauline's role in the Fishers' home foregrounds something unacknowledged by the myth of the family outlined in the primer. The comfort and loveliness of the affluent white home are supported by Pauline's labour, at Pecola's expense. The series of scapegoating incidents we have discussed – a series that chronologically precedes Pecola's rape by her father – implicates everyone in Pecola's mental alienation, her madness.

The chapter of pages 86–102, devoted to Pauline, describes Pauline's history as indissociable from the context of wider historical and social forces and short-circuits any reading that would attempt to focus the blame for Pecola's fate narrowly on Pauline's private inadequacy. This chapter has two narrators: both the third-person narrator and Pauline as a first-person narrator. The two narrations combine to describe Pauline's social castration and neurosis – manifesting itself, for example, in her view of herself and her daughter as irredeemably ugly – as a result of her migration from the rural South to the urban North. This perspective or hypothesis questions and undermines two conventional ideas at the same time. The first is Freud's view that neuroses are the result of events within the family during one's childhood. The second – the African American version of the American dream – is that the urban North was to be a kind of Promised Land for the migrants.

Pauline spends the first 11 years of her life "on a ridge of red Alabama clay seven miles from the nearest road" (86). The third-person narrator insists that her Oedipus-like damaged foot, due to a childhood accident – Morrison's coded reference to Freud, the Oedipus complex and castration – *was not* the cause of her eventual neurosis and "the end of her lovely beginning" (86). Although at the beginning of World War I the family moves to a town in Kentucky (due to an increase in industrial job opportunities generated by the War), Pauline remains insulated from the urban experience and preserves "her country ways and lack of knowledge about city things" (90) because she stays at home to do housework and mind her young siblings while her mother works as a servant. Then Cholly comes along, whistling "[a] kind of city street music" (89), kisses her damaged foot, "enjoy[s] her country ways", but takes her away "up north" (90–91) to Lorain.

Pauline, as her first-person narration reveals, is a born visual artist. She sees the world in terms of relations between lines, volumes and colours and rearranges her domain – from found objects to "jars on shelves" (86) – to make those relations aesthetically pleasing. She also organizes her experience and her memories aesthetically. She understands her happy childhood in terms of a composition of purple, yellow and green – the purple of berries, the yellow of home-made lemonade and the green of Southern "june bugs" illuminating trees at night – and uses this composition to picture her early love for Cholly and their passionate love-making (87, 90, 101–2).

Pauline's Spring is invisible to Northerners, white and black, who look down upon her as a representative of the rural South – blacks "[n]o better than whites for meanness ... 'cept I didn't expect it from them" (91). Her first employer in Lorain is a middle-class white feminist woman who seeks to impose her own world-view on Pauline and is grotesquely blind to the specificity of her experience. She refuses to pay Pauline until she divorces her unsatisfactory husband and claims alimony. Black Northern women similarly view Pauline as lacking their own straightened hair, high heels and Northern city accent. Pauline's recapitulation, the end of her efforts to defy Northern attitudes, her social castration, finally takes place while she watches a Hollywood film.

> I 'member one time I went to see Clark Gable and Jean Harlow. I fixed my hair up like I'd seen hers on a magazine. A part on the side, with one little curl on my forehead. It looked just like her. Well, almost just like ... I was sitting back in my seat, and I had taken a big bite of that candy, and it pulled a [front] tooth right out of my mouth.
>
> (96)

"Well, almost just like": in a "double bind" imposed by mainstream culture, Pauline must desire but cannot have Jean Harlow hair. Hollywood promises Pauline beauty and sexual fulfilment but delivers ugliness. The third-person narrator explains that, in the movies, "Along with the idea of romantic love, [Pauline] was introduced to ... physical beauty. Probably the most destructive ideas in the history of human thought ... In equating physical beauty with virtue, she ... collected self-contempt by the heap" (95). After the emphatic indignity of the loss of her tooth Pauline "settled down to just being ugly" (96). When she gives birth to Pecola, she looks at her and judges her with the weight of her own defeatedness: "I knowed she was ugly" (98) – gradually "into her daughter she beat ... fear of life" (100).

Morrison appropriates a Freudian dream-symbol of castration anxiety – the pulled-out tooth – into a symbol of social castration performed by the "dream industry" of Hollywood. Morrison's lyrical descriptions of the agrarian South reverse the traditional idealization of the North in the black imagination.

Morrison returns to the rural South in the following chapter (103–29), where the third-person narrator describes Cholly's history and, finally, his rape of Pecola. Cholly spends the first 13 years of his life in rural Georgia. Abandoned by his parents at birth, he is other-mothered – informally adopted – by his Great Aunt Jimmy. The narrator conveys Cholly's memory of her "handing him a bit of smoked hoc ... clumsy-like, in three fingers, but with so much affection" (125). The critic Andrea O'Reilly (2004) discusses the African American tradition of other-mothering and community-mothering as a survival of West African collectivism and a valuable cultural resource. This resource seems to be under threat of extinction in the urban North: the County has to intervene to house Pecola, who arrives at the MacTeers's escorted by a white official; Mrs MacTeer's gossip with her friends touches upon other such cases of failure of community-mothering.

Young Cholly is other-mothered by Jimmy and Blue Jack and nourished by Blue's storytelling: passing on important events in African American history such as the Emancipation Proclamation, real-life stories of love and lynchings, ghost stories. When Jimmy becomes ill, she is herself cared for by her friends. On her deathbed Cholly witnesses Jimmy and two female friends turning their pain and suffering into narrative in a "recitative of pain" (107). At the funeral, people are "engrossed in ... reminiscences about dreams, figures, premonitions ... recollections and fabrications of hallucinations" (117). This spring of communal oral culture is privatized and under threat in the urban North. It survives in the household of the three whores; in Mrs MacTeer's soliloquies and her blues singing alone in her kitchen; in the violin playing of Claudia's and Frieda's grandfather in their grandmother's kitchen.

During Jimmy's funeral, Cholly and Darlene walk away into an Arcadian world of "wild wineyard[s]" and "green-and-purple grass on the edge of the pine woods" (114). Then, on the verge of sexual congress in communion with Nature, the pastoral is suddenly invaded by a violent anti-pastoral force: two white men with a cocked gun force Cholly to "get on wid it" (116). While simulating the act, he directs his hate at Darlene, as hating grown white men "would have consumed" a young boy: "Such an emotion would have destroyed him" (118). Cholly runs away to the city (Macon, Georgia) in search of his father. He is rejected by him anew and, straining every muscle to stop the tears, suffers a new humiliation: he soils himself. For a period he becomes "dangerously free" (125), "truly free" and affirms "his own perceptions and appetites" in a "godlike state" (126). But marriage and children finally defeat him, deadening his imagination and curiosity.

Pecola's rape is narrated by the third-person narrator but controversially seen through the perspective of Cholly's feelings: a volatile interplay of love and hate. He returns home, steps into the kitchen, and initially looks at his daughter as he looked at Darlene, hating her because he loves her but cannot protect her. The reader is invited to link Cholly's "rape" by the white men with his rape of Pecola. Then Pecola accidentally repeats a "quiet and pitiful" (127) gesture Pauline was performing with her damaged foot when Cholly first saw her and loved her. "The tenderness welled up in him, and he sank to his knees" (128). Then lust takes over. He observes but is not deterred by Pecola's bodily reactions: the "rigidness of the shocked body, the silence of the stunned throat ... the dry harbor of her vagina. She appeared to have fainted" (128). After the rape, he looks at her with "hatred mixed with tenderness" (129). Readers familiar with the interplay of love and hate in canonical modernist novels such as D.H. Lawrence's *The Rainbow* are disturbed by their mixedness in the context of a rape. Some critics have complained that Morrison risks exculpating the rapist and silencing the victim.

In Cholly, Morrison mobilizes the racist stereotype of the "bad nigger" and brings it face-to-face with the ancient Greek tragic hero who hubristically exceeds his limits: Cholly's descriptions as "godlike" and "dangerously free" (125–26) are equally appropriate for the "bad nigger" and the "tragic hero". As Morrison points out, Cholly is what "I keep calling a 'free man' ... free in his head ... I think it's a way of talking about what some people call the 'bad nigger'" (Morrison 1976a, 19). Cholly "express[es] either an effort of the will or a freedom of the will" (Morrison 1983a, 164).

Barbara Christian, in *Black Feminist Criticism* (Christian 1985), argues that the dominant figure in African American novels has been the "tragic mulatto", the African American who is light-skinned enough to pass as white and to enter white society at a time of segregation and strictly enforced apartheid. *The Bluest Eye* distances itself from this figure; the tragic hero here is the dark-skinned and underclass Cholly and – in the eyes of some critics including Barbara Christian – Pecola herself.

In the chapter of pages 130–45, the third-person narrator describes pregnant Pecola's visit to the charlatan, Soaphead Church, as he is called by everyone. Soaphead's letter to God in this chapter qualifies him as one of the first-person narrators of the novel. Soaphead was born Elihue Whitcomb and added the middle name Micah, an Old Testament name that means "godlike" in Hebrew. Soaphead, a light brown West Indian with a "fine education" (130), is the offspring of a highly educated middle-class family proud to descend from the mulatto bastard of a British aristocrat. In keeping with the white pseudo-scientific racism of de Gobineau, they attribute their intellectual achievements to their white blood.

Just as Geraldine attempts to cut herself off from "niggers" and her own Funk, Soaphead attempts to cut himself off from "niggers" and all bodily excretions – his name (Soap) connotes cleansing. He becomes a paedophile to avoid conventional intercourse and touches little girls' breasts, innocently in his view, in clean and fluidless fun. Nauseated by the mucous excretion around the eyes of his landlady's old dog, he is looking for a way to get rid of it, when Pecola knocks on his door. She has a "little protruding pot of tummy" (137), is not allowed to go to school because of her pregnancy, and says she is in urgent need of blue eyes as a solution to her isolation. Soaphead, in his excessive adherence to white values and to the value of white-ness, only too readily understands the logic of the 12-year-old child's reasoning. Handing poisoned meat to Pecola, he asks her to feed the dog: any unusual behaviour, he tells her, would be the sign that her wish has been granted. The dog's death agony convinces Pecola that her prayer for blue eyes has been answered.

After the incident, Soaphead's letter to God marks him as an author figure. The letter is the beginning of his autocritique. It is "an incisive analysis of his own corrupt being", according to Denise Heinze (1993, 130). Comparing himself to God, it is written from one creator (of imagined blue eyes) to another and from one "bad man" to another (143). Soaphead's acceptance of the mixture of good and evil in everyone, including God, questions and undermines his lifelong effort to whiten himself:

> [W]e were not royal but snobbish, not aristocratic but class-conscious; we believed authority was cruelty to our inferiors, and education was being at school ... Our manhood was defined by acquisitions. Our womanhood by acquiescence.
>
> (140–41)

SUMMER

In the chapter of pages 147–51, adult Claudia narrates Claudia's and Frieda's summer of 1941. While selling marigold seeds all over town in order to buy a new bicycle, from house to house they gather the spreading story of Pecola's pregnancy and reactions to it. Pecola is beaten by her mother, Cholly leaves, and everyone feels an "overwhelming hatred for the unborn baby" (150) because it is "Bound to be the ugliest thing walking" as its parents are "two ugly people doubling up ... to make more ugly" (149). Claudia and Frieda devise a magic ritual for the baby to live: they bury the bicycle money and plant the remaining marigold seeds, incanting magic words. If the seeds sprout the baby will live. But the seeds do not sprout and the baby dies. Thinking that they have failed Pecola, Frieda and Claudia abandon interest in her.

The final chapter (152–64) begins with a long and intimate conversation between Pecola and a hallucinated friend. Pecola's newly acquired blue eyes lend credibility to the idea that she should have a close and loving friend. The conversation allows Pecola to acknowledge the rape and condemn it as "[h]orrible" (158); to acknowledge a second incident with Cholly and voice her fear that it might have elicited a bodily response other than that of pure horror; to reject those who have rejected her – "*I don't like anybody besides you*" says the friend (156); to acknowledge painful truths at a safe distance, including her own madness: "you were right here. Right before my eyes." "*No, honey. Right after your eyes.*" (154).

This conversation finally allows Pecola a sustained voice. Significantly, it also arguably brings about a merging of the novel's two main narrators: the unspecified third-person extradiegetic and objective narrator; and adult Claudia as the first-person intradiegetic and subjective narrator. After the conversation these two narrations formally merge. Previously, chapters narrated by the third-person narrator began with an epigraph extracted from the third, jumbled up version of the Dick-and-Jane primer and were typeset with justified right margins; chapters narrated by adult Claudia in the first person had no epigraphs or other titles and were typeset with unjustified right margins. In this chapter, an epigraph is combined with Claudia's first-person narration and with justified right margins to suggest that the subjective and the objective have come together. This formal merging is replicated in the content of the narration. Adult Claudia, in this chapter alone, is privy to information beyond her experience – information earlier available only to the omniscient third-person narrator. It can be argued that adult Claudia was the third-person narrator all along. Alternatively, it can be argued that the two narrators have merged after Pecola's schizophrenia and even *because of it*. Lynne Tirrell's "Storytelling and Moral Agency" (Tirrell 1990) is devoted to this merging. Tirrell argues that adult Claudia authorizes herself as a moral agent in the very act of telling Pecola's story. According to Tirrell, Claudia initially pursues separately a third-person objective narrative and a first-person subjective narrative, but finally manages to combine the two and tell Pecola's story in a manner that is not "oversimplified by too much involvement and too little distance ... or too much distance and too little involvement" (in Middleton 2000, 19).

The merging of the two voices – objective and subjective – enables adult Claudia to articulate a fuller, multi-layered, composite interpretation of Pecola's fate. Pecola was everyone's waste: "All of our waste which we dumped on her and which she absorbed ... All of us – all who knew her – felt so wholesome after we cleaned ourselves on her ... We honed our egos on her, padded our characters with her frailty, and yawned in the fantasy of our strength" (162–63). Claudia considers everyone personally and actively responsible – including herself and us, the readers – and declares that "we assassinated" the thing that mad Pecola is searching for in the garbage (163). On the other hand, and simultaneously, adult Claudia argues that the iron determinism of an entire social system – "the land kill-[ing] of its own volition" – decided her fate: "the land of the entire country was hostile to marigolds that year. This soil is bad for certain kinds of flowers" (164).

It is important to point out that adult Claudia, in this chapter, argues *both*: her counter-narrative is dialogic rather than monologic and dogmatic. Adult Claudia is equally dialogic in her final account of Pecola's fate. On the one hand, Pecola is a victim crushed by external forces and *A Bluest Eye* is a naturalist novel. (See Furst and Skrine 1971.) "The damage done [to Pecola] was total" (162) and irreversible: "It's too late ... much, much, much too late" (164). On the other hand, Pecola is a tragic hero, freely and willfully crossing the line: "She, however, stepped over into madness, a madness which protected her from us" (163). Most critics adopt the former view; some critics, notably Barbara Christian and Lucille Fultz, adopt the latter view. Pecola's name, pointing to the Latin *pecco*, "I sin", also supports the latter view.

Morrison's strategy in her first novel has been one of bold narrative revision, as a means of engaging with the reader's misconceptions and questioning them effectively. Having conducted the reader away from complacent sureties, the open-endedness of this novel sets the reader a new challenge: to think dialogically.

Sula (1973)

Sula is the story of the interrupted friendship between two black girls, Sula and Nel, in the context of modernity, a context the novel interrogates critically and redefines. Sula is a figure of the modern black woman writer, Nel a figure of the writer's community and audience. Their aborted friendship and Sula's premature death explore impediments to the emergence of the black woman writer and of a fluid and multiplicitous female black self. Some of these impediments are theoretical discourses such as existentialist feminism and black nationalism: the novel investigates their possibilities and limitations and calls for the need to move beyond both. *Sula* intertextually engages with a number of discourses, as we will see: provisionally or ironically endorsing but also questioning them, in a particularly open-ended manner that gives the reader a lot of freedom and responsibility. It is therefore a text in dialogue with itself, but also in dialogue with its readers.

BLACK MODERNITY: THE BOTTOM, CHADRACK, EVA

The first chapter of *Sula* introduces a place as a main character. The Bottom is a black neighbourhood "tucked" into the hills of the small fictional river valley town of Medallion, in Morrison's native Ohio (6; all page numbers in this chapter refer to *Sula* [Morrison 1973] unless otherwise indicated). Thomas Hardy opens *The Return of the Native* with a pagan description of Egdon Heath as an ancient living being on which other small and short-lived creatures, including humans, live. Morrison, by contrast, throws us into the midst of the violent process of the Bottom's death in 1965: already "they tore the nightshade and blackberry patches from their roots" – "nightshade and blackberry", plants black in name or actuality – and soon "They are going to raze" and "level" the buildings (3). This death in the name of "progress" (6) will transform the Bottom into the modern Medallion City Golf Course.

The narrative perspective of the third-person unidentified narrator is extraordinarily mobile in this section. However, the main perspective is the distanced view – "that place", "there" (3) – of a white urban outsider, who "happened to have business" in the Bottom, such as "collecting rent" (4). This perspective romanticizes black poverty and turns it into the fascinating ethnographic spectacle of a picturesque black woman "doing a bit of cakewalk" to a mouth organ in the midst of black people who "laugh and rub their knees" (4). This is exactly the perspective George Eliot rejected forcefully in relation to middle-class representations of the poor in English literature, and against which she defined her "realism" in Chapter 17 *of Adam Bede* and in her essay "The Natural History of German Life". Morrison later rejected her use or *mimicry* of a white perspective here. She argued that it was used to draw white readers into a black world and that this was a compromise she should have avoided. In keeping with Homi K. Bhabha's understanding of "mimicry" (see "Of Mimicry and Man" in Bhabha's *The Location of Culture*), I would argue that her "mimicry" of this white perspective involves its ironization – e.g. we are aware of the administrative doublespeak in: "Generous funds have been allotted to level" the Bottom (3) – and its critique: "it would be easy" for this man "to ... not notice the pain ... the pain would escape him" (4). The white urban outsider's perspective mythologizes and dehistoricizes the Bottom – "there was once a neighborhood" (3). However, those of us who accept the ironic invitation to read the Bottom formulaically as a timeless and picturesque folk community unrelated to modernity will be rudely shaken in the next chapters. The reader is caused to think about how to relate and *not* to relate to the Bottom; and a perspective that can "notice the pain" is subtly elaborated.

We are proleptically promised that in the pages to come we will "notice the adult *pain*" (4, my italics). Witnessing human suffering is the register of Greek tragedy, and its peculiar characteristics were outlined by Plato, Aristotle and Nietzsche. In the *Republic*, Plato has a strange psychological insight that is still with us today: "When Homer or another tragedian represents the grief of one of the heroes ... *even the best of us ... feels pleasure*" (Plato 1998, Book X, 605; my italics). Aristotle builds on this insight with his theory of catharsis in *Poetics* (Aristotle 1942). In *The Birth of Tragedy* Nietzsche, rewriting Aristotle, understands tragedy as the transfiguration of suffering into aesthetic delight. Is the aestheticization of reality compatible with ethics? How should one bear witness properly?

Having witnessed the ignominious end of a long-established dwelling place, the novel is going to be an attempt to return to a lost world whose last vestiges are being obliterated. In this respect, Harold Bloom's description of Morrison as a "poet of loss" – in the tradition of Woolf and Faulkner – is quite apposite for *Sula* (Bloom 1990b, 4). But why go back? When the era of segregation came to an end, black people moved downtown, and black communities such as the Bottom declined. Segregation continued by other means, as the white middle-class moved to the suburbs and set up exclusive spaces such as the Medallion City Golf Course, while black people were trapped in the inner-city ghettoes. (See **p. 19**.) (See Morrison 1976a, 12.) We will see that Morrison is going back to the past in search of cultural resources for the future.

In discussing *The Bluest Eye*, I showed Morrison's use of "narrative revision": mobilizing certain formulaic expectations in the reader only to demolish these expectations as fraudulent. Similarly, the white outsider's perspective discussed above assumed a binary opposition between, on the one hand, modernity and progress; on the other hand, the Bottom as a premodern folk community of "banjos", "mouth organs", folktales, "bare feet" and "head rags" (4–5). Chadrack, whose biblical namesake survived the fiery furnace (Daniel 2), deconstructs this opposition. Chadrack is *of* the Bottom but at the same time modern in an exemplary way. He fought in World War I – the first modern, technologically advanced and industrialized war – and returned from the inferno "ravaged" (7) beyond repair. His story is narrated in the third person but focalized through Chadrack's perspective on the world. He inevitably invites comparison with Septimus Warren Smith, the shell-shocked psychotic World War I veteran and interrupted artist in Virginia Woolf's *Mrs Dalloway*. Chadrack's description of the death of a soldier (8) is in keeping with trauma theory in its dissociation of feeling and unnaturally vivid sensation; but it is also a composition in white (breath), grey (explosions) and red (blood), suggesting he is an artist figure. Because of his artist's eye, the rice (white), meat (grey) and tomatoes (red), each in a triangle of his hospital food tray, allow him to repeat the trauma of the death scene in such a way that its "repugnance was contained in the neat balance of the triangles" (8) – and the unpredictability and disorder of modern reality is artistically mastered. Released from hospital, the psychotic, hallucinating, delirious, amnesiac and dispossessed Chadrack is an exemplary modern self: "hot, frightened, not daring to acknowledge the fact that he didn't even know who or what he was" (12). He returns to the Bottom and continues his "struggle to order … experience. It had to do with making a place for fear as a way of controlling it" (14). On the third of January 1920, with an artist's creativity, he invents a public ritual, National Suicide Day, telling people that "this was their only chance to kill themselves or each other" (14). He is a modern artist figure: both cut off from the people – living on the margins of the Bottom in a shack overlooking the river – and attempting to speak and act for them; searching for utopian aesthetic solutions to escape the nightmare of history.

Eva is an equally modern figure. She kills her only son, Plum, in 1921. Abraham, the biblical patriarch, chose to sacrifice his only son, Isaac, in obedience to God. Eva, the modern African American matriarch, chose to sacrifice her only son, Plum, for his own good, according to her judgement alone. Eva develops into a modern female subjectivity in the 1890s when her husband, BoyBoy, abandons her and their three young children to answer the call of big-city living, the African American dream. A destitute single black mother of three, Eva's confrontation with modernity is more naked than BoyBoy's and demands of her that she summon demonic powers of action to preserve the lives of her children. Eva's modern experience is the discovery of her capacity for action. She leaves her children with Mrs Suggs for a day only to return 18 months later, with only one leg and a "new black pocketbook" (34). It is believed that she put her leg under a train for insurance money. As an exemplary modern worker, she had realized that her body – very literally – was all she had to sell. Like the soldier whose face was destroyed by shellfire and like the "ravaged" Chadrack, Eva's leg is caught in the wheels of modernity. What is extraordinary in her case is that Eva chooses this to ensure the survival of her children. Eva's is a female subjectivity enabled by motherhood.

Eva builds a rambling house where she reigns as "creator and sovereign" (30) over a large brood: her own children, "other children Eva took in" (37), such as the three "deweys", lodgers, and "a regular flock of gentleman callers" who enjoy both her "male" intellectual superiority and independence and her "female" nurturing qualities (42). Eva's son Plum "floated in a constant swaddle" of maternal love until he went to World War I and returned intractably addicted to hard drugs (45).

The detailed description of Eva's killing of Plum provides sufficient textual evidence to support opposing readings of it: as a mercy killing motivated by mother love; or on the contrary as a grotesque over-stepping of one's limits and an egotistical perversion of "mother knows best". Following the reader-response theorist Wolfgang Iser, we can call this a textual "gap": a passage designed to allow several incompatible interpretations and inviting the reader to step in and actively construct or choose their own meaning, and impose their own judgement. Perhaps predictably, the critical controversy has been intense and critics have taken polarized views for and against the act. Morrison herself intriguingly condemned Eva of selfishness in an interview, arguing that she killed Plum because his condition was "too painful for her" (Morrison 1976a, 15–16).

Eva herself understands Hannah's death by fire in 1923 as "the perfection of the judgment against her" for killing Plum (78). However, she defends her decision to kill Plum – he was so infantilized that he "wanted to crawl back in my womb" (71) – and responds to Hannah's misfortune with her capacity for excessive action in relation to her children undiminished: she leaps out of a third-floor window in an attempt to cover Hannah with her body and extinguish the fire.

Morrison's exploration of an alternative androgynous female subjectivity that mixes a "male" capacity for action, a "male" triumph over the world, independence from the subservient or "handmaiden" role of wife and "female" affirmation of the role of mother is an engagement both with the historical experience of poor black women and with the racist stereotype of pathological and pathogenic black matriarchy. The influential 1965 Moynihan Report on the state of the black family revivified this stereotype and gave urgency to Morrison's intervention. Against the Report, *Sula*'s many references to black men's structural unemployment and their exclusion from well-paid working-class employment such as road-building suggest economic reasons for the vulnerability of the black family and the large number of single-parent black families.

THE BLACK MODERN WRITER AND HER AUDIENCE: SULA AND NEL

The point of emergence of Nel's subjectivity is the ten-year-old Nel's train journey to New Orleans in November 1920. She was and will continue to be her mother's daughter in character, but during this trip she also begins a line of deviation from her mother. Nel is a differential, both/and, both self and other, as will become clear shortly. This deviation will enable her to befriend Sula against her mother's wishes. Nel's motherline sends Morrison back to territory explored in *The Bluest Eye*. Her grandmother, Rochelle Sabat, is a Creole whore. Though prettier and wealthier than the three whores of *The Bluest Eye*, she is portrayed with equal enthusiasm. As Heinze points out, "Morrison particularly delights in showcasing the prostitute"; Rochelle is magnificent and, with her "halolike hair, is truly virginal" (Heinze 1993, 46, 81). She is the "woman in a yellow dress" (25), a Morrisonian fetish, and will reappear in *Tar Baby*. Nel's mother, Helene, builds her subjectivity as a fortress to keep out Rochelle; hers is an identity built on the opposition of self and other. She becomes a figure akin to Geraldine in *The Bluest Eye*: she imports white middle-class morality – and "oppressive" (29) cleanliness, uprightness and sexual puritanism – and makes an advantageous marriage, in order to be "as far away from the Sundown House [Rochelle's brothel] as possible" (17).

The white-identifying Helene accidentally boards a "Whites Only" compartment – the Freudian reading would be that this is an unconscious wish fulfilment. She is intercepted by the white conductor: "What you think you doin', gal?" (20). What happens next is an extraordinary crossfire of looks. The conductor looks at Helene, it is suggested, in the same manner in which he jiggles his ear free of wax: in other words, he sees this "pale yellow" (20) black woman in a beautiful brown dress as having both the colour and the value of ear wax. Helene, inappropriately "eager to please" the bestial conductor (20), "Smiled dazzlingly and coquettishly" at him (21). Meanwhile two black soldiers (presumably World War I veterans), whom Helene's glance quickly registers as having "shit-colored uniforms" (21), an unthinking racial slur, witness this. In Nel's eyes, who is looking at the soldiers, they "looked stricken" by the spectacle (21) and responded with a "bubbling ... hatred for her mother" (22). Having to make a choice, Nel identifies with the black male perspective – and recognizes the authority – of the soldiers: she decides that her mother's smile was "foolish"; her mother was "custard" (22), "custard pudding" (28). Her deviation from her white-identifying mother starts here, and upon her return to the Bottom Nel befriends Sula, whose family is unacceptably "sooty" in Helene's eyes (29).

The train scene hinges on the viewpoint of the black soldiers, a proto-black-nationalist perspective. What was it about these black men's participation in World War I and their return home that liberated in them an attitude of antagonism to white authority and the rejection of black submissiveness? (See **p. 10**.) *Sula*'s two black soldiers of November 1920 invite the reader to consider this historical experience.

In this scene the third-person narrator largely conveys ten-year-old Nel's newfound perspective. The problem with this perspective is that it is a harsh male perspective projecting onto Helene the soldiers' own helplessness. Sensing that she is a potential victim of this gaze, Nel endorses its authority while also feeling threatened by it: "She wanted to make certain that no man ever looked at her that way" or "would ever accost her and turn her into jelly" (22). What is beyond her is rejecting both white and black male authority for a black female subjectivity.

Nel and Sula, aged 12, become friends in 1922. In interviews Morrison repeatedly stressed the friendship between Nel and Sula as the major thematic innovation of the book: "[t]o have heterosexual women who are friends, who are talking only about themselves to each other, seemed to me a very radical thing when *Sula* was published in 1973" (Morrison 1993b, 252).

Nel and Sula are ostensibly complementary. Whereas Nel dreams the conventional but inappropriate passive dream of being a princess waiting for a prince, Sula dreams the novel active dream of "galloping" on a horse "through her own mind" (52). Whereas Nel is "consistent" and has a core self, Sula is a creature of moods and "could hardly be counted on to sustain any emotion for more than three minutes" (53). Chicken Little slipping through Sula's fingers, falling in the river and drowning is a metaphor capturing the problematic side of Sula's lack of a stable core self to rely on. The changing birthmark over her eye is a sign of the Protean Sula, lending itself to a wide spectrum of interpretations from other characters in the course of the novel.

Their friendship lasts five years and enables a crossfertilization of their complementary selves: self and other communicate and cross the frontier between them. The quality of their friendship was "adventuresomeness ... a mean determination to explore everything that interested them" (55). There is a common project underlying their complementarity and deconstructing/undoing their divide: "Because each had discovered years before that they were neither white nor male, they had set about creating something else to be" (52). This "something else to be" turns out to be the friendship itself, as old Nel recognizes belatedly in the closing pages of the book.

Morrison questions both Sula and Nel. In 1923 Sula watches her mother burn. Eva "remained convinced that Sula had watched Hannah burn not because she was paralyzed, but because she was interested" (78). The description of Hannah's agony is protracted and unbearably graphic for the reader: sight, sound and smell are stimulated disturbingly. This description might be argued to emanate from Sula's fascinated observation. Sula's "adventuresomeness" begins to be critically explored. Is she too detached or just traumatized?

In 1927 Nel marries Jude Greene. It is a rare middle-class "real marriage" in the Bottom: an expensive marriage in church followed by a reception, conceived and executed by Helene Wright (80). Black men's exclusion from well-paid construction work undermines Jude's masculinity, and he wants to marry to give himself "a someone sweet, industrious and loyal to shore him up ... The two of them together would make one Jude" (83). Nel – or rather a part of her – accepts this role gladly. Her other part – her "sparkle" and "splutter" – would only have "free reign" with Sula (83). But Sula leaves the Bottom in the midst of the wedding reception and that part of Nel disappears from view.

The narrator's perspective, in this section, is feminist. We are reminded of the observation in Woolf's *A Room of One's Own* that a woman is a mirror showing man twice his size. However, Morrison here mainly engages with Simone de Beauvoir's existentialist feminism of *The Second Sex*. Patriarchy forces upon women a role of "being for others": nurturing and living for others and through others (their husband or children) rather than affirming their subjectivity directly. This role is internalized by women, who must reject this pseudo-destiny in order to live authentically. Authentic subjectivity is a deviant subjectivity, breaking away from the endless unwitting reproduction of a state of things and leaping towards another possible future: making oneself anew, reinventing oneself otherwise. It is exactly her potential for free subjectivity that Nel shuts down when she marries Jude and loses Sula. We begin to ask whether Nel's identification with a defiant black male perspective in the train scene impedes her subjective freedom, making her subservient to Jude.

In 1937 Sula returns to the Bottom a university graduate, herself expounding existentialist feminism. When Eva greets her return with a rude put-down: "When you gone to get married? You need to have some babies. It'll settle you", Sula responds in formulaic existentialist language: "I don't want to make somebody else. I want to make myself" (92). Morrison now examines the value and appropriateness of existentialist feminism in the context of a poor black community under siege. She develops a black nationalist perspective from the point of view of which Sula's feminism is an evil and makes the case against Sula strongly. Morrison will, in turn, question black nationalism subsequently.

Upon her return to the Bottom Sula puts Eva in a home for destitute black people run by a white church, and then sleeps with Nel's husband. This is not freedom but licence, the reader might think. To strengthen the case against Sula in the eyes of the readers temporarily, red herrings are used in this section: for example, Nel states as a fact that Jude left her for Sula (110), but this turns out later not to be the case. It turns out that Sula had no intention at all to take Jude away from Nel and settle down with him. The Bottom comes to view Sula as the embodiment of evil and the stemmed-rose birthmark over her eye (52) is now reinterpreted as a "scary black thing" (97–98), "copperhead" (103), "rattlesnake" (104), "Hannah's ashes" (114), "evil birthmark" (114).

Morrison now unfolds the black nationalist perspective. Sula is evil because she threatens the survival of the Bottom. Whites in the same position would set out to stone her and "annihilate" her, but the people of the Bottom tolerate her because they have a "full recognition of the legitimacy of forces other than good ones" (90). Whites have been burning witches and lynching black people, but there is no equivalent behaviour amongst black people, who are morally superior: "There was no creature so ungodly as to make them destroy it … they could not 'mob kill' anyone" (118). Put metaphysically, Western cosmology polarizes good and evil; African and African American cosmologies recognize the coexistence of good and evil.

Having expounded this black nationalist perspective Morrison then exposes it to critical consideration by juxtaposing, ironically, its view of Sula as a devil to what is actually happening in Sula's life in 1939. Sula discovers "possession" not in the demonic sense but in the formulaically feminine sense of wanting to "nest" with Ajax. He smells the "scent of the nest" and leaves her (133). The narrator now looks more closely into the black nationalist argument against Sula: "it was the men who gave her the final label ... the dirt that could not ever be washed away. They said that Sula slept with white men. It may not have been true, but it certainly could have been" (112). The narrator exposes the process of Sula's demonization: it derives from a repressive male perspective, which targets a woman and projects onto her what the community doesn't want to acknowledge in itself: the men's own "willingness" to sleep with white women and everyone's "skin color [which] was proof that it had happened in their own families" (113). Sula is used as a scapegoat. Though Sula's demonization is unjustified, nevertheless it has a socially useful or policing effect on the people of the Bottom, particularly the women, who shoulder the burden of their responsibilities towards others – the traditional female roles of caring for the young, the old and the needy – more willingly.

Sula explores a new modern subjectivity. Modern subjectivity is announced in the nineteenth-century writings of Walt Whitman, Walter Pater, Nietzsche and Oscar Wilde, who emphasize the fluidity and multiplicity of the modern self: "Do I contradict myself? / Very well then. ... I contradict myself; / I am large. ... I contain multitudes" (Whitman 1855, 85). Instead of a stable and unchanging core self one has a "multiplicity of inner states" (Nietzsche 1888, 44), one has "moods" (Wilde 1891, 68, 71, 90–91). For Sula, too, "there was no self to count on ... She had no center, no speck around which to grow" (119). Instead, "There was only her own mood and whim" (121); "she lived out her days exploring her own thoughts and emotions, giving them full range ... hers was an experimental life" (118). For Pater, in *The Renaissance* (1873): "This at least of flame-like our life has, that it is but the concurrence, renewed from moment to moment, of forces parting sooner or later on their ways" (Pater 1873, 150); we find the volatility of modern life intensified when we observe the self: "if we begin with the inward world of thought and feeling, the whirlpool is still more rapid, the flame more eager and devouring" (ibid., 151). The responsibility of the critic–artist "towards the human spirit, is to rouse, to startle it to a life of constant observation" (ibid., 152), Pater writes. Sula echoes this: "What's burning in me is mine" (93) she asserts and sets out to observe it with "tremendous curiosity" and a romantic "gift for metaphor"; she is a modern "artist with no art form" (121). This new subjectivity is not the prerogative of privileged European men; it is open to all those who deviate from or resist dominant morality and fixed social and gender roles.

Sula's own first-person narration momentarily breaks through in an italicized passage where she metaphorically excavates Ajax to find stratum after stratum of precious material: gold, alabaster, and the deep stratum of black fertile loam (130–31). However, she soon hits a dead end: in a monologue spoken aloud, as to an audience, she confides in us her exhaustion – "There aren't any more new songs and I have sung all the songs there are" (137) – and is then interrupted by third-person narration. The next chapter opens with Sula on her deathbed at the age of 30.

Two reasons are suggested for Sula's dead end. First, she had been "looking all along for a friend" but "a lover was not a comrade and could never be – for a woman"; secondly, she was an "artist with no art form" (121). Arguably the two are related. The demise of her friendship with Nel deprives Sula of an audience for her dreams and experiments. Sula and Nel are not only complementary parts of the self, they are also figurations of modern black female artist and community that fail to come together, yet ought to come together. This is an implicit critique of existentialist feminism: community is not a limitation to be overcome by authentic subjectivity nor a situation whose weight hampers authentic subjectivity, but the "speck" and "consistency" around which the modern black female artist can crystallize and grow.

In 1940 Nel visits Sula on her deathbed. She sees Sula's birthmark (and Sula herself) as a "black rose" (139), not as the sign of evil it represents for the community, but can't help being "exasperated with her arrogance" (142). In response to Sula's defiant affirmation, "I got my mind" (143), Nel raises the question of right and wrong and leaves. Sula, the artist, acknowledges her aestheticization of reality: "I stood there watching [Hannah] burn and was thrilled" (147). Are aesthetics and ethics mutually exclusive? Sula then has a nightmare – a recurring one – that provides an indirect answer. The smiling Clabber Girl Baking Powder lady disintegrates into dust. Sula tries ineffectually to stuff the dust into her pockets but ends up covered in dust, swallowing it and choking. Underneath the bright surface of aesthetic delight the artist relates traumatic events – such as beautiful Hannah turning into dust – in order to save and preserve what is irrevocably lost. But this ethical vocation is difficult and threatens to overwhelm the artist.

The novel then momentarily takes a supernatural direction (this is the first instance of the supernatural element that will come to characterize Morrison's subsequent fiction): Sula, impossibly, "noticed that she was not breathing, that her heart had stopped completely ... She was dead" (149). Having witnessed her own death, Sula's last words – "Wait'll I tell Nel" (149) – with their heavy alliteration of "tell" and "Nel" corroborate the link between female friendship and narration. The very recounting of overwhelming events to an audience/friend willing to share in them will preserve the artist. Sula's vital need for Nel is affirmed – even though Sula doesn't explicitly recognize this.

We are now in a position to understand the epigraph of *Sula*, "Nobody knew my rose of the world but me ... I had too much glory. They don't want glory like *that* in nobody's heart" (175). The quotation comes from Act Two, Scene One of Tennessee Williams' play *The Rose Tattoo*, which is set in an American location comparable to the Bottom: a "village populated mostly by Sicilians" (132) recently migrated to America, racially stigmatized as "Wops" (147 and *passim*) by other Americans, including other Italian Americans, and clinging to their cultural heritage. Serafina's glory is her husband, Rosario Dele Rose, or rather her overflowing and idealizing love for him. The rose tattoo on his chest miraculously appears on her breast when she conceives a child by him, she believes. Serafina fills herself up with this perfect love and mourns excessively for the death of her husband in order to counter their racial stigmatization and defy the impermanence of modern life. However, she comes to recognize that her love for Rosario is an act of blindness or wilful evasion of her husband's infidelity – and she falls in love again, somewhat more realistically this time but still in keeping with traditional Sicilian femininity.

The Bottom is a community of pariahs – mostly women, children and disabled men such as Chadrack and Plum – stigmatized by recent immigrants themselves (see *Sula*, 53) and deserted by black able-bodied men such as BoyBoy and Jude. However, Sula's rose, unlike Serafina's, is her own mind; she is independent of men and defiant in the face of impermanence, change and death. Where Serafina wants a husband and children, Sula needs a female friend.

THE CIVIL RIGHTS MOVEMENT AND NEL'S *ANAGNORISIS*

The march to the tunnel under the river being constructed at the exclusion of black labour in 1941 allows Morrison to return to the Bottom and examine its belief that Sula is evil. The Bottom's demonization of Sula now emerges as a blindness to their real situation and to real evils. The people of the Bottom expect Sula's death to lead to a new dawn: an end to their economic discrimination and their exclusion from building the tunnel under the river, an end to segregation. Instead Sula's death ends their uncomplaining bearing of their burden: "A falling away, a dislocation was taking place ... a restless irritability took hold" (153). Chadrack is also changed by

Sula's death. On the mortician's table, the birthmark over her eye looks like a "tadpole" (156) – a creature representing metamorphosis – and he suspects that his yearly ritual to contain change and death, National Suicide Day, is "never going to do any good" (158).

On the third of January 1941, National Suicide Day develops into a demonstration when the people of Bottom join Chadrack on his parade. The crowd's mood is volatile and changes dramatically as they march out of the Bottom, through Medallion and towards the tunnel. They march through the Bottom laughing; they march through "the white part of town whooping like banshees" (160); then they march to the tunnel, confronting their economic discrimination and structural unemployment and "kill[ing] ... the tunnel they were forbidden to build" (161). But as they attacked the tunnel under the river, the earth "shifted" and the walls of the tunnel collapsed, killing many people (162). The Bottom's first political demonstration – a harbinger of the Civil Rights Movement (see **pp. 15–17, 18–19**) – miscarries. However, the people of the Bottom have now joined the fight to end their political and economic disenfranchisement, on the year that America enters World War II and joins the war against fascism.

In 1965, at the height of the Civil Rights Movement, the third-person narrator conveys 55-year-old Nel's perspective on Sula, the Bottom and the end of the segregation era. In 1965 there are increased economic opportunities for black people, and they have moved into formerly all-white parts of Medallion. However, Nel's critical perspective looks out for what is being lost on the way to progress. Black people's social and economic advancement has gone hand-in-hand with an uncritical adoption of white middle-class norms such as the nuclear family – at the expense of the extended family and community other-mothering – and a puritanical sexual morality. The Bottom "had collapsed" and been replaced by "separate houses ... and less and less dropping by" (165); black people begin to send old relatives to old people's homes; and the new generation of black whores are "embarrassed" and "shamed" by their profession (164). Nel's reflections are obviously not a defence of segregation laws and institutionally entrenched discrimination, but a tribute to black communal life during the segregation era. However, this tribute does not falsely idealize the past, and Nel's assessment of the Bottom and of her own past self is unsentimental.

The Bottom's use of Sula – "the most magnificent hatred they had ever known" (173) – was "spite that galloped all over the Bottom" (171). In *On the Genealogy of Morals* Nietzsche outlines his well-known analysis of spite or *ressentiment* or what he calls "slave morality". *Ressentiment* says: you're bad therefore I'm good. The man of *ressentiment* defines himself through the demonization/

degradation of an individual or collective other. According to Nietzsche this "slave morality" was rife in modern Europe: modern European man is a creature of *ressentiment*. German (and European) anti-Semitism – for example, the demonization of the Jew in Nazi propaganda – is an instance of *ressentiment*. The Bottom's demonization of Sula relies on the same pernicious logic. Thus Nel questions the black nationalist argument for the moral superiority of black people.

Nel looks back on her own self/life and belatedly recognizes a misplaced allegiance to her husband Jude and identification with black men, instead of an allegiance to her friend Sula and identification with black women: "all that time, I thought I was missing Jude" – "girl, girl, girlgirlgirl" (174). Her cry for Sula is "circles and circles of sorrow" (174) without issue or response; Sula is gone. It is witnessed by us, the readers, alone. Will we respond?

Nel looks back on her early friendship with Sula and on Chicken Little's death. She now acknowledges "the good feeling she had had when Chicken's hands slipped" (170). In the terms of tragedy, she positions herself as Sula's *audience*, watching a spectacle of suffering and feeling aesthetic pleasure. Nel's position, and its peculiar aesthetic and ethical dilemmas, is simultaneously our position in relation to this book. Will our own aesthetic delight in reading *Sula* bring its own recognition (*anagnorisis*) of painful truths and will it lend itself to ethical questioning of real evils?

Song of Solomon (1977)

Song of Solomon presents a refiguring of masculinity through a revision of the conventions of the story of the hero, particularly in African and African American oral literatures. The hero, Milkman Dead, searches for gold but discovers instead his cultural inheritance. His forefather, Solomon, was commemorated by a song. According to this song, Solomon, a slave, had a supernatural escape from slavery by flying back to Africa. But he left behind his wife Ryna and 21 children, including Milkman's grandfather Jake. Solomon's song is sung by those he deserted. Milkman too leaves and leaves others behind to pursue his quest. But Milkman only takes off, away from his middle-class affluence, materialism and individualism, when he begins to see his interdependence on others and to hold different and incompatible perspectives (both Solomon's and Ryna's). In this new kind of flight he is aided by his "ancestor" – in the strong African sense of foundation, as Morrison explains – his aunt Pilate. A more androgynous Milkman emerges, capable of flying "[w]ithout ever leaving the ground" (336; all page numbers in this chapter refer to *Song of Solomon* [Morrison 1977] unless otherwise indicated). The story is "my own giggle (in Afro-American terms) of the proto-myth of the journey to manhood", Morrison has said (Morrison 1989a, 51).

This third novel is a departure for Morrison because of her turn to oral traditions (a turn that will continue in her next novel), but also because of its male protagonist and focus on masculinity (the protagonists of the first two novels were female), even though its revisionism means that Pilate is more than the traditional expendable helper of the hero and rivals Milkman as the moral centre of the novel. She is herself androgynous. However, the major innovation here – enabled by Morrison's turn to oral literatures – is the mixing of realism (and even "naturalism" in the sense of overwhelming external conditions) and a new supernatural element which will become one of the defining features of Morrison's fiction: Solomon flying, Jake's ghost delivering oracular advice to Pilate. Morrison has called this supernatural element "enchantment" (Morrison 1986, 226). The status of this supernatural element, crucially, remains undecided: it is left open (and for the reader to decide if they feel so inclined) whether it is objectively and literally true or subjectively and metaphorically true. Stylistically, the novel is distinctive in its mix of the supernatural with an intensified realism and intensified use of the conventions of the classic realist novel: unlike the earlier novels, there is very detailed, "thick" description, emphasis on verisimilitude, many minor characters, convoluted plot, greater length and many references to African American history – though this is an alternative history presenting a reality previously buried and unavailable to both hero and reader and unearthed for their benefit. Suitably, a final element in the mix is a "popular", detective-story format: suspense, withholding of information and constant revelations in small doses that keep the reader interested – though unlike the classic format (*The Adventures of Sherlock Holmes*, for example) the supernatural is not dispelled and truth does not prevail against illusion, but rather multiperspectivism is affirmed.

The novel moves forward, following the hero's life from birth to age 32, but with constant flashbacks coming from a variety of characters. Its first part is set in Mercy, a fictional town in the state of Michigan on the shore of Lake Superior, and describes the hero's captivity. The second part follows, in slower motion, the hero's travels between North and South at the age of 32. By travelling South he reverses the historical direction of African American migration from the South to the promised land of the North (the African American version of the American dream), though his movement is a to-and-fro-ing, a dialectic between North and South rather than a migration South.

ANCESTORS, FLYING AND SINGING: PILATE AND JAKE

The novel opens with a man who undertakes to "fly away on [his] own wings" and hits the ground (3). The date is 18 February 1931, the date of Morrison's birth. The heterogeneous black crowd witnessing the event, as well as most readers, interpret Robert Smith's leap as a suicide. The shock of the event sends Ruth Dead, the hero's mother, into labour and the hero is born. But Pilate bursts into a song that accompanies, interprets and transforms Smith's actions into a version of the African American folktale of the flying African slaves. Milkman is born under the sign of this flying/falling man, anticipating the song of Solomon and his own leap that closes the novel.

Morrison has said that her familiarity with the folktale of the flying slaves comes from first-hand aural experience, though she also read slave narratives where they figure prominently (Morrison 1985b, 182). Susan L. Blake, Higgins and Grewal argue that this folktale is specific to the Gullah slaves of Georgia and South Carolina (Grewal 1998, 65; Higgins 2001, 20). According to Blake, Morrison's source is the variations recorded in the collection *Drums and Shadows: Survival Studies Among the Georgia Coastal Negroes* (Savannah Unit, Georgia Writers' Project 1940), in which the names Solomon and Ryna appear; Higgins adds that in one variation Ryna is left behind when her mother Therese flies away, and that a common element in many of the variations is that when a slave's or a group of slaves' suffering becomes overwhelming, magic words are uttered and they fly away (Higgins 2001, 20).

Did Robert Smith, indeed did his African slave predecessors, commit suicide or fly away? On the one hand, historians tell us that many African slaves committed suicide; on the other hand, Wilentz argues that "in the Southern United States and throughout the Caribbean" tales abound of slaves who flew back to Africa, and asks: "Which perception of reality are we to believe?" (Wilentz 1992, 158). Instead of choosing between history and folktales, Morrison turns to folk traditions as a cultural resource for the future, but vitally subjects them to an intellectually and ethically rigorous process of distillation. Many critics pointed out the critical and revisionist nature of Morrison's engagement with African American oral traditions. Awkward influentially argued that, in asking questions about the woman and children Solomon left behind, Morrison shows the "andro-centric" and "masculinist" aspects of myth, including African American myth (Awkward 1990, 71).

If the absence of fathers is a problem, their crushing presence is also identified as a problem. Milkman's childhood is a captivity, a joyless dead-end, because it is dominated by a patriarchal family. The problem, familiar to readers of Morrison's earlier novels, is the uncritical assimilation of white middle-class values or a deadly affluence. Milkman's father, Macon Dead, is a self-made affluent man, and a caricature of the callous landlord and unloving, domineering father and husband. Milkman's mother, Ruth Foster, is a black version – "the underside" – of the ideal Southern lady (Christian 1985, 77): decorative, incompetent, "pressed small" by her own middle-class father, Dr Foster (125). To survive her loveless and sexless marriage she secretly breastfeeds Milkman beyond the usual period of doing so, and this is how the hero gets his name.

A sense of dead-end and captivity – the naturalism of Morrison's earlier fiction – permeates the black community across class divisions, "led" as it is by patriarchs such as Milkman's father. After Robert Smith, Porter gets drunk and attempts to kill himself, but only manages the dubious flight of "pee[ing] over the heads of the women" from the window of his attic room (25); the connection between the two men, their participation in a black terrorist group, will only be revealed later. Their suicidal crises suggest that the "solution" of the terrorist group is itself a dead-end. Chapter 9 explores a way out for the working-class Porter in his unlikely pairing with the middle-class and highly educated daughter of Macon Dead, Corinthians, against her father's wishes and despite his punitive reprisals. Before their encounter, the closest she got to singing was as the servant and typist of a white poetess. What is fruitful in this pairing is its dynamic and dialogic nature in bringing together, in uncomfortable but productive ways, the "top" and the "bottom" of the fractured and class-divided black community.

Another potentially liberating or empowering solution practised by the black community of Southside (Mercy's poor black neighbourhood) is that of symbolic skirmishes with white officials around naming and interpretation. They rename Mains Avenue "Doctor Street", as it is the street where Dr Foster, the first black doctor, lived; when an official announcement insists that the street's name is "Mains Avenue and not Doctor Street" they rename it Not Doctor Street to both "keep their memories alive and please the city's legislators as well" (4). This is one of many instances of the counter-naming Henry Louis Gates has influentially described as African American "Signification" of dominant reality: it is subtly, obliquely, indirectly subversive rather than openly antagonistic, and an appropriate, "guerrilla" tactic for minority or marginalized groups (see **p. 184**). However, Morrison suggests that it is limited and inadequate on its own.

Life in Mercy is a dead-end for Macon Dead himself, it seems. He has expelled his sister Pilate from his life because of her disreputable lifestyle. But one evening he is drawn to Pilate's house against his will: like Odysseus to the Sirens, "Macon walked on, resisting as best he could the sound of the voices" (28), but unlike Odysseus he returns and "surrender[s] to the sound" (29) of three women singing together: Pilate, Reba her daughter and Hagar her granddaughter. He is refreshed by a black oral culture absent from his own home. What Morrison singles out as valuable in this resource is its responsive and reciprocal nature and values, as an alternative to both individualism and antagonism (and the counter-naming discussed above). The creativity and nurturing intersubjectivity of oral black culture is Morrison's focus in the story of Pilate's naming. Her father, the illiterate ex-slave Jake, opened the Bible and chose a group of letters, a word, visually depicting his nurturing/motherly relation to his children; "Pilate": "a large figure that looked like a tree hanging in some princely but protective way over a row of smaller trees" (18), redefining the written word. Homonyms, sounding alike, are especially important for an oral culture, and Pilate will later appropriate "pilot" (in the senses of guiding and flying) as part of her own identity. Men fly/leave and women sing/nurture, but Pilate and Jake are exceptional and can do both.

At the age of 12 Milkman meets his notorious and forbidden aunt Pilate. For Milkman "Pilate is the ancestor", as understood by African cosmologies and then appropriated and redefined by Morrison (Morrison 1984a, 344). Pilate's own ancestor is her father's ghost. When she was 12 Jake was shot by the wealthy Butlers, who wanted his farm in Montour County, Pennsylvania – he had been duped into signing a document transferring his ownership but he refused to accept it.

The "ancestor" is comparable to the helper in European folktales as codified by Propp (Grewal 1998). Higgins describes "ancestors" in African cosmologies as ancestral spirits shared by the entire community as communal mothers and fathers of an extended family. They visit the living in embodied form, protecting but also threatening them: "ancestors can influence for good or for evil" (Higgins 2001, 30). Richard Wright, in *Black Power* (1954), argues that, for the Ashanti, a person's spirit, *kra*, if he or she dies before their time, lingers: "with the *kra* that lingers ... trouble starts" (Wright quot. Higgins 2001, 22); he continues that "the pacification of the dead constitutes one of [the Ashanti's] problems of life" (Wright quot. Higgins 2001, 34).

In inventing Pilate Morrison revises and reimagines the figure of the "ancestor". Pilate is the most unambiguously positive and simultaneously the most paradoxical character in Morrison's entire *oeuvre*, a meeting of contraries – tradition and innovation, flight and singing, man and woman – in their positive aspects. She is both a living woman and a supernatural and mythical figure who has no navel.

Nurtured by her father (her mother died in childbirth), after his death and her separation from her brother she wanders, and keeps getting expelled from the African American communities she settles in because of her navel-less stomach.

> When she realized what her situation in the world was and would probably always be she threw away every assumption she had learned and began at zero ... [S]he tackled the problem of trying to decide how she wanted to live and what was valuable to her ... But most important, she paid close attention to her mentor – the father who appeared before her sometimes and told her things.
>
> (149–50)

She chooses to wander for 20 years, but without abandoning her daughter Reba, and only settles close to her brother to give her granddaughter Hagar access to the "conventional ... things and people Hagar seemed to admire" (151). Her own home is unconventional, however: it is open, restful and in motion. When Macon overhears the three women singing he also sees a house "whose basement seems to be rising from rather than settling into the ground": it combines flight and song (25). When Milkman visits he sees a house with many windows and no curtains (40) and a woman who "looked like a tall black tree" (39), combining roots and heights. His final assessment of her, similarly, is that "Without ever leaving the ground, she could fly" (336). Morrison summarizes Pilate's utopian fusion of contraries by describing her as "the apogee ... of the best of that which is female and the best of that which is male" (Morrison 1984a, 344).

Faithfulness and freedom of interpretation mix in Pilate's relation to her father's ghost. She has to take liberties if she is to make sense of his elliptical statements. "Clear as day, her father said, 'Sing. Sing,' and later ... 'You just can't fly on off and leave a body'" (147). She interprets the former as a call to sing and to engage with African American musical traditions; but Milkman later finds out that her mother's name was Sing, another possible interpretation. Her interpretation of the latter is to carry, throughout her wanderings, the bones of a white man her brother killed in self-defence after Jake's death. Milkman later finds evidence that she has been carrying her father's bones; also that Solomon tried to take Jake, his youngest, with him but dropped him, another possible interpretation. This evidence does not invalidate her creative misunderstandings or the values she has built on them. On the contrary, too literal an interpretation, an excessive attachment to paternal authority, would have been a problem. Her invention of a new life outside white middle-class values is also an immersion in African American traditions, but similarly without blind obedience to this alternative community and authority.

Pilate's interpretations distil her father's legacy as singing *and* flying *and* carrying your burden. Her androgyny is, to a degree, Jake's own, and she passes it on to Milkman. When Milkman travels South and meets the old men of Danville, Montour Country, they describe Jake as "magnificent": he built one of the best farms in Montour Country and "sang like an angel while he did it" (235). Pilate has reconstructed a nurturing/mothering father. Macon, who also saw his father's ghost (168ff.), has reconstructed his legacy as "Own things" (55). (Jake is also Morrison's reconstruction of her maternal grandfather, Solomon Willis see **pp. 12–14.**) Pilate is Milkman's ancestor, not Macon, both because of her intersubjective ethics, as opposed to Macon's individualism, and also because Milkman chooses Pilate over his own parents.

THE "LOVE" OF SEVEN DAYS MEN: GUITAR

Guitar Bains is Milkman's best friend, an unlikely friendship. Guitar's parents moved to Mercy from Florida when he was "five or six" – a clever little boy who could spell "admissions" correctly (7) – but their migration North was unsuccessful (a situation Morrison has already explored in her first novel). His father was cut in half in an industrial accident but the family received no compensation; his mother was unable to cope and took off; so his grandmother, the competent Mrs Bains, moved to Mercy and took on the children's care in spite of her slight financial resources. This friendship across class divisions begins when Guitar defends the younger Milkman from school bullies – out of a paternalist sense of commitment to the weak, it seems – in spite of the fact that Macon Dead had evicted his family. This commitment is confirmed by a story he tells: he was a magnificent child hunter back in Florida but felt nothing but distress when he accidentally killed a doe instead of a male deer: "A man shouldn't do that" (85).

Guitar introduces Milkman, and the middle-class reader, to black working-class life in Southside. He introduces Milkman to Pilate's home but also to a male environment: Railroad Tommy's Southside barbershop, which is both a place of business and place of congregation for the male community. Unlike Milkman, who is protected by his middle-class affluence and respectability, these men were brutally exposed to white racist violence and police violence, with the complicity of the legal system and the media; the barbershop is the place in which *their* side of the story is recounted. In a counter-signifying event à la Gates, they listen to the radio coverage of Emmett Till's racist killing and retell it to themselves, accurately predicting that, though the killers were known, they would be acquitted. (See **p. 15**.)

But this counter-signifying is not enough. Regulars of the barber-shop have been involved in a secret local terrorist group, the Seven Days, "started in 1920" in response to white atrocities against black World War I veterans (155). (See **p. 10**.) It comprises seven members, one for each day of the week. When a white crime against blacks is committed, the man on whose day of the week it happens has to avenge in a like-for-like manner with white victims, as an expression of his "love" for black people. Robert Smith's suicide and Porter's attempted suicide are both related to their membership of the Seven Days and their unlivable form of "love" for the black community (Smith: "I loved you all" (3); Porter: "I love ya! I love ya all. ... I can't take no more love, Lord. ... Just like Mr. Smith" (26)).

Guitar joins the group as the Sunday man, perhaps in keeping with his earlier commitment to the weak, because he "had to do some-thing" (154). The ideology of the group, as he explains it to Milkman, can be described as a black essentialism: white crimes against blacks demonstrate the moral inferiority of all whites (a "disease" they have in their "blood" and "chromosomes"); "under certain conditions they would *all* do it", including President Roosevelt (157). (Another version of black racism was explored in *Sula*.) Grewal describes it as a black male working-class "(aggressively antiwhite) nationalism" (Grewal 1998, 71). A Sunday comes in September 1963 when "Four little colored girls had been blown out of a church" (173). This was the real-life bomb explosion in a black church in Birmingham, Alabama. (See **p. 16**.) Guitar is determined to find the money to fund his counterstrike, but is haunted by a vision of "scraps of Sunday dresses" (173) – the thought that white girls are no different from the black girls, and he is no different from white racist terrorists. Like Smith and Porter before him, Guitar becomes mentally unstable.

Milkman involves Guitar in a search for a horde of treasure young Macon and Pilate saw in a cave when they were in hiding after their father's murder. Milkman promises to share it with Guitar; but when the gold does not materialize, Guitar is convinced his friend has cheated him and sets out to kill him. Instead, he kills Pilate by accident (his second doe) and, in the novel's closing lines, "put[s] the rifle on the ground" (337) – his breakdown over at an enormous cost.

Bouson argued that the text sends "contradictory messages" about Guitar (Bouson 2000, 90). Morrison, however, has asked readers in interview to understand Guitar, alongside the characters of Cholly Breedlove and Sula Peace (in her first and second novels), in positive terms: as tragic characters who exceed their limits and express an effort or freedom of the will (Morrison 1983a, 164).

Guitar's ideology and that of the older working-class men of the Seven Days – a black essentialism that affirms an a priori black moral superiority and white inferiority – was also the ideology of Morrison's father. Morrison described her father's black essentialism in "A Slow Walk of Trees" (Morrison 1976b). *Song of Solomon*, written after her father's death and bearing the dedication "Daddy", aimed at "recreating a time period that was his" and "trying to figure out what he may have known" (Morrison 1987c, 123–24).

WOMEN WHO "LOVE TOO HARD": HAGAR, RYNA, SING

Milkman's first love is Hagar: in love with her since he was 12 and she 17, her lover since he was 17, he dismisses her callously when he's 31. Hagar is unable to move on: she becomes a "restless ghost" (127) haunting him, "stalk[ing]" him (128), ostensibly trying to kill him but unable/unwilling to do so. In a frantic shopping spree, Hagar attempts to match the light-skinned middle-class girl Milkman is now dating, and the white middle-class ideals she aspires to, but when this fails she wastes away and dies. Pilate's and Reba's love for Hagar and their efforts to save her are not enough.

Like her biblical namesake Hagar is expelled. Abraham's marriage to Sarah is childless and Hagar is a slave used by Abraham to give him a child, Ishmael. But when Sarah gives birth to Isaac, Hagar and Ishmael are cast out. Christian versions broadly follow this pattern, while in Islamic traditions Hagar is resettled by Abraham rather than expelled. However, in all versions Hagar survives. This story of a slave and single mother who survives in spite of inimical circumstances has been especially resonant for African Americans. But Morrison's Hagar dies. She does not survive Milkman's casting out because the individual's survival is a collective and intersubjective project: it depends on the help of others as much as on the individual's resources. Morrison boldly suggests that even one's immediate family is not enough for the individual's survival. Collective other-mothering is required. Pilate's and Reba's love for Hagar is not enough in the absence of wider communal love. In the earlier novels Morrison explored three-woman households as a utopian possibility. In an instance of autocritique Morrison here questions their viability. The idyll of the three women singing together, as perceived by Macon and refreshing him (discussed earlier), is exposed as an idealization: the women's interactions with Macon and Milkman shatter their household.

From Macon's perspective, Pilate "seemed to be more interested in this first nephew of hers [Milkman] than she was in her own daughter, and even that daughter's daughter" (19). However, the substantial problem is not that Pilate other-mothers Milkman but that Macon does not other-mother Hagar in reciprocal other-mothering. As Morrison argues: "Pilate had a dozen years of close, nurturing relationships with two males"; but Reba and Hagar experience "a diminution of their abilities because of the absence of men in a nourishing way in their lives" (Morrison 1984a, 344). As Heinze argues: "Morrison's intention is not to suggest that women cannot sustain their own lineage, but that for families to survive, they must include men who ... are feminized" (Heinze 1993, 83).

Macon, unlike Jake, is too male to other-mother Hagar; and Hagar herself, unlike Pilate, is too female. Through the character of Hagar, Morrison offers a critique of certain aspects of femininity – possessiveness and conventionality – that contribute to Hagar's inability to survive. Pilate is aware of Hagar's conventionality and materialism: Hagar was "prissy", "liked pretty clothes" and "seemed to admire" people like Macon: "[p]rosperous, conventional" (150–51). Had Macon not disavowed Pilate's family, Hagar could have been his spiritual heir, an heir to his middle-class values. The problem here is that his values do not include nurturing others.

Hagar's possessiveness towards Milkman connects her to her foremothers, Ryna and Sing. When Solomon flies away leaving Ryna behind, she is unable to survive without him; and "[w]hile [Milkman] dreamt of flying, Hagar was dying" (332), as Milkman belatedly recognizes. Sing or Singing Bird, Jake's Native American wife, is, according to Circe: "Crazy about her husband too, overcrazy. You know what I mean? Some women love too hard" (243). But Jake doesn't leave her: they elope North in a wagon full of ex-slaves. Is Hagar's possessiveness a hereditary propensity in the manner of Thomas Hardy – an especially strong one because it comes from two separate lines – or is it a cultural aspect of femininity across time and across ethnic locations?

THE HERO'S PROGRESS: MILKMAN

At the beginning of A Room of One's Own, her modernist manifesto, Woolf writes: "I should never be able ... to hand you ... a nugget of pure truth" (Woolf 2004, 3). At the end she reformulates this idea: "Truth is only to be had by laying together many varieties of error" (122) – in other words, truth is multiperspectival. Milkman's progress is Morrison's reworking of this core modernist insight. Milkman searches for nuggets of gold but discovers and begins to lay together the many incompatible perspectives of his heterogeneous inheritance.

At his father's prompting, Milkman sets out to find a horde of gold. He involves Guitar in the plan: the gold would be divided equally between the three men. In search of the gold Milkman and Guitar enter Pilate's never-locked house and steal a sack which they mistakenly believe to contain the treasure. Then Milkman travels to the cave in Danville and to Jake's birthplace, Shalimar, in Virginia. What Milkman discovers is a multiperspectival heritage. The perspectives of: Pilate; Ryna and Solomon; Jake and Sing; Macon and Ruth; Guitar and Hagar; in Mercy the barbershop men; in Danville the old men of Danville and Circe; in Shalimar the old men at the hunt, the Native American Susan Byrd and the children singing the song of Solomon. At the beginning of his progress he hears unwillingly the incompatible perspectives of Macon and Ruth on each other. He then discovers an ability to listen: he emerges not so much as a subject speaking, but as a subject, an inter-subjectivity, listening and responding. In the novel's final scene, he responds to Pilate's dying call to "Sing a little something for me" and delivers the song of Solomon with Pilate as the flying hero: "Sugargirl don't leave me here" (336). Milkman begins an attempt to understand each perspective favourably, critique his own, and lay perspectives together, whether in antagonism or as complementary. Milkman therefore becomes not a character – in the sense of a fixed and consistent set of attributes – but a space for the interaction of others' perspectives, the multiple and heterogeneous lines of his inheritance. Because of this heterogeneity of tradition one can't simply be faithful to it, one has to become pluralistic and dialogic.

Milkman's progress mixes enchantment and hard-nosed realism. In Danville he listens to Circe's recollections: she is an impossibly, supernaturally old woman living in her masters' ruined and reeking mansion, but she seduces Milkman with the "sweet spicy perfume" she exudes and "the mellifluent voice of a twenty-year-old girl" that comes out of her "toothless mouth" (240). In Shalimar he listens to the old men and their dogs during the hunt "talking to each other" in total darkness and this attentive listening alerts him to Guitar's creeping up on him and saves his life (277 ff.). The children of Shalimar sing the Song of Solomon and Milkman gives them his full attention and finds out that Solomon could fly. He returns to Mercy elated.

In the final chapter Pilate helps Milkman understand that "while he dreamt of flying, Hagar was dying" (322); and he takes the box with Hagar's hair that Pilate had prepared for him, assuming responsibility for her. In the closing scene, Milkman and Pilate return to Solomon's Leap – "the higher of two outcroppings of rock ... looking over a deep valley" (335) where Solomon took off – to bury Jake's bones. Guitar follows them, stands on the second outcrop of rock, tries to kill Milkman but shoots Pilate instead. Milkman sings to her then stands up to offer his life to Guitar and test him. Milkman had been musing earlier, "Perhaps that's what all human relationships boiled down to: Would you save my life? or would you take it?" (331). Guitar puts down his gun. Milkman leaps.

The final chapter and especially the closing scene are so open-ended, so open to a variety of interpretations that critics have read them in diametrically opposed ways: for some Milkman's quest ends in success, for others in failure.

Carr Lee argues that Milkman finds his "authentic" self through "liberating participation in the corporate life of black community" (Lee 1998, 45); and the novel ends with the "healing of Milkman's brokenness" (47), his "successful connection with a people" and "the triumphant hope of continuation for an interconnected African-American culture and heritage" (60). Awkward, however, argues that Morrison "problematize[s] a strictly celebratory Afrocentric analysis of Milkman's achievements" (Awkward 1990, 85). James Coleman finds Milkman's solution futile because it doesn't affect the community and Sumana agrees: Milkman "never reaches the point where he moves beyond self-healing to other-healing" (Sumana 1998, 94). According to Brenner, Milkman's final leap is "one more gesture of irresponsibility; he flies, indeed, from the burdens of doing something meaningful in life, preferring the sumptuous illusion that he will ride the air" (Brenner 1987, 102).

Valerie Smith argues that Milkman "bursts the bonds of the Western, individualistic conception of self, accepting in its place the richness and complexity of a collective sense of identity"; she reads Milkman's carrying of Hagar's hair positively, as "a symbol of his newly acquired cyclical vision of a past he no longer needs to escape" (Smith 1985, 282–83). O'Reilly similarly argues that Milkman, successfully other-mothered by Pilate, sheds his "masculine individualism and separateness" (O'Reilly 2004, 100) and reconnects with the motherline. Harris, however, argues that Pilate's death − "[t]hat this tower of selflessness should fall, even for an enlightened Milkman" − is "difficult to acquiesce to" (1991, 114); she adds that "Milkman essentially destroys Pilate's family" (Harris 1991, 107). Wilentz agrees: Milkman "[i]ronically ... destroys the foundation of these women's lives" (Wilentz 1992, 146). Many critics argue that Milkman progresses at the expense of female characters. In particular, Hirsch argues that "the male protagonist, alone benefits from the lessons learned" (Hirsch 1995, 89) and that the novel "has not yet found a way to share the son's knowledge with the daughter" (90). Matus argues that the situation of women hasn't improved, Pilate's line perishes, and the Dead women haven't been resurrected: Pilate "has no female descendants who will rise and possess her for their futures" (Matus 1998, 84).

Some critics point to the very open-endedness of the final chapter and scene. Lubiano argues that there is no "closure" (Lubiano 1995, 97) – "The idea of transcendence implied by flight and so beloved by many ... critics ... is by the end not so clear a proposition"; Milkman's final leap "allows for multiple and troubling interpretations" (111) – but then decides that Milkman's leap "over Pilate's body" undermines any optimism (112). Bouson argues that, while Milkman's leap "can be read as a suicidal and nihilistic gesture", simultaneously the text attempts to rescue Milkman and turn shame into pride (Bouson 2000, 100).

Morrison has created a dialogic text that allows or rather that demands the reader's active participation and the continuation of dialogue.

Tar Baby (1981)

LOVE AND WAR

Tar Baby is a contemporary rendition, and revision, of courtly love and chivalric romances: it is an impossible love story between a destitute young chevalier, Son Green, and the unreachable Jadine Childs. (Chrétien de Troyes's *Lancelot*, narrating the impossible love story of Lancelot and Guinevere, is the exemplary chivalric romance.) They come together despite the social chasm that separates them, their antagonistic perspectives clash with increasing violence in their efforts to rescue each other, and they come apart, their love impossible.

The theme of irreconcilable social perspectives impossibly coming together and clashing is replicated among the minor characters. Morrison highlights the theme in the novel's epigraph: "my brethren ... there are contentions among you" (St Paul, I Corinthians 1:11). The paradox of conflict – "contentions" – is that without bonds (the bonds of young lovers or "brethren") incompatible perspectives are blind to each other and completely unrelated: conflict presupposes some mutual recognition, a commonality of sorts. At the beginning of *Tar Baby* perspectives are unrelated: the novel stages their coming together – in conflict.

In the first half of the nineteenth century and while the gap between rich and poor was widening in England, first the Romantic poet Shelley in "A Defence of Poetry" (1821), then the realist novelist George Eliot in Chapter XVII of *Adam Bede* (1859) advocated literature as a means of connecting social groups across a widening chasm and promoting social sympathies. In *Tar Baby* Morrison allows the reader to observe incompatible perspectives invisible to each other: this very observation brings them into the same field and creates a demand, a narrative pressure, for their interaction. The novel then stages antagonistic encounters between them. These perspectives, though embodied by highly individuated characters, point to urgent contemporary global dilemmas: ecology versus development; fraternity versus liberty; cultural ownership versus cultural hybridization.

Tar Baby, while still focusing on African American characters, is Toni Morrison's international novel. It is set mainly on a fictional privately-owned Caribbean island, Isle des Chevaliers (Island of the Knights), and takes place largely between autumn 1979 and autumn 1980, but points the reader to the legacy of European colonialism, the decline of the French and British Empires and the new global role of the USA.

Isle des Chevaliers, an earthly paradise suffering a hidden ecological wound,witnesses secret irreconcilable conflicts of perspective among its human inhabitants: incompatible norms, desires, imaginings, myths. Who are these inhabitants? Valerian Street, a white American retired candy manufacturer from Philadelphia, is the main owner of the island and presides over the rigidly hierarchical world of his mansion, L'Arbe de la Croix (the tree of the cross; "arbe" is a Creole variation of the French "arbre"). Valerian's only natural heir, his son Michael, refused to take over the family factory started by Valerian's "workaholic" Dutch Grandmother Stadt (50; all page numbers in this chapter refer to *Tar Baby* [Morrison 1981a] unless otherwise indicated). Michael is a socialist, an activist who has been working with disenfranchised ethnic minorities, and an environmentalist. His eagerly anticipated visit to the island will not materialize; his non-arrival signals his rejection of his inheritance. Valerian's younger second wife, Margaret, Michael's mother, is a working-class Italian-American former beauty queen who is nostalgic about the trailer she was raised in. Valerian's impeccable servants are the lower-middle-class African Americans, Sydney and Ondine Childs, butler and cook: born and raised in Baltimore, they worked for Valerian in Philadelphia before moving with him to the island. Sydney identifies himself as a "Philadelphia negro": the black professional aristocracy described by Du Bois in his famous sociological study, *The Philadelphia Negro* (1899). Sydney's and Ondine's servants (employed by Valerian for the heavier work) are the black Caribbeans, Gideon, Marie-Thérèse Foucault and Alma Estée. They work in the grounds of L'Arbe de la Croix but live in Queen of France, fictional capital of the semifictional island of Dominique; their ancestors were initially transported to Dominique as slaves for the Caribbean sugar plantations producing the chief ingredient of Valerian's candy fortune. The island still belongs to France but was also a British colonial possession in the past: Gideon, Marie-Thérèse and Alma therefore speak two languages: Creole and English. In this the semi-fictional island of Dominique points to the historical reality of many Caribbean islands. Dominica, also called Dominique, was independent by the time of the writing of *Tar Baby*, but the neighbouring Martinique, birthplace of the postcolonial thinkers Césaire and Fanon, remains a part of France.

Jadine Childs is Sydney's niece and Valerian's possible spiritual heir. Raised by her mother in poverty in Baltimore, she is orphaned at the age of 12. Sydney and Ondine then look after the intelligent light-skinned girl, and Valerian becomes her patron, funding an exclusive education. At the age of 25, she is an Art History graduate of the Sorbonne and the "copper Venus" (115) on the cover of *Elle* magazine. Ostensibly – her secret nightmares aside – she is a highly successful inheritor of European high culture, convinced that "Picasso *is* better than an Itumba mask. The fact that he was intrigued by them is proof of *his* genius, not the mask-makers'" (72). At the novel's opening she is on a long visit to the island: in keeping with her position in the hierarchy, she sleeps in Valerian and Margaret's quarters and eats with them, served by her uncle.

The household is preparing for Christmas and Michael's arrival when, instead of her son's return, Margaret discovers a runaway black man in her closet: Son Green. He has jumped ship due to his longing to return home to Eloe, a small all-black town in Northern Florida, particularly his longing for the pie ladies: the ladies minding the pie table in the church basement, half-remembered, half-imagined. But his *nostos* (homecoming) is interrupted and he finds himself marooned on Isle des Chevaliers. Exercising his authority, Valerian invites the dispossessed intruder to stay as his guest. L'Arbe de la Croix is a hierarchy without real contact perpetuated by an uneasy *détente*. But Son's unclassifiable presence disrupts the hierarchy and acts as a catalyst bringing elements together in explosive interaction. Long-hidden secrets, desires and conflicts come to the surface; antagonistic perspectives, previously unrelated, now come into contact with each other and clash. Is this a gain, an *anagnorisis* (recognition) of sorts? Does conflict go hand-in-hand with an interrelation of the unrelated and therefore potentially lead to progress?

Tar Baby explores differing perspectives and their conflict through a kind of out-of-tune realism, what we can call an "excessive" realism. The reader is offered realistic observation and recording of interminable (both lengthy and unresolvable) verbal conflicts with minimal narratorial intervention and mediation. John Irving (1981) complained of the "excessive use of dialogue" in his review of the novel, but this is an appropriate formal decision. Repressed, unplayed-out conflicts may result in excessive outcomes, such as the excessively violent acts committed by Margaret and Son and revealed in the course of the novel. The third-person external narrator and the characters themselves respond to these excessive events and conflicts with an excess of interpretation. Jadine produces 16 different reasons why her relationship with Son fails, and "[h]aving sixteen answers meant having none" (293).

As in *Song of Solomon*, Morrison mixes realism with "enchantment" in *Tar Baby*, though the relation between the two is very different here, as we will see. In *Song of Solomon* realism and enchantment work together: for example, supernatural characters help Milkman solve the historical puzzle of his multiple inheritance. In *Tar Baby* realism is bound to conflicts between characters; enchantment, on the other hand, is an attempt to imagine peacefully coexisting, conflict-free, univocal groups. Isle des Chevaliers is populated by realist characters clashing. It is also populated by an animist nature, a tribute to African animism and its Caribbean metamorphoses: clouds, river, fish, champion daisy trees, wild parrots and diamondbacks converse peacably (7–8 and passim). Unlike Darwinian nature and unlike the warring humans, this is an Edenic realm of harmony, free interaction and repose. The ontological status of this animist nature in the novel is undecidable: is it an objectively existing enchantment or is it imagined by the third-person unspecified external narrator and some of the characters?

Finally, Isle des Chevaliers is inhabited by mythical humans. Since slavery, black Dominicans such as Marie-Thérèse have imagined it to be inhabited by mythical black blind horsemen, refiguring historical maroons (fugitive slaves). White Dominicans such as Dr Michelin have imagined it to be inhabited by mythical white "chevaliers" (knights, etymologically horsemen) riding their mounts – and have named it Isle des Chevaliers – refiguring the historical military superiority of Europe over the rest of the world in the modern period, which came to an end after World War II and the break-up of European empires. Dr Michelin himself was forced to leave Algeria when it gained its independence, after a bloody and protracted conflict. Both mythical groups, like nature above, are imagined as internally unanimous and univocal and coexisting peacefully with nature, all rivals excluded.

Isle des Chevaliers is an Eden whose serpent is modern development, begun 30 years ago when Valerian bought the island and the building started. The Haitian builders employed witnessed the destruction of the river: its course interrupted, the "brokenhearted" river "became a swamp the Haitians called Sein de Vieilles [old women's breast]. And witch's tit it was: a shrivelled fogbound oval seeping with a thick black substance that even mosquitoes could not live near" (8). But black Dominicans such as Marie-Thérère, transfiguratively turning repulsion into attraction and destruction into love, imagine that it is inhabited by the mythical black swamp women who blissfully couple with the blind black horsemen. Morrison explained in interview that "there is a tar lady in African mythology" whose role is the very positive one of holding things together, as tar itself is a substance that holds things together (Morrison 1981b, 122). Perhaps translating this African mythological figure, black Dominicans have transformed the tar-like "thick black substance" (8) of the swamp into the mythical swamp women. Son brings with him his own utopian and mythical pie ladies. But his arrival on the island and Valerian's invitation change all that, introduce conflict both in the "real" and the mythological world, and bring the hidden interaction between the real and the mythological into view.

Son soon mythologizes the "real" inhabitants of the island, but the mythological template he now uses involves conflict. Son mobilizes a version of the African American folktale of "Brer Rabbit and the Tar Baby", which gives the novel its title. Brer Rabbit invades the forbidden territory of a white farmer. In order to capture Brer Rabbit, the white farmer makes a Tar Baby on whose sticky body Brer Rabbit will get trapped. Brer Rabbit gets caught but, being a cunning "trickster" figure, he fools the white farmer into releasing him into the briar patch, Brer Rabbit's own proper territory. Son reconfigures this: he is Brer Rabbit; Valerian is the white farmer; Jadine is the Tar Baby; his purpose is to rescue the Tar Baby from the white farmer.

All the island's "real" and mythological characters are drawn into this new field of interaction opened by Valerian's invitation. When Son and Valerian clash round the Christmas table: "Somewhere in the back of Valerian's mind one hundred French chevaliers were roaming the hills on horses ... Somewhere in the back of Son's mind one hundred black men on one hundred unshod horses rode blind and naked" (206–07).

SON AND JADINE

Tar Baby opens with Son's first nocturnal landing on Isle des Chevaliers and closes with his second nocturnal landing, his return. Here are the closing lines of the opening section: "he could see very little of the land, which was just as well because he was gazing at the shore of an island that, three hundred years ago, had struck slaves blind the moment they saw it" (6). Son's first landing is already a return. The narrator puts the fugitive Son explicitly in the position of historical Maroons (runaway slaves or Maroons who established their own community on this island after the shipwreck of a slave ship) and mythical blind horsemen (Maroons as mythologized by those who were recaptured or who didn't escape). However, blindness is the sign of another sort of vision: Tiresias, the ancient Greek mythical androgynous prophet "with wrinkled dugs" (T.S. Eliot 2003, *The Waste Land*, l. 228) and seer is blind; the similarly named Marie-Thérèse, a retired wet nurse, who will emerge as Son's spiritual mother, is partially sighted. Son's birth-like emergence from the sea, the life-threatening maelstrom of "the water-lady" (2) suggests the slaves' traumatic arrival in the New World.

Son comes to L'Arbe de la Croix in search of food. Marie-Thérèse senses the presence of a starving man, welcomes him and incorporates him into her world by imagining him to be a blind horseman; to help her in her efforts to feed him Gideon removes a pane of the pantry window. Son stays on and leads a nocturnal existence: every night he watches over Jadine while she sleeps and attempts to breathe into her his legendary "fat black ladies in white dresses minding the pie table" in order to rescue her from her inauthentic life (119). When Son is finally discovered, Margaret, Sydney, Ondine and Jadine initially disown him as the embodiment of the racist myth of the "bad nigger": he is not a blind horseman but a "swamp nigger" (100), a rapist, etc. But Son is a trickster figure (in the Western tradition an exemplary trickster and wanderer would be Odysseus), whose ingenious and dazzling performances tailor his mutable persona to suit each new interlocutor. His physical beauty – aided by his newfound cleanliness and Hickey Freeman suit – soon ensnares everyone.

For Jadine he reserves his ultimate performance, that of his "real" life story, during a picnic *à deux* on the beach. In 1971, "eight homeless years" ago (167), Son killed his wife, Cheyenne, whom he found in bed with a 13-year-old boy. He crashed his car into the wall of their tiny house, the car exploded, he tried to save her but she died, and he had to leave Eloe to escape a conviction for "Murder Two" (177). Son doesn't tell Jadine but we, the readers, know – because the third-person narrator gives us access to his thoughts – that he didn't "look her in the eyes as she died ... he hadn't had the courage or the sympathy and it shamed him" (176). We, the readers, also find out that Son values "fraternity" above all else (169, 206). He is a black nationalist who identifies with his black brethren and espouses a black essentialism that assumes the inherent and a priori goodness of black people, as embodied by his "pie ladies". This novel continues Morrison's exploration of black nationalism and black essentialism begun in *Sula* and *Song of Solomon*.

Son's commitment to fraternity plays itself out in the explosive Christmas scene. Having invited Son but also Sydney and Ondine (for the first time) to share the Christmas meal with him, Valerian announces that he has sacked the Caribbean servants for stealing apples. The scene revises God's expulsion of Adam and Eve from Eden in Genesis. Son contests Valerian's decision and sides with the Caribbean servants. Valerian "had played a silly game and everyone was out of place" (209). A generalized conflict breaks out and Ondine reveals the 30-year-old secret that Margaret abused her baby son: "She stuck pins in his behind. Burned him with cigarettes" (209).

Son and Jadine secretly elope to New York and then visit Eloe. What Son hasn't told Jadine, and what the third-person narrator hasn't revealed to us, is that after Cheyenne's death, her mother, an avid churchgoer and exemplary candidate to mind the pie table, acquired a gun and promised to kill him on sight. Now that he returns to Eloe, his legendary benevolent maternal "pie ladies" are exposed as a screen fantasy ("screen memory", Freud would say) protecting him from the haunting dying eyes of "the best pussy in Florida" (256) and the pie lady who wants to hunt him down. Eloe is a patriarchal community with rigid gender roles and Son's "pie ladies" fantasy is complicit with this patriarchal ethos. The fantasy of nurturing pie ladies polices the lives of real women: it cannot accommodate Cheyenne's sexuality (hence perhaps Son's excessive reaction to her infidelity); her mother's masculine initiative; Jadine's cleverness and desire for self-determination. Son's ideal of fraternity, etymologically referring to brothers, is gender-biased: potentially limiting and even threatening rather than enabling the lives of black women. Eloe stands as Morrison's critique of the hamlet of Shalimar in *Song of Solomon*; it questions her idealized presentation of small rural Southern communities. The madness of Son's sister (madness being a canonical theme in women's writing), despite her talent for running, suggests the unlivability of Eloe's feminine norms.

Back in New York the urban Arcadia of Son's and Jadine's love now unravels in escalating violence and Jadine ends the affair and returns to Isle des Chevaliers, leaving behind all the photographs she has taken of Eloe's women, her own view of them. Son looks at them: "They all looked stupid, backwoodsy, dumb, dead" (275). His vision of Eloe's pie ladies having disintegrated, Son is now self-consciously a cultural orphan in search of a cultural heritage, just like his contemporaries, Michael and Jadine.

In the novel's closing chapter Son travels to Dominique in search of Jadine but finds Marie-Thérèse in her stead, in this novel of substitutions and displacements. Marie-Thérèse, a descendant of the blind horsemen (of those Maroons who were recaptured but never lost their "blindness" or other vision), offers to adopt Son into the race of blind horsemen and to bequeath to him her cultural inheritance. In the closing section Marie-Thérèse navigates her boat from Dominique to Isle des Chevaliers in darkness, replicating the darkness of the opening section and the darkness of birth. Enveloped and witnessed by an animist nature of clouds, fish, hills and trees, she lands the boat on the side of the island legendarily inhabited by the blind horsemen and tells Son: "The men are waiting for you ... You can choose now. You can get free of her" (308). He crawls, walks then runs in darkness: "Lickety-lickety-lickety-split" (309, closing lines). Son has chosen to join the blind horsemen, and in joining them he is also Brer Rabbit returned to the briar patch. Son's solution is a merging, hybridization and crossfertilization of Caribbean and African American myths.

However, Son's solution has its own problems. Once again all conflict is, untenably, disavowed in this new mythological world. Once again the mythological world becomes an escape from reality; rather than leading back to reality and interacting with it, it is a dead-end according to some critics. Jadine, cast in the role of Tar Baby (and so cast off or given up), comes to embody a guilty complicity with the white world, which Son in reality shares. The night before his tête-à-tête with Jadine on the beach, we witness him reflecting on his eight years at sea in the company of "that great underclass of undocumented men" (167): "the day Son bashed the snapper's head in", he recognized in the eyes of his Mexican companion that he was indistinguishable from American violence and aggression towards the rest of the world: "*Americano. Cierto Americano*" (168). His solution untenably projects his sense of complicity onto Jadine. Yet another problem with his solution is that he inherits Marie-Thérèse's cultural capital at the expense of the natural heirs: Gideon, Marie-Thérèse's nephew, and Alma, Marie-Thérèse's young protégée. At the novel's close, Isle des Chevaliers, a Caribbean island, is effectively divided between Valerian and Son, two Americans; in this sense Son becomes indistinguishable from Valerian.

Jadine, like Son, defines herself through her imaginings, fantasies and nightmares: the engine of "real" life, and of *Tar Baby*'s plot, is the life of the imagination. In the course of the novel, she summons three increasingly nightmarish self-questioning – rather than self-affirming – visions of black femininity: the woman in yellow that chases her out of Paris, France; the swamp women that threaten her life in Isle des Chevaliers; and the night women that "impugn [her] character" and "discredit [her] elements" in Eloe (290). Her plotline ends with Jadine on a plane back to Paris, to "tangle with the woman in yellow ... and with all the night women" (292).

Jadine was a student and a model in Paris in the second half of the 1970s. On that doubly triumphant day of 1979 when she gains her degree and becomes cover girl for *Elle*, she encounters a vision of black feminine sexuality and fertility: "skin like tar against the yellow canary dress", she is "too tall", has "too much hip, too much bust" and holds three eggs "aloft between earlobe and shoulder" (42). The woman looked at Jadine and "shot an arrow of saliva between her teeth down to the pavement" (43). This gesture chases Jadine out of Paris, to the safety of Isle des Chevaliers.

Jadine, an academically gifted girl, is grappling with the racist and sexist stereotype of the black woman as (sexualized and procreative) body. Paris after World War II is the site of two intellectual movements that could have offered resources to her: existentialist feminism, the feminism of Simone de Beauvoir; and the *négritude* movement as represented by the Senegalese poet and politician Léopold Senghor and the Martinican poet and politician Aimé Césaire. Jadine, caught between the two, allows Morrison to explore the limitations of both. The *négritude* movement is especially relevant in understanding the woman in yellow. In a reversal of white racist essentialism it reappropriates, defines positively and affirms the value of a black essence. The African woman in yellow could have come out of a Senghor poem celebrating black woman. Jadine's fascination with her shows her unconscious engagement with the *négritude* movement and simultaneous sense of alienation from – her rejection by and of – an essence of black womanhood predicated on sexuality and fertility. To return to the folktale of Brer Rabbit and the Tar Baby, in Jadine's eyes the woman with the "skin like tar" is a Tar Baby ensnaring Jadine, now cast in the role of Brer Rabbit, into a trap: a trap of femininity created by and for the benefit of men.

Jadine's growing attraction to Son in Isle des Chevaliers reactivates her ambiguous relation to her body and to black femininity in a new form borrowed from local material, the black Dominican myth of the swamp women of Sein des Vieilles. After her tête-à-tête with Son on the beach Jadine trips and falls into Sein des Vieilles, sinking deeper and deeper into the tar. The swamp women, "hanging in the trees looked down at her" (183); they consider her efforts to extricate herself from the tar and save herself as her rejection of "their exceptional femaleness ... their sacred properties ... holding together the stones of pyramids ... [T]hey wondered at the girl's desperate struggle down below to be free, to be something other than they were" (184). Jadine summons Caribbean swamp women invested with the socially cohesive and reproductive properties of the Tar Lady of African mythology discussed by Morrison (above); but in relation to her, sinking in the tar, they manifest paradoxically as life-threatening progenitors, as entrapping Tar Babies rather than enwrapping mothers.

In Eloe Jadine recreates the group of threatening female ancestors in the image of familiar women: her dead mother, Ondine, the woman in yellow, Marie-Thérèse, Cheyenne and the women of Eloe. African American, Caribbean and African, they are a cosmopolitan group of black "diaspora mothers" (290). They come to her as "succubi" (260), their breasts bared. Marie-Thérèse seems to have materialized out of Jadine's nightmares when she asks Son to forget Jadine in the novel's closing lines because "She has forgotten her ancient properties" (308). Echoing this, Morrison dedicates the novel to the women of her family "all of whom knew their true and ancient properties". Many critics have joined in and found Jadine's resistance to traditional or mythological femininity very dislikeable.

Jadine refuses to "settle for fertility rather than originality, nurturing instead of building" (271). This is a summary of existentialist feminism as formulated in Beauvoir's *The Second Sex* (1949). Confined to roles of "immanence" and "being for others" (procreation, nurturing, social reproduction), women must reach for freedom, "transcendence" of the status quo and assigned roles, making the leap into originality, creativity and self-fashioning. However, Jadine's nightmares suggest that she cannot fully espouse existentialist feminism: her dreams voice her unease with it and point to its limitations. In the late 1970s a new feminist paradigm emerges in Paris, "difference" feminism. Its inaugural text is perhaps Luce Irigaray's *Speculum of the Other Woman*, originally published in 1974. Articulated by Irigaray, Hélène Cixous and others, it involves a critique of existentialist feminism (see, for example, Irigaray's "Equal or Different?"), reaffirms female sexuality and reclaims traditional female roles. Jadine's conflict invites the reader's engagement with the debate between existentialist feminism and difference feminism, but her visions of black femininity also point to the emergence of black feminism and its distinctive priorities.

Jadine like Sula, her ancestor in Morrison's fiction, triggered critics' moral disapprobation and Morrison herself has been disapproving in interviews. Jadine's worldly success as Valerian's spiritual heir anticipated uncomfortably the individualism, materialism and rapaciousness of the 1980s and became a focus of black and feminist fears of assimilation.

VALERIAN, HIS WIFE, HIS AFRICAN AMERICAN AND CARIBBEAN SERVANTS

Valerian, like most other characters, is not the natural inheritor of his resources. His uncles bypassed their own daughters to leave the factory to him. He has organized his household in L'Arbe de la

Croix along the hierarchical lines of a Southern plantation: the hierarchical distinction between house slaves and field slaves is reproduced in the distinction between Valerian's American servants and his Caribbean servants. Early on in his marriage to Margaret he disallowed her budding friendship with Ondine in order to preserve the distinction between owners and servants. Margaret's enforced isolation is the context in which her abuse of Michael, her deviant mothering, is understood. As Ondine interprets it: Valerian "kept her stupid; kept her idle" (281). Margaret's disorder (forgetting the names and uses of things and, given a name, her inability to summon its image and concept) suggests that someone else named the world for her and she can neither accept this nor impose her own names.

When Valerian discovers Margaret's abuse of Michael, he begins to shake uncontrollably, losing mastery over his own body. However, the unsummoned visitations of Michael's ghost for many years previous to this suggest Valerian's repressed knowledge of the abuse. Finally he recognizes his "crime of innocence": "What an awful thing she had done. And how much more awful not to have known it" (245). He admits that he "had chosen not to know" (245). There are no islands – you can't cut yourself off from the world. This works as a manifesto for the role and responsibility of the reader, our role, in Morrison's fiction.

Valerian's servant Sydney has defined himself through his imaginary identification with the subject of Du Bois's sociological study, *The Philadelphia Negro* (Du Bois 1899). As a Philadelphia Negro from Baltimore, he identifies himself in spirit as the proud scion of the century-old industrious Philadelphia black middle-class described by Du Bois, but is, ironically, blind to Du Bois's criticism of it. In Chapter 18, section 57, "The Duty of the Negroes", Du Bois writes: "the better classes of the Negroes should recognize their duty toward the masses ... This the Negro is far from recognizing for himself; ... the centrifugal forces of repulsion between social classes are becoming more powerful than those of attraction" (392).

Replicating and perpetuating the problem of "repulsion between social classes", Sydney and Ondine sustain this imaginary identification through their symbolic differentiation from the Caribbean servants and from Son. Ondine's view of Son, at least initially, is that Son "wasn't a Negro – meaning one of them" (101–02). Such is the lack of contact and recognition between the American and the Caribbean servants that they don't know each others' names. Sydney and Ondine call Gideon "Yardman"; they call Marie-Thérèse Foucault "Marys", remaining distant to the fact that the series of Marys they have sacked (because they wouldn't work indoors) are in fact the same woman; they don't name Alma at all (38–39).

Jadine's assimilation of white high culture, her elite education, is a choice Sydney and Ondine made and worked for. Her distance from African American traditions is an alienation threatening the African American historical middle class more generally. Du Bois himself supported African American assimilation of high culture. (See **p. 9.**)

Sydney and Ondine's refusal to recognize any affinity with the Caribbean servants is reciprocated by them. They call Sydney "bowtie" (111), Ondine "machete-hair" (111, 156) and Jadine "That yalla" (155). However, this is the denial of their own undeniable hybridity. (See **p. 195.**) They speak both Creole and English; they are not natives in a pristine state but descendants of enforced migrants, African slaves; Gideon was an economic migrant to North America for many years and has American citizenship; Alma's dream is to possess a red wig.

Marie-Thérèse is Morrison's critique of Pilate (Milkman's "ancestor" in *Song of Solomon*). She is a bearer of black Caribbean oral traditions, an active and versatile storyteller and an author figure self-referentially addressing Morrison's role. Sensing Son's presence when he hides in L'Arbe de la Croix, she narrativizes him both as a mythical blind horsemen and, in a contemporary register, as Jadine's lover, disapproved of by bowtie and machete-hair who "Tried to keep them apart" (107). Unlike the idealized virtuousness of Pilate, Marie-Thérèse combines lofty prophetic vision in her relation to her adopted American Son; lying and cheating in her relation to her nephew and natural heir Gideon (she claimed to be wealthy in order to convince him to return to Dominique) and domestic subservience to him upon his return; neglect in her relation to Alma; spite in her relation to Jadine and the American servants.

Son's two visits to Dominique show the degradation and poverty of black Dominicans, in descriptions pointing the reader to Aimé Césaire's Martinique in *Notebook of a Return to My Native Land* (1956). Marie-Thérèse Foucault's name points to the ancient Greek Tiresias, the orphaned princess Marie-Thérèse (daughter of Louis XVI and Marie-Antoinette) and the French philosopher of power Michel Foucault, and signals the continuing legacy of colonialism weighing over her life. She is unable to nourish Gideon and Alma. Gideon, unlike his biblical namesake, is not chosen by God to free his people; and the son who returns to inherit and resurrect Caribbean oral traditions is not Gideon but the American Son.

We can now understand Morrison's comment on *Tar Baby*: "everybody was sort of wrong" (Morrison 1985b, 178). Social and cultural perspectives, as embodied by characters, interrogate each other very critically. Simultaneously *Tar Baby* holds things together, making connections where there were none. First, it stages a field of interaction for these perspectives and thereby relates them to each other and binds them together, however antagonistically. Secondly, it attempts an imaginative mixing and combining of African American, Caribbean, African and European mythological elements in a utopian dialogue beyond cultural ownership that resonates with Paul Gilroy's theorization of hybridity.

Beloved (1987)

Beloved initiates a new phase – at least a new emphasis – in Morrison's work. After the revisionist engagement with African American folktales (as well as with Western and African myths) in *Song of Solomon* and *Tar Baby* Morrison explores an alternative, revisionist historiography in her trilogy: *Beloved*, *Jazz* and *Paradise*. Engagement with seemingly minor historical events in African American history is perhaps the defining element in Morrison's loosely defined trilogy. But Morrison uses such events as access points to history on the largest scale, to the global and world-historical. In *Beloved* Morrison uses Margaret Garner's 1856 infanticide – a *cause célèbre* – as point of access to the "Sixty Million and more": the victims of the Middle Passage and of slavery.

Morrison came across Margaret Garner's story when she was in-house editor of *The Black Book* (1974) (see **p. 22**), which contains Reverend P.S. Bassett's account, "A Visit to the Slave Mother Who Killed Her Child", published in *American Baptist* on 12 February 1856 (Bassett 1856). Morrison's work on *The Black Book* already announces her interest in an alternative historiography. In keeping with the ethos of *The Black Book*, in *Beloved* Morrison pays little direct attention to big events and great heroes. She merely alludes to the Fugitive Slave Act of 1850 (legalizing the capture of slaves in the free states), the American Civil War and the Emancipation Proclamation of 1863. She pays no direct attention to canonical abolitionist slave narratives and their authors, such as *Narrative of the Life of Frederick Douglass, an American Slave Written by Himself* (Douglass 1845) and Harriet Jacobs's *Incidents in the Life of a Slave Girl* (Jacobs 1861). While they inaugurate the African American written literary tradition, *Beloved*'s characters are mostly illiterate. Morrison merely alludes to *The North Star*, Douglass's abolitionist newspaper, the abolitionist Sojourner Truth and the heroine of the Underground Railroad Harriet Tubman through the characters of Baby Suggs, Stamp Paid and Ella. (See **p. 8**.) But these characters' marginality, dead-ends and moral ambiguity – Baby Suggs's breakdown, Ella's infanticide by refusing to nurse her baby, the offspring of a white rapist, Stamp Paid's acquiescence at his wife's sexual exploitation by their owner – highlight Morrison's critical revision of the discourse of abolitionism and of slave narratives as part of her alternative historiography. *Beloved*'s characters claim freedom in improvised and "improper" ways, suggesting that there is perhaps no single formula for freedom and perhaps no proper form for telling the story. Freedom can (continue to) enslave and telling can silence. Morrison's project of an alternative historiography includes acute awareness of the narrative "emplotment" – as Hayden White would say – of historiography and its difficulties and limitations. Critics such as Pérez-Torres have described *Beloved* as a postmodern historiographic novel.

"FREEDOM OR THE GRAVE" (JACOBS 1861, 138–39): REVISING THE DISCOURSE OF ABOLITIONISM

P.S. Bassett's "A Visit to the Slave Mother Who Killed Her Child" (Bassett 1856) is a useful introduction to the discourse of abolitionism. Bassett, a white Christian abolitionist, interprets Garner's infanticide in unambiguous terms. He endorses Garner's act as an act of mother love. The underlying assumption is that death is preferable to slavery and that Garner saved her child. Bassett then uses Garner's case to argue that the institution of slavery cannot be reformed, only abolished. He points out that Garner is a Kentucky slave and Kentucky slavery is generally considered mild, but even this form of slavery is unlivable. Morrison's revisionist gaze will focus particularly on two aspects of Bassett's account: mother love and the distinction between different types of slavery.

In writing *Beloved* Morrison focuses on the theme of mother love and turns the cliché into a disturbing investigation of women's peculiar subjectivity and the dynamics of women's self-sacrifice. In a conversation with Gloria Naylor, while still writing *Beloved*, Morrison explained that Margaret Garner's story and the story of the girl who died to protect her lover in what became *Jazz* were intrinsically connected so that the two novels had began as one. In both cases: "A woman loved something other than herself so much" (Morrison 1985a, 207). "It's peculiar to women" Morrison commented; "the best thing that is in us is also the thing that makes us sabotage ourselves, sabotage in the sense that our life is not as worthy" (ibid., 208). Morrison reiterated the point after publication: "What was on my mind was the way in which women are so vulnerable to displacing themselves, into something other than themselves ... there's still an enormous amount of misery and self-sabotage" (Morrison 1987b, 241).

Morrison's return to Bassett's argument that there is ultimately no distinction between slavery in its most brutal versions and "enlightened" slavery is equally bold. *Beloved* explores the view that, in some respects, there is no difference between Schoolteacher, whose discourse is that of nineteenth-century pseudo-scientific racism and anti-abolitionism; Garner, the Southern slave-owner who defined his slaves as men in the spirit of the Enlightenment but assumed that the privilege of defining belonged to him and not his slaves; the Northern abolitionist Bodwin whose kitchen in 1873 contains a racist household object: a statuette of a black boy kneeling on a pedestal bearing the legend "At Yo Service", his open mouth forming a small receptacle for "coins needed to pay for a delivery or some other small service" (255; all page references in this chapter refer to *Beloved* [Morrison 1987a] unless otherwise indicated). Writing with the benefit of historical hindsight Morrison seeks to address and understand the intractability of racism after the Emancipation Proclamation and the failure of Reconstruction.

The linear progression from slavery to freedom – exemplifying the Enlightenment view of history as progress – that organizes slave narratives gives way in *Beloved* to circularity, the elusiveness of freedom and "unspeakable thoughts, unspoken" (199).

The language of Jacobs's *Incidents* is the Enlightenment language of "freedom" and "oppression". "Give me liberty, or give me death" (Jacobs 1861, 151) is a motto this text shares with white abolitionism as well as with nineteenth-century national liberation movements. (For example, the slogan of the 1821 Greek Revolution was "Freedom or death".) Bassett's wholly positive account of Margaret Garner's infanticide is one of many such contemporary accounts. In 1857 Frederick Douglass declared in a speech: "every mother who, like Margaret Garner, plunges a knife into the bosom of her infant to save it from the Hell of our Christian slavery, should be held and honoured as a benefactress" (quot. Rushdy 1992, 43). Frances Harper's poem on Garner, "The Slave Mother: The Tale of the Ohio" constructs Garner's act in similar terms: "I will save my precious children/From their darkly threatened doom,/I will hew their path to freedom/Through the portals of the tomb" (Harper 1857, 22). In the closing lines the audience is addressed directly: "Will you not, as men and Christians,/On the side of freedom stand?" (ibid., 23). In *The Fugitive Slave Law and Its Victims* (1856), the white abolitionist Samuel J. May had similarly presented Garner as a "noble woman" and "heroic wife" fighting "the oppressor", who had the "admiration of hundreds of thousands" (May 1856, 34–35). Like Bassett he concluded that "the mildest form of American slavery ... was worse than death itself!" (ibid., 36).

In the essay "The Site of Memory" Morrison outlines *Beloved*'s relation to slave narratives in particular. Paying tribute to the over 100 slave narratives published prior to abolition as "a very large part of my own literary heritage" (Morrison 1987c, 104), she then spells out their limitations. Written with the multiple aims of being representative; of contributing to the abolition of slavery; of combating the prohibition against slave literacy; and proving their author's ability to write and think to a high standard, they were in keeping with popular taste at the time in drawing a veil over the extent and nature of the violence of slave life. Significantly "there was no mention of their interior life", perhaps because of the perceived lowliness of African American subjectivity, in spite of literature's programmatic serious attention to "low" social groups ever since Wordsworth's 1802 Preface to *Lyrical Ballads*. (For qualification of this see Peach in Criticism on *Beloved*, **p. 209**.) In an oft-quoted passage Morrison continues: "My job becomes how to rip that veil drawn over 'proceedings too terrible to relate.'" In this task "Only the act of imagination can help me" (Morrison 1987c, 110–11 throughout).

SLAVE SUBJECTIVITIES

The formulaic nature of abolitionist discourse veils historical traumas and obscures the continuing psychic devastation of desperate acts of resistance. In relation to historical trauma Morrison has particularly highlighted the silence that has surrounded the Middle Passage:

> those that died *en route* ... they never survived in the lore; there are no songs or dances or tales of these people ... I suspect the reason is that it was not possible to survive ... and dwell on it ... There is a necessity for remembering the horror, but of course ... in a manner in which the memory is not destructive.
>
> (Morrison 1988, 247–48)

However, remembering and telling appropriately is a difficult task because slavery is "undigestible and unabsorbable, completely. Something that has no precedent in the history of the world, in terms of length of time and the nature and specificity of its devastation" (Morrison 1987d, 235). *Beloved* metafictionally explores storytelling as "the process by which we construct and deconstruct reality in order to be able to function in it" (ibid.).

In relation to acts of resistance *Beloved* deviates from slave narratives and abolitionist discourse in two respects. First, Sethe's infanticide ravages Sethe and her family and meets with African American communal disapproval, in spite of Bodwin's successful abolitionist translation of the act into an exemplary act of infanticide-in-order-to-save and the resultant reduced sentence Sethe receives – "The

[American Anti-Slavery] Society managed to turn infanticide and the cry of savagery around, and build a further case for abolishing slavery" (260). And yet both Bodwin's abolitionist discourse and School-teacher's anti-abolitionist discourse – within which Sethe's infanticide proves that slaves are savages or animals or cannibals (149–51) – fail to appropriate and fully absorb Sethe's act, opening the way to a ghostly remainder, Beloved, and an excess of interpretations. Morrison's deviations from Margaret Garner's story highlight *Beloved*'s project of exploring African American subjectivities. Whereas Sethe repli-cates certain aspects of Garner's life and demeanour, Garner was returned to her owner and resold while Sethe serves a short sentence and then lives in freedom. This alteration shifts focus onto the cost of and impediments to freedom: Sethe's haunting, her guilt that she admits only to Beloved, and the difficulty of her attempts to make amends and move on.

Secondly, *Beloved* explores a wide repertoire of slaves' desperate, excessive acts of resistance or failures to act – instances of too much or too little action – in their moral ambiguity. Morrison especially highlights deviations from nineteenth-century norms of femininity and masculinity. Women's infanticide of rape-babies conceived with whites or running away without their children or committing suicide to escape slavery, and thereby deserting their children, have to be understood against the passive female norm; men's failure to act or madness or vulnerability to rape have to be understood against the ideology of the rational and energetic self-made man. Ella's repressed story of refusing to nurse a baby that took five days to die (259) is echoed in the repressed story of Sethe's mother. Sethe remembers and obliquely tells the story of her unnamed mother, a survivor of the Middle Passage: she "threw away" her rape-babies and only preserved Sethe; then she attempted to escape and was hanged (61–62), the unspoken story being that she deserted Sethe in her escape. Sethe's infanticide can be seen as a response to her mother's repressed and undigested desertion: "I wouldn't draw breath without my chil-dren ... My plan was to take us all to the other side where my own ma'am is" (203). Beloved has a memory of a mother figure jumping in the water and leaving her behind, which can be interpreted as an individual or collective memory of a mother committing suicide during the Middle Passage and deserting her child (211–13). "Heroic wife" (quoted above; Samuel J. May on Margaret Garner) emerges as an inappropriate description of slave femininities in the context of an institution systemically interrupting slave family bonds as a threat to the primary relation between master and slave. (See Hortense J. Spillers, "Mama's Baby, Papa's Maybe: An American Grammar Book".) Margaret Atwood, in her review of *Beloved*, tries to sum up: "The slaves are motherless, fatherless, deprived of their mates, their children, their kin. It is a world in which people suddenly vanish and are never seen again, not through accident and covert operations or terrorism, but as a matter of everyday legal policy" (Atwood 1987).

Beloved's repertoire of slave masculinities is equally revisionist. The distance between Frederick Douglass's slave narrative and Halle's half-told story is instructive. Both men are presented as literate, physically strong and highly capable. But whereas Frederick gradually approximates the white nineteenth-century norm of masculinity, Halle doesn't and displays some traditionally feminine traits. Frederick is an orphan, has no significant family ties, is self-made and owes (or recognizes that he owes) little to others (Douglass 1845, 28–29); Halle works to buy his mother's freedom. Frederick fights back when abused: "I resolved to fight; and, suiting my action to the resolution, I seized Covey hard by the throat … This battle with Mr. Covey was the turning point in my career as a slave. It … revived within me a sense of my own manhood" (53–54); he then escapes on his own. Halle, on the other hand, loses his sanity when he witnesses the milking of his pregnant wife. "He saw them boys do that to me and let them keep on breathing?" Sethe asks Paul D. He responds: "A man ain't a goddam ax. Chopping, hacking, busting every goddam minute of the day. Things get to him. Things we can't chop down because they're inside" (69). Paul D himself has experienced literal invasions of his black male interiority: the bit in his mouth in Sweet Home after his failed escape and then his sexual violation in Alfred, Georgia. When Sixo and Paul D are recaptured by Schoolteacher and his men, Sixo bursts into song and something about his singing convinces Schoolteacher that Sixo has gone wild, that "This one will never be suitable", so he kills Sixo (226). Paul D "thinks he should have sung along" (227).

The hybridized novelty of slave subjectivities – masculinization of women and feminization of men – is explored as a resource, and normative nineteenth-century masculinity and femininity subtly critiqued. At the beginning of *Beloved* Paul D walks into Sethe's haunted house, 124 Bluestone Road, and Sethe explains that the house is haunted by her dead baby daughter. Paul D "had become the kind of man who could walk into a house and make the women cry. Because with him, in his presence, they could" (17). With him "[e]motions sped to the surface" (39), so Sethe tells him about her milking and the tree on her back made by the weals from her flogging and, in a subterranean communication between Sethe and the baby ghost, "The house itself was pitching" (18). This "feminine" quality coexists with a more formulaic masculinity within Paul D and, in a parody of heroic masculinity, he beats up the house to kill the beast he had helped summon in the first place: "holding the table by two legs, he bashed it about, wrecking everything, screaming back at the screaming house" (18). He does this to save his princess, Sethe, but when the ghost is gone Sethe does not feel rescued: Paul D "ran her children out and tore up the house" (22).

Shortly afterwards the baby ghost returns as Beloved, a fully embodied young woman, and a novel family of four is improvised: "They were a family somehow and he [Paul D] was not the head of it" (132). Instead of killing the beast Paul D is "moved" by Beloved against his will and made to touch her "on the inside part" (117) in a disturbing but healing repetition-with-a-difference of his traumatic rape. His closed "tobacco tin" heart opens and he finds himself saying "Red heart. Red heart" (116–17). Paul D echoes and revives Baby Suggs's dormant legacy and becomes its inheritor: More than life, "love your heart. For this is the prize" (89). This is "the heart that started beating" when Baby Suggs crossed the Ohio River and became a free woman (147). "Freedom or the grave" is being redefined as "Your heart or the grave". In *Beloved*'s closing pages Paul D returns to 124, finds Sethe exhausted and offers to bathe her, echoing Baby Suggs's bathing of Sethe after her escape when she first arrived in 124. To Baby Suggs's "Call" he responds by selecting for its usefulness that "feminine" part of him that is interactive and intersubjective. Sethe looks at him and sees once again a man who can "make the women cry. Because in his presence they could" (272).

THE HAUNTING AND EXORCISM OF 124

The opening lines of *Beloved* throw us into the midst of a gothic novel, a ghost story. What can a story of the supernatural possibly have to do with critical historiography and the "Sixty Million and more"? And what can it possibly have to do with psychological realism, the exploration of nineteenth-century African American subjectivity? Is not the supernatural the antithesis of historical and psychological realism? In thinking about literary genres one might argue that there is a major difference to be marked between the gothic novel and the realist novel: the gothic novel is a work of "imagination" or "fancy"; the realist novel a work of "observation".

In fact, the text inaugurating the genre of the gothic novel, Horace Walpole's *The Castle of Otranto* (1764), combines supernatural events and enchantment with a meticulous historicism and with psychological realism. In his 1765 Preface to the second edition Walpole argues that the text was "an attempt to blend the two kinds of romance, the ancient and the modern. In the former all was imagination and improbability: in the latter, nature is always intended to be, and sometimes has been, copied with success" (Walpole 1764, 9). In other words, the gothic novel, in Walpole's view, is an attempt to combine imagination and observation; the old genre of romance and the new genre of the novel. Walpole was aspiring to emulate a characteristic of "all inspired writings": "witnesses to *the most stupendous phenomena*, never lose sight of their human character" (ibid., 10). In a letter he comments that "it was written for this age, that wants nothing but cold reason" (ibid., xxvi). Since its inception the gothic novel was a form attuned to the sublime and the "stupendous" and to bearing witness to the unpresentable: extreme phenomena defying human reason, "phenomena" perhaps such as the modern history of slavery and the Middle Passage.

The gothic element of *Beloved* – it can be described as part gothic novel, part tragedy, part postmodern historiographic metafiction – resonates with African American cosmology. Its appropriateness is due to the fact that slaves had a strong belief in the ghostly. In Morrison's own experience, ghosts continue to be a part of African American cosmology. (See **p. 14**.) As critics have pointed out slave-owners exploited the slaves' belief in ghosts to control and terrorize them (for example, the KKK ghost-sheet outfit); *Beloved* can be seen as a reappropriation of the ghost story: putting it in African American hands for African American use.

The Gothicism of *Beloved* is therefore a means of exploration of African American subjectivity and a part of this novel's new and enhanced historical and psychological realism. The baby ghost of the house at 124 and the adult embodied Beloved are arguably aesthetic forms the inhabitants of 124 use in order to give voice and shape to their traumatic historical experience in their efforts to heal themselves. The haunting of 124 is a form of remembering of their "stupendous" experience of slavery. The task is one of "remembering the horror, but of course ... in a manner in which the memory is not destructive" (Morrison quoted above). The haunting seems initially to have a negative and re-enslaving effect: while Sethe was a runaway slave, her sons, Howard and Buglar, "run away" to escape their haunted house (3); then Baby Suggs, who had given up her Call as a preacher, dies exhausted. And yet it is a vital expression of a collective unconscious, as Stamp Paid claims: "he believed the undecipherable language clamoring around the house was the mumbling of the black and angry dead ... this new kind of whitefolks' jungle was hidden, silent, except once in a while when you could hear its mumbling in places like 124" (198–99).

The haunting of 124 speaks a collective unspeakable. Denver in answer to Paul D's question "You think she sure 'nough your sister?"

responds "At times I think she was – *more*" (266; my emphasis). The question "Who is Beloved?" has continued to preoccupy critics and has received multiple answers. Horvitz has argued that Beloved is both Sethe's daughter and Sethe's mother; Harris and Barnett have argued that she is a succubus; House that she is a real, historical girl. But whoever she might be, the thirty women who gather outside 124 come to witness her and recognize her as Sethe's dead daughter. The haunting of 124 therefore comes to have a binding and unifying role. It is witnessed and attested to by increasing numbers; and becomes a shared communal reality working against the fragmentations and divisions of the community. Furthermore the thirty women's recognition of Beloved as Sethe's dead daughter "come back to fix her" (255) is an implicit recognition of their own traumatic and repressed past – for example Ella's implicit recognition of her own infanticide. The exorcism of Beloved is a collective self-exorcism where the distinction between exorcist and exorcised no longer holds.

In the gathering of the thirty women outside 124 a process reversing Howard and Buglar's running away and Baby Suggs's exhaustion begins. With this gathering "the Clearing had come to" Sethe (261) and Baby Suggs's call-and-response healing ritual is resurrected; then, reversing the boys' desertion, Paul D returns to 124 to do Baby Suggs's work.

W.E.B. Du Bois summarized the failure of Reconstruction as follows: "The slave went free, stood a brief moment in the sun, then moved back again toward slavery" (quot. Franklin and Moss 2000, 288). *Beloved* imagines anew this "brief moment in the sun" and attempts to understand why it didn't last and to save what was valuable in that moment. In the novel's terms the "brief moment in the sun" is Sethe's "twenty-eight days ... of unslaved life" (95), culminating in Baby Suggs's feast for 90 people. Baby Suggs's "celebration of blackberries that put Christmas to shame" (147) is an excessive action answered the very next morning by the community's resentment and inaction – no-one runs to 124 to tell them that Schoolteacher is coming. This is answered by Sethe's infanticide which is answered by the community's inaction – no-one sings, "like arms to hold and steady her on the way", when the sheriff takes Sethe away (153).

In Greek tragedy the hero acts excessively, hubristically, while the chorus comments on the action but is unable to intervene. This combination of the hero's excessive action and the community's inaction is the very diagnosis of the problem in *Beloved*. What is singled out as valuable is the interactive, call-and-response form of Baby Suggs's ritual in the Clearing (88); while the problem is that something has gone wrong in the call and response. This call-and-response form is resurrected when the thirty women gather outside 124. Their call allows Sethe to repeat her infanticide with a difference: when she sees Bodwin coming to get Denver and thinks Schoolteacher has returned, she attacks him; Denver and the thirty women intervene and stop her. The interaction of tragic hero and chorus summons a precarious African American community into existence by performative means: "I will call them my people, which were not my people" (*Beloved*'s epigraph). Critics have pointed out that in the series 124, three is the missing number that points to Sethe's third, murdered child. The thirty women provide the missing number and put community in the place of the murdered girl.

A historian might argue that Morrison's account of the failure and the potentialities of Reconstruction is too subjective to be valid. However, Morrison does not set out to offer an objective account of the past, but an alternative historiography from the point of view of the present and for present use. This resonates with the project of the literary-critical school of New Historicism, which came into prominence in the 1980s, and involves a critique of the "objective" historian in favour of the "effective" historian, as announced in Michel Foucault's "Nietzsche, Genealogy, History" (1971), an essay deeply indebted to Nietzsche's perspectivist historiography.

What is also selected as valuable is the metaphysics that underlies Baby Suggs's rituals in the Clearing. In announcing "we flesh" (88) and relying on bodily performances to heal the spirit, Baby Suggs understands a clear interconnection and interaction of the physical and the spiritual, body and mind. The same non-dualism underlies the haunting of 124: the baby ghost's actions are objectively visible and physical; Beloved is fully embodied. In outlining the principles of a Black art Morrison has identified, as elements, both call-and-response and also a world-view "blend[ing] the acceptance of the supernatural and a profound rootedness in the real world at the same time with neither taking precedence over the other" (Morrison 1984a, 342). In response to the Nietzsche-inspired critique of Western metaphysics as constructing a binary opposition between spirit and body in favour of the former and devaluing the latter, what is on offer is an alternative African and African American cosmology positing the oneness or unity of the two. Barbara Christian, followed by many critics, points out that African cosmology is an important context for the understanding of *Beloved* (Christian 1993b). The ancestor, in West African cosmologies, returns in fully embodied form, eating, drinking and having sexual relations with the living, both benefiting but also threatening the living. In this context Beloved is an ancestor figure. So is Baby Suggs, whose visitation and advice to "know" racism and yet "go on out the yard" (244) enables Denver to step out of 124, seek the community's help and initiate a chain of call-and-response that will culminate in the gathering of the thirty women. Baby Suggs, the embodiment of oral culture, also enables Denver to renew her literacy lessons with Lady Jones who viewed Baby Suggs as "the ignorant grandmother" (237) and attributed the story of Beloved's return to the community's "ignorance" (257); and to accept Miss Bodwin's "experimenting on" her and the prospect of a university education at Oberlin offered by Miss Bodwin (266). Clearly Morrison views the relation between orality and literacy, not as a relation of either/or, but as one of both/and.

BOTH/AND

We have touched on the way in which slave narratives and abolitionist discourse are indebted to Enlightenment thought and occur within its conceptual parameters, most notably the binary oppositions between reason/literacy/civilization/science/freedom versus body/superstition/ignorance/orality/barbarism/enslavement, valuing the former and devaluing the latter. To the extent that it relies on this oppositional thinking Enlightenment thought can be seen to reproduce biases found throughout the history of Christian, Western culture, in spite of the Enlightenment's apparent novelty and radicalism. Even more ominously this opposition underlies and legitimates the blatant racism of some of the greatest Enlightenment philosophers. Relying on this opposition, Hume in 1742 claimed the inferiority of black people and therefore unwittingly legitimated slavery: "There never was a civilized nation of any other complexion than white ... No ingenious manufactures amongst them, no arts, no sciences" (in Kramnick 1995, 629). Kant agrees with Hume in his 1764 essay "Observations on the Feeling of the Beautiful and the Sublime" (Kramnick 1995, 637–39). In 1772 Diderot attacks slavery and colonialism by reversing this opposition, in the sense of reversing the hierarchy and valuing the devalued side of the opposition. He fictionalizes as follows a Tahitian response to Europeans: "We do not want to barter what you call our ignorance for your useless civilization" (Kramnick 1995, 641). Thomas Paine, in his 1775 powerful attack on slavery in the *Philadelphia Magazine*, similarly turns the tables by calling his own nation and other Western nations taking part in the slave trade "barbarous", "inhuman" and "monstrous": "By such wicked and inhuman ways the English are said to enslave towards one hundred thousand yearly; of which thirty thousand are supposed to die by barbarous treatment in the first year ... So monstrous is the making and keeping them slaves at all, abstracted from the barbarous treatment they suffer" (Kramnick 1995, 646–47).

To a certain extent *Beloved* continues this tactic of reversing the binary opposition. It privileges orality and aspires to being an oral text (albeit, of course, in writing). It values what Lady Jones calls "ignorance" – for example, the oral and bodily performances at the Clearing, the sound emitted by the thirty women – as collective art and simultaneously action in the world. It privileges the body as a site of knowledge and human interaction and denounces Schoolteacher's racist pseudo-science. It redefines European civilization as "whitefolks' jungle" (quoted above).

However, *Beloved* also goes beyond the logic of binary opposition, which is a logic of either/or, and embraces a logic of both/and, in keeping with African cosmology. It embraces: spirituality *and* the body; orality *and* literacy; African civilization *and* Western civilization. Denver is the textual representative of this double vision or double inheritance. Sethe chose her name in memory of the white runaway indentured servant, Amy Denver, who helped her reach the Ohio River and give birth to Denver; in a moment of cross-race solidarity the "two throw-away people" (84) did their work "appropriately and well" (85). This is a story told by Denver herself on my occasions, with increasing sophistication and narrative improvisation; these oral storytelling acts position Denver as the inheritor of Baby Suggs, a folk artist with considerable oratorical and performance skills. Simultaneously, Denver is also the inheritor of Halle's literacy and one of Lady Jones's most promising students. Lady Jones's view of Baby Suggs as "the ignorant grandmother" (quoted above) suggests that African Americans selected for higher education run the risk of becoming alienated from their culture, but Denver holds the promise of a bicultural education.

Many critics have pointed out that *Beloved* is multiperspectivist. For example, Sethe's infanticide is narrated through a series of perspectives: the slave catcher's; Schoolteacher's; the sheriff's; Stamp Paid's; and finally Sethe's. The novel also refers or alludes to a multiplicity of forms of knowledge: science; newspapers, pro-slavery and abolitionist; written slave narratives; songs; interactive rituals; oral storytelling but also listening. This multiperspectivism is not a facile pluralism, but is part of an attempt to select what is useful and discard what is unviable. Throughout her essay "The Site of Memory" Morrison stresses that her writing involves "selection" (Morrison 1987c, 111) and "cut[ting] back" (120); she concludes: "Now I know better how to throw away things that are not useful" (122).

In *Beloved*'s concluding section, the ambiguity of "pass on" (274–75) – "to transmit" and "to die" – poses but does not answer the question of whether the story of Beloved should be remembered or forgotten or what parts should be remembered and what forgotten. The novel's characters suffer from an excess or a lack of involuntary remembering and forgetting. What to remember and what to forget? How to remember the past appropriately? How to select the past's potentialities for the future and discard dead-ends? How to repeat, tell, past horrors non-destructively? These are the questions that the novel poses and opens rather than answers.

Jazz (1992)

Jazz is the second novel in Morrison's loosely defined trilogy. The trilogy – *Beloved*, *Jazz* and *Paradise* – attempts an alternative historiography, with each novel taking an ostensibly minor historical event as its starting point. A 1926 photograph of a dead girl in her coffin by African American photographer James Van Der Zee is *Jazz*'s starting point. The photograph was published in Van Der Zee's *The Harlem Book of the Dead* (1978) for which Morrison wrote the Foreword. Van Der Zee's caption comments that the girl, shot by her lover, chose to bleed to death rather than name her killer (see Gates and Appiah 1993, 52–53). The caption includes the comment: "She was just trying to give him a chance to get away" (Van Der Zee quot. Peach 2000, 131). Owen Dodson's accompanying poem suggests that the girl died to escape as well as to protect her lover and that her death can be read as a suicide (Matus 1998, 123 quotes and discusses the poem).

As early as 1985 Morrison commented that she initially saw *Beloved* and *Jazz* as one book. The Margaret Garner story and the story of the dead girl were intrinsically connected. In both cases, "A woman loved something other than herself so much" (Morrison 1985a, 207). "It's peculiar to women ... the best thing that is in us is also the thing that makes us sabotage ourselves, sabotage in the sense that our life is not as worthy" (ibid., 208).

If this oft-quoted comment suggests universal concerns, the novel is also deeply engaged with the locale of Harlem in 1926. The narrative present is 1926, a time of possibility and hope, after World War I and before the Great Depression. Harlem, within the post-Reconstruction context of the Great Migration – the exodus of African Americans to the Promised Land of the urban North – is the black capital of America. Harlem in the 1920s is a cultural Mecca for many reasons: musically the emergence of jazz, the musical form that names the age, from blues; in literature, the writers and intellectuals of the Harlem Renaissance optimistically announcing the New Negro; in politics, a new black pride, combative and activist, in response to white race riots and continuing institutionalized racism. (See **pp. 10–11**.) At least this is the outward history.

Morrison's alternative historiography critically interrogates the high-art discourse of the Harlem Renaissance – the discourse of black modernism – and its ideology of the "new". It turns to jazz – a low-art and semi-disreputable culture at the time – in order to identify, with the benefit of historical hindsight and in view of current needs, historical dead-ends – such as Dorcas's use of jazz – and select, out of its principles, resources to live by. Improvisation is the jazz formal principle Morrison singles out as most valuable.

Morrison's historiography in *Jazz* has a prominent metafictional element, so that the novel can best be described as "historiographic metafiction". *Jazz*'s impossible narrator – impossibly shape-shifting from first-person intradiegetic narration to third-person extradiegetic and omniscient narration – proclaims himself/herself unreliable, keeps highlighting the difficulties of storytelling, and invites the reader to become equally self-aware and equally alert to the difficulties of reading and sense-making. Objectivity and authorized versions are suspect.

BLACK MODERNISMS AND THE ART OF IMPROVISATION

The story of *Jazz* – the love triangle of Joe, Violet and Dorcas – is Morrison's improvisation on the story of Van Der Zee's dead girl. The story is stated briefly in the novel's opening. Like a jazz theme it is then developed in numerous amplifications and variations: in literary terms the narrator and characters return to it in order to elaborate their own perspective on what happened. In this sense, *Jazz* has the quality of jazz.

The jazz principle of improvisation on the given – against the dominant modernist aesthetic of creating the new – could be seen, in this regard, as a modernist counter-discourse. To the extent that returning to and revising, rewriting, the original is often identified as postmodernist, jazz improvisation can be seen as postmodernist *avant la lettre*. Since her first novel, Morrison's has been a postmodern aesthetic of intertextuality: reworking the cliché and revising the canonical, whether ancient Greek, African, modern Western or African American. In *Jazz* Morrison offers a genealogy of postmodern intertextuality: one of its points of emergence is an alternative African American modernism, that of jazz music. By this account, what defines jazz is not its newness and originality, but its intertextual, dialogic and revising relation to the blues and other discourses, as Scheiber argues (see **pp. 220–1**).

Jazz distinguishes between two modernisms. The dominant modernism is defined early on: "I'm strong. Alone, yes, but top-notch and indestructible ... At last, at last, everything is ahead. The smart ones say so and people listening to them and reading what they write down agree. Here comes the new ... There goes the sad stuff. The bad stuff ... History is over, you all" (7; all page references in this

chapter refer to *Jazz* [Morrison 1992a] unless otherwise indicated).
Jazz subjects this avant-gardist ideology to multifaceted critique.
Harlem life offers an individualistic and largely illusory sense of free-
dom from the racist past.

In the spirit of the Harlem Renaissance and Alain Locke's "The
New Negro" (1925), Joe's account of his life is that he reinvented
himself, he "changed into new seven times" (123). He declares "I've
been a New Negro all my life" (129). He thinks he is "free to do something wild", but the narrator comments: "That's the way the City
spins you ... All the while letting you think you're free" (120). As Joe
trails and kills Dorcas in unconscious repetition of his early attempts
to trail his mother, Wild, the reader might well conclude that while
Joe thinks he's free to make himself new he is unwittingly compelled,
haunted, controlled by the past. Joe, Violet and Dorcas have all been
orphaned by a violent racist past that still haunts them. Wild's "terror"
(144) when she sees Golden Gray for the first time is an elliptical
reference to her terror of whiteness. Violet's mother, Rose Dear, commits suicide in a delayed response to her dispossession. Dorcas's parents
are killed during the notorious St. Louis white race riots (see **p. 10**).

The "new" is suspect in an African American context and connotes
the enforced migration of the Middle Passage and the dispossession
of slavery. African Americans experienced modernity – Marx's "All
that is solid melts into air" – very early and in highly traumatic
fashion. The Great Migration North was freely chosen. The period
between the end of World War I and the Depression displayed a new
African American political anger and activism that anticipated 1950s
and 1960s activism and the civil rights movement. But Harlem life in
the 1920s was new in its boldness and appetite *and simultaneously*
haunted by the "specter ... left behind" (33). In Morrison's reading
the Harlem Renaissance constructs a false opposition between a free
urban Northern present and future and a compromised and tainted
rural past onto which problems such as continuing institutionalized
and internalized racism are projected. (By this reading jazz would not
be absolutely new, and opposed to the tainted blues, as the Black
Aesthetic Movement claimed (see **pp. 220–1**.) Zora Neale Hurston
was an atypical member of the Harlem Renaissance in exploring the
cultural resources of the rural South and can be considered Morrison's precursor in this.

The other modernism Morrison explores is the alternative modernism of jazz. Alice "knew from sermons and editorials that it wasn't
real music – just colored folks' stuff: harmful, certainly; embarras-
sing, of course; but not real, not serious" (59). For Morrison, on the
other hand, jazz improvisation is a viable alternative to the false
dilemma of the new versus the unconscious repetition of the old: it is

an artful, ironic or critical engagement with the past and the given. More than a formal principle it is potentially a way of life that replays the past differently, recomposing and reconfiguring it. By this reading jazz would be steeped in the past and emerging out of the blues *as well as* distinctly new *as well as* an ancestor of postmodernism.

In this novel jazz improvisation is generalized. The second triangle of Joe, Violet and Felice is an instance of improvisation: it is neither new nor a repetition of the first triangle, but replays the past differently and defies the narrator's expectations. In another instance of improvisation, Felice's father loves talking back to the black New York weekly press, such as the *Amsterdam News* and the *New York Age*. Felice comments: "The good part for him is to read everything and argue about what he's read" (199). *Beloved*'s characters were mostly illiterate. Denver, the character embodying historical possibility, pursued literacy with tremendous appetite in the 1870s. Literacy is the great project in Frances E.W. Harper's novel *Iola Leroy, Or Shadows Uplifted* (1893). In the 1920s, the generation following Denver's has become literate. Alice reads newspapers regularly, Malvonne "lived alone with newspapers and ... books" (40) and Dorcas's father poses in a photo "holding a book" (200). But this is no longer enough. The father's literacy didn't save his life during the St. Louis riots, and Alice lives in fear.

Harlem offers its inhabitants a burgeoning black press, beauty industry, entertainment industry and music industry. In interviews Morrison has said repeatedly that music nurtured African Americans in the past, but since its commercialization and wide dissemination, the novel is the art form that has taken over this role (Morrison 1981b). In *Jazz* she develops a more nuanced argument. Commercialism, consumerism, fashion, ever-new styles, a love of surfaces and self-styling are omnipresent in Harlem, but they can nurture or harm depending on the use you make of them: will you simply replay the record or are you able to talk back and improvise? In *Jazz*'s background minor characters play or sing on rooftops, sidewalks and in front of open windows – this is where possibility lies. Stave comments: "The metaphor of the needle in the groove of a record, which is referenced repeatedly throughout the text, stands in contradiction to the concept of a jazz performance, in which the music will always vary from earlier iterations of it" (Stave 2007, 65). The skin whitening and hair straightening of the black beauty industry, in which Violet and Joe work, is an instance of replaying the record, in the sense of repeating white standards of beauty.

Improvisation is both a way to claim a degree of authorship and to question authority and fake objectivity. The narrator keeps revising his or her account of Golden Gray: "How could I have imagined him so poorly?" (160). Violet, Joe and Felice improvise and escape the narrator's confident announcement of a new "scandalizing three-some" and new shooting (6). The narrator gives up earlier claims of omniscience and omnipotence suited to the authorial persona of an author-God – "well, it's my storm, isn't it? I break lives to prove I can mend them back again" (119) – and acknowledges the characters' improvisational flair: "It never occurred to me that they were thinking other thoughts, feeling other feelings, putting their lives together in ways I never dreamed of" (221).

"CRACKS ... IN THE GLOBE LIGHT OF THE DAY" (22): FREUD AND THE BLACK SELF

We have been describing improvisation as artful repetition, repetition with a difference, of the past and the given. The particular difficulty of this project for *Jazz*'s characters is that the past and the "given" is unavailable and unlivable. On the surface Harlem in 1926 is "good times and easy money" (9). But the glittering surface half-conceals "ill-glued cracks ... beyond which is anything" (23). The past is an amorphous and terrifying monster threatening to erupt from the depths of the unconscious. Jazz improvisation cannot stand securely on the foundation of the past in order to build something new because "there is no foundation at all" (23). The past has to be actively reconstructed in the present to be made available for improvisation – and this is what begins to happen in the novel, while parts of the past will remain beyond reclamation.

Violet and Joe intuit this lack of foundation – that any search for roots is going to reveal rootlessness – and capture it in an image. Violet's image is a memory trace. During the dispossession from their home, "all of us children put one foot on the other" (98). The ground has just been taken from under their feet, their mother, Rose Dear, is broken and unable to help them, so they give form to their helplessness in this gesture – and help themselves by using one foot as the ground for the other so becoming their own foundation, at the cost of a split self (divided into helpless orphan and helping surro-gate mother). Joe has also turned a memory trace during his fruitless search for his mother, Wild, into an image to capture his own "inside nothing" (37), his mother's desertion of him – his own lack of foundation. Close to Wild's "sheltering rock" home (176), while searching for Wild, Joe comes across an oak tree with exposed roots, which bears traces of her. The tree "grew in unlikely soil – entwined in its own roots" (178). The tree "whose roots grew up its trunk" (180) symbolizes his condition. He is the tree "whose roots grew backwards as though, having gone obediently into earth and found it barren, retreat[ed] to the trunk for what was needed. Defiant and against logic its roots climbed. Toward leaves, light, wind ... the ground was as porous as a sieve. A step could swallow your foot or your whole self" (182). In the absence of a solid foundation, the trunk feeds the roots – the search for roots is an act of the imagination reconstructing the past. In Morrison's novels Joe's "inside nothing" is characteristic of the African American self across the generations. Dorcas "knew ... what that inside nothing was like" (37–38) – but so did Baby Suggs in *Beloved*.

Violet's putting one foot on another returns in a mid-life breakdown. She has never told Joe about her past; now she experiences Freudian slips of the tongue, when her everyday speech is interrupted by another rogue speaker inside her but beyond her control. She makes herself speechless to silence this other "renegade tongue" (24) but she experiences "cracks". She sits "in the middle of the street" (17) then tries to steal a baby with a "butter-colored face" (19) then tries to cut Dorcas's "creamy" (5) face in her coffin during the funeral. She experiences those acts as done by the other Violet, *that* Violet. Violet is a split self.

The beginning of the twentieth century is the era of Freud and psychoanalysis. His "discovery" of the unconscious fragments the self. This fragmentation of the self, the Freudian drama in general, takes place within the context of the nuclear family. But the family in *Jazz* is open to history or blown open by history – family dramas turn out to be historical dramas. Violet's father is on the run because of his political activism; Rose Dear's experience of dispossession is so structural and institutionally embedded that it is shared by many African Americans; Joe's birthplace, Vienna – an ironic reference to Freud's Vienna – is burned to the ground and its entire black population dispossessed and forced to leave. Violet returns to the past to "discover" the unassimilable fact of her mother's suicide. She also "discovers" that True Belle, her grandmother and the family's saviour, transmitted to her an adoration of Golden Gray which is unlivable for the "very dark, bootblack" Violet (206), but which she repeats in her attempt to steal the "butter-colored" baby. Freud has no language and no cure for the splitting of the self because of internalized racism. Du Bois called it "double consciousness" in *The Souls of Black Folk* (1903), but the working-class Violet hasn't read Du Bois and needs to improvise.

As in *Beloved*, reconstructing the past in *Jazz* involves selection. Violet reconsiders the limits of her self and revises what she had unwittingly included and excluded. She comes to include the crazy Violet – "*that* Violet is me!" (96) – and decides to kill the golden boy inside her. Golden Gray is "another you inside that isn't anything like you" (208). In a fantasy of reparation she sets out to make herself into the kind of woman her mother would have liked as a friend – and who might have saved her. Violet also includes, in a livable form, Rose Dear's "Seeing bleak truth" (101). Felice sums her up: "She doesn't lie, Mrs. Trace. Nothing she says is a lie the way it is with most older people" (205).

The narrator participates in this process. The self he or she sheds is the omniscient narrator: "my know-it-all self covered helplessness" (220). The narrator then claims an illusory, delusional or rather imaginative loving proximity with the unavailable and speechless Wild. The narrator claims impossibly that the terrified and terrifying Wild, who would not mother Joe, "has seen me and is not afraid of me. She hugs me" (221). Wild is included into the narrator's self.

CALL AND RESPONSE

Blues call and response or antiphony, inherited by jazz, has a prominent role in this novel. Morrison's novels have been increasingly multi-perspectival and dialogic. *Jazz* continues this trend to explore the possibilities of unlikely and antiphonic duos and trios. Particularly in *Jazz*, historical possibility lies in couplings that are dynamic, differential and non-stereotypical – transgressing lines of race, colour, class and generation. The unlikely coupling of Violet and Alice, Dorcas's aunt, is exemplary in this respect. Violet takes her cracks and slips of the tongue to the seamstress Alice, who stitches and mends for her. Violet and her voice of the unconscious meets the severely repressed Alice.

Alice has internalized white middle-class values and is sexually repressed. Like Geraldine in *The Bluest Eye*, Helene Wright in *Sula* and Ruth Dead in *Song of Solomon*, she is the sort of character who would not have been allowed change and development in Morrison's earlier novels. But her friendship with Violet causes her to change in her fifties: "something opened up" (83). In the past she could hear a "complicated anger" and "appetite" in jazz music but could not recognize it as her own (59). But she now senses inside her "a new thing – anger" (75). Her auto-critique follows: she "had chosen sur-render and made Dorcas her own prisoner of war" (77). The acme of her development is a moment that mixes creation and destruction. "I'm saying make it, make it!" she tells Violet, while burning the fabric she is ironing, unintentionally but with all the heat of her emerging new self (113).

Morrison has been exploring the great potential of female friendship since her early work, especially in *Sula* with the interrupted friendship between two young girls, Sula and Nel, taking place in the 1920s and broken off in 1927. In *Jazz* Morrison returns to this theme with the unlikely friendship between Dorcas and Felice, interrupted in October 1925 when Felice meets Joe. Felice remembers that "the girls in my school bunched off according to their skin color. I hate that stuff – Dorcas too. So me and her were different that way" (200–01). The two girls get into fights often to defend their friendship. In both novels young female friendship is interrupted because of men, but whereas the semi-rural Nel is looking to get married, Dorcas, the Harlem girl, has discovered desire.

Felice's account of Dorcas turns her into an enigma. She has an easy-going personality and ought to have been good-looking but "She just missed ... it missed somehow ... All together it didn't fit" (201). This is a version of the *hamartia* of Greek tragedy: missing the mark, a flaw in an essentially good character. Intriguingly Felice tells us that Dorcas's death was a suicide: her wound was not so severe but she "let herself die" (204, 209). Felice finally called the ambulance against Dorcas's explicit wishes but it comes too late and Dorcas bleeds to death "because it was colored people calling" (210). Felice understands Dorcas's suicide as a desertion of her: "Her best friend, I thought, but not best enough for her to want to go to the emergency room and stay alive" (213). In her final days Dorcas's most prominent feeling is one of triumph with regard to female rivals for Acton's attention. Felice declares that all the girls she knows are looking for men, but she wants a job instead. Stave concludes that Dorcas died because she broke off her friendship with Felice: "In choosing to privilege her relationship to Joe and later to Acton rather than to Felice, Dorcas ... denies herself the strength that she requires to continue to live" (Stave 2007, 62).

Morrison connects Dorcas's sexual appetite and sexual boldness to the notorious East St. Louis white race riots that killed her parents. During the burning, by arson, of her home that killed her mother: "wood chips – ignited and smoking – exploded in the air. One of them must have entered [Dorcas's] stretched dumb mouth ... the bright wood chip sank further and further down until it lodged comfortably somewhere below her navel" (60–61). Dorcas's pursuit of sex – embodying and exemplifying the spirit of the Jazz Age – is, on this reading, the inadequate expression of something more primary which her "dumb mouth" is unable to articulate: the terror and grief of racism. Morrison reverses Freud's order. In Freud the libido has primarily sexual aims and is secondarily sublimated into higher non-sexual activity: social and cultural life. In Morrison's reading on the other hand the sexual liberation of the Jazz Age is a displacement. It is not really a liberation, but an historical dead-end, hence Dorcas's suicide.

Morrison's critique of 1920s sexual liberation is reminiscent of Herbert Marcuse's critique of 1960s sexual liberation in *One-Dimensional Man* (1964). Against the dominant view that 1960s sexual liberation was also a political liberation, he argued that it was a lamentable and "repressive" displacement of political activism. Engaging with Freudian terminology critically he called 1960s sexual liberation "repressive desublimation".

Within the context of 1920s Harlem, Morrison seems to conclude that, for African American women at least, sexual liberation does not carry much historical potential. The historical problems of the particular time and place are identified as individualism and speech-lessness – and the alliances selected (Violet and Alice; Violet, Joe and Felice) improvise successfully on these problems. However, *Jazz* still overflows with sexual desire, which spills over in the sensuality of the narrator and in the nineteenth-century sections improvised by the narrator. Morrison is far from suggesting a disapproval of sexual desire *tout court*.

Sexual appetite and perhaps something more brings together Vera Louise and Henry Lestory or Hunter's Hunter. The non-stereotypical nature of this desire is all too apparent to those who have read *Beloved*. In *Beloved* the race barrier is crossed routinely in the rape or sexual abuse of African American women by white men in positions of power. Morrison alludes to this history in *Jazz* as well. It is suggested that Vera Louise's father also fathered "seven mulatto children on his land" (141). The narrator's elliptical reconstruction of the escapades of Vera Louise (of Wordsworth, Vesper County) and Henry Lestory (of Vienna, Vesper Country), riding together in the woods, is a counter-narrative of un-coerced desire flowing between an upper-class white woman and a rustic black man before the Civil War. (Wordsworth is a reference to the Romantic poet who famously put his faith in "low and rustic life" in the Preface to *Lyrical Ballads* (Wordsworth 1802, 650).) Their child, Golden Gray – the child of an unlikely free union rather than the stereotypical rape – can boast an alternative and more promising genealogy for the mixed-race figure (see **pp. 226–8**).

Vera Louise kept Golden Gray, which was "a renegade ... thing to do" (139). Her one concession to social norms – to avoid the social ostracism of "fallen women" at the time – was that she presented him as a white orphan she had adopted. Golden Gray could "pass" because "his flesh was radiantly golden and floppy yellow curls covered his head" (139), but "passing" also involves a long process of racialization, a becoming white. Golden Gray's upbringing as a white gentleman, undertaken by Vera Louise and True Belle, involved being dressed "like the Prince of Wales" (140), underwear monogrammed with blue thread and perfumed baths but also a repertoire of gestures and facial expressions. The black boy who meets him outside Henry Lestory's little house is convinced he is white because of his "smile-less smile" (156). But Golden Gray's desire deviates from the norm of "passing" and identifying with white ideals. He follows True Belle's advice to search for his father.

The figures of Vera Louise and True Belle are internally dialogical or antiphonic, in that they combine conformity and non-formulaic desire. True Belle, a name ironically pointing to the white upper-middle class figure of the "Southern belle" Vera Louise was destined to be, both stereotypically adores the golden hair and skin colour of Golden Gray and harmfully transmits this colourism to Violet and counter-stereotypically encourages the golden boy to look for his black father. Moving against the main current of African American history, where elevating the race involved acquiring literacy and formal education, Golden Gray sets out to meet his rustic father, then meets and chooses the "uncivilized" Wild. Desire, as Deleuze and Guattari have argued in *Anti-Oedipus*, is a certain investment or *cathexis* (in Freud's language) of an entire sociopolitical field: it might invest the most repressive social formations or it might invest "revolutionary" and alternative ways of life. Sexual choices involve sociopolitical choices. Golden Gray, in his journey, has to face and attempt to overcome his racism; an element of physical repulsion when he encounters Wild points to this racism. The movement of repulsion and attraction in relation to Wild, the, as it were, slow-motion rising of attraction and falling away of repulsion, enacts the shedding of his racism.

The light-skinned African American who desires and invests or cathects white middle-class norms is a staple character in Morrison's fiction: Geraldine in *The Bluest Eye*, Helene in *Sula*, Ruth in *Song of Solomon*, Jadine in *Tar Baby*. In *Jazz* the light-skinned Dorcas seems to hit a dead-end because her desire for Acton, based on his desir-ability to other girls, is too formulaic. Against Morrison's own *oeuvre* and the readers' expectations, Golden Gray's mixed-race origins do not condemn him to internalize racism inescapably. This revision of attitude towards the mixed-race figure is performed by the narrator in front of our eyes. From one narrative revision to the next, the narrator's attitude changes from hostility and distrust to active ben-evolence (143–61): "Not hating him is not enough ... I have to alter things ... I want to dream a nice dream for him, and another of him" (161).

Wild, in her encounter with Golden Gray, also seems to undergo a process of overcoming her terror of whiteness. The two seem to disappear from the novel, from its history together. However they survive, as legendary figures, in the narrator's speculating and inventing and in sections focalized through Henry Lestory and Joe. It is Henry Lestory who names Wild and turns the encounter of Wild and Golden Gray into a supernatural love story. For many years after their disappearance local people "caught a glimpse" of Wild: "instead of resting she was hungry still. Though for what, exactly, he couldn't say, unless it was for hair the color of a young man's name. To see them together was a regular jolt: the young man's head of yellow hair long as a dog's tail next to her skein of dark wool" (167). His hair is now too long for a white gentleman (see page 143), the suggestion is that he is going wild too. Joe's jealous perception of the couple is that of a heated and illicit sexuality – wild in this sense. He finds traces of Golden Gray under what he considers to be Wild's sheltering rock and concludes that she is "holed up with" Golden Gray (182). The accounts of Henry Lestory, Joe and the narrator are too elliptical to be unambiguous, to determine what "actually" happened to them. They certainly survive in the sense that the narrator, Joe and Hunter's Hunter all claim the antiphonic couple of the ultra-refined upper-class Golden Gray and the primitivist/Africanist Wild as "ancestors".

WORLDLINESS

In *Jazz* the reader of Morrison's *oeuvre* finds a momentary near-total eclipse of the supernatural. Since *Sula* Morrison's novels have combined realism and a supernatural element which she has called "enchantment". This mix will return in *Paradise*. In *Jazz* the only trace of an enchanted world-view is the very brief reference to Henry Lestory's Wild as a spirit (quoted above). But this moment only highlights and accentuates the worldliness of the novel's 1920s narrator and characters.

In the narrator's and Joe's view there is nothing supernatural about Wild. However, the reader is intrigued by the similarities between Wild and Beloved. Beloved, heavily pregnant and unassimilable, is "exorcised" and disappears from the outskirts of Cincinnati, Ohio – and Wild, heavily pregnant and unassimilable, appears in Vesper County, Virginia. It can be argued that in *Jazz* Beloved returns as an historical girl gone Wild because of her terror of whiteness, summoned as an "ancestor" by a worldly and angry generation. Wild will return as Dorcas in 1920s Harlem: scarred again by the terror of whiteness, living for the moment and in this world, but once again unassimilable.

When the narrator looks back at Rose Dear's suicide in 1892, he/she attributes to her the narrator's own disenchanted view of the world: "Seeing bleak truth" (101). Morrison has relied on the figure of the third-person omniscient narrator in her novels. However, *Jazz*'s narrator is divested of this conventional, though supernatural, all-knowingness. 1920s Harlem is a modern nihilistic world where all enchantment has been dismissed as illusion, a world of bare "existence" to use Sartre's language. The "evil [that] run the streets" (9) and the "specter" (33) from the past is racism, outside and internalized.

What takes the place of the supernatural in *Jazz* is acts/flights of the imagination where the dreamer is aware that the dream is his or her dream, in disjunction with bleak historical actuality. Jazz improvisation, antiphony, open-endedness, as performed by the narrator and characters, is the "supernatural" and anti-historical or counter-historical element in this novel. What also takes the place of the supernatural is the enigmatic and elliptical, anti-realist elements which provoke the reader to step in and dream his or her own dream. The reader of *Jazz* becomes aware, sooner or later, that any solutions he or she brings to the many unresolved interpretative questions illuminate something about themselves as well as the novel.

Paradise (1998)

Paradise completes Morrison's postmodern historiographic trilogy. *Beloved* was set mainly in the mid-nineteenth century, before and after the Emancipation Proclamation of 1863, close to the Ohio River, frontier between North and South. *Jazz* was set mainly in Harlem during the 1920s: the Jazz Age or the era of the New Negro and the Harlem Renaissance. *Paradise* is set mainly in a fictional all-black town in Oklahoma in July 1976: two hundred years after the Declaration of Independence on the 4th of July 1776; one hundred years after the end of Reconstruction in failure in 1877. The year 1976 is arguably the year of the decline of the Civil Rights Movement or the "second Reconstruction" (Widdowson 2001, 319). *Paradise* mobilizes these historical references and others. It combines a multiplicity of historical contexts of differing scale.

In July 1976 nine men led by the Morgan twins, the New Fathers of Ruby – an all-black town established in 1949 as a utopian alternative to surrounding racism – attack a neighbouring commune of stray women, the Convent, to fight the evil, as they see it, threatening Ruby's existence. Morrison examines the unfulfilled promise of political utopias and identifies the exclusivity that tends to characterize thinking about paradise:

> I was interested in the kind of violent conflict that could happen as a result of efforts to establish a Paradise. Our view

of Paradise is so limited: it requires you to think of yourself as the chosen people ... Which means that your job is to isolate yourself from other people. That's the nature of Paradise: it's really defined by who is not there as well as who is.

(Morrison 1998b)

Morrison elaborates in her *Nobel Lecture in Literature*, written in 1993, whilst she was writing *Paradise*:

The conventional wisdom of the Tower of Babel story is that ... it was the distraction or the weight of many languages that precipitated failed architecture. That one monolithic language would have expedited the building, and heaven would have been reached. Whose heaven ... ? And what kind? Perhaps the achievement of Paradise was premature, a little hasty if no one could take the time to understand other languages ... Had they, the heaven they imagined might have been found at their feet. Complicated, demanding, yes, but a view of heaven as life.

(Morrison 1993a, 202)

We have been imagining paradise as a space of univocity, agreement, seclusion, and exclusion of the unworthy – we should perhaps re-imagine it as an open space of heterogeneity, dissent and inclusion.

A COMPLEX HISTORIOGRAPHY

After the failure of Reconstruction a black exodus began, from the rural South to the urban North and West. Migrants West – to Kansas and Oklahoma – were called "Exodusters" (see p. 9). *Paradise* locates this movement as one of the origins of Ruby as well as of the attack on the Convent. According to Morrison, a starting point for *Paradise* was a post-Reconstruction newspaper "feature in the *Herald*" inviting black migration to all-black towns in the West with the cryptic headline, "Come Prepared or Not at All" (13; all page references in this chapter refer to *Paradise* [Morrison 1998a] unless otherwise indicated). Morrison found out that it was intended to deter ex-slaves from migrating West without capital, and read about how "two hundred freedmen and their families were turned away from an all-black town by other ex-slaves because they lacked such resources" (Bouson 2000, 192). In *Paradise* the ancestors of Ruby, the nine Old Fathers, respond to this headline by leaving Mississippi and Louisiana in 1890 to migrate West and settle on "unassigned land" (6) with their families. Rejected by new towns, including the all-black town of

Fairly, for being too poor or too dark-skinned or both, the Old Fathers move "into Arapaho territory" and found Haven in Oklahoma, aided by "signs God gave to guide them" (14). They are led by the visionary Zechariah otherwise known as Coffee Morgan or Big Papa. When Haven declines, the New Fathers, led by the twins, Deacon or Deek and Steward Morgan, grandsons of Big Papa, found Ruby in an isolated location.

Morrison explores the Exodus narrative underlying the black Exoduster movement, particularly in its problematic aspects: a Chosen People leaves bondage behind for the Promised Land, according to God's will. The Exodus narrative had already been made use of by those claiming American exceptionalism; now it was taken on by the black Exoduster movement. Morrison suggests that this narrative has historically involved exclusions. Neither the Pilgrim Fathers who boarded the *Mayflower* for the New World nor the Founding Fathers and their Declaration of Independence abolished slavery. Their Promised Land was already populated by Native Americans; the "unassigned lands" claimed by the Exoduster movement were already someone else's home. Exodusters were in this sense conquerors/colonialists (see Flint 2006). In *Paradise* the founders of Fairly expel and "disallow" the Old Fathers of Ruby in 1890 (189); the New Fathers of Ruby, led by the Morgan twins, set out to kill the Convent women in 1976. The Declaration of Independence is still unfulfilled: "We hold these truths to be self-evident, that all men [*sic*] are created equal, that they are endowed by their Creator with certain unalienable Rights, that among these are Life, Liberty and the pursuit of Happiness."

A second and earlier historical context for the attack on the Convent is that of the Puritan witchcraft trials of Salem, Massachusetts, in 1692–93 and the execution of 19 people, mostly women, for witchcraft. The critics Dalsgård (2001) and then Fultz (2003) develop this argument. Fultz points out that the witch trials were partially motivated by the desire to take over property owned by women without male relatives. In *Paradise* Sargeant Person takes part in the attack because he wants the Convent land (277).

A third historical context in *Paradise* is that of neo-imperialism, as discussed in Edward Said's *Culture and Imperialism* (Said 1993). The "civilizing mission" of European colonialism is being continued by an American "civilizing mission" throughout the Americas. Mary Magna, an American Catholic nun doing missionary work in Latin America, abducts nine-year-old Latin American (probably Brazilian) Consolata/Connie – a light-skinned and green-eyed black girl – to save her from the squalor of her life. She moves Consolata (if this is her original name) to a new location, the Convent, where she is given a new language, English, and a new religion. Mary Magna continues her missionary work in the Convent. The Convent is a mansion originally built by an embezzler who soon vacates when he is apprehended for his crimes. In its second incarnation it houses Catholic nuns with a mission to educate and civilize Native American girls – a kind of embezzlement authorized by the church and the state. Arapaho and Algonquian girls are renamed Penny or Clarissa, Christianized and linguistically dispossessed, though they can be heard "singing forbidden Algonquian lullabies" (237). The racism that permeates this education is visible in Connie's position in the Convent. In spite of Connie's religiosity and the love between her and Mary Magna, she is a maid and sleeps in the cellar. The cellar in this mansion might be a reference to the slave narrative, *Narrative of Sojourner Truth* (Truth 1850). Sojourner's master, Charles Ardinburgh, moves to a "new house, which he had built for a hotel ... A cellar, under this hotel, was assigned to his slaves, as their sleeping apartment".

When the mission dissolves Connie and Mary Magna, now frail with age and confined to her room, stay on in the deserted mansion. Connie initiates the Convent's third incarnation: a refuge for stray women. Connie continues to sleep in the cellar but she becomes critical of the separation of body and soul and the devaluation of the body in Christianity. Appropriately, she makes the cellar the location for the staging of a ritual which attempts to overcome this dualism. This is the Convent nine Ruby men attack in 1976.

A fourth historical context in *Paradise* is that of the Civil Rights Movement. Reverend Misner, a newcomer to Ruby, has been an active participant in the Movement. Misner and Anna Flood are committed to the political education of Ruby's youth. Signs of this new political education – such as the black fist with red fingernails painted on the Oven (101), a Black Power salute – provoke a hostile response from the Morgan twins who perceive a threat to their authority, and antagonism between youth and Ruby's leaders mounts. Gigi, one of the Convent women, was involved in the Civil Rights Movement, but became alienated from it. For Gigi, the Convent and her emerging friendship with another Convent woman, Seneca, are more nourishing. Female activists and critics have argued that the Civil Rights Movement and Black Power organizations marginalized black women and replicated the sexist behaviour of wider society. *Paradise* invites engagement with this critique. K.D. slaps his pregnant girlfriend Arnette, and the way in which the politically progressive Misner addresses both the unplanned pregnancy and the slapping outlines the continuing problem of sexism. Misner presides over a meeting of men – K.D. Morgan (father of Arnette's unborn baby); his uncles, the Morgan twins; and Arnette's father and brother,

Arnold and Jeff Fleetwood – and brokers an agreement among the men about Arnette's future in her absence, sealing it with a prayer: "'Gentlemen. Brothers. Let us pray.' They … listened obediently to Misner's beautifully put words and the tippy-tap steps of women who were nowhere in sight" (61).

The Vietnam War is a fifth historical context active in *Paradise*. Soane and Deek Morgan's boys died in the Vietnam War, while Jeff Fleetwood, father of four damaged children, is a Vietnam veteran. Tally has suggested that Jeff might have been exposed to Agent Orange, a defoliant used in the war that causes "malformation in offspring" (Tally 1999, 27).

A sixth historical context alluded to in *Paradise* is the emergence of "black women writers" and of black feminism in the 1970s. Morrison has both identified herself as a "black woman writer" and worked hard to establish this new category. Her relation to black feminism, on the other hand, has been ambiguous.

In her *Nobel Lecture* Morrison represents the writer as a blind old black woman living in the outskirts of town – a figure effectively describing Consolata. Consolata is Morrison's figure of the "black woman writer" in *Paradise*. Consolata is blind but has the supernatural gift of "stepping in" or "seeing in" or "in sight" (247) – she is able to see "what took place in the minds of others" (248). This has of course often been seen as the writer's gift. In pages 262–66 Consolata fully emerges simultaneously as both an artist and as the spiritual leader of the Convent women. She devises a multimedia, collective and interactive healing ritual. The ritual mobilizes "body" as well as "spirit" (263): the women trace outlines of their bodies on the floor, practise "loud dreaming" (263), but also the ability to listen and "step easily into the dreamer's tale" (264). Morrison is here self-referentially outlining her own aims as a "black woman writer" as well as outlining her ideal reader.

With regard to the emergence of 1970s black feminism, *Paradise* explores it through the emergence of a feminist sensibility in Gigi, Billie Delia and Anna Flood. For Gigi an etching of Saint Catherine of Siena is the image of a woman giving herself up "to a lord" (73). She reinterprets her own overtly sexual appearance not as a claim to liberated sexuality but as a sign of subservience to men. Later she breaks with K.D. and turns to Seneca. Billie Delia witnesses the male battle of interpretations surrounding Arnette's pregnancy and thinks that "the stallions were fighting about who controlled the mares and their foals" (150). Ruby witnesses a public battle of interpretations between old men and young men surrounding the Oven motto, "The Furrow of His Brow" (83–87). The leaders of Ruby interpret this as a command to the young men to obey their authority: "Beware the

Furrow of His Brow" (86). Young rebellious men interpret the motto as: "Be the Furrow of His Brow"; in other words, "We [the young men] *are* the power" (87). They make this interpretation explicit in graffiti on the Oven reading: "We Are the Furrow of His Brow" (298). Anna Flood thinks to herself of another possibility: "Be the Furrow of *Her* Brow" (159). After the killing of the Convent women and the mysterious disappearance of the bodies, Billie Delia thinks: "When will they return? When will they reappear, with blazing eyes, war paint and huge hands to rip up and stomp this prison calling itself a town?" (308). Then she refuses to choose between Brood and Apollo.

THE METAHISTORIOGRAPHIC ELEMENT IN *PARADISE*

Historical narrative and interpretation, in a variety of forms, is at the heart of the communities of Ruby and the Convent. At the Convent "loud dreaming" is a form of communally shared auto-biography. *Paradise* outlines and interweaves three kinds of historical narrative in Ruby. Firstly, "official" (188), "controlling" (13) and public historical narratives: the official story of the "Disallowing" (189) – the exclusion from Fairly – and the founding of Haven through Big Papa's visions of the "walking man" sent by God to guide him (97); and the "two editions of the official story" of the attack on the Convent (296). The Morgan twins view themselves as faithful guardians of these narratives, pride themselves on their perfect memories, and claim that "Between them they remember the details of everything that ever happened" (13; see also 12–17 and 95–100).

The Morgan twins claim objectivity and obedience to the narrative authority of their grandfather, leader of Haven, as a means of defending their own authority, as the leaders of Ruby. Their own "official story" of Ruby is then "elaborated from pulpits, in Sunday school classes and ceremonial speeches" (188). Michel Foucault famously distinguishes between the "objective" historian and the "effective" historian in his essay "Nietzsche, Genealogy, History" (Foucault 1971): the "objective" historian, while ostensibly prostrating himself before the authority of facts, in fact only conceals his own interests; the "effective" historian explicitly looks at the past from the point of view of his own current project in order to serve contemporary ends (86–90). While ostensibly faithful to the old ways and the old stories, the Morgan twins have abandoned the collectivism of Haven and early Ruby (see 108–09 and 116). For example, the Morgans' bank recently foreclosed on the loan for Menus's house.

Light-skinned schoolteacher Patricia's secret written historiographic project is an historical counter-narrative. She develops the story of

Ruby's reverse colourism. According to Pat's narrative, Fairly excluded the nine founding families because they were very dark-skinned – Pat calls them eight-rock or 8-R, "a deep deep level in the coal mines" (193). The men of Ruby responded with a reverse colourism, which set out to disallow light-skinned newcomers such as Patricia's mother, Delia. In Pat's view, her mother and unborn sister died because the men of Ruby were unwilling to seek medical assistance for a woman whose skin colour signified "racial tampering", though the women of Ruby "begged" (197). Also Menus was pressured to give up his light-skinned bride-to-be. While Pat's narrative is self-consciously subjective, it is not effective: Pat keeps it secret and then burns all her papers. Even worse, Pat has internalized the reverse colourism she attributes to Ruby's men, and directs it against herself and her light-skinned daughter, Billie Delia. Pat almost kills Billie Delia with an electric iron before she becomes aware that she is unthinkingly reproducing the men's association of light-skinned women with sexual promiscuity (202–04). (This reflects the way that the historical sexual exploitation of female slaves by slave-owners was blamed on black women's promiscuity by white and black alike.) Pat's counter-narrative ends in failure because of her own self-defeating conformity and silence. She shares a thoughtless and overeager consent with the majority of the women and men of Ruby. Roger, her father, married the light-skinned Delia but remained anxious for the town's approval. Menus allows them to dissuade him from marrying his light-skinned girl (200–02).

As we have already seen, Ruby's narratives are split between male public discourse and female internal monologue and secret writing. The reader is given privileged access to the private thoughts of Ruby's women as counter-narratives and counter-interpretations. Soane articulates a silent critique of her husband Deek for not helping Menus (107). But silence is complicity, as Soane comes to recognize: "If only she had talked twenty-two years ago. Just talked" (288).

Paradise simultaneously excavates a minor tradition of women speaking up, centred on Fairy and Lone, arguably Ruby's female counter-leaders. When Roger Best marries light-skinned Delia, Steward Morgan's response is "He's bringing along the dung we leaving behind" (201). Fairy condemned this response in the strongest terms: "God don't love ugly ways. Watch out He don't deny you what you love too" (201). She speaks out, even though as a woman she is "easily ignored by good brave men on their way to Paradise", as Pat comments (201–02). Lone, Fairy's adopted daughter, teaches Connie how to use the gift of "stepping in" they share, as well as teaching Connie her own alternative Christian ontology – "Don't separate God from his elements" (244) – which resonates with Connie's own thinking about reconnecting body and spirit. (Christian tradition and its literature do not uniformly expound the dualism of body and spirit and do not lack other visions of the relation between the two. For example, to mention one highly influential imagination of paradise, see the embodied form of the angels in Milton's *Paradise Lost*, Milton 1674, 5.433–39 and 8.622–29.) Eighty-six-year-old Lone emerges as an alternative leader of Ruby during the attack on the Convent. In response to Lone's rhetoric, the "citizens" of Ruby, including Soane and Dovey Morgan (287), go to the Convent to stop the nine men, led by the Morgan twins. Afterwards, unlike Pat, Lone is willing to make public her version of the events at the Convent; she is deemed unreliable by some men though supported publicly by others (297–98).

Fairy's and Lone's bold counter-narratives qualify them as female counter-elders of Ruby. They embody a black female voice, agency and radicalism well predating the 1970s generation of black women writers and black feminists. (bell hooks famously pays tribute to the radicalism of nineteenth-century black women in the opening pages of *Ain't I a Woman*, hooks 1982, 2–4.)

VISIONS

If in *Paradise* Morrison shows that historiography involves narrative, narrative in turn is indissociable from the imagination – a world of visions. Visions are what gather together and make sense of external/objective and internal/subjective reality, belonging to both. In Morrison's historiography, history, reality, facts are inseparable from stories, myths, sublime visions, mystical experiences, catastrophic delusions. Characters in this novel are partly defined by their visions and delusions.

"Ruby", the novel's first section, explores from the inside the delusional perspective shared by the nine men who attack the Convent. The men are not named and individuated until much later (277–78). They are looking for "witch tracks" (4) because they imagine the Convent women as "Eves unredeemed by Mary" (18). Their attack on the Convent is a fight against evil, "For Ruby" and with "God at their side" (18). The men figure Ruby women and Convent women as mutually exclusive. One of the nine men, unidentified, thinks about Convent women: "these were women like none he knew or ever heard tell of" (8). Implicitly the Convent women are figured as Eves, the Ruby women as Marys. The nine men's perspective is certainly the dominant perspective in this section, but it is also subtly questioned. We, the readers, are forced into the men's perspective – "obliged", "startled" and "unnerved" (3) with them – and faced with a dreamlike or rather nightmarish world, initially uncertain as to whether it is real or imagined. Is the unnatural chill of the Convent real or imagined by the men? References to dreams in this section suggest that we too are caught in their murderous dream.

Subsequent sections systematically expose the men's perspective as a delusion, by demonstrating the bonds connecting Convent women and Ruby women and thereby undermining the men's binary opposition of Eves and Marys. For example, Soane and Connie are shown to be very close (43), with Deek warning Soane against her friendship with Connie (105); Billie Delia helps Pallas (175); Seneca tries to help Sweetie (126ff.); Lone tries to save the Convent women (269). Billie Delia, Arnette, Soane, Sweetie and even Menus (165) have taken refuge in the Convent in the past and received help from Convent women, to their mutual benefit.

Lone, as a Christian, shares the nine men's language, but uses this language to opposite effect: to condemn the men's attack on the Convent as "devilment" (269) and try to save the Convent women in accordance with God's will (273). Is Lone's vision of reality and version of Christianity more true than the nine men's? Christianity in *Paradise* is a spacious context amenable to a variety of quite singular visions – from Big Papa's "walking man" to Dovey's "Friend" (93) – whose "truth" or "falsity" can only be judged by their effects.

In *Sula* Morrison had explored the following black nationalist argument for the moral superiority of African Americans: black people, unlike white people, tolerate what they view as "evil" rather than setting out to destroy it; she suggested that the very process of demonizing someone as "evil" is problematic. In *Paradise* the attack on the Convent further responds to *Sula* that African Americans are just as capable of the desire to exterminate those they label "evil". In response, Lone's reversal – naming the nine men's action "devilment" – is not enough. Consolata's alternative theology, against the oppositions of spirit (good) and body (evil), Mary (good) and Eve (evil), offers another ethical option: "Never break them in two ... Eve is Mary's mother" (263).

Paradise is overpopulated by individual and collective dreams and nightmares: visions invested with desires or fears, revealing and confronting or masking and avoiding reality, enabling or disabling the dreamers, avidly embraced or discarded or transmuting into other visions. These visions have material effects. Both Ruby and the Convent began as visions of safe haven. In making one's vision public and collective, consent or dissent must come into play. Big Papa's "walking man" is accepted collectively as a true vision and thus becomes effective. Conversely, the vision of the nine men who attack the Convent is met with dissent by the citizens of Ruby who go to the Convent to stop the nine.

After the death of her infant twins, Mavis suffers from a paranoid delusion that her remaining children are plotting to kill her because she is unable to confront her husband's brutality, with ambiguous effects: she propels herself to escape from her husband, but deserts her children who have to face his brutality without her. At the Convent she generates a new vision, the ghosts of her twins who live with her and continue to grow. The Convent women facilitate her recovery by consenting to the reality of Mavis's vision and her healing is further enabled by participation in Consolata's "loud dreaming" sessions. As a result, when she returns to her daughter Sal in the concluding pages of the novel, she can confront her husband's abuse and her own desertion of her children. Dovey, on the other hand, does not communicate her vision of the "Friend": her conversations with the male Friend allow her to articulate her thoughts but also act as a substitute for the public discourse she is unwilling to enter into. Consolata also generates the vision of a male supernatural Visitor, with very different effects. (One might compare these male Friends to Sojourner Truth's account of her idiosyncratic visionary talks with Christ in her narrative.) Consolata's Visitor is a male version of herself – he has her "tea-colored" hair and green eyes (252) – summoned by her to initiate and authorize (with his male authority) her ritual of "loud dreaming". In contrast to Saint Catherine of Siena submitting to "a lord", once the collective regeneration of Convent women promised by her ritual is under way, her vision transmutes into a female, maternal very dark-skinned singing figure, Piedade. The novel's final scene reimagines the *Pietà*: Mary holding Christ's dead body is replaced by Piedade holding Consolata's living body – Consolata as a living Christ.

Desire is fluid, changing form, and even contradictory. The Morgan twins witness the spectacle of 19 lady-like and affluent black women in their youth and invest it with the power of a vision for Ruby women (109–10); and yet Deek desires Consolata (231) and fails to stop and help Sweetie (114). K.D. witnesses a swimming pool full of white children and turns it into a vision of "purest happiness"; to him Gigi is the fulfilment of this vision (57). Gigi is propelled by visions of sexual ecstasy (63–66), possibly in response to her traumatic participation in the Civil Rights Movement and the "boy spitting blood into his hands" in a demo (64); and yet sexual ecstasy with K.D. is not enough and she chooses Seneca's friendship. But did she do the right thing in abandoning political activism or in deserting her grandfather in Alcorn, Mississippi (65)?

Delusion and error is an ever-present possibility with potentially lethal effects. Sweetie sees Seneca, who is trying to help her, as "sin" and "demon"; in her "state of grace" (129) she imagines the Convent women as evil spirits who "snatched" her (130) away from home because she cannot acknowledge the desertion of her children. In this instance, the text distinguishes clearly between her delirious perspective and objective reality. The Convent women are so caught up in their visions that they don't heed Lone's warning that the men are coming to kill them (269). The "enchantment" and "rapture of holy women dancing" in the rain is also a blindness to reality (283). Connie's "light-blindness" after Deek's desertion of her (242) is an ambiguous sign both of her Tiresias-like powers and her inability to face reality. Visions could be an avoidance of bare truth, traumatic experience or plain disagreeable reality. Is Lone's and Consolata's gift of "in sight" a delusion? Did Consolata save Scout Morgan with her gift or is this a collective delusion (245)?

What are we to think of the disappearance of the Convent women, Pallas's baby and the Cadillac? Does the novel here affirm a supernatural perspective? What are we to think of the supernatural return of the Convent women? Does it happen only in the eyes of those who witness it or summon them and is it therefore purely subjective or even delusional? Gigi seems visible only to her father and the reader yet she is fully embodied, her hair growing (309–11). Jean, Seneca's mother, misremembers their life together and their meeting miscarries – and yet Seneca is bodily enough to bleed (316–17). Mavis is visible to her daughter Sal and the waitress and her "side hurts" (315). In the context of Morrison's *oeuvre* since *Song of Solomon*, the Convent women have become African "ancestors": the dead returning to the living fully embodied.

In the midst of this fluid, multiperspectival landscape, Morrison seems to be proposing some guiding principles. First, take responsibility for your own imagination and visions. This is outlined in the bifurcation in the Morgan twins' response after their attack on the Convent. Steward continues to insist that "The evil is in this house"; Deek, on the other hand, affirms "This is our doing" (291). Deek recognizes, in their vision of the Convent as evil, the work of their own imagination. As Morrison commented in her interview with James Marcus: "I tried to make it possible to think that Paradise was within our imagination" (Morrison 1998b) – as is Hell. When Deek, one of the New Fathers of Ruby, takes responsibility for his own visions, he allows for alternative visions and effectively allows for dissent and challenges to his authority. Taking responsibility for one's visions takes a very different form for the women in the novel. Their condition has been silence, secrecy and living in their own inner worlds. Consolata's ritual therefore aims to allow the women to make their visions public and to provide them with a responsive audience. Transformations undergone by both male and female characters are processes of democratization.

These processes find a parallel in Reverend Misner's theology. Reverend Pullian views God as an external authority; just as the Morgan twins initially claim to be utterly faithful to the authority of the past. Misner, as a civil rights activist, on the other hand, views God as an "interior engine" (142). For Misner "He *is* you" (147). This Feuerbachian view of God as a projection of our own powers is reflected in the theological views of Ruby's dissident youth: "We *are* the power" (87) – "We Are the Furrow of His Brow" (298). Once the spiritual/supernatural realm is reincorporated as of this world, the Platonic–Christian separation and opposition of this world and the Other World – whether as Paradise or as Hell – comes to an end. Paradise is "down here" (318). The ontologies of Misner and Consolata at this point come together. They differ in that Misner and the young men who claim the motto of the Oven proclaim their own strength and their faith in the future, while Consolata invents and talks to the Convent women about Piedade (284–85), an "ancestor" figure come to aid them.

The final guiding principle is that of the value of dissension – but without exclusion. If, in the novel's terms, Deek made the right decision and Steward the wrong one, Steward nevertheless must not be demonized, repudiated and excluded from the community. Coffee Morgan or Big Papa "walked barefoot for two hundred miles rather than dance" for the white man (301), but walked away from his twin brother, Tea Morgan, and in proud repudiation of Tea's wrong decision (302). Deek's "barefoot walk" (300), on the other hand, is towards Misner and towards his brother – in defiance of Big Papa (303). Billie Delia also points to an inclusive and experimental future by refusing to choose between the brothers, Apollo and Brood Poole, or between Ruby, the Convent and the world outside.

INCLUSIVITY

Paradise explores critically and compares two social spaces: the all-black Ruby and the all-female Convent. Many critics have read *Paradise* as a feminist novel, some as a stridently feminist one overvaluing the Convent and undervaluing Ruby. Many critics have interpreted Morrison's strategy of making it impossible for the reader to identify the white Convent woman as Morrison's endorsement of the abolition of the category of race and the coming of a world beyond race, announced by the Convent as an all-female race-blind utopia. However, one might argue that, instead of selecting the Convent against Ruby as the more viable vision of life, the text doesn't choose between the two but selects inclusivity and rejects exclusion.

Unlike the patriarchs of Ruby (and some critics), Morrison includes the mixed-race and light-skinned figure in Ruby's renewal. The patriarchs of Ruby pride themselves on their racial purity as a sign that they "bowed to no one" (99), even though the Blackhorse family's "stick-straight hair" (198) suggests the "racial tampering" (197) they can't tolerate. Deek cannot recognize what he shares with the light-skinned Consolata: "I've traveled. All over. I've never seen anything like you" (231). Consolata, on the other hand, recognizes that she belongs with Deek – "he and I are the same" (241).

In Morrison's early novels, light-skinned black women such as Helene Wright in *Sula* or Ruth Dead in *Song of Solomon* were stereotypes of "assimilationism" and capitulation to white middle-class values. The novelty of *Paradise*, on the other hand, is that the light-skinned Consolata and Billie Delia embody positive powers of transformation. Billie Delia – like Denver in *Beloved* and Felice in *Jazz* – embodies the future.

The attack on the Convent is the appalling catalyst for Ruby's renewal, in that it triggers Ruby citizens' active dissent and Deek's process of transformation. The killing of the Convent women turns them into "ancestors" whose legacy will revitalize Ruby. The Convent women's dance in the rain in deep enchantment completes Consolata's vision and the Convent women's transformation – "they feel saved" (Morrison 1998b). Billie Delia calls for their return to Ruby for her sake and Ruby's. In calling for the return of the Convent women, she summons the power of dissension without exclusion, as a viable form of identification and belonging.

Love (2003)

It is difficult to determine the story and genre of *Love*. Early reviews of the novel are widely at variance with one another and point to this generic instability. To give some examples, Laura Miller (2003) described the novel as "like 'What Ever Happened to Baby Jane?' with two Bette Davises". Elaine Showalter (2003) commented that the relationship of Christine and Heed is "almost gothic in its ferocity and passion, as if they were African-American female versions of Cathy and Heathcliff". Michiko Kakutani, in a negative review, described the novel as "a gothic soap opera, peopled by scheming, bitter women and selfish, predatory men" (Kakutani 2003). Ron Charles (2003) singled out the "humor" and "gothic comedy" of the novel.

Reading *Love*, the early descriptions of the two old women are darkly comic Dickensian caricatures, using metonymy to describe characters: Christine's 12 diamond rings and initialed silver spoon;

tiny Heed's deformed hands and illiteracy: "most folks I seen had perfect hands, you know, because that's the way we was taught … no X-type people came, of course" (26; all page numbers in this chapter refer to *Love* [Morrison 2003a] unless otherwise indicated). But Heed's setting of Christine's bed on fire and L's intervention (86, 134) might point the reader to *Jane Eyre* where Bertha Mason, the madwoman in the attic, sets Rochester's bed on fire and Jane comes to the rescue.

Is *Love* a novel about two cantankerous old women, Heed and Christine, fighting each other viciously for the title of "sweet Cosey child" (79) – each claiming a special relation to Bill Cosey 25 years after his death? Or is it a novel about the interrupted love of two little girls? Is this a novel about Bill Cosey's posthumous influence? Or is it a novel about misrecognized female ancestors: L and Celestial?

ANAGNORISIS AND THE READER'S EXPERIENCE IN *LOVE*

At the heart of *Love* is Morrison's revisioning/refashioning of the *anagnorisis* (recognition) of Greek tragedy. Morrison offers an *anagnorisis* of love and describes the process of emergence of *anagnorisis* out of its opposite: misrecognition, blindness, forgetting and, in psychoanalytic terms, repression and screen memories. Who is the lover? Who the beloved? Who is entitled to count as a lover? Who is entitled to being loved?

Morrison has written a meticulously crafted novel designed to inveigle the first-time reader into a world of misrecognition. She makes use of a third-person extradiegetic narrator, but the narration is focalized through characters that turn out to misrecognize reality. Readers are trained to interpret the third-person extradiegetic narrator as objective, and this narrator's failure to alert us to the focalizers' unreliability plunges us into a world of misreadings and, as our reading progresses, drastically revised interpretations. We are forced into our own movement from blindness to *anagnorisis*.

There is a second narrator in the novel, the ostensibly intradiegetic narrator L. Morrison exploits the reader's training in interpreting intradiegetic narrators as subjective. She withholds until the last pages the information that L is a ghost and therefore (at least partially) extradiegetic; and she carefully defers the reader's understanding that L's narration is the main site of *anagnorisis* in the novel. Only in the final pages of the novel do Heed and Christine emerge out of their blindness and know this; while Junior is only beginning a process that might lead to *anagnorisis*.

L's initial narrations are carefully crafted in order to be read differently by the first-time and the second-time reader. For example, L's announcement of *"a story that shows how brazen women can take a good man down*" (10; all sections narrated by L are in italics in the original). The first-time reader understands this to hint that the Cosey women took Bill Cosey down. The second-time reader understands this as the positive task of knocking down the myth of the Good Man, and also interprets this as a reference to L's killing of Bill Cosey, only revealed by L in the final pages: Cosey was "*an ordinary man ... I had to stop him*" (200). Early reviewers described L's role in the novel as choral: like the ancient Greek tragic chorus, she witnesses and passes judgement. Morrison herself commented on L: "I wanted her to function as a witness, as someone with judgement" (Morrison 2003c). But L exceeds the role of chorus by acting on her judgement and killing Cosey.

When L discovers that Cosey disinherited the Cosey women – May, Heed and Christine – and bequeathed all his fortune to Celestial, she kills him, destroys his will, and forges a deliberately ambiguous will in favour of the "sweet Cosey child" – thereby referring to both Christine and Heed – intended to give them "*a reason to stay connected*" (201). Her confession of murder invites the reader to judge her in turn but throws our judgement into perplexity. Reviewers and critics have commented that the letter of her name stands for Love. The first-time reader is subtly led to assume that the novel's section titles – Portrait, Lover, Friend, Benefactor, etc. – refer exclusively to Bill Cosey: for example the title "Portrait" seems to refer to Bill Cosey's portrait above Heed's bed. However, the second-time reader knows that L (as well as other characters) also has a claim to being the protagonist referenced by the titles. L loves, befriends, benefits and other-mothers the variously orphaned Bill Cosey, Heed and Christine. The reader is asked to consider – as in *Beloved* – a murder inspired by love.

The first breakthrough in *anagnorisis* takes place halfway through the novel. L intimates that the hotel's "*ruination*" began when Cosey "*chose a girl already spoken for ... she belonged to Christine and Christine belonged to her*" (104–5). L clarifies this in the final pages of the book: "*when children fall for one another*" they open themselves to "*a mix of surrender and mutiny they can never live without*" (199). L chooses to valorize the love of young Heed and Christine for each other. Their friendship is a mutiny because it crosses class, money and colour divides: the dark-skinned underclass Heed; the light-skinned, grey-eyed affluent Christine.

L's reference to St Paul's "*First Corinthians, chapter 13*" (199) invites the reader to compare L's judgement to St Paul's, as Benjamin Burr argues. St Paul writes:

> When I was a child, I spake as a child, I understood as a child, I thought as a child: but when I became a man, I put

away childish things. For now we see through a glass, darkly; but then face to face; now I know in part; but then shall I know even as I am known.

(quot. Burr 2006, 167–68)

St Paul's metaphor of child and man assumes that children, unlike men, are only capable of a poor reflection of each other and cannot know each other fully. L, on the other hand, suggests that children, because of their very youth, have privileged access to such knowledge. Morrison explored this potential in *The Bluest Eye* and *Sula*: Claudia and Frieda can befriend dark-skinned underclass Pecola because they haven't yet imbibed social prejudices. Sula and Nel's friendship is interrupted in their late teens by Nel's conventional marriage.

From the very beginning of her narration, L repeatedly connects wanton women and mutinous children: "*loose women*" and "*disobedient children*" (5); "*wicked females and … unruly children*" (10). The second-time reader understands that L embraces and is mindful of protecting the special powers of both. The novel offers an analysis of the external and internal threats to such powers, at an historical point following the Civil Rights Movement.

AFTER THE CIVIL RIGHTS MOVEMENT: CLASS DIVISIONS AND ASSIMILATIONISM

Cosey thoughtlessly abuses his economic power in effectively buying an 11-year-old for $200 as his bride (193) and in disinheriting the women whose labour built his hotel. L's narration reveals that his capitalist power and charisma depend on his father's dirty money and the work of May and L: May and L were "*like the back of a clock*" while Cosey was its "*face*" (103). Simultaneously, *Love* investigates explicitly the women's complicity and willing self-enslavement. L comments that May made herself the Cosey men's "*slave*" (102). She is supported by Christine and Heed's belated self-critique. As Christine tells Heed: "we sold ourselves to the highest bidder" (185).

The first-time reader is misdirected into thinking that Cosey is the centre of the novel – lured into resting on his or her own patriarchal and capitalist assumptions. The novel works like the glass panels of the hotel's double doors that "*mirror your own face as well as the view behind your back*" (7). In the course of the novel characters and readers recognize that the legendary Cosey is a ghost of their own making, exorcise him and summon the ghosts of L, Celestial and Heed. Cosey is dead and Celestial sits on his grave.

Cosey died in 1971; Christine returned to One Monarch Street in 1975; May died in 1976; Christine and Heed have been living in One

Monarch Street on their own, hating each other and obsessed with Cosey's legacy, for 20 years. Why? In interview Morrison hinted at the importance of historical context. In part Christine and Heed's relationship "disintegrated because of the internal pressures of desegregation" (Morrison 2005, 228). Ironically desegregation exacerbated class, money, colour and education divides within African American communities. In 1976, Christine and Heed find themselves on opposite sides of a widening divide, and can summon no resources for overcoming their animosity. Is this a failure of imagination on the part of Christine and Heed? (See **p. 19.**)

Through Romen *Love* explores a male femininity and an alternative, critical/resistant masculinity. During the gang-rape scene, Romen sheds "girlish tears" (46) for Pretty-Fay and feels compelled, almost against his will, to interrupt the obscene male bonding ritual. He intuits "the connection between them ... As though he *and* her had been tied to a bed; his legs *and* hers forced open" (48). Romen breaks ranks and crosses boundaries – his name sounds like "roaming" – and is punished with a beating and ostracism for not "doing his gender right", to quote Judith Butler: "Discreet genders are part of what 'humanizes' individuals within contemporary society; indeed, we regularly punish those who fail to do their gender right" (Butler 1990, 139–40). Morrison commented: "The first thing I wrote was that gang-rape scene ... to the contempt of his friends, he releases the girl" (Morrison 2003b, 214).

Romen and Junior are an African American post-segregation-era version of Romeo and Juliet and their crossing of social boundaries. As Morrison has commented in interviews regarding the emergence of class differences with desegregation: "The Civil Rights Movement of the sixties suddenly released Black people into their own class society. Before, they had all lived together ... The unity was shattered" (Morrison 2004, 224).

Romen lives in Monarch Street. Junior lived in the Settlement, which is "a planet away from One Monarch Street", the address of her new employers (53). The Settlement was formed out of both black and white populations after World War I: "the black ones because they had no hope, or the white ones who had no prospects", living together and "marrying one another" (54). In their eyes, "the only crime was departure" and Junior's escape from the Settlement was "treason" (55). Leaving the Settlement and rendering herself homeless has already cost her "mangled toes" (179), reform school and prison. The 14-year-old Romen's perceptions and emotions are divided and contradictory. Initially he perceives Junior as an "alien", but is drawn to her "sci-fi eyes" and would "kill to join [her] on the spaceship" (115). Unable to recognize her properly, he sees her damaged foot as a bestial sign of the devil, a "hoof" (154). In a moment of breakthrough in the novel, he intuits the real context of her mythological hoof and humanizes it. The hoof is the pitiable reality of "mangled toes" and he kisses them (179).

One of the *topoi* of African American criticism has been colourism within the African American community. Historically the African American middle class has been light-skinned, the African American poor dark-skinned, with dark-skinned women especially devalued (see Alice Walker 1982). African American intellectuals and activists saw the need to affirm the value of dark-skinned African American women and Morrison has contributed to this in most of her novels. In *Love* Morrison explores the Settlement as a new mixed-race underclass enclave disowned by everyone, including the African American community. Junior is a new type in Morrison's literature: the light-skinned underclass black woman.

Morrison describes the encounter between the Settlement and a school principal on an official visit in terms ironically evoking a parallel with Hernando de Soto's expedition to Florida in 1539–40. De Soto, born in extreme poverty, explored Florida in search of gold for Spain, with the aid of his guides, Ortiz and Perico, introducing Native Americans to European brutality and European diseases lethal to them. In the "late fifties" (54) – the late 1950s was already a time of rapid desegregation – the school principal comes to the Settlement in order to expel the Settlement boy Otis Rick (hear Ortiz and Perico) from his school because of the boy's brutality: "he had loosened a child's eye in the playground" (54). The principal travels to the rural Settlement in his DeSoto car to enact the expulsion; he is not made welcome by the natives: "The DeSoto was towed back to town by State Troopers because nothing could make its owner go back to retrieve it" (54). Morrison chooses not to use Settlement characters as focalizers, with the exception of the one character who leaves the Settlement, Junior. As a result she increases the reader's sense of distance from the Settlement, which remains unknown directly. In a crisis of confidence, the third-person extradiegetic narrator gives several possible reasons as to why Junior's uncles wanted to stop her from leaving, running her over and damaging her foot (57).

Love, whose narrative present is the mid-1990s on the East Coast (possibly Florida), vividly resurrects a segregation-era world that no longer exists. Cosey's up-market seafront hotel for black people, established in the 1930s, during the Depression, as a *"playground"* for those who *"studied ways to contradict history"* (102), is now deserted; the black working-class Up Beach is now *"twenty feet underwater"* (7), and Cosey's *"Santa Claus"* role in Up Beach (103) a thing of the past. While resurrecting the past, the novel, ironically, acknowledges its powerlessness to understand a present-day community, the Settlement. However, it does ask insistently: is it "*too late*" for Junior, who has left, to be understood and to understand herself (200)?

Junior's itinerary in the novel mirrors Christine's and Heed's itinerary from misrecognition to *anagnorisis*. Junior comes under the spell of Cosey's ghost soon after moving to One Monarch Street. The monarch here is Cosey and Junior identifies him as her "Good Man": a father figure who "promised to hold a girl steady on his shoulders while she robbed apples from the highest branch" (30). Junior sees and hears Cosey in the house, but also enters a process of becoming Cosey, by donning his tie and his "undershorts" (119). In *Paradise* Morrison examined this process of female self-authorization and self-legitimation by recourse to a male supernatural figure in her depiction of Consolata's Visitor. In *Love* Morrison critiques Junior's myth of the Good Man and her identification with Cosey as an error – in ancient Greek tragedy, the untranslatable *hamartia*: swerving from the right course, missing the mark, misunderstanding. This error authorizes her desire to steal Cosey's fortune, abandon Heed and Christine at the deserted hotel, and join the affluent and propertied middle class.

Romen, when he kisses Junior's foot in the bathtub, precipitates in her a "slipperiness" or "inside slide" (196) that helps release her from her fixation on Cosey, and she confesses her plan to Romen. (In Morrison's *oeuvre*, Romen joins *Beloved*'s Paul D. Paul D, when he first enters the house at 124 and encounters the ghost, imagines himself as a monster-slaying hero on a mission to save Sethe; but develops into a carer bathing Sethe, modelled on Baby Suggs.) However, this change in Junior was initiated earlier by Junior herself, taking the form of a contest between Cosey's ghost and L's ghost as rival ancestors for Junior, as the second-time reader comes to understand. When Junior goes to the deserted hotel with Heed, Junior smells L's bread (175) and wonders if her Good Man is here: "She can't tell. The cinnamon bread is not him" (176). Having forged Heed's will to benefit herself, Junior's own unconscious rejection of the act takes dream-like form: "The aroma of baking bread was too intense … [Cosey] wasn't there" (177). She returns to One Monarch Street, unthinkingly turns off Christine's overheated oven and saves the house, as L saved the house when Heed set Christine's bed on fire many years ago. She confesses to Romen, he arrives at the deserted hotel (195), and Junior senses that "the Good Man vanished" (196). Junior, without knowing it, has rejected Cosey and chosen L as her ancestor. And yet, Junior depends crucially on Romen's intervention and Christine's response. Romen rescues Christine and locks Junior in L's room; and Christine, in dialogue with Heed's ghost, deliberates:

"Should we let her go … We should let her stay … She knows how to make trouble. So do we. Hey, Celestial" (198).

L AND CELESTIAL AS ALTERNATIVE ANCESTORS: CHORUS AND TRAGIC HERO

As Morrison has repeated in interviews, her novels explore the dialectic of chorus and tragic hero in an African American context and as one of the constituents of her Black art (Morrison 1985b). Particularly, she has been exploring the failure of community and tragic hero to come together in reciprocal determination. In *Beloved*, for example, Sethe's excessive action is mirrored by the community's failure to act, to alert Sethe that Schoolteacher is coming. Community and tragic hero come together, belatedly, when the thirty women gather outside 124 to help Sethe. In *Love*, *hubris*, exceeding one's limits, takes the form of wanton women and unruly children. The excessive friendship of Christine and Heed as little girls – excessive because it crosses social boundaries – is a tragic act. But this friendship is interrupted when Cosey marries 11-year-old Heed Johnson.

Why was this marriage allowed to take place? One of the focalizers answering this question is Sandler Gibbons: Cosey's younger and poorer friend, Romen's grandfather, ex-resident of Up Beach, member of a black blue-collar "aristocracy". Sandler belongs to an aspiring, relatively successful but vulnerable social group: he is affected by de-industrialization; his daughter and son-in-law are affected by limited career choices and have to leave Romen to his grandparents' care in their efforts to progress; Romen is threatened by unemployment and the criminalization of black youth, and Sandler is worried that he might attract police attention (15). (See **p. 19**.) Sandler argues that Heed's Up Beach family, the Johnsons, were "not typical" of Up Beach (147). If Up Beach was the middle, Cosey and the Johnsons were the top and bottom of the local African American community. The top and the bottom were similar in that they wouldn't be "monitored": "Nobody swooped down on" the Johnsons (147). Sandler accuses Cosey and Heed's father, Wilbur Johnson, of abuse of patriarchal power. Heed didn't have a choice: "Was there someplace Cosey and Wilbur Johnson couldn't reach?" (147). The first-time reader might concur with Sandler. However, the second-time reader is likely to question his reliability and ask why the community did not act on Cosey and Wilbur Johnson to prevent the marriage. Did Sandler not invest them with an imagined excessive power far beyond the reality to excuse the community's inaction? L's poisoning of Cosey can be seen as a belated activation of the community's power to intervene.

Chorus – the community's power to intervene and pass judgement beyond a complicitous replication of the status quo – and tragic hero – freedom of action – work together twice in *Love*: in the relation of L and Celestial; and in the relation of Romen and Junior.

In the novel's closing lines L and Celestial come together while visiting Cosey's grave. The scar-faced prostitute, Celestial – as she emerges out of L's narration and sections focalized by Christine and Heed – is a free woman. She is associated with a space without dividing lines, the ocean. In L's narration we see her as a little girl fishing by the ocean, "*casting into the waves. For what, who knows*"; then "*the wind turned and the homemade fishhook hooked her*" (101), but not for long. Nor did the knife-attack on her face deter her. L and Heed contribute forgotten fragments of Celestial's lifelong and even posthumous love affair with Cosey. L's narration describes Cosey and Celestial together on the beach, and lingers on Celestial: Celestial is "*wading out into black water and I could tell she wasn't afraid … of anything*" (106). Celestial then makes a sound that L "*wanted to answer*" (106). L tells us that Celestial's singing and humming – her power of "*the tongue*" (201) – is salutary and freeing. L believes that, had Celestial inherited Cosey's fortune in accordance with the will that L destroyed, she "*would have given it away … would have blown [the hotel] up rather than let it stand as a reminder of why she was not permitted to mount its steps*" (201).

In the novel's closing lines Celestial sits on Cosey's grave – hiding the false epitaph "*Ideal Husband. Perfect Father.*" – and sings to him (201). L reciprocates: "*I join in. And hum*" (202). L's narration can be seen to emanate from – to be made possible by – Celestial's humming. (L's destruction of Cosey's written will and her writing of a forged will can also be seen as an extension of Celestial's power of the tongue.) Junior's use of language reminds L of Celestial: when Junior meets Theo – the most eager participant in Pretty-Fay's gang rape – she answers his "*hateful stare*" with verbal abuse (67).

Since their childhood Christine and Heed have connected Celestial with a capacity to act in a "bold, smart, risky" manner – their revision and reversal of May's condemnation of her: "There is nothing a sporting woman won't do" (188). "Except … for a language they called 'idagay,' 'Hey, Celestial' was their most secret" and self-empowering language (188). In the novel's climactic scene, when Christine and Heed resurrect their friendship and the power to talk to each other, they share their memory of Celestial on the beach, her "head held high", winking at them (188). They had named their beach playhouse – a "keeled-over row-boat" (190) – Celestial Palace. The last words they share before Heed's death are "Hey, Celestial" (190) – an exclamation affirming their friendship and their power of the tongue. Heed's obsessive bathing can be interpreted as a longing for the sea, for Celestial and for Celestial Palace.

At the beginning of the novel Heed does not remember Celestial and her authorizing, liberating wink: Junior "winked, startling Heed into a momentary recall of something just out of reach, like a shell snatched away by a wave" (27); the second-time reader recognizes this forgotten something as Celestial. Heed and Christine, in the final words of their recorded posthumous dialogue, affirm Junior's, and their own, Celestial heritage: they want Junior to stay because "She knows how to make trouble. So do we. Hey Celestial" (198). Heed and Christine's *anagnorisis* of a buried past, and their reviving of their childhood language, is the "bold, smart, risky" thing to do.

In a free association *Love* links up the ocean, waves, sound waves, the voice, the tongue, language and contrasts them to stone, stony reality, crushing inexorable conditions, the Necessity of Greek tragedy. In a depressive moment anticipated by Baby Suggs's breakdown in *Beloved*, Christine thinks: "the veil parted to expose a wide plateau of lifeless stone" (132). When the resurrection of Heed's and Christine's friendship is about to happen and they are about to resume their childhood conversation, the third-person extradiegetic narrator comments: "The landscape beyond this room is without color. Just a bleak ridge of stone and no one to imagine it otherwise ... An unborn world where sound, any sound ... is a gift" (184). Language, or at least the language that is the vehicle of the enlivened imagination, envisages things otherwise and is, therefore, closely connected to excessive action.

The relation of Junior and Romen is the second instance of chorus (as subversive or transgressive intervention and judgement in relation to the status quo) and tragic hero (as freedom of action) working together in *Love*. Romen's and Junior's respective capacities for subversive intervention and freedom of action have been established before they meet. During the gang-rape Romen had released the girl, breaking ranks with his friends and even his conscious, intentional self. Romen's subversive feminization (discussed above) continues the unfinished revolution of the Civil Rights Movement. Morrison points to the negative role of a patriarchal, dominating masculinity within the Civil Rights Movement through the incident of the rape of a female student volunteer (166–67). Fruit effectively condones it; Christine's response is ineffectual.

Junior leaves the Settlement in spite of her uncles' brutality during her first attempt at escape. She also "upend[s]" the Administrator sexually harassing her "over the railing" of a first-floor balcony in spite of the proximity of the date of her release from "Correctional" and tells the Committee what happened (117). Through such actions

Junior lays claim to an alternative female masculinity. Romen's sub-versive intervention in his relation to Junior (kissing her damaged foot, driving to the hotel in order to stop the realization of Junior's plan) prevents Junior's female masculinity from collapsing into the dominant, patriarchal masculinity in acts of abuse of power. Junior comes close to repeating the dominant, patriarchal form of masculinity: she is sexually voracious and preys on 14-year-old Romen; and she preys on Christine and Heed with an eye on Cosey's fortune – the ghost of her Good Man is a personification of her greed. Then Romen kisses her damaged foot ...

Junior's arrival in One Monarch Street triggers the resurrection of Christine and Heed's friendship and their own capacity to act subversively. In recognition, Christine is willing to offer Junior a home – in itself a demonstration of Christine's renewed capacity to act. The underclass Junior is as socially inappropriate a guest as Heed was a socially inappropriate friend many years before; Sandler and Vida do not at all welcome Romen's association with Junior.

The Cosey family has been in the black hospitality business since 1930, with Dark's money made out of informing on black people to the Police. Young Christine – in the free spirit of L and Celestial – drastically reinterprets this hospitality in her friendship with Heed; and the legacy of this free spirit and this friendship lives on in old Christine's offer to let Junior stay.

A Mercy (2008)

In *Paradise* Morrison critically engaged with the dominant American narratives of the Pilgrim Fathers and the Founding Fathers. *A Mercy* sets out to narrate the beginnings of the United States in terms that decentre and interrupt these two narratives.

Paradise was the final text in a trilogy – *Beloved*, *Jazz*, *Paradise* – best described as a project of alternative historiography. *A Mercy* arguably extends the earlier trilogy into a quartet. Many reviews described *A Mercy* as a prequel to *Beloved*. For example, Michiko Kakutani described it as "a kind of prelude" to *Beloved* (Kakutani 2008). These novels develop like crystals around a seemingly minor historical event, and *A Mercy* is no exception. The historical event here is Bacon's Rebellion in the colony of Virginia in 1676 (a century before the beginning of the American War of Independence in 1775). The novel's third-person extradiegetic narrator describes the event through Jacob Vaark, who is the focalizer: "an army of blacks, natives, whites, mulattoes – freedmen, slaves and indentured – had waged war against local gentry led by members of that very class"

(8; all page references in this chapter refer to *A Mercy* [Morrison 2008a] unless otherwise indicated). The rebellion failed but the fear this "people's war" (8) inspired in local gentry led to the passing of new laws designed to break this emerging solidarity across lines of class and race. There are no doubt a variety of ways in which to narrate Bacon's Rebellion. For example, an historian might focus on the rebels' aim to expel all Native American tribes from Virginia; and the perception of all Native American tribes as a common enemy by those taking part in the rebellion. Jacob Vaark is travelling through Virginia in 1682. He identifies himself as a "commoner" (23) and his account of the Rebellion focuses on it as a rebellion against hereditary privilege. Toni Morrison, in her interview with Lynn Neary, similarly focuses on the attempt to overthrow the Royal Governor of Virginia, Sir William Berkeley (Morrison 2008d). In this account Bacon's Rebellion manifests a seventeenth-century spirit of liberty and democratization. It is an inheritor of the forces whose struggle against absolute monarchy led to the English Civil War and the temporary abolition of the monarchy; and anticipates Thomas Paine's modern democratic notion of the "people" as it underpinned the American Revolution.

In Jacob's view, the new Virginian laws – "eliminating manumission, gatherings, travel and bearing arms for black people only; ... granting license to any white to kill any black for any reason", etc. (8) – are "lawless laws" (8–9) working against the "common cause" (9). (Morrison here possibly alludes to Thomas Paine, who uses the phrase "common cause" in his *Common Sense* [Paine 1995, 6], one of the most influential and widely read documents of the American Revolution, written in early support of independence.) Morrison has commented that these laws brought about an "immediate division ... between the various levels and kinds of poor people, and the benefit was only to the rich" (Morrison 2008g). Against the forces working towards a new society, a new commonwealth, "Any social ease between gentry and laborers, forged before and during that rebellion, crumbled beneath a hammer wielded in the interests of the gentry's profits" (8). From the point of view of the present, what is particularly significant is that the new laws "separated and protected all whites from all others forever" (8). This is nothing less than an early moment in the creation – the institutional construction – of racism. Bacon's Rebellion is only alluded to, never named, and appears peripheral to the plot, but the possibility it raises of alliance, an artificial family or society across lines of class, race and gender, is central to this novel.

Morrison's argument in *A Mercy* is that "whiteness" (as the privileged term) and "blackness" (as the devalued term) are a modern invention constructed in the New World in the seventeenth century. Her argument resonates with Michel Foucault's influential understanding of power in *Discipline and Punish*. Foucault argues that power is not negative – it doesn't stop us from doing what we want – but *productive* – it makes us who/what we are. *A Mercy* depicts a New World before "whiteness" and "blackness": the second half of the seventeenth century in what was to become the United States is a pre-racist world in the process of race-ing itself. The term "racist" is used in the particular sense of discriminating against people of African descent, though racism can take other forms. In the terms of Morrison's *Playing in the Dark* (Morrison 1992b), the novel explores the emergence of "American Africanism". (See **pp. 146–50**.)

A Mercy decentres the role of New England Puritans – the Pilgrim Fathers – as we find them in canonical American narratives. The novel narrates the early years of the colonization of North America as a Babel of nations, languages, religious denominations and classes: the Swedes, the Dutch, the French, the Portuguese; Presbyterians, Anabaptists and Catholics; Angolan slaves, English transported convicts, indentured servants and peons, Dutch patroons, free Africans. Florens's first-person narration unfolds in a defamiliarized language that evokes what must have been the chaotic multilingualism of seventeenth-century America. Her mother spoke the language of her African (possibly Angolan) tribe; then Portuguese in Barbados; Portuguese and some Latin and English in Maryland. The mother addresses Jacob Vaark in English when she asks him to take Florens. Florens's first language is Portuguese: her name for her mother is "a minha mãe" (1, 99, 135–36, 159) – *minha mãe* means "my mother" in Portuguese. A Catholic priest teaches mother and daughter reading and writing, using Latin religious texts such as the Latin version of the Nicene Creed. Owned by Vaark, Florens migrates to upstate New York and enters a small English-speaking community. Lina is raised in the language and religion of her Native American tribe. After the devastation of her village from smallpox, a European disease, when Lina is a small child, she is rescued by French soldiers; she then becomes a servant to English-speaking Presbyterians, who sell her to Jacob Vaark. (The brief references to French soldiers and to the tribe's "sachem" or chief (52) suggest that Lina belongs to the Algonquins.) In *Common Sense* (1776), one of Thomas Paine's arguments for independence from Britain was that the colonies were not British but multicultural: "Not one third of the inhabitants, even of this province, are of English descent. Wherefore I reprobate the phrase of parent or mother country applied to England only, as being false, selfish, narrow and ungenerous" (Paine 1995, 23). *A Mercy* confirms and displays the linguistic and cultural dispossession, nomadism and pluralism of the American colonies in the seventeenth century. Morrison presents a vision not of a facile or sentimentalized multiculturalism but of the often violent and brutal contact of individuals with alien cultures and with large-scale uncontrollable forces.

AGAINST THE IDEOLOGY OF THE "SELF-MADE MAN"

One of the insights or perhaps hypotheses of the novel is that, in this pre-racist world, very little separates enslaved Africans, white indentured servants and poor "unmastered women" (56). Morrison develops this insight in dialogue with contemporary scholarship and has cited Don Jordan and Michael Walsh's *White Cargo: The Forgotten History of Britain's White Slaves in America* (2007) as one significant text (Morrison 2009a).

Willard Bond is an English indentured servant. At the age of 14 he is sold for seven years to a Virginia planter, and works as part of a group of men in bondage: "Six English, one native, twelve from Africa by way of Barbados" (146–47). But his "seven years stretched to twenty-some" (55) and is very likely to stretch indefinitely. His status is lower than that of the free African blacksmith and, Willard comments, "No law existed to defend indentured labor against" free Africans (149). He is unaware that such laws are being put in place, for example in Virginia after Bacon's Rebellion. Willard's younger companion, 22-year-old Scully, is an English indentured servant who has inherited his mother's "indebtedness" (151). She was transported to the colonies for "lewdness and disobedience" and didn't live long enough to finish her indenture (55). Scully hopes to be free before his death but is Kafkaesquely unaware of the terms of his contract.

Rebekka, Jacob Vaark's wife, is the daughter of a poor London waterman whose family live "eight people in a single room garret" (84). She crosses the Atlantic under conditions comparable to those of Florens's enslaved mother. She remembers her passage, one of eight women travelling steerage and living for "six weeks" (70) in a small five-foot high "dark space below next to the animal stalls" (79). Food reaches them through a hatch over their heads in a basket tied to a rope, and they share one tub as a lavatory (79). They spend one hour per day on deck (71). In the delirium of her illness Rebekka recollects her group of co-travellers that "planks separated ... from the [animal] stock" (82). Judith and Lydia, prostitutes, and Dorothea, cutpurse (pickpocket), were sentenced and "ordered to choose between prison and exile": they would be indentured servants in the colonies to repay the costs of their transportation (80). Anne is sent off to the colonies because she is pregnant – a fallen woman.

The nightmarish transatlantic voyage of the eight women, focalized through Rebekka, and the account of indentured servitude in the colonies, focalized through Willard Bond and Scully, can be read productively against Daniel Defoe's *Moll Flanders* (Defoe 1722). Considered by many to be the first novel in English, *Moll Flanders* oscillates between romance and the realism of the new novel form. In 1683, in the first person, Moll Flanders narrates her life which includes an early sojourn in Virginia and her later conviction and transportation back to Virginia. During her early stay Moll encounters her mother, who was herself convicted and transported to the colonies. In a passage hovering between realism and fantasy the mother simultaneously gives a grim account of indentured servants – "Servants, *such as we call them*, my Dear, *says she*, but they are more properly call'd *Slaves*" – and evokes the great expectations that accompanied the English migrant experience – "many a *Newgate* [London prison] Bird becomes a great Man" (Defoe 1772, 86; see 86–88 and 361–63). Moll's mother herself has seen her fortune transformed and is a female version of the "self-made man": she married her master and then greatly improved his plantations after his death, "by her Diligence and good Management" (88).

Moll's account of her transatlantic voyage as a convict is equally divided. On the one hand, her first night in steerage is hellish: "We were … clapt under Hatches, and kept so close, that I thought I should have been suffocated for want of Air" (306); and she reports her husband's expressing the opinion that for a gentleman the death penalty is preferable to transportation and servitude (301–02). On the other hand, having accumulated a lot of money after her life of crime, she soon buys herself a luxurious passage and her freedom upon arrival. Moll and her husband then "bought us two Servants, (*viz.*) an *English* Woman-Servant … and a *Negro* Man-Servant" (331). Clearly the important distinction here is between masters and servants – no distinction is being made between white indentured servant and black slave. Finally they buy a plantation "to employ between fifty and sixty Servants" (332).

The criminal source of Moll's capital and her reliance on the slave labour of 50 people might be read as comment on the ideology of social mobility through "Diligence and good Management" – the ideology of the "self-made man" ostensibly rising through his own efforts alone. *A Mercy* launches a multifaceted attack against this ideology. Willard Bond and Scully, as indentured servants, have no legal protection in practice against exploitative masters. Florens, on her journey to the blacksmith, encounters a group of white indentured servants re-leased by their master to a tannery for some years: "They are certain their years of debt are over but the master says no" (38). They decide to run away. Further on her journey Florens encounters an early small town or village of Puritan farmers. She remembers

Jacob Vaark's view that such communities are not economically profitable: "Mistress says Sir says ... farming will never be enough in those parts" (103). In the novel the model of economic advancement in the New World changes into that of the large-scale sugar cane plantations in Barbados reliant on African slaves (27–30). Senhor D'Ortega's grand mansion, Jublio, in Maryland is supported not only by his tobacco plantation, but also by his slave trafficking, and he runs into financial trouble when his slave ship sinks. Jacob Vaark sets out to be a self-made man but his freedom and money increasingly involve the bondage of others.

JACOB VAARK'S "FAMILY": JACOB, LINA, REBEKKA, SORROW, WILLARD BOND AND SCULLY

A *Mercy* focuses on a miniature society of seven people, a fragile artificial family in the wilderness of upstate New York, created around the benevolent Jacob Vaark – a sort of Noah's ark, as his name suggests, seven miles from the village of Milton (31). (Morrison points the reader to the poet Milton, his role in Cromwell's Commonwealth of England, his republicanism, etc.) Jacob's "family" embodies the ideals he discerns in Bacon's Rebellion in that it is an alliance of white, black, Native American and mixed race, of free, indentured and slave, under his leadership. After his death the members of the "family" each attest to their commitment to the family, and yet it is falling apart (57, 132, 142, 153–54). The novel unfolds the perspectives of each member of this family: the Anglo-Dutch Jacob Vaark, his English wife Rebekka, the Native American Lina, the African Florens (the race of her father is withheld), the mixed-race Sorrow, the English indentured servants Willard Bond and Scully. The novel's narrative present is, for the most part, 1690, the year of Jacob Vaark's death. Any new alliance, any new family will now have to be initiated from below.

The narrative centre of the novel is Florens, a 16-year-old slave girl. Morrison thereby shifts the centre of gravity within the family from Jacob Vaark to Florens. Florens narrates alternate sections in the first person and present tense, beginning with the first section – six sections in all. (We can number them 1, 3, 5, 7, 9, 11.) Morrison has commented in several interviews – for example, in Morrison 2008d – that she used the first person and present tense for "immediacy". Other sections are narrated by a third-person extradiegetic narrator, but each section is focalized by a different member of the family. I will discuss Florens's narration last.

Jacob Vaark is the focalizer in the second section, which narrates his 1682 journey through Virginia to Maryland. His destination is

Senhor D'Ortega's plantation where he buys Florens as a mercy – the novel's title – in response to her mother's plea to choose Florens, as part-payment of Ortega's debt to him. (The name Florens points to florins, Portuguese coins of small value; Morrison 2009a.) The Anglo-Dutch Vaark's fateful encounter with the Portuguese Ortega and his splendid mansion is a clash of the forces of democratization and social cohesion against the forces of capitalist accumulation. However, this turns out to be a clash, an antinomy that Vaark internalizes and lives out. One part of him is inheritor of the Dutch tradition of freedom of thought, inheritor of struggles to establish parliamentary democracy in England, and ancestor of Thomas Paine and the American Revolution; the other part of him desires to own a house to rival Ortega's mansion, Jublio – dreams of "a grand house of many rooms" (32).

Jacob has no notion of common whiteness or European-ness, but perceives and invests emotionally in intra-European class and religious antagonisms. His enemies are gentry and Catholics. He distrusts all religious denominations – including Anglicans and Dissenters – and is looking to marry an "unchurched" woman (18). Instead of perceiving and evaluating Florens's African mother along racial/racist lines – instead of race-ing her – he perceives her as pleasantly "clove-smelling" (18). Jacob and Ortega are both white, free, land-owning men – Jacob inherited his Dutch uncle's 120 acres of "dormant patroonship" in upstate New York (9–10) – and yet the great social fissure that Jacob is aware of is that between himself and Ortega. (Patroons were seventeenth-century Dutch colonial landowners appointed by the Dutch West India Company in the colony of New Netherland in today's upstate New York.) However, their encounter and transaction implicates and corrupts the disgusted Jacob. He rejects Ortega armed with the ideology of the Protestant work ethic and the "self-made man": "his own industry could amass the fortune, the station, D'Ortega claimed"; he "sneered at wealth dependent on a captured workforce" (26). But he has bought Florens and, earlier, Lina.

Jacob rejects Ortega's reliance on slavery for its lack of "restraint" (23) and "excess" (25); and wishes to become rich through his own efforts, in a manner that is "fair … pure, noble even" (25). This aspiration is not fulfilled. In fact he only becomes rich when he invests in the Barbados slave economy. His justification is that "there was a profound difference between the intimacy of slave bodies at Jublio and a remote labor force in Barbados" (32), but participating at a distance in slavery does not absolve one of participation. (Jacob's is the crime of innocence Morrison initially explored in Valerian Street in *Tar Baby*.)

The novel's fourth section is focalized through Lina, bought by Vaark in the early days. In those days Lina and Jacob were, in a sense, indistinguishable, twins of sorts. Both orphans, they worked hard, side by side. However, the narration focuses on the recent past and the feverish building of Jacob Vaark's large house, funded by his Barbados investments. The large house is ready in every particular, including its grand wrought-iron gate, with the exception of its window panes, when Vaark dies of smallpox. It is one of a series of paradoxical houses in Morrison's *oeuvre*, both fenced in and open.

Lina's perspective on Jacob Vaark develops further the duality of his nature. On the one hand Lina observes, in Vaark's interactions with the black blacksmith, his commitment to the ideal of fraternity later glorified by the French Revolution: "Sir behaved as though the blacksmith was his brother" (58). On the other hand his large house, his third and last, was excessive, according to Lina, and brought on his demise. The "second one was strong ... There was no need for a third" (41). The third house "required the death of fifty trees" (41), and "Killing trees in that number without asking their permission ... would stir up malfortune" (42). Lina disapproves of the prideful pleasure he took in building a "monument to himself" (42); and pays tribute to the collectivism of her tribe where "everyone had anything and no one had everything" (58).

Morrison seems to be referring here to the well-known tale of "The Three Little Pigs", particularly the pigs' three, increasingly more substantial, houses. Morrison is arguably critiquing the tale and its underlying ideology. Lina's perspective can be read productively against Bruno Bettelheim's interpretation of the tale in *The Uses of Enchantment*. According to Bettelheim the tale is teaching us that "we must not be lazy ... , for if we do, we may perish. Intelligent planning and foresight combined with hard labor will make us victorious over even our most ferocious enemy – the wolf!" (Bettelheim 1991, 42). The wolf, "wild and destructive ... stands for all asocial, unconscious, devouring powers against which one must learn to protect oneself" (ibid.). Bettelheim reads the three little pigs and the three progressively "more substantial" houses they build as "symbolic of man's progress in history" (ibid.). The first two pigs have less substantial houses because they are still "Living in accordance with the pleasure principle" and "seek immediate gratification" (ibid.).

Bettelheim implicitly reads the tale as advocating the ideology of the "self-made man", the Protestant work ethic and the Enlightenment ideal of human progress through the exercise of Reason. Lina's perspective on Vaark's third house critiques this ideology. The third house does not represent a higher stage of rational development, maturity and positive adjustment to the reality principle, but represents Vaark's corruption by an economic system generating great wealth through the enslavement of other humans and the environmentally unsustainable overexploitation of nature.

Lina's perspective reveals her as a cultural hybrid who has chosen her own versions of loyalty and solidarity across race and class lines. She other-mothers Florens. Initially hostile to the "Europe wife" (50), Rebekka, she then forms a close bond with her and states simply that they "became friends" (51). In the narrative present of the fourth section, Vaark has just died and Rebekka, infected by him, lies dying. Lina administers medicine and cares for her tirelessly (48). She also offers help to a group of white runaway indentured servants and promises not to betray them (50).

The sixth section is focalized through Rebekka Vaark, surveying her life in a delirious state as though suspended between life and death. This condition is the result of her illness, the loss of her beloved husband and protector, and also, following his death, the situation she now finds herself in without him, since "a widow was in practice illegal" (96). Her delirium reveals her to be oscillating between two paths. Which one should she trust herself to? On the one hand, there is her friendship with Lina, her particular version of Deism – her belief that God created the universe but does not interfere in the world – and the example of her shipmates: self-reliant women who "trusted their own imagination" (96). On the other hand, there is the belief in God's protection, the patriarchal and racist views of the Anabaptist women of the neighbouring village of Milton and the healing power of the blacksmith.

On the one hand, in a "moment of clarity", Rebekka acknowledges her female servant Lina as "the single friend she had" (71) and allows Lina to treat her. On the other hand, she trusts in the blacksmith, a freeman, to cure her and sends Florens on a perilous journey to secure his help. She revisits her heretical belief that God is unconcerned with humanity (78) and concludes that "Only Lina was steady" (98); but also considers the opposing belief of the Anabaptist women – who "obeyed" men (96), distrusted "lesser peoples" and claimed that "Natives and Africans had access to grace but not to heaven" (96–97) – that they were God's chosen people (90). In this way Rebekka struggles with opposing ideas, without resolution: "That was Lina. Or was it God?" (98).

Rebekka recalls her girlhood in London. Morrison has cited Emily Cockayne's *Hubbub: Filth, Noise & Stench in England, 1600–1770* (2007) as a source for *A Mercy* in her interviews (for example, Morrison 2008f). I have found several echoes of *Hubbub* in the novel rather than direct or sustained reference. Cockayne's discussion of female beauty as "plump" (25); washing once a year (60); the wearing of wigs and the connotation that men wearing them were "deformed and emasculated" (66–67); the law of not beating your wife after nine in the evening (112); arguably the Great Fire of London following the Great Plague (118); the "Cut-purse" (162), etc., have found their way into different sections of *A Mercy*.

To return to Rebekka's section, she alludes to her family's support for the restoration of the British monarchy in October 1660 and for the subsequent public executions of so-called Fifth Monarchists, who threatened the re-established monarchy, in January 1661. Unlike her family, Rebekka at 16 thinks, speaks and acts against the established order of things: she has a "rebellious mouth" and is "stubborn" (72). Her ability to think differently is revealed in the approval shown towards her delinquent shipmates, including a cutpurse and two prostitutes, and in her religious beliefs. Her version of proto-Deism highlights her scepticism towards "higher" authority, and anticipates the Enlightenment call to think for oneself. (Deism emerged in the seventeenth century in dialogue with the scientific revolution and influenced several Enlightenment thinkers and Founding Fathers; Thomas Paine expounded Deism in *The Age of Reason*.) This had been Rebekka's early path – and is now one of two paths she faces in the midst of her delirium.

The eighth section is focalized through Sorrow, a mixed-race schizophrenic girl given to Jacob Vaark. The reader of *The Bluest Eye* will compare Sorrow to Pecola. In the midst of a shipwreck, Sorrow creates an exact double of herself, Twin, as her "safety, her entertainment, her guide" (117). Pirates have probably attacked the ship to steal its cargo and have murdered everyone aboard except Sorrow (114–15). Sorrow is a creature of modernity: all that is solid dissolves into water in her case, to modify Marx. Her father – biological or adoptive – was the captain of the ship and her mother possibly an enslaved African woman transported to the New World. During her first 11 years she did not once set foot on land and was raised by her father as a "crewman-to-be" (125) dressed in men's clothing (116). Twin tells Sorrow glorious stories transfiguring the catastrophe she witnessed into its opposite, such as the story of the "thousandfold men walking the waves" (120).

Twin's loyalty and protectiveness towards Sorrow mirrors Lina's relations to Rebekka and Florens. This section follows the disintegration of these parallel relations after Rebekka's recovery from smallpox. Sorrow witnesses Rebekka's betrayal of Lina. The blacksmith arrives, notices Lina's medicines and pronounces Rebekka cured. Rebekka now needs to decide whom to count as her saviour. She thanks the blacksmith many times and prays to God in thanks.

Her former belief that God has no interest or involvement in human affairs – and that our lives and the human world are our own responsibility – gives way to its opposite: Sorrow reports her saying that "God alone cures" (131). Also, Rebekka's friendship with Lina and acknowledgement of Lina's care of her gives way to the blacksmith's authority. Sorrow, astutely, "understood that servants … their care and devotion did not matter to" Rebekka now (127–28). Rebekka has voluntarily re-entered in the New World the hierarchical system she left London to escape: "curtseying, curtseying, curtseying" (75).

The reader notices an irony in Rebekka's development: as she is cured of smallpox, she becomes infected by racist and patriarchal ideas. She comes to this "Fresh and new England" (88) only to be infected by a (new) moral corruption in the New World. In biblical terms this is the expulsion from the Garden of Eden, the Fall. Rebekka remains unaware of her fall, while Sorrow – an incarnation of her earlier self – discerns it and gains from her knowledge. Otten (1989) has analysed the role of the fortunate fall and the value of experience in Morrison's earlier novels.

Sorrow's perspective combines a critique of Rebekka's betrayal of Lina with a critique of Lina's loyalty. As a result of Sorrow's double critique the beginning disintegration of Lina's and Rebekka's friendship emerges as undecidable: positive and negative at once. Lina fashions herself by selecting and even reinventing aspects of her dual – Native American and Presbyterian – cultural heritage. Morrison endorsed this process of self-assembly in Song of Solomon's Pilate; here she explores the potential dangers of "self-invention" (48). Lina believes that the mentally ill and singular-looking Sorrow – with black teeth, red "wooly hair" and alarming "recurring boils" (49, 51–52) – is "bad luck in the flesh" (51). The very strength of her loyalty to Rebekka impels her to decide that the deaths of Rebekka's four children (19) were "Sorrow's fault" (122). The Presbyterians who took Lina in as a child believed that Lina's tribe was devastated by an epidemic as the "first sign of His displeasure" (45); her tribe believed that some people attract bad luck (53) – Lina's views are no less deluded and possibly a mixture of the two. But Lina acts upon her belief: she keeps Sorrow away from Florens and, excessively, kills Sorrow's newborn baby. At least this is what Sorrow suspects.

Pregnant for the second time and about to give birth, "Twin was absent" (130) and Sorrow becomes her own guide. She gives birth with some help from Willard and Scully and thanks them for it, but she is also "convinced that this time she had done something, something important by herself" (131). Twin and Sorrow have merged in this self-healing act, and Sorrow acknowledges this by calling herself

"Complete" (132). The sea and ship she sees in her new daughter's eyes can be read as an intimation of her intention to run away (132). For the reader of A Bluest Eye it is as if Pecola has just cured herself and is leaving Lorain.

Thus Rebekka and Sorrow, daughters of watermen, are moving in opposite directions. Rebekka enters the novel with a rebellious mouth and ends up enslaving herself; Sorrow enters the novel mad and seemingly crushed by overwhelming forces and ends up healing herself and preparing to free herself.

The tenth section is focalized through the indentured servants, Willard Bond and Scully, in contemporary terms, a gay couple. Couples, almost programmatically, are not enough for each other in Morrison's fiction, and this couple is no exception. They are both trying to find a place in a wider context. Will values the "camaraderie" across race lines he experienced among workers in different states of bondage in a Virginia plantation (146–47). He has resisted his exploitative masters, and has experienced Jacob Vaark's household – to which his master leased him out – as a kind of family. Scully reiterates the realization of other focalizers (Lina and Sorrow) that, after Jacob Vaark's death, their small society is falling apart: "They once thought they were a kind of family" but Scully "saw nothing yet on the horizon to unite them" (153–54). This section, together with the pages on Rebekka's transatlantic voyage, can be fruitfully read in dialogue with Jordan and Walsh's White Cargo.

FLORENS AND "A MINHA MÃE"

From the very first sentence of A Mercy Florens's addressee is an initially unspecified "you" that draws the reader in. Florens narrates her journey to the free black blacksmith she worships and, through this journey, her life in Vaark's household and her traumatic separation from her mother, which she understands as her mother's betrayal of her. The two poles of her narration are the free male black blacksmith, the model she desires but cannot emulate because she is female and a slave; and her mother, who comes to her in a recurring dream, trying to tell her something Florens cannot hear: the mother is "always wanting to tell me something ... I look away from her" (99); "I tell her to go" (135).

The seventh section – or the fourth section narrated by Florens – is especially important, in that it narrates the moment of Florens's raceing. In spring 1690 Florens enters a Puritan village and interrupts a witchcraft investigation two years before the beginning of the Salem witch trials in February 1692. Jane Ealing, Widow Ealing's daughter, is suspected of being the minion of "the Black Man" (107, 109).

Readers of Nathaniel Hawthorne's *The Scarlet Letter* (1850) will recognize "the Black Man" as the devil's appellation in that novel, set in Boston from 1642 into the second half of the seventeenth century. Brian Harding, editor of the World's Classics edition, comments that this was "a common appellation for the devil in the seventeenth century" (Hawthorne 1850, 285). Jane realizes the financial motive underlying her persecution: the male head of the family is dead and "It's the pasture they crave, Mother" (107). Morrison is here advancing an argument historians have made in relation to the Salem trials. Florens interrupts this scene and takes Jane's place. Because of the colour of her skin, the villagers announce that *she* is the Black Man's minion. Florens comes face to face with a performative utterance that forces upon her an instantaneous but drastic incorporeal transformation. Before this scene she was a slave whose skin colour was incidental to her enslavement; after this scene, her skin colour becomes a sign of the devil and thereby eternally justifies her enslavement. The villagers are looking at Florens without human "recognition" (111) – "I am a thing apart" (113). Once again, to extend Jane's argument, one can discern the financial motive. The scene is an allegory of the simultaneous emergence of racism and transition to an economy systematically relying on African slaves in the American colonies. In this scene, Jane embodies the forces resisting this process: she thinks for herself and helps Florens escape. Like the heroine of *The Scarlet Letter*, Hester Prynne, she is capable of a "freedom of speculation" or "amplitude of speculation" (Hawthorne 1850, 164, 199). Rebekka initially possessed but then loses this freedom, perhaps because of the precariousness of her position as a widow. Jane, the widow's daughter, is yet another reincarnation of Rebekka's youthful rebelliousness, yet another daughter inheriting her spirit and ensuring the survival of the forces countering tyranny and human bondage.

In the ninth section – or the fifth section narrated by Florens – Florens reaches the blacksmith and finds him committed to other-mothering a dark-skinned, possibly mixed-race orphan, Malaik. The blacksmith rejects her in favour of the little boy. Florens now finds herself denied all external authorization and legitimation. In the course of her journey she is raced and denied human recognition by the Puritans, who withhold the letter that Florens has been carrying, written by Rebekka and authorizing Florens's journey; Malaik then takes away the protective boots of Jacob Vaark in which she has been travelling; and now the blacksmith rejects her love: "Own yourself … You are nothing but wilderness. No constraint. No mind" (139). Florens is now existentially naked without recourse to any source of external aid. Her response is the beginning of her emerging subjectivity. First, she summons Jane Ealing as a resource in a dream of self-authorization. She dreams of a lake where she looks for her face: "my face is not there ... Daughter Jane is kneeling next to me [and telling me] ... Oh, Precious ... you will find it" (135–36). Secondly, she mobilizes Lina's eagle story – see pages 60–61 – in order to struggle with the blacksmith and claim her subjectivity: "Feathers lifting, I unfold. The claws scratch and scratch" (140). In Lina's story on Man and a mother eagle protecting her eggs, the mother eagle claws at Man who claims dominion over her world, Man strikes the mother eagle, she is falling, and her eggs hatch alone. Morrison here feminizes the symbol of the United States. Florens reshapes Lina's story and figures herself as simultaneously an eagle egg hatching alone and her own mother clawing Man.

The eleventh section – the sixth and final section narrated by Florens – continues the violent struggle between Florens and the blacksmith: "Our clashing is long" (155). This struggle can be read as a Hegelian dialectic between master and slave, necessary for Florens's independence from the blacksmith and her claiming of her own subjectivity. This Hegelian dialectic of intersubjectivity (see "Lordship and Bondage" in Hegel's *Phenomenology of Spirit*) has influenced Marxists, existentialists and postcolonial thinkers such as Frantz Fanon. Florens recognizes that there is no outside protection – she is her own protection and her own guardian/avenging angel: "I have ... no home" (156). Willard and Scully thought they saw at night Jacob Vaark's ghost haunting the empty big house he built. The reader now experiences a jolt of recognition: Florens is the spirit haunting the house built out of his profits from slavery. She has disobeyed Mistress – she who had been too eager to please – and entered the forbidden house, and has been writing her entire narrative on its floorboards with a nail at night and sleeping "among her words" (156).

Florens's narration gives her a voice through which to judge herself and others, reorder her relations and choose her alliances. She has become a smith after all – a word-smith forging her life through writing. She rejects Mistress's new assumption of superiority and authority in relation to Lina as the behaviour of an *unfree* freewoman, "an ass in the skin of a lion" (158), and places the responsibility for her behaviour firmly with Rebekka herself. If Mistress behaves "as she believes her piety demands", Florens asserts that "These rules are her own" (157). She then compares the blacksmith and Jane Ealing, and chooses Jane. The blacksmith is jealous of his own freedom – "A lion who thinks his mane is all" – but Jane is jealous for everyone's freedom and "risks all to save the slave you throw out" (158). Florens here anticipates the Enlightenment and becomes the embodiment of

Revolution – an African American personification of *Liberté*. She plans to burn down the big house and believes that "Lina will help. She finds horror in this house" (158). She affirms her new alliance with Sorrow and intends to run away with her and her baby. Stuart, in his review of the novel, describes Florens – in her "prettify ways" (*A Mercy*, 2) – as a "wanton" or "outlaw" woman in the Morrisonian tradition (Sula, Celestial, Junior) (Stuart 2008). We could argue that wanton woman, artist figure and political consciousness potentially come together in Florens's emergence. Her "prettify ways" can be read as a reference to the writer's aestheticization of life – a longterm theme in Morrison's *oeuvre* since *Sula*.

Florens has been addressing her narration to the blacksmith, but her critique of him culminates in abandoning him as an addressee and addressing her mother: "Mãe, you ... " (159). In the final words she addresses to the blacksmith Florens declares "You are correct ... I am become wilderness" (159), while boldly redefining its meaning and connotations: "wilderness" has to be understood as a response to a certain kind of civilization. "Wilderness" is perhaps the most multivalent symbol in *The Scarlet Letter*, accruing a number of positive and negative connotations, and Morrison nods in assent and continues this work.

The novel's final section is a first-person narration by Florens's mother, addressing Florens. Their separation is irrevocable and Florens cannot possibly hear her but *we* can, so we the readers witness a magical moment. Florens thought that her mother betrayed her. The mother now reveals to Florens, whose ear we have become, her real motive for asking Vaark to take Florens: he "saw you as a human child" (164).

Mirroring Florens's race-ing by the Puritan villagers, the mother describes her earlier race-ing in Barbados: "It was there I learned how I was not a person from my country, nor from my families. I was negrita [black girl] ... it was as a black that I was purchased by Senhor" (163). Vaark's recognition of Florens's humanity does not share in this de-humanizing and objectifying, race-ing gaze – and the mother concludes that "There is no protection" for a female slave "but there is difference" (164). Is there difference? Was Jacob Vaark different? – the reader inevitably asks. The readers know that the mother didn't prevent Florens's eventual race-ing. (This is a question Morrison initially raised persistently in *Beloved* in relation to the owner of Sweet Home, Mr Garner.)

While hoping that there is a difference, the mother also asserts her experience of the universality of bondage, inhumanity and patriarchy. In Africa "The men guarding we and selling we are black"; in the New World white men whip black slaves but also "lash their own" (162). In Africa women are goods for men, as they are in the New World (161). The mother's reading of patriarchy is perhaps Morrison's tribute to Gayle Rubin's well-known 1975 essay, "The Traffic in Women: Notes on the 'Political Economy' of Sex". Morrison might also be inviting a comparison with Olaudah Equiano's uncritical account of African patriarchy in his canonical 1789 slave-narrative, *The Interesting Narrative of the Life of Olaudah Equiano, or Gustavus Vassa, the African, Written by Himself* (Equiano 1789, 21).

The mother's advice to the readers, her surrogate children, is a version of Enlightenment radicalism to come: "to wrest dominion over another is a wrong thing; to give dominion of yourself to another is a wicked thing" (165). Thinking for yourself – Kant's advice in "What is Enlightenment?" – is not enough. You need to free yourself as well.

FREEDOM AND "COMMON CAUSE"

In *A Mercy* freedom and community are not opposed but, on the contrary, presuppose and strengthen each other. Independence and self-reliance go hand-in-hand with chosen social alliance and collaboration, often in resistance. We have discussed some of the instances in this novel of an actively forged social bond in an alliance across class, race and gender: the Catholic priest who risks punishment to teach Florens and her mother to write; the runaway white indentured servants who offer to take Florens with them (63), and whom Lina supports in turn in a double alliance; the Native American boy who gives Florens water to drink (100–01); Jane risking her life to help Florens escape; the new alliance of Florens and Sorrow, as they plan to escape; Willard Bond's alliance with English, African and Native American workers in the Virginia plantation.

The weaving of a social bond requires acknowledgement of the labour of others, recognition of their equality and fellow subjectivity. Florens repeatedly recognizes Jane's help as Jane herself recognizes that Florens's race-ing by the villagers benefited her, in that it suspended her own persecution. The characters live amidst a gathering historical storm – the racist legitimation and institutionalization of the African slave trade – but they live at a time just prior to this, at a time when the situation is still fluid. Whose labour and human value will be recognized, and whose will not; and how and why? The fantastical stories of cane growing miraculously by itself in Barbados that Jacob hears in 1682 in Virginia misrecognize the slaves' labour; it becomes invisible, nonexistent (29). Rebekka initially recognizes Lina's generously (and in this sense, freely) offered labour (98), but then recognition fails and she sees only her debt to the free blacksmith and to God. Sorrow cures herself by recognizing her own labour (131).

The novel's title, *A Mercy*, is open to a variety of interpretations, depending on whose act of mercy the reader is prepared to recognize. Yes, the title can be interpreted as Vaark's act of mercy, but it can also be interpreted as the mother's or even Jane's. The mother thought she sacrificed her own chance of a better life for her daughter. Vaark, tellingly, fails to recognize the mother's act of mercy (see 24, 30, 32) and assumes – why, the reader wonders – that the mother was "throwing away" (32) a child that "mattered less than a milch cow" to her (30). The reader, on the other hand, can see that the mother's act is an act of freedom, as redefined in the novel: freedom as fighting for the freedom of others. In a world of contingency and overwhelming historical forces, the measure of the individual's freedom is his or her acts of solidarity.

In *A Mercy* Morrison is rethinking the political ideals of the modern Western world. The novel is set in 1690 but urgently addresses the writer's and the reader's responsibilities today in what is her most political work to date.

Published in the month Barack Obama was elected president, *A Mercy* is pre- and post-racist, looking back and forward at the same time. It returns to the history of slavery, while asking us to think about our own freedom and unfreedom.

In a narrowly realist historical novel relying on verisimilitude, acts such as Florens's and Sorrow's alliance and their plans to run away would have been accorded their historically likely outcome of defeat. But Morrison's is a *virtual* realism, reclaiming the pure potential of the past for the sake of our future.

Selected nonfiction

We have been referring to the broad spectrum of Morrison's nonfiction – from interviews to newspaper articles to scholarly essays – throughout this book. In this section we will return to a selection to demonstrate the variety but also the continuities and evolution of Morrison's nonfiction, as well as the uninterrupted communication between it and the novels. Morrison has been doing a lot of her theorizing in her novels; she has also been using narrative in her nonfiction.

"WHAT THE BLACK WOMAN THINKS ABOUT WOMEN'S LIB" (22 AUG. 1971)

This long article is interesting for at least three reasons. First, it is an early document in the emergence of African American feminism, calling attention to the situation of African American women and their traditions of resistance, buried under negative dominant stereotypes. Morrison discusses Geraldine, a stereotypical black female character "highly offensive to black women" (Morrison 1971b, 23) developed by black comedian Flip Wilson. Morrison argues that it is possible to read such a negative stereotype against the grain in order to release, "under the stupidity and the hostility, the sweet smell of truth" (22). In the case of Geraldine, "for defensive read survivalist; for cunning read clever; for sexy read a natural unembarrassed acceptance of her sexuality; for egocentric read keen awareness of individuality; for transvestite ... read a masculine strength" (23). The way Morrison reads Geraldine illuminates a significant aspect of her novels: her fictional project of reworking racist and sexist stereotypes, begun with her very first novel and discussed throughout this book.

Secondly, the article illuminates aspects of *Sula*, the novel Morrison was writing at the time – particularly *Sula*'s critique of existentialist feminism, perhaps the dominant feminist paradigm at the time. (The article was written before the emergence of French "difference" feminism; Irigaray's *Speculum of the Other Woman* was published in 1974.) Morrison voices the widespread mistrust black women felt towards the white middle-class feminist movement, but concludes on a hopeful note – "the air is shivery with possibilities" (30) – once certain conditions are met.

Implicitly rejecting the idea that white middle-class feminists can liberate black women, she argues rhetorically and polemically that, if white feminism succeeds, white women will lead the kind of lives already led by black women, who (in terms perhaps ironically recalling the language of existentialism) "frequently kicked back ... [O]ut of the profound desolation of her reality [the black woman] may very well have invented herself" (24). Morrison argues that historically black women have been taking jobs outside the home as well as heading households in a hostile world, while white women have escaped such responsibilities and remained children. Implicitly demanding white feminists' engagement with African American history, she takes two segregation-era signs – "White Ladies" and "Black Women" – and turns them wittily into proof of her argument: ladies are all "softness, helplessness and modesty" (18); women are "tough, capable, independent and immodest" (19). In this sense, "Women's Lib", if it succeeds, will turn white ladies into black women. Morrison was of course aware that her description of white women applies with greatest force to affluent middle- and upper-class women. In her novels Morrison greatly complicates her argument to explore black women's internalization of white middle-class values.

Not only is this a highly rhetorical text, it also uses novelistic techniques familiar to the readers of her novels, such as Morrison's distinctive use of narrative suspension. For example, in *A Mercy* the reader has to wait until page 34 to discover the identity of the "you" – the addressee – of Florens's narrative. In this article readers have to wait for nearly 100 words before being told that the initial, unspecified "They" refers to public signs in the racially segregated U.S.: "White Only", "Colored Only", "White Ladies" and "Colored Women". This is Morrison's way of formally highlighting the specificity of African American women's experience.

REVIEW OF *WHO IS ANGELA DAVIS?* BY REGINA NADELSON (29 OCT. 1972)

This short review of Nadelson's biography of the well-known African American intellectual and activist Angela Davis, who was imprisoned at the time, announces Morrison's ethical commitment to multi-perspectivism. The issue here is race and the voice is angry that Nadelson, a white woman, focuses exclusively on Davis's white intellectual influences and her allegiance to the Communist party, while ignoring her black influences and remaining deaf to Davis herself. Morrison rejects Nadelson's biography of Davis because it is monoperspectival rather than multiperspectival: it has a "Cyclopean view" – a reference to both the Cyclops's one eye and his feeding on human flesh, which Morrison suggests are connected.

The angry voice is, I believe, very deliberately chosen, and the article carefully crafted. For example, the unannounced gap between the penultimate and the last paragraph and the unmarked change of perspective at the beginning of the last paragraph perplex readers to highlight differences of perspective. This prepares readers for Morrison's concluding point that a mono-perspectival account of Davis is exploitative – only a multiperspectival account will do.

"REDISCOVERING BLACK HISTORY" (11 AUG. 1974)

This article was written in connection with the publication of *The Black Book*, a project of alternative African American historiography for which Morrison, then working in publishing, was the in-house editor. *The Black Book* is a massive compilation resembling a scrapbook and documenting the lives of mostly anonymous black people, rather than the conventional heroes of history, with material largely provided by collectors. The article mainly presents *The Black Book*. It also articulates Morrison's critique of black political correctness from the late fifties onwards, and especially her critique of the Black Power movement (see **p. 26**). Morrison rejects the Black Power slogan, "black is beautiful", from a black woman's perspective already developed in "What the Black Woman Thinks" (see above). The slogan equates black (female) beauty with virtue and endorses escapist models unhelpful to black women: "when Civil Rights became Black Power, we frequently chose exoticism over reality" (41). Instead Morrison advocates the kind of contact with reality and with the past that she feels *The Black Book* offers.

"A SLOW WALK OF TREES (AS GRANDMOTHER WOULD SAY), HOPELESS (AS GRANDFATHER WOULD SAY)" (4 JUL. 1976)

In this article about the black experience (see **p. 12**), Morrison returns to her theme of multiperspectivism, outlined in her article on Angela Davis discussed above.

Morrison explores opposed views held by her grandmother, Ardelia, and grandfather, Solomon, as to whether the life of African Americans would improve; and then the opposed views held by her mother, Ramah, and father, George, as to whether the moral fibre of white people would improve. Instead of choosing, Morrison argues, dialogically, that her own outlook is indebted to all these views and the resources they bring with them: cynicism and pessimism (Solomon); strong acts of will and optimism (Ardelia); reasonableness (Ramah); an aggressive reversal of colour prejudice against whites, an ethic of work and self-help (George).

"ROOTEDNESS: THE ANCESTOR AS FOUNDATION" (1984)

In this influential article Morrison outlines her Black art and the principles towards which it aspires:

- an oral quality;
- an "affective and participatory relationship" between writer and reader;
- gaps for the reader to step in and actively contribute to the meaning of the text – "What is left out is as important as what is there";
- the presence of a chorus "commenting on the action";
- the presence of ancestor figures as a legitimating and sense-making resource;
- a hybrid genre combining the powers of the imagination and realism: "blend[ing] the acceptance of the supernatural and a profound rootedness in the real world".

(341–43)

We have been discussing these principles throughout the book.

PLAYING IN THE DARK: WHITENESS AND THE LITERARY IMAGINATION (1992)

Morrison describes *Playing in the Dark* as "a serious intellectual effort to see what racial ideology does to the mind, the imagination, and behavior of masters" (12). *Playing* is based on three William E. Massey, Sr. Lectures given at Harvard University in 1992. "Unspeakable Things Unspoken: The Afro-American Presence in American Literature" (Morrison 1989a) is an early version of the perspective developed in *Playing*.

Morrison had already begun the exploration of the effects of racism on the "behavior of masters" in *Tar Baby* (1981), in her sketch of Valerian's fetishization of the black washerwoman of his youth. On the traumatic day of his father's sudden death, he is simultaneously exposed to the trauma of racism. Comforted by the black washerwoman who involves him in her work in an outhouse, he is immediately separated from her: his family sacks her for her inappropriate behaviour. Valerian memorializes the washerwoman in a shrine, a duplicate outhouse built on his Caribbean estate. His fetishization of the washerwoman is just as problematic as racist loathing – it is another form of racial othering. This is why it doesn't stop him from repeating in his later life, over and over, the racist incident of his youth. He interrupts, as inappropriate, the budding friendship between his white wife, Margaret, and their black cook, Ondine. He later sacks the washerwoman's contemporary equivalents, Gideon and Marie-Thérèse, when they steal some apples.

To return to *Playing* Morrison here argues that European Americans constructed an "Africanist" presence, a savage and subjugated "other", as the polar opposite against which they defined themselves as free, new and powerful. European Americans saw African Americans through the stereotype of this Africanism. Instead of concerning themselves with African Americans as unfamiliar human beings and setting out to know them, they used this stereotype to buttress their own identity and protect it from the contradiction at the heart of early American society: champion of freedom, yet defender of the institution of slavery. As a result American national identity has been constituted through the exclusion of African Americans. This is in effect Morrison's redefinition of American racism.

Morrison focuses on the effects of racism on the white American writer and white American literature. The contradiction at the heart of American society – espousing inalienable human rights but excluding African Americans from them – strains the white American writer's imagination. Recourse to a constructed Africanist presence gives the writer a shorthand and an escape into Africanist stereotypes, but the stress is still felt at the margins of texts bold enough to allow hidden contradictions to register.

At its most promising white American literature is "unsuccessful" in a deconstructive sense; in the sense that the unity of the text is interrupted by "slips" (58) and "disturbances" (84), disrupted by lapses, shattered and "slash[ed]" (45) by contradictions. It simultaneously "held, resisted, explored, or altered" racist notions (11). It was "complicit in the fabrication of racism" but also "exploded and undermined it" (16). It both participated in and resisted racist constructions. In such texts "Africanism often provides a subtext that either sabotages the surface text's expressed intentions or escapes them through a language that mystifies what it cannot bring itself to articulate but still attempts to register" (66).

At its least promising white American literature reproduces Africanist stereotypes. Whether the Africanist presence stands for "limitless love" or for "dread" (x), the "symbolic figurations" (ix) of blackness, the "metaphorical shortcuts", the "shorthand" (x) are "a language that can powerfully evoke and enforce hidden signs of racial superiority, cultural hegemony, and dismissive 'othering' of people" (x).

The writer's difficult task is to undo stereotypes and thereby to "free up the language" and make it new (xi). By defamiliarizing perception and language that has become "lazy" (xi), the writer will bring to light the unfamiliar and truly enter "what one is estranged from" (3–4). If this doesn't happen – if, for example, one relies on the routine shortcuts of American Africanism – the "foray" of the writer's imagination is "disable[d]" (4). Morrison concludes that the "ability of writers to imagine what is not the self, to familiarize the strange and mystify the familiar, is the test of their power" (15).

The classic modern statement on literature as "defamiliarization" is a text by the Russian Formalist critic Viktor Shklovsky, "Art as Technique", written in 1917, in the midst of the outbreak of the Russian Revolution. This was a fervently creative, experimental and innovative time for Russian artists, writers and critics. Shklovsky advocates literature as defamiliarization. We tend to take the world for granted but what we recognize as the world is only our own routinized and conventionalized perception of it. Art should aim to disrupt routine perception and language in order to make the familiar "unfamiliar" – in order, to use one of Morrison's key terms, to re-enchant the world.

Mikhail Bakhtin emerged out of Russian Formalism, and responded vigorously to the increasingly centralized and oppressive Russian policy on the arts that followed the Revolution. In "Discourse in the Novel" (1933–34) he defines the novelist's task as familiarizing the unfamiliar and marginalized voices of society (Bakhtin 1981). He sees both society and literature as swept, on the one hand, by dominant forces trying to impose their own perspective (Bakhtin calls them the forces of "monologism") and, on the other hand, a multiplicity of marginal voices – "heteroglossia" – and dialogism. The task of the novel is to intensify the forces of heteroglossia and dialogism.

In *Playing in the Dark* Morrison is alluding to Shklovsky and Bakhtin, without naming them. However, her main interlocutor is Edward Said, though he also remains unnamed. (Morrison very briefly refers to Said's *Orientalism* in "Unspeakable Things Unspoken", Morrison 1989a, 29.) In *Orientalism* (1978) Said describes the self-definition of Europeans through the construction of a polar opposite, "the Oriental". The discourse of Orientalism is "the nexus of knowledge and power creating 'the Oriental' [as an "essence" or a stereotype] and in a sense obliterating him as a human being" (Said 1978, 27). Morrison describes American Africanism as working in this manner; and Said's understanding of literature's complex positioning, simultaneously reproducing and resisting Orientalism, clearly resonates with Morrison's own understanding. Said calls this method of reading "contrapuntal" in his sequel to *Orientalism*, *Culture and Imperialism* (Said 1993). Said was delivering sections of *Culture and Imperialism* widely from 1985 (Said 1993, xxxi), and Morrison, herself an academic, is very likely to have been aware of his developing work. Said himself acknowledges Morrison as an interlocutor by opening Chapter One with an epigraph from *Playing in the Dark* (Said 1993, 1).

The decision not to name Said is perhaps related to Morrison's decision to focus on what is "uniquely American" (38). This decision lends her formidable cultural authority to studies of American Africanism, but implicitly withholds her involvement from studies comparing European and American forms of racial othering. By insisting on the "uniquely American" Morrison may risk reproducing the white American narrative of American exceptionalism. Her decision to focus exclusively on Africanism in white American literature also rules out an engagement with African American uses of Africanism, as Awkward (1994) argues (see **pp. 253–4**).

What Morrison does offer is a map for future research in the exploration of American Africanism in white American literature. This map includes topics such as the Africanist persona as "surrogate and enabler" (51) – as "the vehicle by which the American self knows itself as not enslaved, but free; not repulsive, but desirable; not helpless, but licensed and powerful; not history-less, but historical; not damned, but innocent; not a blind accident of evolution, but a progressive fulfillment of destiny" (52). Another suggested topic is "the manipulation of the Africanist narrative (that is, the story of a black person, the experience of being bound and/or rejected) as a means of meditation ... on one's own humanity" (53).

Morrison also offers a series of suggestive readings in American literature showing the flexibility and great variety of the negotiations between a deployment of Africanism and resistance to it – each literary text negotiating this tension in a singular manner. I will now discuss these readings.

Willa Cather's *Sapphira and the Slave Girl* is "trying to come to terms with ... the power and license of a white slave mistress over her female slaves" (18). However, Nancy, the unnamed slave girl of the title, is not only the victim of her mistress, Sapphira. She is also "the unconsulted, appropriated ground of Cather's inquiry into ... the reckless, unabated power of a white woman" (25): Cather uses her self-reflexively to think about white female identity. As the invalid Sapphira uses black bodies in an exercise of "power without risk, so the author employs them in behalf of her own desire for a *safe* participation in loss, in love, in chaos, in justice" (28).

The so-called "failures" of the text (and the text's exclusion both from the American and the Cather canon) are due to Cather's willingness to explore a repressed subject – "the interdependent working of power, race, and sexuality" (20) – as this willingness clashes with Cather's own Africanism, which imposes strict limits on her imagination. However, Morrison praises Cather for "undertak[ing] the dangerous journey" (28).

Morrison also turns to romance and Mark Twain's *Huckleberry Finn*. She argues that romance is the definitive American genre because, while white Americans were claiming their "newness", they were "haunted" (35) by "the terror of human freedom" (37). American romance used slaves as "surrogate selves for meditations on problems of human freedom" (37). Emerson's call for a new white man was met with a "fabricated" and "mythological American Africanism" (47) that used a "bound and unfree, rebellious but serviceable, black population" (45) against which to shape the components of the identity of the white American man: "autonomy, authority, newness and difference, absolute power" (44).

The relationship of Huck and Jim – whom "[n]either Huck nor Mark Twain can tolerate ... freed" (56) – shows the hidden "interdependence of slavery and freedom" (55). What makes Jim an exemplary Africanist presence, a white invention, is his "limitless ... love" for white people and his recognition of their superiority and his "inferiority (not as slave, but as black)" (56–57). On the other hand, Morrison discerns a "contestatory, combative critique" of antebellum America, "disguised ... by humor and naiveté" (54). She concludes that *Huckleberry Finn* both reproduces and makes visible the "parasitical nature of white freedom" (57).

Morrison then turns to Ernest Hemingway and argues that the difference between his earlier *To Have and Have Not* and his posthumous *Garden of Eden* points to a wider cultural "transformation" of American Africanism "from its simplistic ... purposes of establishing hierarchical differences to its surrogate", self-reflective or metaphorical role (63) – for example "to articulate and imaginatively act out the forbidden in American culture" (66). Morrison concludes that today "race has become metaphorical" (63). She repeats this argument in "Friday on the Potomac" (Morrison 1992d) and "Dead Man Golfing" (Morrison 1997b): questions of national importance are inscribed on the surrogate bodies of African Americans.

In her reading of *To Have and Have Not* Morrison points to the dehumanization of the character described as "the nigger" in the first part of the novel, and argues that humanizing this character would seriously undermine the positioning of the white character, Harry, as "knowing, virile, free, brave, and moral" (70). In Part Two, on the other hand, the black man is given a name, Wesley, and speech, but the "serviceability" of his speech is "transparent": "What he says and when he says it are plotted to win admiration for Harry" (74). Simultaneously, Morrison discerns "lapses" in this text (76), for example when Wesley criticizes Harry: these lapses radically reposition Harry as "a figure of antihuman negation and doom" (76).

In Hemingway's *Garden of Eden*, Morrison argues, blackness (because of its association with strangeness) is actively appropriated by the white Catherine for herself and David, in order to affirm a bond between them "unifying them within the estrangement" (87). Simultaneously, there is a tension between the outmoded Africanist story – of Africa "under white control" – that David is writing (89); and the new Africanist story of Catherine's self-blackening that Catherine performs and Hemingway writes.

"INTRODUCTION: FRIDAY ON THE POTOMAC" (1992)

Morrison's essay examines the Clarence Thomas and Anita Hill media controversy, as a point of access into the subtle forms that racism takes in 1990s America. Morrison summarizes the case herself: "a black male nominee to the Supreme Court was confirmed amid a controversy that raised and buried issues of profound social significance" (Morrison 1992d, x). Professor Anita Hill, an African American, initiated the controversy when she accused Thomas of sexual misconduct.

In an analysis that deploys the contemporary critique of binary oppositions, Morrison exposes the presence of a pervasive form of racism in the US government and mass media. Black people are deindividualized, their bodies (as with women) become legitimate objects of voyeurism and they are classified into two interchangeable stereotypes: either they stand for love and "servile guardianship" (xv); or they stand for madness and anarchic sexuality. In this case, the media, politicians and Thomas himself focused on Thomas's body – for example, his weightlifting and his laugh – the latter as a "clearly understood metonym for racial accommodation" (xiii). The confirmation hearings cast Thomas as the loyal servant (servile guardian); the Senate Judiciary Committee and the press saw Anita Hill as mad and anarchic. Those who disagreed merely reversed the roles.

Pointing out that a white candidature would hardly have been allowed to go ahead under the circumstances, Morrison argues that once again issues of critical national importance were played out "on the bodies of black people" (xi). One of the issues raised and buried by the controversy was that of "racial justice and racial redress" (xix): was Clarence Thomas – "bleached, race-free, as his speeches and opinions illustrated" (xviii) – the right black candidate for the Supreme Court of a racist country?

To address this question Morrison has recourse to the story of Friday in Defoe's *Robinson Crusoe*. Crusoe rescues him and indebts him but makes demands without limit upon him, without ever showing awareness of the fact. Friday recognizes Crusoe as his master, gives up his name, his language, those who loved him as well as those who threatened his life within his own culture, and fully internalizes Crusoe. Morrison makes the comparison with Thomas: both men "are condemned first to mimic, then to internalize and adore, but never to utter a single sentence understood to be beneficial to their original culture, whether the people of their culture are those who wanted to hurt them or those who loved them to death" (xxix). She calls upon us to "appraise and benefit from Friday's dilemma" (xxx). She stresses that what is required is not a definitive answer but, on the contrary, "multiple points of address and analysis" (xii).

THE NOBEL LECTURE IN LITERATURE, 1993

Morrison retells an African American variation of a story found in many cultures – and in the process explores and reworks it for her own purposes. A blind old African American woman, "daughter of slaves" and living "alone in a small house outside of town", is renowned for her wisdom (Morrison 1993a, 198). A group of city children visit her and one of them asks: "Is the bird I am holding living or dead?" (199). The woman answers: "what I do know is that it is in your hands" (199).

Morrison acknowledges the openness of the story, lending itself to ever-new interpretations, and then interprets it in her own way. The bird is language and the blind old woman is the "practiced writer" (199), suspicious of her visitors and worried about the death of language. Language is dead when it is "[u]nreceptive to interrogation" or when it "cannot form or tolerate new ideas, shape other thoughts, tell another story" (200). It dies in the hands of those − politicians, journalists, scientists, scholars, etc. − who make language "unyielding ... censored and censoring ... policing" (200), in the service of dominance and obfuscation. They are "accountable for its demise" (200). Such "lethal discourses of exclusion blocking access to cognition" (202) must be "rejected, altered and exposed" in all their many guises (201). Morrison comments that "[t]he conventional wisdom of the Tower of Babel story is that ... it was ... the weight of many languages that precipitated failed architecture. That one monolithic language would have expedited the building, and heaven would have been reached" (202); she argues that the opposite is the case. (See my brief discussion of this passage in the section on *Paradise*, the novel Morrison was writing in 1993, the time of this address.) Morrison's underlying Bakhtinian position here is that a living language and genuine thinking are exploratory, provisional, multiperspectival and dialogical − and that the writer must be committed to those values.

Morrison concludes that, instead of setting out to "'pin down' slavery, genocide, war", language should "reach toward the ineffable" (203). It would be fruitful to compare Morrison's aesthetics of the ineffable to Jean-François Lyotard's aesthetics of the sublime. In "Answering the Question: What is Postmodernism?" (Lyotard 1982), Lyotard, French-Jewish poststructuralist philosopher and one of the protagonists of the postmodernism debate, links postmodern aesthetics with the acute problems of presentation posed by overwhelming events such as the Holocaust. He asks: how can writers and artists present an event such as the Holocaust in such a way that its terror is not reduced and domesticated, and in such a way as to make its repetition less likely? Lyotard's answer to this question is a postmodern aesthetics of the sublime: an art of allusion presenting the unpresentable in its unpresentability. The alternative, an art that claims clear adequation between itself and its object, is a totalitarian "fantasy to seize reality" (82). To avoid a repetition of totalitarian terror, the task of the postmodern writer is "to invent *allusions* to the conceivable which *cannot* be represented ... [L]et us be witnesses to the unpresentable" (Lyotard 1982, 81–82, my italics).

Morrison then turns her attention to the old woman's visitors: "Who are they, these children?" (203). Shifting perspective she reinterprets: "Suppose nothing was in their hands" and their visit and their question were in the hope of interrupting "the adult world, its miasma of discourse about them, for them, but never to them?" (204). Perhaps their question to the woman meant: "Could someone tell us what is life? What is death?" (204). Morrison then gives direct speech to the children. We hear nothing but their voice, Morrison dropping "they said" until the penultimate paragraph. The children respond to the woman by questioning her distanced answer, asking many questions, and urging her to tell them a story: "Is there no context for our lives? No song, no literature, no poem full of vitamins, no history connected to experience that you can pass along to help us start strong?" (205). Their calls – "Tell us" ... "tell us" (206) – self-reflexive, they burst into the narrative they long to hear: a wagonload of slaves transported in harsh winter stops outside an inn. A little girl steps into the wagon, gives them food and "something more": "a glance into the eyes of the one she serves ... They look back. The next stop will be their last. But not this one. This one is warmed" (207).

The structure of this story's telling is reminiscent of the beginning of *The Iliad* – a collectively authored oral epic – where the narrator calls upon the Muse, the "Immortal one" (1), to sing her song of Achilles' memorable deed, as a way of kick-starting the narrative. Here the city children appeal to the blind old woman as a way of emerging as new storytellers. The memorable deed they describe is the look of human recognition shared between the little girl and the slaves.

The blind old woman listens to the children's story and responds: "I trust you with the bird that is not in your hands because you have truly caught it" (207). The call-and-response language of looks their story describes and their very act of storytelling capture the dialogic nature of a living language.

Morrison's interpretation of an African American variation of an open-ended cross-cultural story is itself open-ended. My own interpretation is that the blind old African American woman can be read as the literary tradition and the city children as Morrison's generation of black women writers, including Morrison herself as one of those children. Morrison's text can be fruitfully situated in relation to canonical texts on the relation of the writer to the literary tradition. These texts would include: T.S. Eliot's "Tradition and the Individual Talent"; Harold Bloom's reworking of Eliot in *The Anxiety of Influence*; and Sandra M. Gilbert and Susan Gubar's feminist critique of Bloom in *The Madwoman in the Attic*. What is new in Morrison's text is the figuration of the literary tradition – figured as white and male in the previous texts – as an African American woman; and the emphasis on the collective nature of literary innovation, in Morrison's figuration of the new writer as a group of children.

"THE OFFICIAL STORY: DEAD MAN GOLFING" (1997)

Extending her analysis of contemporary forms of racism in "Friday on the Potomac" (Morrison 1992d), in this essay Morrison seeks to expose the racism underlying the "official" story of O.J. Simpson's guilt; and to highlight the silencing of alternative stories, in keeping with her multiperspectivist ethos.

As Morrison had explained in "Friday on the Potomac", one form that contemporary racism takes is that black people are deindividualized and made to fit the stereotypes of either faithful dog or wild and dangerous animal. Morrison here turns to Melville's "Benito Cereno" (1855) to show this process at work. In this story the white captain initially assumes that the Senegalese man is a faithful dog; but the Senegalese man is "in rebellion" and the captain then flips to the alternative view of the man as a wild and dangerous animal "snakishly writhing" (Melville quoted Morrison 1997b, x).

The official O.J. Simpson story, as the white captain's narrative in Melville, outlines a racist view: "We thought he loved us" (vii) but he is a "wild dog" (viii), *both* cunningly calculating *and* (impossibly) a "mindless, spontaneous killer" (ix). The contradiction goes unnoticed because black people have been used as the very sign or symbol of contradiction and incoherence. For example, according to the 11th edition of the *Encyclopedia Britannica* (1911), "the negro" is characterized both by "dog-like fidelity" and "acts of singular atrocity" (*Encyclopedia* quoted Morrison 1997b, xi). The racist assumption of black incoherence has meant "the absence of a rational analysis of behavior" (xii) in the official Simpson narrative.

An official narrative was constructed quickly, "so powerfully insistent on guilt, so uninterested in any other scenario, it began to look like a media pogrom, a lynching with its iconography intact" (xiii). And yet, the official story saw itself as race-free, accusing African Americans who didn't assume Simpson's guilt of "ethnic bias" and whites of "liberal paralysis" (xix). Morrison points to the official story's exclusion of Simpson's African American family and the branding as "conspiracy" paranoia of any suggestion of police tampering with evidence – even though two major cases of police malpractice were being investigated at the time (xxii). She detects in the official story a "longing for a living black man repeating forever a narrative of black insufficiency" (xxvi).

Morrison compares the official narrative to the white supremacist film *The Birth of a Nation* (1915): the official narrative is "a newer, more sophisticated national narrative of racial supremacy" (xxvii). She argues that Melville's story works very differently. Deploying the literary theoretical framework she developed in *Playing in the Dark*, she reads Melville's "Benito Careno" as ultimately enabling. While it is not an anti-racist text, it is a dialogical text fighting against its own racism: it *both* "tells the story of an innocent white captain while simultaneously critiquing the racist foundations of that innocence" (x).

THE DANCING MIND (1997)

In this speech Morrison argues that the sort of writing she wants to do cannot be thought without its partner, reading. She uses the metaphor of two people dancing together to illustrate the proximity and interdependence of writer and reader. However, the two partners cannot come together and the dancing cannot take place, unless reader and writer each claim their freedom. Reading, in its finest state, is "the dance of an open mind when it engages another equally open one" (Morrison 1997a, 7), but the reader needs to claim this. Morrison offers an anecdote to illustrate the act of claiming the reader's freedom. A male PhD student at a prestigious university, who has spent his life training his academic mind, like an athlete his body, fully supported by loving parents, finally interrupted the peculiar "terror" (13) of his privileged background and education and "taught himself, forced himself to be alone with a book he was not assigned to read" (10). Morrison now turns to the writer's freedom and reminds her audience that unpoliced writing – offering "the fruits of [one's] own imaginative intelligence" (15), without the "encroachment of private wealth, government control, or cultural expediency" (16–17) – has often required the writer's willingness to put himself or herself at risk. Morrison offers a second anecdote to illustrate the risks involved in claiming the writer's freedom: a female writer who leaves Morrison "awestruck by her articulateness" and erudition appeals to Morrison to help the women writers of her country, "sh[ot] down in the streets" by the state for writing in an "unpoliced" manner (12).

3

Criticism

The Bluest Eye

Michael Awkward's influential "'The Evil of Fulfillment'" (1989) argues that *The Bluest Eye* situates itself within the African American written literary tradition. Morrison opens her novel with the Dick and Jane primer in order to engage with the customary introductions by white writers appended to eighteenth- and nineteenth-century slave narratives and other black literary texts. She uses the primer in order to reject traditional white authorizations and authentications of the black voice; and to demonstrate "her refusal to allow white standards to arbitrate the success or failure of the Afro-American experience" (180). Morrison critiques "the bourgeois myths of ideal family life ... as wholly inapplicable to Afro-American life" (179).

A Bluest Eye offers a substantial engagement with Du Bois's concept of "double consciousness". Du Bois defined "double consciousness" in *The Souls of Black Folk* (1903): "One ever feels his twoness – an American, a Negro; two souls, two thoughts, two unreconciled strivings; two warring ideals in one dark body, whose dogged strength alone keeps it from being torn asunder" (Du Bois 1903, 11). Pecola's schizophrenia is Morrison's figuration of "double consciousness" as a "debilitating state" (176). The final merging of the voice of the extradiegetic narrator and the voice of adult Claudia is the desirable resolution of "double consciousness". When the two voices merge, Claudia achieves an "informed black perspective" (183). The overcoming of "double consciousness" occurs "as a direct function of Pecola's own schizophrenia" (207). However, most characters use the "survival technique" (189) of splitting themselves into a good "white" self that they own and a bad "black" self that they disown and project onto Pecola: "the improved self-image of the community ... results from its sacrifice and projection of the shadow of blackness onto Pecola" (207).

Awkward also situates *The Bluest Eye* in relation to Zora Neale-Hurston's *Their Eyes Were Watching God*; Richard Wright's *Native Son*; Ralph Ellison's *Invisible Man* and "The World and the Jug"; and James Baldwin's "Many Thousands Gone". Awkward's argument, that Cholly's rape of Pecola is Morrison's revision of Jim Trueblood's incest with his daughter in Ellison's *Invisible Man*, has been influential. Unlike Ellison who treats the effects on the daughter as insignificant, Morrison "details Pecola's tragic and painful journey" (201).

Trudier Harris, in *Fiction and Folklore* (1991), situates *The Bluest Eye* in relation to folktales. The novel is "an inversion" (11) of the structure of folktales, as outlined in Vladimir Propp's classic Formalist account, *Morphology of the Folktale*. According to Propp, some folktales involve a questing hero ("seeker") whose quest encounters obstacles but is eventually successful; others involve a "victimized" hero who is eventually rescued (Propp 1968, 36). In spite of the variety of *dramatis personae* and "functions" (actions or plot lines), folktales "of the most dissimilar peoples" involve trials but end happily for the hero (Propp 1968, 64). In *The Bluest Eye*, however, "the ugly duckling does not become the beautiful swan" (11). Pecola is on a "modern quest for a holy grail" (42–43) – a quest for beauty – but her quest fails. This is Morrison's response to the excessive optimism of the 1960s "Black is beautiful" rhetoric.

In relation to Western folklore, the infertility of the land in the novel can be read against the Arthurian legend of the Fisher King, keeper of the Holy Grail, whose roots lie in pagan Celtic mythology. When he is wounded and rendered impotent, the entire kingdom becomes a wasteland. In some versions he is eventually healed by a knight. T.S. Eliot refers to the Fisher King in *The Waste Land* (Eliot 2003), another intertext for the novel.

In relation to African folklore, adult Claudia is a *griot*, a West African storyteller, whose storytelling performances are important communal events. In relation to African American oral traditions, Claudia's telling of Pecola's tragedy is "in the tradition of blues narrative" (26) and "holds out the possibility for the exorcising function of the blues" (27).

John N. Duvall, in *The Identifying Fictions of Toni Morrison* (2000), argues that the intertextual communication between Ellison's *Invisible Man* and *The Bluest Eye* is more extensive than Awkward acknowledged. Ellison's protagonist and Pecola are both invisible, in the sense that people see not them but a stereotype. Soaphead's letter to God is Morrison's letter to Ellison, claiming a place in the African American tradition for giving a voice to little girls silenced by Ellison's masculinist bias: "The Purpose of this letter is to familiarize you with facts which either have escaped your notice, or which you have chosen to ignore" (*Bluest Eye* 176).

Elihue Micah Whitcomb/Soaphead, who enters "authorship" through the letter, is a self-reflexive artist figure, as is Claudia: both figures are self-critical (28). Soaphead, in his isolation and perversion, points to the isolation of the writer and the writer's "implication in what she critiques" (43). The letter to God, therefore, "encodes Morrison's ambitions and anxieties regarding her authorial identity" (28).

Duvall, who discovered that Morrison's middle name was not Anthony (hence Toni) but Ardelia, argues that Soaphead's confession that he invented his middle name, Micah, points to Morrison's own invention of the middle name Anthony for herself. He speculates that Morrison chose the name Toni for its "connotations of elegance and newness" (38) and rejected her first name, Chloe, for its connotations of "servility in the agrarian South" (38) – in *Uncle Tom's Cabin*, Uncle Tom's wife was called Chloe, for example. Duvall claims that, while fashioning herself as urban and new, in *The Bluest Eye* Morrison paradoxically identifies small Southern agrarian communities (such as Aunt Jimmy's community) as sites of authentic blackness; another site of authentic blackness is the home of the whores around whom Morrison builds a cult of true black womanhood, while demonizing middle-class African Americans.

Linden Peach, in *Toni Morrison* (2000), situates the novel at the intersection of several discourses. First, resonating with Roland Barthes and Louis Althusser, Morrison's use of the Dick and Jane primer shows that language is "enmeshed with power structures … [I]deology is … embodied in language and in social institutions" such as the family (34–35). The particular ideology exposed by Morrison in the primer is the dominant discourse of the white middle-class nuclear family. The novel contrasts "the isolation of the white, nuclear family with the community of the South – evidenced in the attention Aunt Jimmy receives from her neighbours during her illness" (43). Morrison, secondly, questions a black nationalist discourse that assumes the homogeneity of black experience, silencing black women in the process. Adult Claudia turns her thoughts to her mother and places herself in a female line (6–7). Thirdly, Morrison engages with the racist stereotype of the black Jezebel, though she runs the risk of "confirming" it (40). The novel stages an "ironic interplay" (47) of different discourses. As adult Claudia increasingly takes over as narrator, the marginal or ex-centric moves centre stage.

FEMINIST READINGS

The pioneering **Barbara Christian**, in *Black Feminist Criticism* (1985), views Pecola as a tragic hero or existentialist rebel, comparing her to the overtly rebellious Sula: "[Pecola and Sula] are women who become scapegoats in their communities because they look at the truth of things ... , becoming the dumping ground for those feelings of help-lessness and horror people have about their own lives" (26). They will not or cannot take their proper place in the order of things – they will not "learn how to do the white man's work with refinement" (*The Bluest Eye*, 64). The Lorain African American community in *The Bluest Eye*, on the other hand, is too assimilated and lacks its own standards. Morrison critiques the oppressive unnaturalness of the equation of beauty with virtue and of love with romance.

Madonne M. Miner, in "Lady no Longer Sings the Blues" (1985), argues that *The Bluest Eye* is structured by the classical myths of Persephone and Philomela and the "sequence of rape, madness, and silence" (85) underlying both. According to the myth of Persephone, Pluto, god of the underworld, abducts Persephone and takes her underground, where she loses sight of the surface of the earth and of her mother, Demeter, goddess of agriculture. Demeter imposes a similar sensory deprivation on humans by making the earth infertile. In the Homeric "Hymn to Demeter", quoted by Miner, "the earth didn't yield a single seed" (91), as the marigolds do not grow in *The Bluest Eye*. The myth of Philomela makes the rape explicit and stres-ses, not the rape victim's deprivation of her sight by the rapist, but the deprivation of speech: Tereus cuts off Philomela's tongue. In both cases, the rapist imposes his subjectivity and denies the subjectivity of his victim.

Pecola suffers violation, not only in the hands of her father, but also in the hands of Mr Yakobowski, Junior, Bay Boy and friends, and Soaphead. They assert themselves at Pecola's expense and, as their worlds expand, Pecola's world shrinks. What we find is a distribution of "presence/absence, language/silence, reason/madness along sexual [gender] lines" (90). The men affirm their vision, impose it on Pecola, and deny her vision, with the collaboration of women such as Pauline, who "projects a white male vision" (95) on Pecola and finds her ugly. Pecola is ultimately "incapable of defending herself against visual distortion" (95). However, while Pecola disintegrates, adult Claudia and Morrison herself speak and affirm their vision: "although the novel documents the sacrifice of one black woman, it attests to the survival of two others" (98).

Karla F.C. Holloway and **Stephanie A. Demetrakopoulos**, in *New Dimensions of Spirituality* (1987), see their work on Morrison as an experiment in "feminist, biracial scholarship" (6): Holloway within an African and African American context; Demetrakopoulos within a Western context. Holloway reads *The Bluest Eye* in relation to the African concept of *nommo*: naming or the power of the word to bring things into existence. Holloway interprets Mrs MacTeer's blues singing and soliloquies as finding a voice in the midst of African American voicelessness.

Karen Carmean, in *Toni Morrison's World of Fiction* (1993), distinguishes between the assimilated Maureen and Geraldine, on the one hand; and the more authentic voices of the blues-inspired Claudia and Mrs MacTeer, on the other hand. The former have internalized the racist and sexist stereotype of the oversexed black woman and, hence, associate Pecola's blackness with licentious sexuality (*Bluest Eye*, 55–56 and 72).

Andrea O'Reilly, in *Toni Morrison and Motherhood* (2004), focuses on the contrast between Pauline Breedlove and Mrs MacTeer. Through Pauline, Morrison studies the destructive consequences of the absence of black mothering in the traditional mould. Pauline internalizes a white model of marriage (the patriarchal nuclear family) and a white model of femininity predicated on female beauty. Her disconnection from the black "motherline" makes her unable to mother Pecola (58). Pecola's obsessive milk-drinking from the Shirley Temple cup shows, not her adoration of Shirley Temple, but her "longing to be mothered" (56). Pauline, ironically, succumbs to the ideology of female beauty partially because of her very "artistic sensibilities" – her "soul of a poet and ... eye of an artist" (50); partially, she is disconnected from the motherline because of her migration to the urban North. Traditionally kitchens are safe havens in African American life. Morrison heightens the irony and highlights the disconnection from tradition by staging Pauline's expulsion of her daughter in the Fishers' kitchen and Cholly's rape of Pecola in the Breedloves' kitchen.

O'Reilly argues that critics have failed to appreciate the value of Mrs MacTeer's mothering because of their unthinking adoption of the middle-class "sensitive mothering" model, where all work becomes play between mother and child (31). This model presupposes affluence and should not be used to label as bad mothers those who have to struggle to keep their children alive. Morrison "foregrounds the importance of preservation", and Mrs MacTeer is exemplary of "preservative love" (32).

PSYCHOANALYTIC READINGS

Ed Guerrero, in "Tracking 'The Look' in the Novels of Toni Morrison" (1990), takes the work of psychoanalytic feminists on "the look" as his starting point: women are turned into objects to be consumed by the dominant male gaze. (See, for example, Laura Mulvey's "Visual Pleasure and Narrative Cinema".) Morrison explores a more complex understanding of "the look": society's dominant gaze is racist and classist as well as sexist. For example, when Pauline goes to the cinema, "[w]hile many white feminist critics argue that women suffer negation of self by having to identify with a sexual object displayed for the pleasure of the male gaze at the screen, Pauline ... must suffer this negation in a compounded sense ... She is ... forced to look at and apply to herself a completely unrealizable, alien standard of feminine beauty" (30). Morrison shows that not only women but African American men as well are turned into objects by the dominant gaze. Adolescent Cholly's first sexual encounter is interrupted "by two racist white men who force him to copulate in the glare of their flashlights and their voyeuristic, sadistic gazes" (31).

Jill Matus, in *Toni Morrison* (1998), offers a psychoanalytic interpretation of racism as historical "trauma". Pecola, Claudia and Frieda are exposed to the trauma of racism and react to it very differently. Pecola's reaction is shame, which internalizes the world's devaluation of her and leaves her defenceless. Claudia's and Frieda's reaction is anger, which allows them to resist their devaluation. However, nine-year-old Claudia's anger later turns to "fraudulent love" (16) and other forms of accommodation, as adult Claudia acknowledges. Also, while young Claudia gets angry with Pecola and Maureen Peel, adult Claudia acknowledges the question of appropriate anger, anger that is not misdirected at the weak: "all the time we knew that Maureen Peel was not the Enemy. The *Thing* to fear was the *Thing* that made *her* beautiful" (see *Bluest Eye*, 57–58; original emphasis).

Morrison's description of Pecola's rape, a personal trauma, is in keeping with the reactions of real-life trauma victims. Pecola's silence during the rape is a traumatic "collapse of witnessing" (50). This failure to own and acknowledge what is happening to her continues in Pecola's dialogue with her imaginary friend, which is "in no way ... a therapeutic dialogue" (48). Adult Claudia, on the other hand, witnesses the traumas of racism and rape and draws the reader in as co-witness and "co-owner of the trauma" (48).

J. Brooks Bouson, in *Quiet as It's Kept* (2000), argues that, through Cholly's rape of Pecola, Morrison "invokes" (29) and "repeats" (36) the racist stereotype of the "bad nigger" – the black underclass as pathological, degenerate and dangerous, as rehashed by the notorious 1965 Moynihan Report. Morrison undermines the stereotype by showing that Cholly and Pauline are deeply shamed by the white world and transfer their shame – their self-perceived "ugliness" – to Pecola. Cholly, Pauline and especially Pecola are also intra-racially shamed: other African Americans displace their own racial shame onto the dark-skinned and poor Breedloves.

Cholly, Pauline, Claudia and Morrison herself adopt a variety of anti-shame tactics: Pauline becomes an exemplary servant and aggressively

Christian; Cholly develops an "oppositionally defined and shameless identity" (35); young Claudia cultivates a "reactive rage" (30) against Maureen Peel and others. Morrison herself – in presenting the rape from Cholly's point of view, in inviting sympathy for Cholly, and in "silenc[ing] and background[ing] Pecola" – "partly denies the horrors she sets out to describe" (28) and "counteract[s] and aestheticize[s] the raw shame and pain" (28, 45). But she also "risks shaming her readers" (41) by positioning them as voyeurs in a scene presented from the point of view of the violator rather than the humiliated victim. As a result, critics are drawn into a drama of shame/blame attribution – some blaming Cholly, others the African American community or white society, others even Pecola.

Lucille P. Fultz, in *Playing with Difference* (2003), substantially extends Guerrero's argument (discussed above). Aunt Jimmy and her friends as well as Pauline and Pecola are "perceived solely as victims", but "attempt to subvert the objectifying gaze" of the world (46) by affirming their subjectivity and their own perspective on the world. See the "recitative of pain" (109) on Aunt Jimmy's deathbed; and Pauline's first-person narrative of "lost pleasures" (55). Fultz argues that Pecola's "single-handed attempts to change other people's perceptions of her" are often overlooked (55). Pecola's conversation with her imaginary friend is a "dialogue with herself" and a "counternarrative" (59) subverting other people's representations of her.

SELECTED OTHER CRITICISM

An existentialist reading

Terry Otten, in *The Crime of Innocence in the Fiction of Toni Morrison* (1989), argues that Soaphead becomes a paedophile to hold on to his "innocence" (*Bluest Eye*, 132), while adult Claudia incriminates herself in relation to Pecola. (See **p. 191.**) Pauline falls when she moves to Lorain but denies her knowledge and clings to her innocence and the Fishers' paradise. Cholly falls from innocence during his first sexual encounter, watched by the two white men. He then becomes dangerously free "beyond good and evil" (18).

Otten is dissatisfied with Morrison's handling of Pecola. Pecola's fall from the garden of Eden is protracted: she walks down "Garden Avenue" (35) and is existentially negated by Yacobowski; she enters Geraldine's garden and is expelled so that Geraldine can hold on to her innocence; she is raped. However, as the fall (autumn) brings "death, not harvest" (10), Pecola's fall brings no knowledge: her "violent passage from innocence to experience results in the perpetual innocence of insanity" (9). As a result, Pecola's story is "melodrama ... not high tragedy" (16). Otten takes for granted – perhaps wrongly – that Morrison portrays Pecola as "victim ... [u]nable to commit a saving sin" (23) and that Pecola's insanity is the opposite of knowledge.

A reading developing the work of Kathryn Hume

Denise Heinze, in *The Dilemma of "Double-Consciousness"* (1993), uses Kathryn Hume's distinction – in *Fantasy and Mimesis* (1984) – between a "literature of disillusionment" where reality is unknowable; and a more didactic "literature of revision". The itineraries of Cholly, Pecola and Soaphead belong to a "literature of disillusionment": all three characters "resort to ... fantasies in which they depart from consensus reality" (153). Cholly is insane in that he is "alone with his own perceptions" (126). Pecola, faced with the equation of white beauty and goodness, "[c]hooses goodness" and with "remarkable strength of character goes insane to convince herself of her ... worth" (156). Soaphead views himself as "an inevitable participant in an evil system": God's (157). As these characters become insane, the "world becomes unknowable" (153) for the reader. The reader, self-reflexively, "is faced with ambivalence, uncertainty, conflict, and guilt" (157).

A Bakhtinian reading

Philip Page, in *Dangerous Freedom* (1995), argues that *The Bluest Eye* thematizes fusion and fragmentation, finds them both inadequate and moves beyond both. This is an implicit critique of Awkward's discussion of "double consciousness", perhaps also a critique of Du Bois (see discussion of Awkward above): the solution to splitting and "double consciousness" is not to merge into one.

Many objects are split open in the novel: the Breedloves' split-open sofa; Pauline's tooth, pulled out of her mouth and impairing "her power of *nommo* [naming things]" (42); the burning-hot berry pie that falls and bursts out on the floor. The central example is Pecola's rape. Sometimes this is actively pursued – as, for example, with young Claudia's dismemberment of blonde, blue-eyed dolls to discover the secret of their overvaluation. Such instances of fragmentation can have positive/pleasurable or negative/painful effects or both. Instances of fusion are three groups of women – the three whores; Mrs MacTeer gossiping with her friends; Aunt Jimmy and her friends – and the third, joined-up version of the Dick and Jane primer.

Page offers a Bakhtinian reading of *The Bluest Eye*. (See p. 183.) The novel moves beyond both fragmentation and fusion in that it assembles many voices and perspectives (it is dialogic, to use

Bakhtin's term): the primer, Pauline, adult Claudia. Adult Claudia herself both assumes responsibility and "blames 'the earth, the land ... the entire country'" (*Bluest Eye*, 160); she cannot be pinned down and remains internally dialogic. The novel moves "toward recognition of the necessity for a pluralistic perspective" (55). "[R]e-solution" – in the sense of a unification or fusion of perspectives – "in a divided culture ... is a false hope" (58).

A postcolonial reading

Gurleen Grewal, in *Circles of Sorrow, Lines of Struggle* (1998), reads *The Bluest Eye* as a study of *domestic* or *internal* colonialism: African Americans are colonized by white middle-class America and "internalize a dominant culture's values" (21). The novel links the colonial (West Indian) educated middle-class Soaphead and the American middle-class Geraldine, showing them both to be uncritically and passively mimicking white hegemonic norms. The use of the Dick and Jane primer in three versions foregrounds the idea of mimicry. The distinction between the second and third versions is one between middle-class/second-world black mimicry of white middle-class norms (Soaphead, Geraldine)and a grossly unlivable working-class/rural/third-world black mimicry (Pauline, Cholly, Pecola). The reader is "meant to see the debilitating effect of priming" and "miseducation" (25) on Pecola and others. In this sense, the novel is an "anti-*Bildungsroman*" (23).

The novel makes "an impassioned case for decolonizing the mind" (21), through Claudia – "the portrait of the black woman artist as a young girl" (22) – who "struggles to claim ownership of her freed self" (20). Young Claudia and the three whores escape normalization. The three whores – especially Miss Marie – exemplify Bakhtinian "grotesque" realism or the "carnivalesque" (Bakhtin's terms): they represent the spontaneous transgressive/anti-authoritarian potential of the underprivileged (39–40). Adult Claudia, on the other hand, is an example of resistance as "nothing less than a transformation in con-sciousness" (36). This is why the chapters narrated by her are free of the coercive Dick and Jane epigraphs. Claudia articulates and advocates "the interests and desires" of the uneducated rural and working-class black people (40–41).

The novel is complex in its intervention. First, it responds to and corrects Ralph Ellison and Richard Wright with a feminist sensibility and a critique of the educated black middle class. Secondly, it compli-cates the exclusive concern of white feminists such as Luce Irigaray with sexual difference by addressing other forms of difference. Thirdly, written and published in the heyday of the Black Power movement, and its slogan "Black is beautiful", it goes beyond the logic of simple counter-assertion and "lays its own claim to represent the subaltern" (34).

Sula

There have been two major themes in criticism on *Sula*:

- *Sula* as a critique of both white feminism and black nationalism in order to open a new space for black women writers.
- *Sula* as a critique of the binary oppositions of self/other and good/evil in order to explore a multiple, fluid and changing black female self.

FEMINIST READINGS

Sula was published as the postwar Women's Movement gathered momentum. It is instrumental in the emergence of a new category, that of the "black woman writer", and calls for a space that didn't yet exist – that of black feminism. This is the view of many critics writing on *Sula*. Feminist readings have been the most prevalent approach to this novel.

Barbara Smith's "Toward a Black Feminist Criticism" (1977) has been greeted by critics as an inaugural document for both black feminist literary criticism and for lesbian literary criticism. Smith proposes directions and principles for black feminist criticism. First, whereas Marxism prioritized class, black nationalism prioritized race, and white feminism prioritized gender, black feminist criticism will posit the inter-implication of race, class, gender and sexuality: "the politics of sex as well as the politics of race and class are crucially interlocking factors in the works of Black women writers" (2304). Secondly, Smith calls for the "assumption that Black women writers constitute an identifiable literary tradition" (2307). The critic will situate texts within this tradition and "not try to graft the ideas and methodology of white/male literary thought" upon black women's art (2308). Instead of situating Morrison in relation to William Faulkner or Virginia Woolf or Ralph Ellison, the black feminist critic will situate Morrison in relation to black women writers such as Zora Neale Hurston. This might prove restrictive if applied too rigorously and dogmatically. However, it is intended as a political intervention correcting the lack of attention towards, and devaluation of, black women writers; helping to construct a new canon of African American women writers, and paying attention to the previously unexplored resonances among them due to the commonality of their experience.

Smith argues that *Sula* "works as a lesbian novel not only because of the passionate friendship between Sula and Nel but because of Morrison's consistently critical stance toward the heterosexual institutions of male–female relationships, marriage, and the family" (2308). As this oft-quoted statement already suggests, Smith desexualizes, politicizes and expands the term "lesbian" to include: "bonding ... between Black women for the sake of barest survival" (2310); bonding between heterosexual women which doesn't call itself feminist; heterosexual feminists who are consciously "woman-identified" and who consciously critique patriarchy; and lesbian (by sexual orientation) women who argue that heterosexuality is a social institution that perpetuates the inequality and oppression of women. Smith's redefinition of "lesbian" has been influential. Adrienne Rich, in her well-known essay, "Compulsory Heterosexuality and Lesbian Existence" (1980), renames women's bonds and identification with other women the "lesbian continuum".

In interviews Morrison has explicitly denied a sexual attraction between Sula and Nel, stressing instead their heterosexuality. Smith acknowledges this and suggests that Morrison, as a black woman, is especially reluctant to abandon her "heterosexist assumptions": "Heterosexual privilege is usually the only privilege that Black women have" (2313).

Hortense J. Spillers, in "A Hateful Passion, a Lost Love" (1983), follows Smith and situates the character of Sula in relation to Janie Starks in Zora Neale Hurston's *Their Eyes Were Watching God* (1937) and Vyry Ware in Margaret Walker's *Jubilee* (1966). However, rather than looking for resonances and commonalities, Spillers' model is a Hegelian dialectical one: Vyry is the thesis; Sula is her antithesis; Janie is the contradiction between them (with no Hegelian synthesis in view). Vyry exists "for the race" (211) and is the virtuous victim of a powerful white world, leaving no space for "ambiguity or irony or uncertainty" or "individualism" (220). Sula on the other hand is "woman-for-self" (211) and a figure of "moral ambiguity" (212). She is not situated in relation to a powerful white world but, on the contrary, "circumscribed by the lack of an explicit tradition of imagination or aesthetic work" (212–13). Her relations to Eva, Hannah and Nel are far removed from a utopian feminist "simple, transparent love" between black women; Nel as well as the female reader react to Sula with "emotional ambivalence" (226). Janie is an unresolved contradiction, an "entanglement of conflicting desires" (222): on the one hand, she is submissive and her desires are "male-centered"; on the other hand, she is "independent in her own imagination" and ready "to make her own choices" (221).

The three characters are *not* mutually exclusive, but *"angles onto* a larger seeing" (232). This is also how Spillers understands the relation between Sula and Nel – and she readily agrees with Morrison's statement that Sula and Nel are parts of the same self. For Spillers too Sula is "not the 'other'" but one of the many facets of the black female self (Morrison 1976a, 232).

Barbara Christian, in *Black Feminist Criticism* (1985), reads *Sula* as a feminist critique of the Bottom. The Bottom has uncritically adopted the world's oppression of women and its restrictive "definition of woman, her span and space" (53). The people of the Bottom conform to the wider societal norm that "the bearing of children or the relationship to males be central in a woman's life" (54). They view Nel's role of handmaiden to Jude as good, Sula's resistance to such a role as evil. Such views harm the Bottom, as the Bottom "expends its energy" on hating Sula instead of focusing on "the evils of racism and poverty" (50). Sula could have benefited the Bottom with her ability to "look at the truth of things" (26), her "insistence on knowing oneself, the urge to experiment and thus move forward" (54). However, Sula has "no concern for" community (78). Between the Bottom and Sula there is a shared failure to connect, nourish and be nourished. As a result Sula dies from "boredom and spiritual malnutrition" (27).

Houston A. Baker, Jr., in "When Lindberg Sleeps with Bessie Smith" (1989), attempts to develop an innovative perspective that is at once feminist and black male; the results are both stimulating and disturbing. Baker focuses on Ajax's relationships to Sula – especially the sex scene between them – and to his female ancestor, his "conjure-woman" mother. Troublingly, Baker rewrites Ajax as the hero of *Sula* and casts the two women as his helpers. Ajax's claim to feminism is that he is not "his own man", but the "offspring of his mother's magic" – she is "the Place ... that provides conditions of possibility for successful heterosexual bonding" (252). However, underneath the flattering rhetoric, Baker turns Ajax's mother into a stepping-stone for his sexual and emotional satisfaction. Similarly, Baker recasts Sula as a woman who can help Ajax define himself and reclaim his masculinity. In the sex scene she is a masculine woman on top of Ajax for his benefit: in making love to Ajax she "rewrites the 'joke' of capitalism that emasculates" black men; and in her first-person narration imagining that she digs deeper and deeper into Ajax's strata until she finds fertile loam, she is Ajax's symbolic cleaning-lady: "ritual blues purifier and cleaner of congestive layers whose excavation leads, finally, to fertile and reclaimed 'dirt'" (251).

Baker is aware that capitalism's joke was played on black women as well as black men; he comments on Eva that to "defeat capitalism's 'joke,' she subjects herself to dismemberment" (241). However, he thoroughly exculpates black fathers – "the actual fathers are disappeared by a 'nigger joke' in *Sula* that emasculates them and denies them any legitimate means of production" (246) – while condemning Eva as "self-absorbed" (243). Baker thus reproduces a misogynist binary opposition: bad "self-absorbed" black woman (Eva) versus good black woman for the benefit of black man (his reading of Sula and Ajax's mother).

Baker argues that *Sula* breaks with the African American dream of progress through migration to the urban and industrial North – a dream in which the canonical African American literary tradition of Wright and Ellison participates (244). Instead *Sula* allows black men to confront their economic emasculation and then summons "a potentially redemptive heterosexuality" which only fails because of Sula's sudden possessiveness (253). Casting *Sula*'s women in folk, domestic and male-helper roles, Baker misrecognizes their own confrontation with capitalism and economic emasculation, makes exorbitant demands upon them, and threatens them with rejection if they don't meet them.

Denise Heinze, in *The Dilemma of "Double-Consciousness"* (1993), offers a feminist critique of *Sula*. While Morrison is accepting of black men who refuse to settle down, she "does not acknowledge a similar need in women"; she often presents women who wander as "aberrant and self-serving" (99). Sula, as a result, is an "unattractive" character (99). Heinze, on the other hand, endorses Morrison's three-woman families – such as the three Peace women in *Sula* – and Morrison's critique of nuclear families.

Gurleen Grewal, in *Circles of Sorrow, Lines of Struggle* (1998), argues that *Sula* begins the difficult emergence of black feminism out of black nationalism. The attempt is only partially successful and Grewal echoes Heinze's feminist critique of Morrison. Sula is the "iconoclastic figuration of black feminism attempting to break through nationalist consciousness"; her premature death figures the "absence of a viable feminist space within black collectivity" (46). Even the independent and masculine Eva greets Sula with "When you gone to get married … " (49). Nel's affirmation of her interrupted friendship with Sula – her "emergent consciousness" – is the only breakthrough in the novel (47). Adopting Victor Turner's influential distinction between "communitas" and "structure", Grewal argues that their friendship is an instance of communitas, while the Bottom women's internalization of patriarchal gender roles and power imbalance is an instance of structure. Sula alone risks "the free fall from the social web of proscriptions" (54). However, Morrison doesn't allow Sula the degree of freedom Ajax enjoys. Further, in an implicit critique of

Houston Baker, Grewal argues that Ajax deserts Sula not because of her possessiveness, but because of his "inability to identity with Sula's own rejection" of structure (55).

Andrea O'Reilly, in *Toni Morrison and Motherhood* (2004), reads *Sula* as a critique of the existentialist feminism of Simone de Beauvoir. Existentialist feminism, in its emphasis on *self*-affirmation, is inappropriate and harmful to black women. What nourishes them is connection to the motherline, the line of female ancestors. In keeping with her idealized view of the motherline, O'Reilly problematically embraces enthusiastically Eva's killing of Plum: Eva "claimed maternal power to protect and nurture her son the only way she could" (147). Sula ought to have remained connected to her motherline, and when she "kills the ancestor by putting Eva into a home, she also kills herself" (63). O'Reilly denies any value or agency in Sula's exploration of her subjectivity: in embracing existentialist feminism Sula falls pray to "dominant standards" (61) – a hegemonic white feminism – that cannot nourish her.

Toni Morrison, in interviews, has repeated that Sula is "male" (for example, Morrison 1985b, 185). Cholly (*The Bluest Eye*), Ajax and Sula are alike: they are versions of the "'free man' ... free in his head"; Morrison's versions of "what some people call the 'bad nigger'" (Morrison 1976a, 18–19); all three "express either an effort of the will or a freedom of the will" (Morrison 1983a, 164). This has been an aspect of "black male life" – often condemned but now rehabilitated by Morrison: "the fact that they could split in a minute just delights me. It's part of that whole business of breaking ground, doing the other thing"; Sula is "masculine" in this sense (Morrison 1976a, 26). Morrison makes a connection between this black masculinity and the tragic hero exceeding limits: Sula is a "law-breaker"; while Nel "lives by the law, she *is* the community" (ibid., 14). Morrison argues that the singers Billie Holiday and Bessie Smith were masculine women, in this sense – "They were outside of that little community value thing" (ibid., 17). These black masculine women are Sula's real-life female ancestors.

UNDOING BINARY OPPOSITIONS: AFRICAN-AMERICANIST, EXISTENTIALIST, POSTSTRUCTURALIST AND DECONSTRUCTIVE READINGS

One of the dominant themes in scholarship on *Sula* has been the way in which the novel critiques "binary oppositions". A binary opposition posits two terms as mutually exclusive: the one term is what the other is not; one of the two terms is positively valued, the other is devalued. Man/woman, white/black, self/other, good/evil are examples of binary oppositions. The critique of binary oppositions by post-structuralist thinkers – Jacques Derrida, Roland Barthes, Luce Irigaray, Hélène Cixous, Henry Louis Gates, Jr. – is far from exclusive to them. African cosmologies, African American trickster tales, Romantic Gothicism, Hegel, Du Bois, the existentialism of Sartre and Beauvoir emerge as unlikely allies of the poststructuralist critique of binary oppositions, as I hope will become clear in this section.

Deborah E. McDowell, in "'The Self and the Other'" (1988), surveys the debates in African American criticism as to how the black self is to be represented. In 1926 Du Bois advocates representations of a positive black self, while Langston Hughes rejects such representations. In 1977 Addison Gayle, Jr., once again, calls for representations of a positive black self, as do other prominent figures in the Black Aesthetic Movement. However, the Black Power movement's "positive" representations were troubling to black women in that they "rendered black women prone or the 'queens' of the male warrior" (152). From the late 1970s onwards, Henry Louis Gates, Jr. critiques the very idea of a "unified, coherent, stable, and known" self (150). In this Gates resonates with a strong tendency in contemporary thought – in particular McDowell reminds us of the critique of binary oppositions in feminist thought, particularly by Luce Irigaray. A positive black self can only reinforce the oppositions "black/white, positive/negative, self/other" (151).

In this context, *Sula* is "rife with liberating possibilities in that it transgresses" binary oppositions; and "demands a shift from an either/or orientation to one that is both/and" (152). McDowell credits Spillers for being the first critic to discern this. Moving beyond binary oppositions, Morrison develops Sula to explore the "assumption that the self is multiple, fluid, relational, and in a perpetual state of becoming" (153). In particular Sula's sexuality is "in the service of the self-exploration that leads to self-intimacy" and of "creativity as seen in the long prose poem she creates while making love to Ajax" (156); McDowell is implicitly critiquing Houston Baker here.

Potentially, the novel can act on the reader as an education in non-binary-oppositional thinking: Morrison "threatens the reader's assumptions ... at every turn" (159). In writing the character of Sula, Morrison "deliberately provides echoing passages that cancel each other out, that thwart the reader's desire for stability and consistency" (160). This is a potentially transformative process enabling the reader to abandon their "static and coherent conception of SELF" (158) and acknowledge their multiple, fluid and changing self. This is mirrored in the process Nel undergoes: "After years of repression, Nel must own ... the disowned part of herself": Sula (158).

Terry Otten, in *The Crime of Innocence in the Fiction of Toni Morrison* (1989), argues that Sula falls from innocence when she accidentally kills Chicken Little and when she overhears her mother saying that she doesn't like her. (See **p. 191**.) Nel tries unsuccessfully to preserve Sula's innocence and manages to preserve her own until the very end of the novel. Nel creates a specious garden of Eden, a "fortress of her innocence" (40), by choosing the role of innocent victim and wronged wife. However, this is an inauthentic and self-harming choice. In the final pages of the novel, Nel is liberated by her acknowledgement of "her other self" (43), Sula. Otten argues that "only by confronting and somehow assimilating the other can Morrison's protagonists achieve a degree of existential freedom" (28).

Otten finds three intellectual allies for his project: African cosmologies, where good and evil coexist; psychoanalysis (according to Freud, Eros and Thanatos, love and hate coexist in the unconscious); and Romantic Gothicism: Sula is Nel's double in the Romantic Gothic sense of the dynamic, demonic, regenerative Other, "the Romantic villain ... whose seeming evil generates good" (37).

Barbara Johnson, in "'Aesthetic' and 'Rapport' in Toni Morrison's *Sula*" (1993), offers a deconstructive reading. When Nel walks in on Sula and Jude having sex, her reaction is strangely detached: "I waited for Sula to look up at me any minute and say one of those lovely college words like *aesthetic* or *rapport*" (*Sula* 105). This is one of several traumatic events witnessed in the novel: "horrible images, painful truths, excruciating losses" (171). Sula's manner of witnessing her mother's burning is also detached – and Eva accuses her of watching it as an aesthetic spectacle rather than taking action. In effect Eva accuses her of "privileging ... aesthetics over rapport" (171); as Nel also seems to do when she contemplates Sula and Jude and thinks of the words "aesthetic" and "rapport". The reader of this novel is in a comparable position: "Do we just sit back and watch? What is the nature of our pleasure in contemplating trauma?" (171).

The underlying assumption here is that aesthetics and rapport are mutually exclusive, a binary opposition: "aesthetics is taken as the contemplation of forms, implying detachment and distance, and rapport is taken as the dynamics of connectedness" (170). However, Morrison deconstructs this very opposition: she "makes the aesthetic inextricable from trauma" (171).

Freudian psychoanalysis has taught us that a dissociation of event and affect is characteristic of trauma: the traumatic event is not properly speaking experienced or owned at the time and is only accessed through a repetition compulsion and long-delayed effects. Morrison's treatment of trauma is very much in keeping with psychoanalytic insights on trauma: "The dissociation of affect and event is one of

Morrison's most striking literary techniques in this novel, both in her narrative voice (in which things like infanticide are not exclaimed over) and in the emotional lives of her characters" (168). The *circularity* underlying the linearity of the novel can be explained in psychoanalytic terms as the return of repressed traumas. However, Morrison also critiques psychoanalysis and "both displaces and deconstructs" core psychoanalytic concepts (167). The story of Eva's self-mutilation recontextualizes castration in the context of the institutionally entrenched economic and political emasculation of African Americans: "the historical experience of some people is the literalization and institutionalization of the fantasies of others" (168). Morrison is taking Freudian concepts such as penis envy and castration, and "recontextualizing them in the framework of American racial and sexual arrangements" (167).

Denise Heinze, in *The Dilemma of "Double-Consciousness"* (1994), follows Gates and reinterprets Du Bois's concept of "double consciousness", not as a debilitating condition, but as an enabling strategy embracing both/and, rather than either/or. (See **p. 184**.) Morrison's use of *both* linear time *and* cyclical time in *Sula* is an instantiation of double consciousness. On the one hand, as Morrison's chapter titles make clear, time moves forward in a chronological and unidirectional line; we can call this the Western, Enlightenment view of history. On the other hand, the novel moves in circles, in the manner of an African cyclical conception of time: the novel begins in the narrative present and returns to it at the end; Sula returns to the Bottom; Nel returns to her friendship with Sula at the end of the novel. Morrison resists resolution between linear and cyclical time, though the novel's end – "circles of sorrow" – supports cyclical time (123).

Philip Page, in *Dangerous Freedom* (1995), argues that *Sula* engages with a series of binary oppositions – self/other, Nel/Sula, Bottom/Medallion, linearity/circularity, etc. – "modifying ... refiguring ... subverting" them (66). Morrison is playing on the Western "motif" of binary oppositions (66), and this is how jazz compositions work: they play on a motif, modifying, refiguring and subverting it. In other words, jazz, an African American musical tradition, has an affinity with Euro-American deconstructive critique. In making this argument Page undermines the binary opposition of Euro-American and African American traditions.

In *Sula* there is a play between "linear chronology and circularity" (64). Morrison also experiments with non-oppositional "conceptions of selfhood" (69). Sula is a fluid self beyond the binary opposition between self and other, and resists univocal interpretation in either positive or negative terms: she "remains open for interpretation" (74), exceeding "narrow formulations of self, woman, or black" (75).

Linden Peach, in *Toni Morrison* (2000), views *Sula* as problematizing the binary oppositions of self/other and good/evil aided by the resources of African American folktales. *Sula* resists the interpretation of Sula and Nel as binary opposites. Instead characters are fluid and changing. Sula, especially, "defies a single and unified reading" (54) and has overtones of the trickster figure in African American folktales, in whom good and evil coexist in ongoing negotiation. Similar trickster characters – for example, Odysseus – can also be found in the Western tradition. In pointing this out Peach, like Page, avoids the pitfall of supporting a binary opposition between African American and Western traditions.

PSYCHOANALYTIC READINGS

Jill Matus, in *Toni Morrison* (1998), comments that Freud's account of trauma in *Beyond the Pleasure Principle* (1920) was a response to traumatized World War I veterans. *Sula*'s train scene suggests the peculiarly difficult position of African American veterans like Chadrack and Plum.

Sula's recurring nightmare of the Baking Powder lady suggests that she was traumatized by her mother's death, as Eva's haunting by Plum suggests she was traumatized by the killing of her son. However, Sula does not seek to avoid painful feelings (Matus points us to Sula's conversation with Nel on her deathbed, but the passage on page 118 might better be cited in support of this). Nor does Sula look at things aesthetically to avoid feeling; on the contrary, "Aesthetic pleasure ... becomes a key that unlocks further feelings" (68).

J. Brooks Bouson, in *Quiet as It's Kept* (2000), argues that *Sula* attempts to reclaim shaming racist stereotypes but at times repeats those stereotypes; its repeated enactment of black-on-black shaming and contempt also points to Morrison's unconscious internalized racism. Through the shameless character of Sula, Morrison engages with and "flaunts" (48, 55) the stereotype of the black Jezebel (the oversexed black female) – a stereotype that had its origins in slavery economics and the use of female slaves as breeders – in the context of the late 1960s and early 1970s climate of sexual liberation. On the one hand, the text "sympathizes with Sula's rebellious wildness and uses her to flaunt, parody, and ... counteract the debased stereotype" (67); the text also defends her by emphasizing her friendship for Nel when she's dying – "Wait'll I tell Nel" (*Sula*, 149). However, on the other hand, the text's "struggle with internalized racism" is perhaps most evident in the case of Sula: as a "primary carrier of the text's rage and contempt", she is "prematurely ushered out of the text" (67). In other words, her painful and premature death can be read as a "textual staging" of internalized racial loathing (70). Simultaneously, the deaths at the tunnel can be read as an enactment of Sula's own contempt for the people of the Bottom, counter-shaming the Bottom for having cast her in the role of pariah.

The Peace family is the epicenter of this cycle of black-on-black contempt. Once again the "explicit agenda is to provide a counter-narrative to shaming racist stereotypes" (55). Morrison engages with the racist stereotype, strengthened by the Moynihan Report, of the black matriarchy as responsible for the pathological degeneration of the black family. *Sula* attempts to reclaim this stereotype but the Peace family comes at times too close to "racist myths" (55). The violent deaths in this family can be read as enactments of the family's self-contempt. Though the text aestheticizes Plum's death and insists that Eva loved him, he is associated with excrement both as an infant and an adult and dies as a result of his mother's "contempt-disgust" (59). Hannah's death is also related to her mother's contempt-disgust towards her: she dies significantly just after Eva scorned her question, "Mamma, did you ever love us?" (61; *Sula*, 67). Sula in turn watches her mother's death with "secret pleasure" in revenge for her mother's shaming dislike of her (65). Critics themselves have been caught in this cycle of shaming and counter-shaming, shaming some characters and defending others.

INTERTEXTUAL READINGS

Of the critics discussed above, **Baker** situates Morrison in relation to an African American "male precursor", Jean Toomer, and compares *Sula* to Toomer's *Cane* (1923) (243–44). **Grewal** situates Morrison in relation to Anglo-American modernism and compares *Sula* to Virginia Woolf's *Mrs Dalloway* (1925) and T.S. Eliot's *The Waste Land* (1922).

Trudier Harris, in *Fiction and Folklore* (1991), explores *Sula*'s ironic and revisionist use of oral literature. Whereas in folktales fire and water purify, in *Sula*, ironically, they kill. Sula is a revisionist character appropriating attributes of male folktale heroes. Borrowing from European folktales, Sula is "as active as Jack the giant killer"; borrowing from African American folktales, Sula is "as amoral as Brer Rabbit the trickster" (54). Female tricksters are rare in folktales and tend to act for the good of their families, unlike Sula.

Formally, *Sula* engages with the ballad: in focusing very selectively on major events, it adopts the "leaping and lingering" structure of both European and African American ballads (57). Formally, it also engages with jazz compositions: death is the stable point or theme to which the novel returns and around which it elaborates many improvisations and variations.

Harris comments on the singing of "Shall We Gather at the River" during Sula's funeral. Popular among African Americans, it was written by the white pastor of a Baptist church in 1864 and refers to the heavenly river of Revelation 22: 1–2. Morrison puts it to ironic use, in that it proleptically announces an "apocalyptic" event: the 3 January 1941 National Suicide Day parade to the river tunnel, the collapse of the tunnel, and the many deaths that ensue.

A MARXIST READING

K. Sumana, in *The Novels of Toni Morrison* (1998), views the relation between Nel and Sula in Hegelian Marxist terms: Nel is the old or the "thesis", Sula is the new or the "antithesis", but Morrison offers no "synthesis" between the two (75). *Sula* responds critically to the sexism of the Black Power movement and focuses on "the struggle for ... women's rights in particular" (68). However, because of Morrison's "weak class analysis", Sula fails to enter into the struggle to change society (78). Morrison's suggestion that Sula is hampered by the lack of an art form is "an idealistic solution that reflects Morrison's own idealism, her own immature analysis of the role of capitalism" (78).

A METAFICTIONAL READING

John N. Duvall, in *The Identifying Fictions of Toni Morrison* (2000), argues that Sula and Chadrack are artist figures. Sula has an aesthetic detachment. She uses sex as Morrison has said she uses writing: to define and reclaim the self. She has the masculinity traditionally associated with the artist. Chadrack shares the attributes of an earlier artist figure in Morrison's fiction, Soaphead Church. Like Soaphead he has a ritualistic role within the community but is isolated from it. Chadrack's National Suicide Day is a community ritual performed by him alone. The twin artist figures of Sula and Chadrack "encode Morrison's anxieties about identifying herself as an artist" (54).

Song of Solomon

AFRICANIST AND AFRICAN-AMERICANIST READINGS

Many critics read *Song of Solomon* within Africanist and African-Americanist contexts: African cosmologies and mythologies; African American culture, oral traditions, written literary traditions and musical traditions.

    Joyce M. Wegs, in "Toni Morrison's *Song of Solomon*" (1982), explores the novel's engagement with blues music. Morrison "takes on the role of a blues singer" to "explore folk values" and "describe variations on traditional male and female roles" in a search for what is valuable today (166). As with the blues, in this novel men leave (fly away) and women are left behind to sing the blues; but extraordinary men and women both fly and sing. Jake and Pilate are the "role models in the novel" (178). Jake both excelled other men and "sang like an angel" (*Song of Solomon*, 237). Pilate both wanders and sings, flies and touches the ground, pilots both in the sense of flying and guiding (180). This is the lesson Milkman learns: "With Pilate's guidance, Milkman finally realizes that a genuine blues man does not really fly solo" (178); and as Pilate lies dying he begins to sing the blues.

References to the blues abound. Pilate's version of the song of Solomon, "O Sugarman", points to "an old blues song about Sugarman" (167) – Wegs is probably referring to "Sugar Man Blues" – and there are references in the novel to blues singers Muddy Waters, Lead Belly and rhythm and blues pioneer Bo Diddley. Hagar's lament that Milkman doesn't love her is a "blues lament"; answered by Pilate and Reba it follows a "traditionally African cry-and-response pattern" (171). The children's version of the song of Solomon in Shalimar "resembles the shout, an ancestor of the blues utilized by field slaves whose knowledge of English was minimal" (174).

Lucinda H. MacKethan, in "Names to Bear Witness" (1986), argues that Morrison's treatment of the theme of naming in this novel is "squarely within" the canon of African American written literature since slave narratives. This "dominant tradition" is summarized by Ralph Ellison in his essay "Hidden Names and Complex Fate" (1964): "Our names, being the gift of others, must be made our own" (quoted in MacKethan 1986, 186). African Americans must retro-actively give their own new meaning to names fortuitously acquired or imposed by others so that they bear witness to their own life and actions. Pilate, for example, gives the meaning "pilot" to her name.

Catherine Carr Lee, in "The South in Toni Morrison's *Song of Solomon*" (1998), places the novel's theme of naming in the Western African context of *nommo*: naming as expression of essence, and this in the African American context of slavery and the ban on marriage between slaves and family names for slaves. Lee reads Milkman's travelling South to find himself as wholly successful both for himself and for the future of African American culture. Milkman's quest deviates from European folktales in this: instead of a polarization of the hero and his enemy and the text's siding with the values of the hero, Milkman flies into the arms of an enemy–friend, Guitar. Guitar is "teacher as well as an enemy" (51).

Trudier Harris, in *Fiction and Folklore* (1991), relates aspects of *Song of Solomon* to African American cultural contexts. She understands the novel's mix of enchantment and realism in the context of African American spirituality, which "presupposes an intertwining of the secular and sacred realms of existence" (87). (This is in keeping with Morrison's own comments.) Harris understands the novel's perspectivism in the context of African American storytelling: in "blur [ring] the line between one person's right and another person's wrong", Morrison adopts the "essence of the African-American story tradition", which involves "the presentation of everybody's versions of events … – frequently contradictory" (95). (Joseph T. Skerrett, Jr. in "Recitation to the *Griot*" and other critics also made this argument.) Milkman is similar to heroes of African American folktales: "Like Brer Rabbit, he has experienced the flexibility of morality. Like John the slave … he has been as much manipulator as manipulated" (95).

Morrison reverses the modern folk pattern of migration from the South to the North in allowing Milkman to find fulfilment in the South, in "a journey that works" (95). However, Harris is critical of Morrison's treatment of female characters and objects to "Female sacrifices for male identity" (107).

Gay Wilentz, in "Civilizations Underneath" (1992), argues that in this novel Morrison is "formulating her discourse within an Afrocentric world view" (139). Morrison uses "African values, characteristics, and community" as an alternative to both assimilation and separatism (138). Adopting the position of the African griot (storyteller), she retells the tale of flying African slaves "to keep her traditions alive on paper" (141). Within the novel Pilate plays the role of griot as do other female characters; Morrison explores "the orature of women" who stay behind as culture bearers safeguarding the "continuation of the group" (143). Also the novel's interactive relation with the reader uses the format of African "dilemma tales": they have "unresolved endings which call for community response" (144). Yet another Afrocentric element is Pilate's "obeah" (voodoo) practices (147). Finally, Milkman can be read as a reincarnation of Solomon, in keeping with African beliefs in reincarnation.

Linda Krumholz, in "Dead Teachers" (1993), compares *Song of Solomon* to two African epics, the Mwindo epic and the Kambili epic, both available in translation when Morrison was writing the novel. On the one hand, the two epics "inscribe heroism as a specifically male province" and relegate women to "the role of helper" (216). On the other hand, the Mwindo epic resonates with Morrison's novel in "Mwindo's conversion from a proud boastful fighter to a wise, generous, and benevolent ruler"; and the moral concluding this epic "corresponds to Morrison's reconstruction of heroism in Milkman" (217). The Kambili epic is relevant in its exploration of the "relationship between individual ambition and collective values" (217). While the hero wants to make "a name for himself", Maninka (the people whose epic the Kambili epic is) beliefs pose the question of the relationship between male memorable deeds (*fa-den-ya*, "father-child-ness") and female social bonds (*ba-den-ya*, "mother-child-ness") (219). The hero is potentially "asocial" and "disrupts the stability of the collective" (219), but can also bring about needed change. This is also the dilemma of *Song of Solomon*: "how can we ... valorize an ethics of collectivity and social responsibility *and* work to ... challenge the social order?" (219).

Morrison "revises the myth of the African-American man" (204). Milkman "becomes the true ancestor" (208) and his name is redefined as nurturer: "men must also recognize their role as nurturers, as 'mothers' supplying their 'milk' to future generations" (209). However, because dominant modern culture still values male over female characteristics, Morrison is cautious in feminizing Milkman: "the 'mother-child-ness' that gives him his name must be repudiated, and his masculinity reinforced, in order to situate him as hero ... Morrison proceeds more cautiously in feminizing Milkman ... than she does in masculinizing Sula" (220) in her previous novel.

Joyce Irene Middleton, in "From Orality to Literacy" (1995), argues that this is a novel that paradoxically "privileges" (29) the values of oral culture. "Merging Greek, biblical, and African American oral traditions ... Morrison brings orality and literacy face to face" and stages a confrontation between them (36). The way the illiterate Jake chooses the name "Pilate" for his daughter amounts to an appropriation of the Bible. Instead of "automatically submit[ting] to the authorized version of the biblical text" (26), he "reveals a unique creativity" (27). Similarly, in naming Mains Avenue "Doctor Street" and then "Not Doctor Street" the black community of Mercy asserts its oral traditions against the literate authorities in a "political conflict over naming" – in "an agonistic expression of signifying" as Henry Louis Gates would say (27).

Listening is a crucial part of oral culture and Morrison's use of homonyms – "Pilate" and "pilot"; Solomon and Shalimar (pronounced Shalleemone [*Song of Solomon*, 261]) – enhances the oral quality of her work by speaking to the reader's ear. In Shalimar Milkman learns how to listen as "a seminal part of his experience" (29). His song to Pilate is a kind of monument to her, though not one set "in stone" (35). This is because of the creativity and interactiveness Morrison attributes to oral cultures.

Gurleen Grewal, in *Circles of Sorrow, Lines of Struggle* (1998), argues that this novel "harkens back to the blues tradition" (61). It records and takes the place of the *griot* (African story-teller) Pilate – who dies at the end as storytelling dies in modernity – so that the bourgeois art form of the novel becomes "a performance containing council and wisdom" (63). It belongs to a group of novels that have "documented and refashioned ethnic identities" in the US since the 1970s (65). It critiques the "individualist, self-reliant model celebrated in American society" (74): Milkman – against his initial middle-class assimilationism or whitened (Milk) identity – is helped by many and in the closing lines has a "cultural transfusion" of blood from Pilate (71). He also recognizes his Native American heritage (73) and attempts to understand the working-class Guitar.

Slave work-songs and spirituals already appropriated biblical stories for resistance. This novel appropriates the biblical Song of Solomon and redefines the African American motif of flight: "the theme of the biblical Song of Solomon, 'love is strong as death,' merges with the African American motif of flight, redefined as engagement rather than escape" (75).

FEMINIST READINGS

Gerry Brenner's "*Song of Solomon*" (1987) is a caricature of feminism rather than a feminist reading, and attributes this caricature to Morrison herself. Brenner (mis)understands feminism as setting out to mock and humble men. He compares Otto Rank's description of the hero's monomyth (essential universal aspects of the hero, from Oedipus to Moses to Gilgamesh) to Morrison's treatment of Milkman and concludes that "she skillfully mocks him and the novel's other men" (96). He claims Morrison's "delight in humbling the hero" (100) and her "disdain for Milkman because of what he fails to learn ... – that in his gene pool also swims the congenital habit of desertion" (101). He sides with Morrison's perceived disdain.

Michael Awkward, in "'Unruly and Let Loose'" (1990), argues that this novel values the role of African American folktales for "black survival", while simultaneously "critiquing their frequent androcentrism" (75). In asking whom Solomon and Milkman left behind, the text records female "immeasurable pain" as well as male flight (89), interrogating Afrocentrism from a woman-centred perspective. In this the novel enables the "fruitful interaction" of "Afrocentric ideology with feminism" (90).

Morrison confronts the problem that traditional myths, including African American ones, "inscribe ... a subordinate and inferior status for women" (73). Subjectivity, the ability to transcend one's situation and heroic action are reserved for men. The main problem is the denial of subjectivity and transcendence to women: the "timeless figuration of woman as object" (83), the "female exclusion as subject" (74) and the "failure to inscribe usefully transcendent possibilities for the female" (85). (Awkward's concepts of subjectivity and transcendence come from the existentialism of Sartre and Beauvoir.) Another problem is the disconnection of male heroic action from social responsibility: Solomon's "apparent absence ... of social responsibility" (69) destroys Ryna (as Milkman destroys Hagar). Morrison interrupts Milkman's heroic quest with Hagar's death; for his quest to continue he has to acknowledge his maltreatment of Hagar.

This novel is in keeping with the "female-centred" perspective of Morrison's earlier novels, but, unlike the earlier novels, does not embrace "the feminist idea(l) of exclusively female communities" (77), such as the female household of Pilate, Reba and Hagar.

Marianne Hirsch's "Knowing Their Names" (1995) argues that the novel focuses on fathers and their effects on their children's lives; it explores the extremes of their domineering presence and traumatic absence: Solomon and Guitar's father are painfully absent, while middle-class Macon is oppressively and patriarchally present. Jake is the only father who is "neither too close nor too distant" (77). He nurtures his motherless daughter Pilate and works alongside his son Macon. But his murder, like Solomon's flight from slavery and the industrial accident that saws Guitar's father in two, creates an historical "puzzle" – the African American father's powerlessness – that the children have to solve (82). The relation to the father is "embedded in larger social and economic forces" (81).

A way out of the extremes of the father's absence or presence is to claim one's dual inheritance: masculine/paternal but also feminine/maternal. In singing Pilate claims the inheritance of her foremothers (including her mother Singing Bird), as does Milkman when he sings to Pilate. However, in this novel none of the female characters, only the "male protagonist", benefits from this dual inheritance (89–90).

Andrea O'Reilly's *Toni Morrison and Motherhood* (2004) compares Ruth and Pilate and their respective relation to models of femininity and motherhood. The motherless Ruth is taught by her father to emulate the hegemonic white middle-class model of marriage, where the wife is submissive to her husband. Ruth's breastfeeding of Milkman until the age of six and her inedible cooking are instances of her resistance to patriarchy (142–44). In Morrison "resistance against patriarchal motherhood is conveyed either as 'deviant' maternal nurturance ... or as failed maternal nurturance", as with Ruth (34, 118). The problem is that O'Reilly does not distinguish at all between failed and resistant motherhood: is every instance of failed motherhood in Morrison an act of resistance?

Pilate rejects the white middle-class model of motherhood: chaste, selfless, passive, domestic; she is both feminine and masculine, both ship and safe harbour (105). In keeping with the communitarian traditions of black mothering, she other-mothers Milkman. But these traditions are under threat. Hagar dies because of the absence of a community of other-mothers, female or indeed male: "fathers are seen as an integral part of the larger nurturant community. Their role is that of communal othermother" (83). Pilate's other-mothering of Milkman guides him towards that role.

The quest of the *Bildungsroman* is learning and integration in society. Milkman's quest – an anti-*Bildungsroman* – involves unlearning, breaking with dominant values, divesting himself of power: Milkman sheds his "masculine individualism and separateness" to reconnect with the "motherline" (100). In accepting Pilate's teaching that you "can't fly on off and leave a body" (*Song of Solomon*, 147), Milkman "has chosen kinship over flight" (104). (One might object to O'Reilly that Milkman leaps and leaves Pilate's body behind in the closing scene.)

DIALOGIC READINGS: DU BOIS, BAKHTIN, GATES

Philip Page, in "*Dangerous Freedom*" (1995), offers a Bakhtinian reading of this novel. Bakhtin distinguishes between "dialogism" and "monologism". Dialogism is the "orchestration" of a multiplicity of voices whose spectrum of relations to each other spans from "resonance" to "dissonance". Monologism is the dominance of one language/perspective at the expense of all others. (See Bakhtin 1981, "Discourse in the Novel".) With the exception of Pilate and Milkman, "characters remain trapped in their ... monologic approaches" (95). Milkman "operates dialogically" (104) in that his is a "miraculous" (85, 106) putting together of many different perspectives, in response to the "heterogeneity of his environment" (85), an environment which includes incompatible figures such as Macon, Ruth and Guitar. The novel "details ... the necessary but arduous process of attaining a viable pluralism" (106).

Page repeatedly describes Pilate, Milkman and the novel itself as "fusional". Milkman fuses characters' competing definitions; as well as African American perspectives and the Native American perspective of Susan Byrd. The novel fuses African, classical and Christian mythologies; and it is the "attempted and ambiguous reconciliation of the divided parts" (84). The problem with Page's use of "dialogic" and "fusional" as interchangeable terms is that it reduces dialogism to "resonance" (reconciliation) alone at the expense of "dissonance" (antagonism, lack of reconciliation). Bakhtin's dialogism, on the other hand, includes both resonance and dissonance as we discussed. In addition, what Bakhtin calls "internal dialogism" is a dialogism with other languages/perspectives *within* each language/perspective and *within* the self.

Thirty years before Bakhtin, W.E.B. Du Bois in *The Souls of Black Folk* (1903) famously diagnosed a condition akin to Bakhtinian "internal dialogism" as the painful predicament of African Americans, "double consciousness". (See **p. 158.**) Du Bois and Bakhtin resonate in their emphasis on conflict, within the self, between socially dominant and minority perspectives. Henry Louis Gates's concept of "Signifying" is an original rewriting of Du Bois and Bakhtin: it appropriates "double consciousness" and "internal dialogism" as a tactic or resource for African Americans and other marginalized groups. "Signifying" (capitalized), the indirectly subversive practice of marginalized groups, sustains an *ongoing dialectic* with "signifying" (the dominant language/perspective).

Gates's poststructuralist delineation of an actively pursued strategy of "double-consciousness" as resignification – what Gates calls "Signification" – is akin to a Bakhtinian dialogization of a word or utterance. It decolonizes and pluralizes the world "by inserting a new semantic orientation into a word which already has – and retains – its own orientation"; it suggests that "a simultaneous, but negated parallel discursive (ontological, political) universe exists within the larger white discursive universe"; it proclaims "the symbiotic relationship between the black and white"; it posits a "vertiginous relationship between ... *signification* and *Signification*, each of which is dependent on the other" (Gates, *The Signifying Monkey* quot. Heinze 1993, 6).

Denise Heinze's *The Dilemma of "Double-Consciousness"* (1993) argues that this novel shows "double-consciousness" in the Gatesean sense I just explained: for example, Jake's "philosophy is a mix of the African view of his role as custodian of the land and the American view of ownership and exploitation" (132). The novel departs from "consensus reality" and Signifies "the difference between culturally imposed ways of seeing" as well as "inciting powerful overflow of emotion and thought" without "prescribing a remedy" – it does not didactically affirm the rectitude of a new point of view (159). For example, Morrison doesn't aim to establish the literal existence of the supernatural (which is presented "ambiguously"), "but to create this *ongoing dialectic* between the seen and the unseen, the known and the unknown, the signified and the Signified" (160, my emphasis). Heinze, unlike Page, stresses the lack of reconciliation between languages/perspectives.

Wahneema Lubiano, in "The Postmodernist Rag" (1995), offers a Gatesean reading of the novel. "Signifying", as defined by Gates, is characterized by the subversive indirection and slipperiness that is also characteristic of postmodernism. This novel is both postmodernist and "Signifying" in that it subtly undermines commonsense reality and meaning, centred identity, and clear-cut solutions: it resists "the dangerous and simplistic pleasures of authoritative coherence" (95) in favour of constant revision, irony, indeterminacy, obliqueness and complexity in relation to the norm and the dominant. It does not "allow the reader to ferret out the 'truth'" (97); on the contrary, the "text has left the reader to flounder about" (100). All the naming and subversive renaming (renaming Mains Avenue "Doctor Street" then "Not Doctor Street") is "a naming that unnames as a guerilla tactic" (102). Unified and "centered subjectivity" is questioned (99): "Guitar's identity is as unified and untroubled by doubt as Macon Dead's is – and ultimately as wrong" (109). Milkman, on the other hand, is "almost without identity" (110); indicative of the "exploitation of the possibilities of indeterminacy in form and content" (98) is that "whatever consciousness is achieved by the protagonist ... is problematic" (102); the novel does not "valorize self-transcendence" (99). However, Lubiano argues that Pilate, not Milkman, is the most successful figure around whom "political possibilities cohere" (113); her death undercuts hope.

Marilyn Sanders Mobley's "Call and Response" (1995) argues that Bakhtinian "dialogism" is "indigenous to the African American expressive tradition" (58), as understood by Gates. For Gates the black tradition is "double-voiced": "between black vernacular discourse and standard English discourse" (Gates quoted by Mobley); the black vernacular "signifies on" – indirectly and imaginatively revises, resignifies – dominant norms (45). Mobley begins with a Bakhtinian/Gatesean reading of this novel. The African American community is "a dynamic, complex, multivoiced network of ongoing dialogues" (42). The voice of the male hero, Milkman, and the voices of the community are in a relation of both/and, not either/or – hence the "complex forms of dialogue that are embedded within the character of Milkman" (43). Milkman "gives up ... individualism ... and comes to understand the connection between language, identity, and community" (61): "a dialogic reading of *Song of Solomon* encourages us to question Western notions of autonomy and individuality as the white male constructions that they are" (63). Milkman's voice is also a dialogue between his parents: his father's "oppressive voice" and his mother's "repressed voice" and "the inner dialogue that develops between these external voices and the voice that is in the process of becoming his own" (53). (See Bakhtin's "internal dialogism" discussed above.)

Mobley then argues that to Bakhtin and Gates we must add a feminist attention to gender and silenced women's voices. In this novel we must distinguish between, on the one hand, a Bakhtinian/ Gatesean "Signifying" or critiquing voice which is usually male: in the barber shop scene, for example, there are differences of opinion and "multiple signifying" (56) – "on one another and on the hegemonic media" (57); and, on the other hand, a female listening and "responsive" voice (57). For example, Pilate, Reba and Hagar singing together in call and response: "the responsive voice in a community of women" is a voice that "fosters intersubjectivity and creates community" (58). Macon "resists the responsive voice" (59) in order to maintain his privileged position. With Milkman, on the other hand, Morrison "deconstructs notions of manhood predicated on illusions of self-sufficiency and on the repression of other voices ... of marginalized subjects": Morrison affirms Milkman's "ability to engage in active listening" (60).

PSYCHOANALYTIC READINGS

Jill Matus, in *Toni Morrison* (1998), points out that Jake, Macon, Pilate and Guitar have been traumatically separated from their fathers. Trauma causes "dissociation of feeling" (75) in Macon and "distortions in memory and obstacles to interpretation" (73) in Pilate.

J. Brooks Bouson's *Quiet as It's Kept* (2000) argues that in this novel the supernatural – "the comforting world of magic and folklore" – is used "reactively and defensively" to divert attention from historical trauma: it acts to transform trauma and shame into pride (78). The novel "deliberately carries out an antishaming agenda" (87). It contrasts the light-skinned and middle-class Ruth with Pilate in clear favour of Pilate, thereby reversing the colour and class hierarchy (85); and, in the glowing portrayal of Pilate, it "interrogates degrading stereotypes of the black underclass woman" (87). Nevertheless critics fail to understand that Pilate is trauma-haunted: she is navel-less as a sign of maternal loss and is haunted by the shooting down of her father (94). Arguably Pilate is shot dead in an "uncanny repetition of family trauma" (99). Similarly, with Milkman critics miss that the "golden treasure of his family's roots" actually involves trauma and shame (93): the killing of Jake but also Solomon's desertion of Ryna and his children – this is "the secret shame that haunts Milkman" (80). The novel also counter-shames whites: it suggests that members of the Seven Days suffer mental breakdown by replicating the terrorist actions of white racists (93).

AMERICANIST READINGS

Below are readings particularly situating the novel in the context of canonical American literature.

Linden Peach's *Toni Morrison* (2000) focuses on American romance. The romance, originally a medieval form, embraces folklore, myth, the anti-rational and instinctual and is the basis of white American literature: it addresses white fears and anxieties of losing control in the New World and projects them onto blackness, as Morrison herself argues in *Playing in the Dark* (Morrison 1992b). American romance, Morrison argues in *Playing*, was preoccupied with the American as a "new white man". *Song of Solomon* is a romance concerned with black fears of assimilation: it "uses romance conventions" (67) to explore the appropriateness of white middle-class values for African Americans. Peach agrees with many other critics that *Song of Solomon* is dialogic. However, he goes on to argue that "a hierarchy of favoured positions emerges in the course of the text" (83).

John N. Duvall's *The Identifying Fictions of Toni Morrison* (2000) argues that this novel completes a first phase in Morrison's work predicated on modernist authenticity: a search for authentic or essential blackness, a black nature presumed already-there and waiting to be discovered by the alienated individual. The novel moves from alienation to authenticity: Milkman was born on the same date as Morrison and achieves a breakthrough to authenticity in 1963, when Morrison began writing her first novel after the collapse of her marriage. Morrison reclaims American canonical modernism in a dialogue with Faulkner's *Go Down, Moses*. Unlike Faulkner's novel, Milkman breaks "free of ... Western patriarchal social organization" (81) by travelling to Shalimar. Morrison once again "seems to equate black authenticity with black poverty" (83). However, Morrison's next novel will offer a critique of Shalimar and of essentialist authenticity itself.

In Pilate's re-evaluation of her life, Morrison engages with the Transcendentalism of Emerson and Thoreau.

SELECTED OTHER CRITICISM

An existentialist reading

Terry Otten's *The Crime of Innocence in the Fiction of Toni Morrison* (1989) reads this novel through the biblical story of the fall, understood in existentialist terms as a salutary fall into knowledge. Milkman initially challenges his father but does not want knowledge. However, "Under the influence of the snakelike Pilate and his Other", Guitar, Milkman leaves the false Eden and the false innocence of his father's garden and undergoes a protracted fall which becomes indistinguishable from flying (53). Pilate is also an Eve figure – in that she's navel-less – and Milkman's true ancestor, hence Ruth's surname, Foster: "Pilate alone can rescue Milkman" (53). In Shalimar we witness Milkman's "understanding of Guitar's demonic power and so his escape from it" (58); also Milkman's "embracing of his Cain-like brother" (58). Guitar tries to kill Milkman to silence that part of him that "rebels against his cruelty to whites" and thus to "preserve his [false] innocence" (61).

A Marxist reading

K. Sumana, in *The Novels of Toni Morrison* (1998), is pleased to note that Morrison has caught up with her studies and is "more aware of the importance of dialectical and historical materialism – the role that capitalism plays in the African's exploitation and oppression"; Milkman's class consciousness undergoes a development in stages, reaching a "full state" (89) when he joins Shalimar's hunters and "commits class suicide" (91). Because of the "qualitative leap" in Morrison's "ability to analyse the nature of capitalism" this novel is "qualitatively better" than her earlier work (94). However, while Milkman's "race and class consciousness develops sufficiently to allow him to recreate himself, it never reaches the point where he moves beyond self-healing to other-healing" (94). Sumana projects Milkman's immaturity onto the author: Morrison "has not yet sufficiently matured to understand that ... [the African American's] economic exploitation forms the basis of his national oppression" (95). And of course "[w]ithout such an understanding, Morrison cannot propose a viable solution to the eradication of capitalism" (95).

Sumana argues that the "economic system of slavery, an early form of capitalism, is the cause of racism and sexism rather than the result of it, as ably demonstrated by Eric Williams, [Kwame] Nkrumah, and [Walter] Rodney" (146); "class, not race and gender, is the African's greatest enemy" (151).

One might object that Morrison sets out to explore problems rather than solutions, perspectives rather than the Truth: she neither seems to have Sumana's certainty of possessing the truth nor is as didactic as Sumana wants her to be, in the sense of creating characters that are models to be copied or feel-good plots with exemplary solutions. One is inclined to feel that Sumana's "maturity" has little to do with Morrison's artistry.

Tar Baby

AFRICANIST AND AFRICAN-AMERICANIST READINGS

Barbara Christian's reading of *Tar Baby* in *Black Feminist Criticism* (1985) is effectively in agreement with Morrison's 1985 comment that "everybody was sort of wrong" (Morrison 1985b, 178). Jadine is imbued with white middle-class patriarchal values "without any concern for social justice" (79), but so are Sydney and Ondine and perhaps black Western culture more generally: "The critical questions that Morrison asks in this novel are whether there is a functional black culture in the present-day West ... Are blacks essentially upwardly mobile?" (68–69). Historical evidence suggests that house slaves did not separate themselves from field slaves, whereas now middle-class blacks separate themselves from the less fortunate. Son represents yet another dead-end, in that he "refuses to contend with the social forces that deprive him of fulfillment" (79).

While Christian doesn't mention Marie-Thérèse by name, her discussion of the mammy figure can be usefully extended to this character. (Marie-Thérèse made her living breast-feeding French babies.) In white American, especially Southern, literature, the mammy is a dominant black female stereotype. The mammy – big, strong-bodied and unambiguously benevolent towards whites – is sunk in the corporeal and the antithesis of the ethereal and decorative ideal white woman. The black mammy addresses and simultaneously "contain[s]" men's unconscious fears of women's bodies (2). African American slave narratives, on the other hand, subvert the mammy stereotype and speak from within the mammy's own experience: "Mammies kicked, fought, connived, plotted, most often covertly, to throw off the chains of bondage" (5). Marie-Thérèse is such a resistant mammy figure, nurturing Son with oppositional values.

For **James Coleman,** in "The Quest for Wholeness in Toni Morrison's *Tar Baby*" (1986), *Tar Baby* is a "failure": Morrison's "unclear directions and garbled messages leave the reader in a muddle in the end" (72). Coleman approaches the novel with a set of prescriptions rather different from Morrison's own aims and the assumptions of later critics such as Page who praise the novel. Coleman is looking for a positive presentation of black folk values, but also for worldly success and advancement in the modern world. He reads the love story of Son and Jadine as promising a marriage of black folk values and worldly success; and reads the failure of the relationship as a failure of the "quest for wholeness", in this sense. Coleman is equally dissatisfied with the positive tone of the novel's ending, when Son enters a black mythological world: it "suggests a positive outcome for him that a close analysis of his situation does not support", in that he is unable to "adapt his folk ways to the modern world" (71). Coleman is finally dissatisfied with what he views as Morrison's disapprobation of Jadine, given that she is the one figure promising successful integration into the world. Coleman seems to ask of Morrison that she write in an instrumental way to fulfil a didactic role of creating positive role models and outcomes, but such criteria are inimical to her own vision of her art. (See Metafictional Readings below.)

Trudier Harris's *Fiction and Folklore* (1991) elucidates Morrison's use of the folktale of "Brer Rabbit and the Tar Baby". The tar baby story, whose earlier versions come from India and Africa (124), is "informed by the [African] trickster tradition": "a forbidden territory is invaded by an outsider [Brer Rabbit] who attempts to get away with valuable property" (116). Brer Rabbit has the amorality, ambiguity and freedom of the trickster figure or, more recently, the "'crazy nigger' or the 'bad nigger' of [African American] oral tradition" (121). He is trapped by a sticky tar baby constructed by Brer Fox and the other animals he stole from. Brer Rabbit hits the tar baby with his paws, which stick fast. Brer Rabbit "begins many versions of the tar baby story by being the aggressor; he then degenerates to victim"; and finally he either escapes or gets eaten (116). Morrison's treatment intensifies this "element of uncertainty" (116); Son is both Brer Rabbit and tar baby (see *Tar Baby*, 120 for Son as tar baby), as is Jadine. For example, Jadine is arguably Brer Rabbit in Eloe; and is explicitly viewed as tar baby by Son in *Tar Baby* 219–20 and 270.

In Son's initial encounter with Valerian, Son successfully controls language and racial stereotypes for his own purposes (121–23) and displays "the trickster's power of words" (122). (He starts to lose this control in his interaction with Jadine.) Another positive element of Son is his closeness to nature. His ability to see in the dark, like the blind horsemen, in the novel's closing lines is not altogether new but a return, in that when he first lands on the island he wanders at night and survives outside. Jadine as Brer Rabbit, on the other hand, only "retain[s] the negative traits of the trickster without mitigating positive ones" (126). Harris's feminist critique of Morrison is that she stays too close to folklore in her portrayals of women: they "share a striking male-centered perspective" (185). Morrison's women are either too self-sacrificing, to the point of victimization, or demonized, or rejected and put down for claiming an excessive masculinity: "Is there any female character in Morrison's work who can fulfill herself and not be destroyed, or not be judged for doing so? Must all women be subsumed under some community standard, or ostracized if they do not adhere to such standards?" (189). Harris argues that "Jadine's talents are undercut by the negative response written into the text in evaluating her reactions" (188).

Therese E. Higgins, in *Religiosity, Cosmology and Folklore* (2001), provides the African context of the African American folktale "Brer Rabbit and the Tar Baby": "The trickster tales, among which the 'tar baby' tale can be numbered, are popular throughout many

African countries" (45); African versions of the "tar baby" tale feature Hare or Spider and Rubber Girl, a sticky girl.

Richard Wright discussed African animism in his non-fictional *Black Power* (1954): "spirits dwell in trees, rivers, in fact, in all inanimate objects" (Wright quot. Higgins 2001, 22). These spirits are anthropomorphic and, if not controlled, will take one over. In *Tar Baby*, Morrison revives these spirits, in the island's animist nature and in the "swamp women", spirits living in the trees of the swamp.

INTERTEXTUAL READINGS IN RELATION TO THE WESTERN CANON

Terry Otten's "The Crime of Innocence in Toni Morrison's *Tar Baby*" (1986) argues for the centrality of the biblical myth of the fall in Morrison's novels and most explicitly in *Tar Baby*. Isle des Chevaliers is a garden of Eden but, like Valerian's greenhouse, a "specious garden" (155). Morrison explores the value of a salutary fall from innocence: for Morrison "no greater crime exists than innocence ... [I]n a culture run by an oppressive order not to sin perpetuates an immoral justice ... [I]nnocence is itself a sign of guilt because it signals a degenerate acquiescence" (153). The salutary fall is a paradoxical "victory in defeat", in that those who "sin against the flawed order become the agents of experience and so run the risk of freedom", while those who don't are "often doomed to moral entropy" (153).

The snake in this specious paradise is Son. The inhabitants of Isle des Chevaliers find in Son those parts of them long repressed; Son enables the return and articulation of their own unconscious "forbidden desires" (157). Initially they "scurr[y] to protect their innocence" (156); but then "confrontation with a serpent emanating from the self" leads to "a frightening self-awareness" (155). Son, both "Criminal and hero", therefore displays the "ambivalence of the serpent figure: forbidden but unconsciously willed, possessing healing powers but potentially destructive" (158).

Morrison avoids a happy ending for the protagonists, Jadine and Son: "Jadine's 'fall' leads to no recovery" and Morrison "allows Son no victory separate from the timeless world of legend and darkness"; Son "retreats from a world where he can find no reconciliation, no solution to his fallen humanity" (163) back to the unconscious where he came from.

For **Patricia Magness**, in "The Knight and the Princess" (1989), Morrison uses the European late-medieval model of courtly love, as developed in Chrétien de Troyes's *Lancelot*, as a template for the relationship between Son and Jadine (86). Both *Lancelot* and *Tar Baby* include: a "nearly unattainable woman" (86); a man as "worshipper" (87);

"humiliation of the knight" (88); "an enchanted island, a generous king, and a princess who needs to be rescued" (91); the knight's entry into the enchanted world and the freeing of the princess; "a secret world of love" (93); a "rigid class structure" (94). (See also Morrison's many references to European royalty, chivalry and courtly love in this novel.) However, Morrison mobilizes the courtly love model "to show its inadequacy" (98); for example, Morrison questions the model of courtly love by welcoming the crossing of class lines (95). Morrison's aim is to stage a clash between a white mythic structure – courtly love – and black mythic elements – the black pie ladies, the black blind horsemen, etc. – in order to interrogate both. Morrison deliberately refrains from a "comforting conclusion in this clash" (99).

For **Gurleen Grewal**'s *Circles of Sorrow, Lines of Struggle* (1998) *Tar Baby* rewrites Shakespeare's *The Tempest*. Valerian can be read as Prospero, the magician in exile; Jadine would be Miranda, Prospero's daughter; Sydney and Ondine would be the superior and airy servant Ariel; Son and Gideon would be the inferior and earthly servant Caliban; Marie-Thérèse would be Caliban's mother Sycorax, Prospero's adversary. As *The Tempest* "ends with Miranda's departure, leaving Caliban to regain the island for himself" (86), *Tar Baby* ends with Jadine's departure and Son's reclaiming of the island.

Morrison "indict[s]" Jadine (90) and, following Fanon's *The Wretched of the Earth*, sees education as potentially alienating the black middle class from black traditions of resistance: "education and assimilation have served the race-class structures of society" (93). Instead, the novel "valorizes the strength ... of peasant women's cultural traditions ... These rural black women have no need for the gains of a liberal feminism, whose ideal of equality Jadine defends" (88–89). Morrison "provides more sympathy for Son" (82), though he also receives authorial criticism (89). Son's return to the island "offers a disidentification with Propero's ordering of the world" and "identification with a legendary past as a testimony of a burgeoning awareness" (94–95) of black history. In identifying with the blind horsemen, Son identifies with the "legend of a slave insurrection" (93). However, *Tar Baby* remains a "troubled and troubling novel" (82) that "doesn't offer any viable routes" (80).

FEMINIST READINGS

Marilyn Sanders Mobley, in "Narrative Dilemma" (1984), argues that Morrison "indicts" Jadine (followed by Grewal in 1998) and "affirms" traditional black femininity (290). The novel is "a cautionary tale for those like Jadine, who define themselves ... against their past in the interest of self-fulfillment" (286). The novel "shows that the black woman who denies her 'historical connections' and 'sacred properties' risks psychic chaos and alienation from the very sources that could empower her" (291).

Peter B. Erickson's "Images of Nurturance in *Tar Baby*" (1984) once again claims Jadine's "indictment" (299) by Morrison for rejecting an ideal of femininity as maternal nurturance. Jadine is "an exception to ... Morrison's infinite tolerance and sympathy" (301). Son, on the other hand, is endorsed for his "submission" to maternal nurturance and to "a benevolent maternal sponsor", Marie-Thérèse (302).

Erickson critiques Morrison for "gender polarization": the "exclusion of 'androgyny'" in favour of a "male/female differentiation" (305), such that women nurture and men are nurtured. As a result, Morrison does not endorse Jadine's experiment with masculinity and does not allow Son "to experiment with nurturance [with nurturing rather than being nurtured] in any substantial way" (306). Son "does not achieve a nurturant identity of his own, but rather fuses with the nurturance" offered by a maternal figure (306).

Jill Matus, in *Toni Morrison* (1998), objects to what she views as Morrison's reductive treatment of Jadine and endorsement of Son; for example, his "crusade to save Alma Estée ... seems a little hollow" (101). Matus further argues that the "nature and specificity" of black women's "ancient properties" (*Tar Baby*, 308) is "largely unexamined" (99). It is also unclear what the "night women" represent. The group includes Cheyenne, Ondine and Marie-Thérèse, but Cheyenne has no connection to mothering, while Ondine and Marie-Thérèse are antagonistic to each other.

For **John N. Duvall**, in *The Identifying Fictions of Toni Morrison* (2000), *Tar Baby* is a feminist rewriting of *Song of Solomon*. It questions Milkman's "triumphant achievement of completed authenticity ... and the valorization of the black agrarian community" (98). Milkman's achievement of authenticity in Shalimar was not gender-neutral; the African American woman has a more difficult relationship to the agrarian past: while Shalimar men include Milkman by sharing Sweet, the Shalimar prostitute, with him, Eloe is patriarchal and polices Jadine. Son's killing of Cheyenne is of a piece with Eloe's patriarchal ways.

In view of the success of *Song of Solomon*, Morrison uses *Tar Baby* to negotiate her own and others' doubts as to her authenticity, while questioning the idea of authenticity itself, especially as defined by men. Jadine is closer to Morrison than critics and Morrison herself have allowed. Morrison's race consciousness, by her own account, developed in 1957–58, when she was older than the 25-year-old Jadine. Jadine on the plane back to France "seems poised at the same moment of Thoreauvian self-scrutiny" that Pilate and Morrison herself must have experienced (116). Jadine's vision of a "hard-working ant-matriarchy, with a self-isolating queen in its midst" can be read as a self-referential figuration of "nascent ... artistic consciousness" (116).

Son, on the other hand, is far more problematic and his mentoring of Jadine is "fraught with danger" (109). Duvall attempts to show, through close reading, that Son rapes Jadine in *Tar Baby* (270–72). Previously unnoticed by critics, this alluded rape was "rhetorically constructed to deny the reader's awareness of the violence" (104). Unlike most critics, Duvall argues that, in joining the blind horsemen in the novel's final lines, Son is "relegated to the trash heap ... of mythology" (116).

Andrea O'Reilly's *Toni Morrison and Motherhood* (2004) argues that, unlike the role of women in the white patriarchal nuclear family, black femininity is built on traditions of "matrifocality", "social activism" and "othermothering"; black mothering has been a "site of agency" and "resistance" (19, 29) – a "political undertaking" (32). O'Reilly warns of the danger of abandoning traditional black femininity in favour of white feminist liberation as self-realization.

Morrison's novels pursue a strategy of highlighting the value of black mothering through absence – by studying the destructive consequences of the absence of black mothering in the traditional mould (43, 46, 172). Ondine has cut Jadine off from the black motherline, leaving Jadine to identify, wrongly, with a white model of female liberation. Son then attempts to other-mother the motherless Jadine but fails. Promisingly, Son is "introduced through images of birth" (108) and "associated with nature and fertility"; and he returns to the maternal/foetal and "pre-Oedipal" world of the naked and blind horsemen (109). However, close attention shows that Son lives his life according to "patriarchal masculinity", especially in his violence towards women, which is "trivialized" by the text (114). As a result, he can't be a "male mother" (115) to Jadine and her reconnection with the motherline fails.

O'Reilly argues that Margaret's abuse of Michael can be read as resistance against her objectification by her husband (145); and makes the wider argument that "[i]n Morrison resistance against patriarchal motherhood is conveyed either as 'deviant' maternal nurturance ... or as failed maternal nurturance" (34, 118). However, as I previously commented, this turns all acts of deviant and failed motherhood into acts of resistance and makes it impossible to distinguish between the two.

The main blind spot in O'Reilly's reading of *Tar Baby* is her unwillingness to consider that Morrison might here be exploring models of traditional black femininity *critically* rather than simply endorsing and celebrating them.

POSTCOLONIAL READINGS

Tar Baby addresses colonialism and postcolonialism explicitly and invites a postcolonial reading. **Paul Gilroy**'s influential *The Black Atlantic* (1993) offers tools for such a reading. Though Gilroy doesn't offer a reading of the novel, his theory can illuminate the novel's mixing of African American, European and African mythic elements; the relation between the African American Son and the Caribbean Marie-Thérèse; and the relation between Jadine and Valerian.

Gilroy views black experience as an exemplary modern experience, in that it has been an experience of displacement and ongoing hybridization. He objects to those who advocate African American particularism: those who view African Americans as a clearly delimited, homogeneous group due to their common origin in an idealized African past. Gilroy calls this Africentricity. He argues that a black identification with Moses and Exodus (and the trope of travelling as a way of figuring slavery) is more helpful than an identification with Egyptian pharaohs. He suggests that African Americans have no exclusive rights to African (or indeed ancient Egyptian) heritage and their version of it is not definitive. He proposes that the countercultural pursuit of mixing intellectual and cultural lines (for example, Richard Wright's move to Paris in 1946) – countercultural alliance – is more effective than the escape from modernity sought in an African American cultural nationalism safeguarding lines of separation and presenting tradition as unproblematically available and necessarily helpful. He insists that recognizing the multiple heritage of black thought and culture is important, and reads the search for its origin in exclusively black sources as a perverse reaction to the mainstream neglect of black thought and culture and indifference to black history.

In response to "those who fear that the integrity of black particularity would be compromised by attempts to open a complex dialogue with other consciousnesses of affliction" (215), Gilroy stresses: the "heterology of black cultures" (194); "exchanges ... that call the very desire to be centred into question" (190); the incessant interaction between so-called white and black thought and culture; the relation of "antagonistic indebtedness" (191) of black countercultures to modernity and their status both as inside and outside. In response to those who "present immutable, ethnic differences as an absolute break in the histories and experiences of 'black' and 'white' people", he advocates a "more difficult option: the theorization of creolisation, *métissage*, *mestizaje*, and hybridity" (2). Gilroy sees Morrison as an ally in his project.

Julia V. Emberley, in "A Historical Transposition" (1999), reads *Tar Baby* together with Fanon's *Black Skin, White Masks*. Emberley argues that Jadine's is a new identity related to the "increasing expansion of U.S. power in the form of political and economic globalization and a shift from the political activism of the 1960s and 1970s to the symbolic powers of multiculturalism and identity politics in the 1980s" (416). Jadine's identity is a "limit case in identity politics; her white, black, and copper masks are not simply facades that, once disclosed, will reveal an original identity. There is no hidden essence underneath the make-up of her subjectivity. She is a transnational first-world black woman" (427–28). But Morrison does not allow us to forget "the indigenous women on the island, represented by the figures of female domestic labor": Jadine's "freedom and enlightenment candidacy ... come at the expense of these colonized domestic laborers" (427).

Yogita Goyal's "The Gender of Diaspora in Toni Morrison's *Tar Baby*" (2006) argues against critics' reading of the novel as a "defense of tradition" (393). This black nationalist position is one of two antithetical positions explored critically in the novel, the other position being the anti-essentialist understanding of the black diaspora articulated by Paul Gilroy (see above). Black nationalism stresses unity and common roots; Gilroy stresses hybridity, discontinuity, contentions, misunderstandings and ambivalence. In *Tar Baby* these two discourses are represented by "two distinct generic strains, those of myth and realism" (394). At the mythic level of the blind horsemen, the swamp women, the night women and an animist nature there is timeless unity; at the realist level there is restlessness and disunity between African Americans and Caribbeans, North and South, urban and rural, men and women: "At the historical, realist level, diaspora exists as contention and fracture, ... subject to class and all the tensions and hierarchies of power" (408). Gilroy's conception of diaspora resonates with *Tar Baby* "at the realist level" (408). These two levels, mythic and realist, cannot be synthesized, leading some readers to a "sense of paralysis" (410).

Morrison examines Son's black nationalism from a feminist perspective to show its masculinism, gender-bias, policing of gender roles and sexuality and to question his fetishization of tradition as an objectification of women; she examines Jadine's mobility and cosmopolitanism from a black nationalist perspective to question her rejection of tradition. From a black nationalist perspective – and the perspective of many critics – Jadine is a "race traitor, or the tar baby captive to white culture" (399). The novel offers an "ambivalent" reading of tradition, suggesting that "the past may threaten individual identity as well as nurture it" (399). Goyal concludes that "in the dramatic conflict between Son and Jadine, neither can be upheld as a reliable authority on race or gender" – Morrison uses them against each other to "reveal their limitations" (406).

DIALOGIC READINGS: DU BOIS, BAKHTIN, GATES, ETC.

Du Bois's concept of "double consciousness resonates with Bakhtin's theory of "heteroglossia" and "dialogism"; as Gates's concept of "Signification" (indebted to Du Bois) resonates with poststucturalist and deconstructive tactics of resignification, play, the deferral of the signified (as theorized by Jacques Derrida et al. and indebted to Bakhtin).

For **Denise Heinze**'s *The Dilemma of "Double-Consciousness"* (1993) Morrison "Signifies upon" the dominant model of beauty (15): reversing "colorism" (the overvaluation of the light-skinned and undervaluation of the dark-skinned), the light-skinned Jadine is "entirely unappealing" (21), while the very dark-skinned woman in yellow is an "image of beauty capable of lifting people out of the corporeal into the spiritual" (46). (See **p. 184.**) Morrison also Signifies upon black masculinity, advocating "feminized" men (83); Son represents "an integration of (culturally produced) gender roles" (90). Finally, through Morrison's use of the supernatural, double-consciousness, as redefined by Gates, becomes "as much [the readers'] psychic state of being as it is hers" (185); a realist and a supernatural perspective are no longer polarized. Valerian and Jadine, the two most educated and "sophisticated" characters, have an intense relation to the supernatural as "a chance to reflect on what they may have missed in their endeavor to embrace the status quo" (172).

For **Philip Page**, in *Dangerous Freedom* (1995), while initially L'Arbe de la Croix is hierarchical and "resembles an antebellum [pre-Civil War] plantation" (112), once Valerian's authority begins to unravel, characters engage in power struggles in order to impose their perspective and make others in their image. Control, hierarchy, authority, who owns the house, who is on whose side: these are the issues (120). As a result of these power struggles, hierarchy gives way to "contention and dissolution" (108).

Morrison counters both hierarchy and power struggles and introduces a Bakhtinian dialogism by formal means. These formal means include: Morrison's "opening of the tar baby myth into ambiguous multiplicity"; Morrison's use of "suspension" (hinting at an event and periodically returning to it, as in jazz music); and her use of "image refrains" (131). Morrison thereby creates "internal dialogue within the text" and the "reader is required ... to fuse ... the linguistic fragments" (131). These techniques open into "greater flexibility, inclusiveness, and harmony" (132).

Linden Peach's *Toni Morrison* (2000) argues that one of the generic intertexts of this novel is Southern romance. It engages with the alliance between whites and a slave elite that identifies with white values in Southern romance (84); and explores the situation of African Americans caught in an "alienating language" (85). Working against the model of Southern romance, meaning in *Tar Baby* is infinitely deferred – and Michael, quite appropriately, never arrives. This deferral of meaning and of resolution resonates both with the work of Derrida and with the open-endedness of the "Tar Baby" folktales. Similarly, in *Tar Baby* the self is multiplicitous, both in resonance with postmodern literature and in order to highlight the experience of African Americans at the "interface" of cultures (101).

For **Joyce Hope Scott**'s "*Song of Solomon* and *Tar Baby*" (2007) *Tar Baby* "exemplifies Bakhtin's carnivalesque" (32). The carnivalesque can be defined as blasphemous, transgressive, producing "subversive acts of language and representation" that parody and undermine "official cultural authority" (32). In *Tar Baby* the marginalized African American trickster Son, his black vernacular and his "Tar Baby" tale, together with a sentient Caribbean nature and a Caribbean mythic world of blind horsemen and swamp women, are "in contestatorial dialogue with the white master narrative" of Valerian (32). The novel stages the "dialogic interaction of the marginalized and the dominant" (33). The horsemen's blindness is a "'trope of the carnivalesque' – a trope of the alterity of their perspective on the world" (39).

If Bakhtin's theory is based on the European tradition of carnival, this novel mobilizes the "idea of carnival as it emerged in the Caribbean, as a manifestation of the spirit of African resistance seen in maroon communities of runaway slaves and freed Africans" who appropriated European carnival (33–34).

METAFICTIONAL READINGS

Judylyn S. Ryan's "Contested Visions/Double-Vision in *Tar Baby*" (1993) argues for the need for metafictional readings of Toni Morrison's novels: readings addressing Morrison's self-referential exploration and theorization of her art within her literary texts (598). Ryan's starting point is Barbara Christian's influential essay, "The Race for Theory" (Christian 1988), which argues that, instead of reading black women writers through an established theoretical framework that might misunderstand their aims, we should pay attention to their own metafictional theorizations. Morrison herself seems to support Christian's project in *Playing in the Dark*: "Criticism as a form of knowledge is capable of robbing literature not only of its own implicit and explicit ideology but of its ideas as well" (quot. Ryan 1993, 597).

Linda Krumholz, in "Blackness and Art in Toni Morrison's *Tar Baby*" (2008), offers a fully developed metafictional reading of *Tar Baby*. Morrison engages with inherited white constructions of blackness – as either absence or excess – and translates them in "aesthetic choices" and "rhetorical strategies" of her black aesthetic (267). In *Tar Baby* she uses an aesthetic of absence in a variety of ways: non-arrival of a main character, Michael; use of "secrets and untold stories" such as Michael's abuse; use of "allusions and elision", particularly allusion to large-scale historical events, such as the history of sugar as a large component of colonial (and neocolonial) economies in the Caribbean and the Southern USA (268). These absences invite readers to fill in the gaps and participate actively. Morrison's brief allusions to African concepts of the mask and of *nommo* – the "generative", shaping and transforming power of words (274) – in *Tar Baby* point to a conceptual framework endorsing active relations between author, reader and world (267). African masks, worn over generations, are part of a conception and practice of art as effective, functional, "shaped by history" (276) and interactive: involving an "active relation" between mask maker, actor and audience (274). Morrison points to this aesthetic when she describes *Tar Baby* as "a piece of mask sculpture" in "Unspeakable Things Unspoken" (quot. Krumholz 2008, 275).

Morrison also uses excess. The woman in yellow haunting Jadine is described as "too much". Morrison creates an "excess of meaning" (271) around certain words, for example the word "tar", which takes new and positive meanings beyond the established and negative racist connotations. Excess makes straightforward interpretation difficult and goes hand in hand with a certain "ethics of reading" (270): we are made aware of our "responsibility for the meanings we create" (271). Morrison also uses a destabilizing "excess of literary allusions" (270).

The plot of *Tar Baby* "works as a metafiction about the ... purpose of black art": to reveal the intersection of art, politics and economics, "transform cultural meanings" and "transform readers" (267). Son is a metafictional "representation of black art" (277), Valerian's house represents white culture, and Valerian represents the "white liberal" humanist view of culture that "mask[s] the relation between culture and power" (283). Margaret, in her associations with sugar (for example, when Valerian first meets her she is dressed like a Valerian candy), might be seen to represent the liberal humanist view of culture as "sweetness and light" (Matthew Arnold), while her abuse of Michael represents culture's hidden links to power and economics. Margaret "dramatizes" the difficulty of narrating what is "unspeakable" without aestheticizing it (288). Son's new respectable clothes and haircut represent the anxiety of "black and subaltern writers who find that when they are put in a position to speak for the folk, they are already set at a distance from them" (282). In the Christmas-meal scene, Son's role in exposing Margaret's abuse but also large-scale historical exploitation constructs Black art as an alternative and transformative "way of seeing" (286). *Tar Baby* is ultimately about the need for metafictional awareness (290).

The main problem with this interesting reading is its selective focus on particular scenes and characters in the first part of the novel. For example, it marginalizes the role of Jadine and relations among black characters in the novel.

SELECTED OTHER CRITICISM

A Marxist reading

K. Sumana's *The Novels of Toni Morrison* (1998) argues that Son's individual solution – in that "he does not join with others, bringing about any change" (107) – is idealistic and "undesirable" (111). (See **p. 188**.) Morrison "does not provide a viable alternative existence … Eradication of the plight of African people demands … collective class struggle against capitalism" (112). One can object that Morrison sees her role as one of posing and exploring problems, not one of providing stock Marxist solutions.

A psychoanalytic reading

For **J. Brooks Bouson**'s *Quiet as It's Kept* (2000) *Tar Baby* is a text divided. First, it associates blackness with both pride and shame (130). It also counter-shames whites: "drawing on essentialist racist discourse … the narrative actively projects onto whites the shame they have long projected onto blacks" (106). Secondly, "tar baby" is racist slang for a black girl (as Morrison herself has pointed out) and Morrison appropriates and redefines tar in positive terms, as a substance that holds things together; however, at the same time, the presentation of threatening female ancestors "undercuts" the positive redefinition of tar and black female mothering (104). Thirdly, while the mythic discourse of blind horsemen, swamp women and pie ladies counters the realist "shaming racial discourse", it also problematically "inscribes the white-constructed and shaming myth of an earthy and natural – and intellectually and culturally inferior – black primitivism" (121). *Tar Baby* therefore sends "mixed messages" (passim). Bouson observes that critics have been tempted to resolve this ambivalence and take sides.

Beloved

PSYCHOANALYTIC READINGS

Psychoanalysis has been, arguably, the dominant discourse in secondary criticism on *Beloved*. A great variety of psychoanalytic concepts have been mobilized.

Deborah Horvitz's "Nameless Ghosts" (1989) argues that Beloved is not only Sethe's daughter but also Sethe's mother, whose own mother leapt into the sea during the Middle Passage. The history of these women is one of maternal loss and perceived "abandonment" and "betrayal" (59). The novel advocates the "imperative to preserve continuity ... between generations of Black women" (64). From a psychoanalytic perspective Beloved is the "embodiment of Sethe's memories" of her dead daughter and mother, enabling Sethe to "remember and tell the story of her past" (66).

Linda Krumholz's "The Ghosts of Slavery" (1992) describes slavery as an individual and "national" trauma (108). Beloved is an "eruption" of the traumatic and repressed past: she "catalyzes the healing process for the characters and for the reader", but simultaneously "foreclos[es] the possibility of a complete 'clearing'" of the past (110). Beloved is both the trauma and its psychic cure: she is "like an analyst, the object of transference and cathexis that draws out the past, while at the same time she is the past" (114).

Ritual is central to the process of healing in *Beloved*. Baby Suggs's ritual in the Clearing is a "model" for this process (114). The gathering of the thirty women is a similar "cleansing ritual" that brings Sethe back to the original scene of infanticide and "enables her to relive it with a difference" (118–19). There are similarities between the psychoanalytic cure and ritual healing in *Beloved*; Morrison suggests that Freud's "theories are modern European derivations from long-standing ritual practices of psychic healing" (111).

For **Jennifer FitzGerald**, in "Selfhood and Community" (1993), the psychoanalyst Melanie Klein, describing the pre-Oedipal phase dominated by the infant's relation to the mother, illuminates Beloved's ambivalent relation to Sethe. Unable yet to distinguish between its own self and the mother as an independent person, the infant projects its own ambiguous feelings of intense love and hate for the mother onto a "good" idealized mother attracting the infant's adoration and a "bad" mother attracting the infant's aggression. For Klein the normal path of development is as follows: projection gives way to introjection and the child recognizes the imagos of the mother as of its own making; the self emerges as separate and autonomous; the mother is recognized as a separate and autonomous being. The perceived end of "normal" psychic development is to emerge as an autonomous subject. Paul D initially attempts but fails to live up to a model of masculinity privileging the autonomy of the subject. FitzGerald argues that in killing her daughter Sethe adopts a similar model of motherhood: in the context of the nuclear family the mother is an autonomous subject with exclusive responsibility for her children.

Morrison critiques the "normal" development of the self in the context of the nuclear family and outlines an alternative announced by Baby Suggs's "discourse of communal self-love" (121). Instead of Sethe's "outrageous claims to *exclusive* responsibility", the African American community provides "communal mothering" as an "alternative to the individualism and autonomy" privileged by psychoanalysis in its focus on the nuclear family. Identity is "constructed not within ... the hegemonic nuclear family but in relation to the whole community" (122). Paul D's washing of Sethe continues Baby Suggs's work, rejects dominant masculinity and contributes to an "alternative version of mothering" (118).

For **Jean Wyatt**, in "Giving Body to the Word" (1993), Morrison revises Jacques Lacan and proposes an alternative to his distinction between the maternal "imaginary order" and the paternal "symbolic order". Wyatt calls this alternative the "maternal symbolic".

Lacan differentiates between a preverbal order of "imaginary" corporeal fusion between infant and mother; and the order of language or "symbolic order" following it. Language is, for Lacan, an order of symbolic differentiations and substitutions. Beloved and Sethe belong to the former order: Beloved's language undoes demarcations, differentiations and separations to assert: I am you; Sethe refuses to substitute words for her dead daughter, hence her daughter's return as a ghost and then as the fully embodied Beloved. While Lacan "opposes bodily connection and verbal exchange" and presents us with an "either-or choice between bodily presence and abstract signifier" (477), Morrison treats this as a false dilemma and envisages the interaction between "a maternal order of nurturance and a paternal order of abstract significations" (482). In joining the community, Denver joins a "social order of language and exchange that both feeds her and teaches her to read" (482). Denver's progress "from the imaginary of mother-daughter fusions to the symbolic order of language and society ... does not entail abandoning maternal intimacy"; however, the community "demands ... a reciprocal nurturing" (483). Against Lacan, Morrison doesn't see a necessary developmental sequence from bodily proximity to language: Denver's "'original hunger' is not for the mother's body but for words" (482).

The gathering of the thirty women and Paul D's return enable Sethe herself to enter the symbolic order and tell her story. "She left me" is Sethe's acknowledgement of Beloved's absence and "puts a signifier there, where the child's body had been" (484). Again revising Lacan, "acts of maternal care" (483) by the thirty women and Paul D are the "necessary support" (484) for Sethe's entry into language.

Denise Heinze's *The Dilemma of "Double-Consciousness"* (1993) argues that *Beloved* can be read as literature of the "uncanny, defined by Schelling as 'the name for everything that ought to have remained ... secret and hidden but has come to light'" (174–75). Heinze implicitly refers to Freud's canonical essay, "The Uncanny" (1919). Beloved is Sethe's uncanny "double": she "seems more a projection of Sethe's imagination than a reincarnation of her daughter" (176). When the initial period of Sethe's "self-love" ends (177), Beloved becomes Sethe's "own unforgiving memory, growing obese with Sethe's guilt" (179). In that others see Beloved, she is also "the projection of repressed collective memory of a violated people" (179).

Peter Nicholls, in "The Belated Postmodern" (1996), points out that the "return of the repressed" in psychoanalysis is not the simple recovery of a repressed content but the retroactive reconstruction of a traumatic event that remains inaccessible. Freud's concept of *Nachträglichkeit* ("belatedness") captures this retroactive logic. The return of the repressed is an "interpretive elaboration or working through whose role is to weave around the rememorated element an entire network of meaningful relations that integrate it into the subject's explicit apprehension of himself" (135, Nicholls quoting Laplanche and Leclair). This is what Sethe has been *failing* to do.

Nicolas Abraham and Maria Torok distinguish between psychic "incorporation" and "introjection" of the dead by the bereaved, in favour of the latter: whereas "introjection assimilates to the self what is lost, incorporation perpetuates the existence of the lost object as something alive and foreign within the self" (140). Abraham and Torok's concept of the "crypt" describes the pathology of incorporation as a failure to mourn properly: "In this crypt reposes – alive ... – the objective counterpart of the loss, as a complete person" (140–41, Nicholls quoting Abraham and Torok). Beloved's return in the flesh can be understood as Sethe's incorporation of Beloved. Sethe has to move from incorporation to introjection: a return of the repressed that reconstructs and recognizes Beloved's loss.

Gurleen Grewal's *Circles of Sorrow, Lines of Struggle* (1998) points to psychoanalytic critic Cathy Caruth, who defines "trauma" as "the literal return of the event against the will of the one it inhabits" (98; Grewal quoting Caruth). Ghostly possession or hauntedness is "trauma". Whereas Harriet Jacobs' *Incidents in the Life of a Slave Girl* (1861) and Frances Harper's *Iola Leroy* present happy individual resolutions, Morrison's "revisionary slave narrative" (98) presents widespread trauma. The traumatic event is not, properly speaking, experienced while it happens – its experience can only be belated. When history is traumatic, "historical experience itself is belated experience … the representation of a historical trauma … relying on … conditions, such as the climate of political and literary receptivity" (103). Morrison stresses the communal and interactive nature of the representation of trauma. The plot re-enacts the infanticide "with a saving difference" – the gathering of the thirty women (115). Having lifted the veil, the novel "must also eventually draw the veil" (116), but this is "forgetting enabled by a therapeutic working-through of the repressed material of historical trauma" (117).

While pursuing a psychoanalytic reading, Grewal points out the cross-cultural references of the figure of Beloved: reminiscent of the Jungian archetype of the maiden, within a West African context Beloved is an *abiku*, a dead child returned to "plague the mother" (106; Grewal quotes a poem, "Abiku", by Wole Soyinka). In a Christian context Beloved redefines St John 1:14 – "And the Word was made flesh" – and Song of Songs 6:3 – "I am my beloved's, and my beloved is mine" – and takes the place of the Holy Ghost in a female trinity of mother, daughter and ghost. In an ancient Greek context, the story of Beloved as a child whose mother jumped ship during the Middle Passage leaving her behind and who was later kept prisoner by a man revises the story of Demeter, Persephone and Pluto (112).

Jill Matus's *Toni Morrison* (1998) argues that Morrison's novels "testify to historical trauma" (1). The traumatic past is unassimilated and is not experienced as past; one repeats it compulsively, and any one account will be fragmented and incomplete. Current definitions of trauma include: long-term exposure to a situation; "insidious trauma" that goes unrecognized by dominant culture and is possibly perpetuated by it (28); and trans-generationally transmitted trauma. Trauma theorists highlight the role of a sympathetic listener/audience in therapy, and this is confirmed in *Beloved* (for example, Paul D, Denver and the community begin to listen to Sethe's story). However, Morrison questions the possibility of completely redeeming the past (for example, Beloved's exorcism leaves Sethe exhausted rather than healed).

Sethe suffers from an overactive memory beyond her control and aestheticizes scenes of racist violence against her will. The lack of feeling on her back, her inability to perceive colour and Denver's deafness are bodily symptoms of trauma. Sethe hasn't forgotten her infanticide, but her account of it is blocked, delayed and fragmented. The non-linearity, discontinuity and fragmentariness of *Beloved* and the return of Beloved enact trauma as a "disease of time" (111).

Sethe's most repressed memories are those of her mother's escape without her and her sense of abandonment; they are the repressed context in which to understand Sethe's infanticide.

J. Brooks Bouson's *Quiet as It's Kept* (2000) endorses recent psychoanalytic work on trauma that has expanded its definition to include: entire "victim-survivor populations" (8); and protracted exposure (3). Trauma would therefore include the Holocaust, anti-Semitism, slavery as well as the post-emancipation treatment of African Americans as a "racially inferior and stigmatized Other" (6, 12–13). In line with trauma theory, Morrison presents traumatic events and their "speechless terror" in "highly visual scenes" and with "a detached perspective" – what trauma theorists call "dissociation" (7); and captures the involuntary, unpredictable and invasive nature of traumatic memories.

Sethe's account of "rememory" (*Beloved*, 36) – her idea that the picture of a catastrophic event stays in the world, is waiting for you and will make the event happen again – captures the involuntary flashes of invasive memory suffered by trauma victims (135, 149). Sethe's near-strangulation by Beloved in the Clearing can be read as Sethe's rememory of cutting her baby's throat (151). Beloved's experience of falling to pieces is in keeping with current literature concerning the fantasies of traumatized children.

Beloved is "using the device of the ghost to convey the power of trauma to posses and trap its victims" (134). However, at the same time the ghost-story element distracts readers from the real horror of slavery presented to them (136). For example, *Beloved* aestheticizes the much more unpalatable story of Margaret Garner (137). The novel therefore "alternates" between uncompromising realism and aestheticization (142).

Collective trauma includes the shaming of a stigmatized group and this group's internalization of the shaming. This is the experience described by Du Bois as African American "double consciousness", and by Fanon as the black person's internalization of racism and resultant "doubleness of experience" (14): as himself and as a despicable other. Though the Civil Rights Movement attempted to interrupt the intergenerational transmission of shame and replace shame with pride, this inveterate shame has not yet been fully overcome.

Morrison "stages scenes of inter- and intraracial shaming"; "struggl-[es] with internalized racism"; aestheticizes the traumatic and the shameful in "the reactive desire to cover up or repair"; constructs "antishaming and restitutive fantasies" usually involving African American ancestors; counter-shames white people and "constructs whiteness as a sign of pathological difference" (ix, 5, 18–19, 21). Morrison's ambiguous characters and endings draw critics into a cycle of shame, as the secondary literature reveals. Critics attempt to rescue one character and listen sympathetically to their story, while they condemn another, shaming and counter-shaming (20). The ambivalent presentation of Sethe's infanticide is "designed to force readers to participate in the shame-and-blame drama" (147) – as is Sethe's ambivalent attack against Bodwin (158). The presentation of Beloved is equally ambivalent: she condenses black collective suffering and simultaneously steers close to the racist stereotype of the black Jezebel (152). *Beloved* is therefore a text of "split perceptions" (160).

Kathleen Marks's *Toni Morrison's* Beloved *and the Apotropaic Imagination* (2003) combines psychoanalysis and Classical scholarship. In ancient Greek culture there is a place for a particular kind of "apotropaic" acts. The apotropaic (preventing evil) literally means turning away from evil, but can take the form of defending yourself from evil by means of the evil itself, as in Oedipus's self-blinding, Antigone's suicide, and the accommodation of the old gods (the Furies) within the context of the new order of the Olympian gods in the *Oresteia*. This kind of apotropaic act manifests human resistance to outside evil but also, according to psychoanalysis, resistance to threatening unconscious memories. It is intended to be preservative but is "a flawed way of seeing reality" (3). Marks makes a distinction between apotropaic and therapeutic – the latter involving selection and discarding of aspects of the past – in favour of the latter. Memory involves a therapeutic discarding role: "it distinguishes between what ought truly to be resisted and what needs to be remembered" (24).

Sethe's infanticide is an apotropaic act, but so is Beloved's return. Marks presents Sethe as Persephone. In Homer's "Hymn to Demeter", Persephone, daughter of earth goddess Demeter, is abducted and raped by Pluto, god of the underworld. Demeter suspends all germination and natural growth until her daughter is returned. Zeus allows Persephone to live above ground for two-thirds of the year, but she has to return to the underworld for the remainder of the year. Persephone is a paradoxical figure: both queen of the underworld and its enemy; both apotropaic and therapeutic. For example, in the *Odyssey*, Odysseus descends to the underworld where he encounters the shadows of illustrious men and women now dead, including his mother, and is reluctant to leave. But Persephone dispels those apotropaic images of her own making: having captivated him with those appalling images, she now therapeutically enables him to return to life.

Sethe's Persephone-like abduction happens when she overhears Schoolteacher discussing her as an animal; to preserve herself a demonic apotropaic power rises in her and she takes on animalistic properties, becoming "Like a snake. All jaws" (*Beloved*, 31). Marks argues that Beloved isn't Sethe's daughter returned to life. She is a false image, a Gorgon's head, created by Sethe in an apotropaic act defending her from "the horror of her own action" (48). Beloved is Sethe's uncanny double. She is pregnant not with child but with her desire to "consume Sethe" (95), i.e. with a suicidal desire, as she *is* Sethe. The Gorgon Medusa could turn men who looked at her directly into stone and Perseus escapes this fate by looking at her in his mirror-like shield. Paul D, following Perseus, keeps his eyes on the silvery lard can when looking at Beloved and lives (*Beloved*, 116). As a "Gorgonian being" (70), Beloved is "what must be turned away, what may not be preferred" (66). Beloved was a "false incarnation" of the past (120). Sethe, Denver and the thirty women come to realize this and to move from the apotropaic to the therapeutic. What is required is to return to the past and, as an artist, wilfully discard and select and imaginatively reorder into a whole, which is what Morrison does in *Beloved*.

Baby Suggs's message of self-love is gradually identified as the part "lying fallow" (43) and in need of selection and reimagination – and which finally sends Denver to the outside world. Denver becomes Persephonic-therapeutic in that she "initiates a kind of spring in the community" (108); while the thirty women become Persephonic-therapeutic in "scattering the image of nothingness before them, the figure of Beloved ... transforming memory ... into an artistic mode of selection that is rooted in the present and insists on life" (111). The community "recognizes the figure's insignificance to its present" (122) and "Beloved" is redefined by the text to refer primarily to Sethe. Baby Suggs's message should therefore be reinterpreted as "only those parts of the past that offer life ought to be loved" (54). The Clearing is a metaphor for this discarding process.

AFRICANIST AND AFRICAN-AMERICANIST INTERTEXTUAL READINGS

Marilyn Sanders Mobley's "A Different Remembering" (1990) reads *Beloved* as a revision of slave narratives, focusing on Morrison's creative deviations from them. While slave narratives move forward from slavery to freedom, *Beloved* "challenges the Western notion of linear time that informs ... the slave narratives" (51). While slave narratives tell the story of one individual from that individual's perspective, *Beloved* "contains not only Sethe's story" but a multiplicity of stories and perspectives – "fragments ... which speak to and comment on one another" (52). While slave narratives highlight the author's literacy, *Beloved* values orality and performs "the call and response pattern of the African-American oral tradition" (52). While slave narratives treat memory as a "monologic, mechanical conduit for facts and incidents", Morrison questions the objectivity of memory and "foregrounds the dialogic characteristics of memory along with its imaginative capacity to construct and reconstruct the significance of the past" (51).

Susan Bowers, in "*Beloved* and the New Apocalypse" (1990), argues that Morrison "fuses Christian notions of apocalypse with West African beliefs" to create a "revised" apocalypse (210). "Apocalypse" means revelation or unveiling. Traditionally apocalyptic writing has been an anticipation and revelation of the future, in keeping with a linear notion of time, but Morrison introduces a West African circular temporality to create an apocalypse that unveils the return of the past in the present. Beloved's return brings about an "apocalyptic demolition of the boundaries between the earthly and spiritual realms, an invasion of the world of the living by the world beyond the veil" (211) – it has "the effect of Judgment Day" (218). However, within a cyclical temporality, there is no end of time: "apocalypse is repeatable and survivable" (212); "judgment can be endured and redemption still achieved" (218). Denver is the "redemptive figure" in the novel (221): she is an "intermediary between spirits and [the] living" (222) and makes possible the exorcism of Beloved by the thirty women. The "primal sound" of the thirty women "takes them all outside of linear time" (224) and "creates the moment of redemptive transfiguration" in *Beloved* (225). Morrison does not offer an "anticipation of the messianic age – the time of freedom and redemption" (214); redemption is a moment and not a permanent final state.

Maggie Sale's "Call and Response as Critical Method" (1992) reads *Beloved* in the context of African American oral traditions, paying particular attention to "improvisation and call-and-response patterns" (42). The novel rewrites slave narratives – which inaugurate the African American written tradition – "with an oral rather than literary style" (45), and presents the experience of a largely illiterate population "in a style more appropriate to that experience" (45). An oral and communal aesthetic of improvisation and call-and-response "encourages multiple ways of seeing and interpreting" (44). Unlike canonical historiography *Beloved* questions "notions of objectivity" (46) and "master versions of history" (42) and moves the "marginalized ... to the center"; but unlike other revisionist projects, the "center presented in *Beloved* is multiple, contradictory" (49).

Beloved values an "interactive, dialogic model of interpretation" (49). In a European context this is a Bakhtinian model; in an African American context, this is an oral, call-and-response model. The novel thematizes and values the "interaction between the perspectives and needs of teller(s) and listener(s)" (46); values Denver's developing "ability to participate in the community" and "to move between positions" (48); asks of readers to refuse to "rest on any single element" (47); and invites the readers' participation by leaving stories "unfinished or unclarified" (43).

Linden Peach's *Toni Morrison* (2000) focuses on *Beloved*'s continuities with the African American literary tradition. *Beloved* "retains" many aspects of slave narratives: "the narrative is oblique, there are silences within it, and it is based on recollection" (25). While Morrison argued that in slave narratives "there was no mention of their interior life" (Morrison 1987c, 110), Peach argues that some slave narratives anticipate Morrison's attention to interiority; for example, *Narrative of the Life and Adventures of Henry Bibb, an American Slave* (1849) represents the protagonist's "internal conflicts" (103). Following Hazel Carby, Peach argues that African American women writers of the 1890s – and texts such as Frances Harper's *Iola Leroy* (1892) – anticipate Morrison. For example, Paul D's femininity has a precedent in nineteenth-century African American women's writing.

Beloved simultaneously interrogates texts and narratives embedded in slave narratives: the narrative of the North as Promised Land (Morrison has pointed out that in the aftermath of slavery the North failed to deliver); and the Bible as both an instrument of indoctrination of slaves and a resource for resistance (116). *Beloved* displays a generic instability: it moves between "slave narrative, folklore, myth, ghost story, autobiography, confession, romance, historical 'realism'" (120). Its effect is to destabilize and to suggest African Americans' fractured memory.

Therese E. Higgins's *Religiosity, Cosmology and Folklore* (2001) argues that Beloved is an African "ancestor". For the Mende of Sierra Leone, after death one's spirit undergoes a process called "crossing the water" (30–31). In keeping with this view, Beloved emerges out of the water and finally re-enters the water. The role of the community in *Beloved* can be understood in the context of African cosmologies, which feature one's clan and village rather than nuclear family: "This concept of interdependency and shared wealth ... is one held by many African societies ... [M]any African peoples ... use the word 'family' in a much broader sense" (77).

Justine Tally's *Toni Morrison's* Beloved (2009) argues that Morrison's references to Africa are a narrative enactment of Michel Foucault's project of giving voice to silenced, suppressed and subjugated knowledges. Foucault's project itself emerges out of Nietzsche's critique of Truth in favour of multiperspectivism. Tally highlights the importance of fertility and regeneration in African cosmologies and in *Beloved*. Sethe has a trace memory of her African mother dancing an antelope dance with other slaves. This might be the "celebration of the 'Ci-wara,' the antelope god who brought agriculture to the Bamana (or Bambara) people of Mali" (44). The Ci-wara ritual "simulates the mating of two antelopes" to celebrate the god who "taught men ... the regeneration both of the soil and of human beings" (121). The antelope is a "symbol of fertility" (129) and Sethe figures Denver and her kicks as an antelope and her hoof-kicks. Beloved, black, pregnant and naked, resembles a "fertility idol used in the Neolithic age, ritually buried in the fields to make them fertile" (137); such idols are still used in Mali for the rites of the Bamana people.

Critics have read Amy as a white indentured servant. Tally suggests that Amy is the ghost of the child of a white indentured servant mother and a black slave father – Amy is an African ancestor come to help Sethe. Tally reads Ella's comment – "I know what kind of white that was" – as confirmation of this. "Amy Denver" points to the French words *aimée* (beloved) and *d'envers* (from the other side).

Tally goes on to develop a black nationalist perspective indebted to the controversial work of Cheikh Anta Diop. She pursues a number of tenuous ancient Egyptian associations (for example, Denver's birth in the Ohio River, reddening the water, points to the annual rising of the Nile, red with sediments that fertilize the land). Tally continues to make the claim – for purely ideological reasons, in my view – that the "foundations of ancient 'Egyptian' culture [lie] in black Nubia" and, bizarrely, that African mythology is the origin of *all* mythologies (127). At the least, these claims are incompatible with Foucault's Nietzschean critique of (one) "truth" and (one) "origin" and are, on Tally's own admission in the first chapter, incompatible with Morrison's project.

AMERICANIST AND WESTERN INTERTEXTUAL READINGS

For **Lori Askeland**'s "Remodeling the Model Home in *Uncle Tom's Cabin* and *Beloved*" (1992) Morrison wrote *Beloved* as "a conscious parallel" to Harriet Beecher Stowe's *Uncle Tom's Cabin* (1852) (176) – particularly its "ideology of domesticity" (160). Stowe constructed "idealized matriarchal domain[s]" (162). *Beloved* shows the lack of autonomy and hence vulnerability of these domains. Mrs Garner has to invite Schoolteacher to run the tellingly named Sweet Home after Mr Garner's death; and her intercession on Sethe's behalf is worse than ineffectual and leads to Sethe's beating. Morrison suggests that Stowe's "matriarchal ideal does not finally alter the basic structure of the patriarchy" (175); Morrison however attempts to "alter irreversibly the power structure of the patriarchal home" (176).

The layout of Bodwin's home – parlour at the front and kitchen at the back, accessible through a back door – is that of a model nineteenth-century house, in keeping with the nineteenth-century ideology of domesticity that values privacy above all else. This ideology effectively hid and "separate[d] the woman who worked [in the kitchen] from the True Woman who reigned" in her front parlour (168). In *Beloved* Baby Suggs enters Bodwin's home through the back door and stays in his kitchen, while he receives slave-owners through the front door and in the front parlour (167). Baby Suggs changes the layout of 124 to abolish the back door and move the kitchen to the front. There is no separation in her home between work on the one hand and "community and spirituality" on the other hand: both are located in the kitchen (169). Furthermore, Baby Suggs's version of Christianity, unlike Stowe's, does not ask the powerless to be meek but rather to love themselves. However, Baby Suggs's success is very limited. *Beloved*'s return and haunting of 124 is a "patriarchal possession", keeping Sethe and Denver prisoners in the house (174). Baby Suggs might have changed the layout of the house but 124 is still owned by Bodwin. Ominously, Beloved disappears when Bodwin, the "more permanent possessor/ghost has returned to his domain" (174).

For **Rafael Pérez-Torres**'s "Between Presence and Absence" (1999) *Beloved* is exemplary of a "resistant and critical" (193) postmodernism coming from the margins and giving voice to the previously silenced (as theorized by Foucault). Linda Hutcheon had developed a similar argument about postmodernism in *The Politics of Postmodernism* (1989). Pérez-Torres rejects Fredric Jameson's and Hal Foster's view of postmodernism as ahistorical and argues that *Beloved* metafictionally exposes "history as narrative ... implicated in ideology" (183) and also "revises perceptions of the past ... in an implicit critique of contemporary social formations" (184). Pérez-Torres also rejects the view of postmodernism as lighthearted and politically unmotivated linguistic "play". The linguistic "play" of *Beloved* – for example, the resignification of "color" in Baby Suggs's pondering of "color" – involves a "deadly serious" (184) decoding of dominant language and resistant resignification. *Beloved* is exemplary of postmodernist "multicultural texts [that] place in the foreground the relation between language and power" (186). Finally Pérez-Torres rejects Jameson's view of postmodernism as uncritical "pastiche". *Beloved* offers a pastiche of a multiplicity of discourses on slavery – dominant and marginal, oral and written – but "dehierarchize[s]" them (196), privileging none. As a result it is an exercise in "disrupt[ing] authority" (197), and is exemplary of "critical postmodern pastiche" (194).

John N. Duvall's *The Identifying Fictions of Toni Morrison* (2000) explores *Beloved*'s dialogue with *Uncle Tom's Cabin*. The latter develops a Christian and simultaneously patriarchal worldview shared by Tom. In *Beloved* both Schoolteacher and Bodwin show allegiance to patriarchal Christianity. This worldview is answered by the pregnant Beloved, "a figure for the religious thinking of Baby Suggs" (125). Sethe's infanticide and the sound collectively emitted by the thirty women show allegiance to Baby Suggs's religion of the flesh, the "maternal body" and the sound that precedes language and God's word (130). Baby Suggs is the first accomplished artist in Morrison's novels and anticipates Morrison's role of public intellectual since the 1980s. Baby Suggs's prosperity (as demonstrated by her feast for 90) is also new in Morrison's work. Through Baby Suggs, Morrison continues her ongoing thinking about her art.

FEMINIST READINGS

Trudier Harris, in *Fiction and Folklore* (1991), focuses on folk elements in *Beloved*. The story of Denver's birth is fantastic – a folktale. The story of Sweet Home, whose characters are larger than life and legendary, is reminiscent of folktales of slave wish-fulfilment such as "Master's Gone to Philly Me York", where the slaves eat well when the master is away (176–77). Baby Suggs is a figure of the African American call-and-response tradition. Morrison presents storytelling as a creative power, grand and threatening: "Sound eventually drives Beloved out" (169). When Baby Suggs gives up this "creative role" she "become[s] just another victim of slavery" (175).

Folk tradition views women as fearful and demonic. For example, tricksters bravely enter "the vagina to break" its teeth (153). In the character of Beloved, Morrison also demonizes women because she is unable to take a distance, in this respect, from folklore. Beloved is a "traditional succubus, the female spirit who drains the male's life force even as she drains him of his sperm" (157). Beloved is demonized in her relation to Paul D and in her fight against Sethe's (masculine) parental authority. Beloved's exorcism resonates, for Harris, with the use of pans and sticks to drive out evil spirits in Frazer's influential anthropological study, *The Golden Bough* (1890).

Deborah Ayer Sitter's "The Making of a Man" (1992) offers a Bakhtinian feminist reading of *Beloved*, focusing on Paul D's "possessive love" of Sethe (18). *Beloved* stages a "debate over the meaning of manhood and the possibility for enduring heterosexual love" (18). Paul D has internalized a heroic individualist male ideal unwittingly inherited from the "culture of the white slaveholder" (24). This dominant – Bakhin's "centripetal" – model casts women in the role of maidens to be rescued. He attempts to rescue Sethe from the baby ghost when he arrives at 124, but his models of masculinity and femininity cause him to misrecognize Sethe's experience and "the woman she is" (23). Paul D's initial response to her infanticide cannot acknowledge her capacity for "male" behaviour but instead condemns her as "an animal" (25). Paul D comes to understand that there is no substantial difference between Garner and Schoolteacher and recognizes his "enslavement to [their] ideal of manhood" (18). In search of a livable masculinity, he retraces Sixo's African model. Sixo's "centrifugal" (Bakhtin) model involves respectful and "dialogic" coexistence with the natural world and the supernatural world, as well as Sixo's dialogic and egalitarian relation with the Thirty-Mile Woman.

Ashraf H.A. Rushdy's "Daughters Signifyin(g) History" (1992) argues that *Beloved*'s response to the debate as to whether slaves resisted or acquiesced in their enslavement, is to develop a "double perspective" (45). The two perspectives are embodied by Sethe's two daughters: Beloved represents "the need to forget" (48); Denver comes to represent "the need to remember" and tell the story: she becomes "the signifyin(g) daughter" (48). The novel's revisionist feminist historiography emphasizes oral storytelling and listening. Gradually Denver "overcom[es] her deafness" (59); listens to her mother's stories; develops a larger historical context for her mother's killing of her sister; and switches her allegiance from Beloved to Sethe. Denver then tells her mother's story to the community in her effort to save her; and the community listens and responds with Beloved's exorcism. Sethe herself becomes a signifyin(g) daughter when she remembers, understands within a larger context, and tells her mother's forgotten story.

While **Barbara Christian**'s "Layered Rhythms" (1993a) does not discuss *Beloved*, Christian's observations on the role of maternal love in Morrison's fiction are helpful in reading Sethe's "too thick" love. Morrison had to kill the "mammy in the Big House" (23), the stereotype of the bodily, acquiescent and happily servile black woman. African American women were presented as mammies in white fiction and even in African American male fiction, and the African American women's tradition was not yet fully recovered when Morrison was writing the novel; maternal love was therefore a powerfully counter-stereotypical theme. Morrison emphasizes the value of maternal love as a freedom historically denied and now claimed.

Pamela E. Barnett, in "Figurations of Rape and the Supernatural in *Beloved*" (1997), reads Beloved as a succubus, a sexually predatory female demon (like Harris above). Beloved rapes Paul, vampirically kisses Sethe's neck in the Clearing and later "sucks Sethe dry" (78). These sexual assaults are traumatic re-enactments of earlier assaults by white male rapists: Sethe's milking; and Paul D's repressed and shameful sexual violation in Alfred, Georgia. Paul D's sexual violation is especially unspeakable because "his shame as a male rape victim is too great" (83). He is unable to tell his story and unable to "join the community" of thirty women (83); critics refer to it "euphemistically if at all" (83). Morrison, however, reconfigures rape to suggest that "sexual exploitation is not only the black woman's story of slavery" (84).

Andrea O'Reilly's *Toni Morrison and Motherhood* (2004) views Sethe's mothering, including the infanticide, as resistance – "a radical act of defiance" (131) – in the face of an institution, slavery, which systematically sought to break the bond between mother and child. While a slave was "seldom allowed to nurse her babies" and only after white babies (129), Sethe's escape is a "heroic quest" where the Holy Grail is "to get milk to [her] baby girl" (133; *Beloved*, 16). The infanticide is "an act of preservative love" (136) (see Marks above), and Sethe asserts her mother's "right to decide what is best for her children" (135).

HISTORICIST READINGS

The first of the essays below is a traditional historicist reading; the second outlines a postmodern historiography.

Elizabeth B. House's "Toni Morrison's Ghost" (1990) argues that Beloved is "not a supernatural being … but simply a young woman who has herself suffered the horrors of slavery" (17). House's close reading of *Beloved* assembles this girl's story: the capture of her and her mother by slave traders in Africa; her mother's leap into the sea to escape and the death of a father figure; and her sexual exploitation in America by white men. *Beloved* is a story of "mistaken identity" (22) made possible by Sethe's longing for her dead daughter and Beloved's longing for her dead mother.

Mae G. Henderson, in "Toni Morrison's *Beloved*" (1991), examines *Beloved* in the context of contemporary historiographic theory on "discourse and narrativity" (84), particularly the work of Paul Ricoeur, R.G. Collingwood and Hayden White. Morrison's "imaginative and reconstructive" retrieval of the past resonates with their understanding of historiography as a narrative art (84). Sethe uses what Collingwood calls "the 'constructive imagination' as a means of re-membering a dis-membered past" (90). Sethe "shapes 'rememories' of the past … through a process of narrativization described by Ricoeur as *configuration* and White as *emplotment*" (90). Morrison's emphasis on "personal narrative, or storytelling" resonates with Collingwood's view of the historian as a "storyteller" (90).

Sethe needs to reconfigure what has been configured inappropriately by others. She uses the metaphor of maternity to construct a counternarrative of her history "along 'motherlines'" (95). Against the dominant metaphors of her infanticide as "animality" and "cannibalism" (97), she reconfigures her infanticide within a "family story of [maternal] infanticide" and within a "context of sacrifice, resistance, and mother-love" (96). Sethe's re-enactment of her infanticide within the transformative context of a community of thirty women resonates with Collingwood's notion of "'history as re-enactment' of past experience" (98). Within Ricoeur's model, Sethe's actions are the "prefigurative" moment; her storytelling, the "configurative" moment; and her re-enactment, the "refigurative" moment where the world of action and the world of narrative interact (100).

SELECTED OTHER CRITICISM

A Foucauldian reading

April Lidinsky's "Prophesying Bodies" (1994) mobilizes Michel Foucault's argument in *Discipline and Punish* that modern power is productive (as opposed to the conventional idea that it is negative, constraining, repressive) and that the individual is an invention of modern power. Modern power constructs individuals as highly disciplined and self-disciplined bodies in a one-to-one vertical relation with authority. Resistance for Foucault is the deployment of collective horizontal (dehierarchized) relations. Collective action undoes compulsory individualization.

Lidinsky comments on the chain gang of Alfred, Georgia and the initial obedient self-chaining of each prisoner that the "Soldier-like discipline seems ... to be the 'miracle' enabling three white guards to achieve such control" (101). There follows a "horizontal redirection of power" (101). Individualization and obedience turn into collective action and resistance, in keeping both with the Foucauldian model and the African American model of call and response: once the men begin listening to each other, "collective action becomes a possibility" (101). They develop a language of "tugs" with which to talk to each other through their chain, "transforming the very device that keeps them partitioned" into a means of collective resistance (101). Resistance is an ongoing collective process. Paul D has to unlearn the iron disciplining of his body that has turned his heart into a sealed tin can; Sethe "must unlearn the choke-hold of the 'circle of iron'" (103). Like the chain gang members, Paul D and Sethe come to develop a "call-and-response connection", involving "practices of collaborative storytelling" and "new somatic literacies" (104).

A Bakhtinian reading

For **Philip Page**'s *Dangerous Freedom* (1995) *Beloved* emphasizes healing accomplished through *nommo*, the African power of the word to bring the world properly into existence: telling stories but also "empathic listening" (145). In this process Bakhtinian "heteroglossia" – not just the coexistence but the interrelation or dialogization of different perspectives – is crucial. For example, Sethe's and Paul D's "memories and minds synchronize ... the point of view alternates between the two, Sethe can read Paul's thoughts ... and nonverbally they share the same memory of the loose corn silk" (154). In *Beloved* telling a story depends on the listener as "active co-creator" (155), providing an active "model for the reader's role" (156). Morrison makes increased use of "cohesive" (134) techniques such as narrative suspension (postponing clarity and resolution in order to enhance the reader's attentiveness and active involvement) and the use of repeated phrases and images, as in African folk narratives, which are "built on repetition of words, phrases, motifs, and stock situations" (142). The self-reflexive image of circularity is especially important. See Beloved's rebirth; Sethe's spinning in her kitchen trying to explain; the circles of community and family, both enabling and threatening (136–39).

A reading using Elaine Scarry's work

Kristin Boudreau's "Pain and the Unmaking of Self in Toni Morrison's *Beloved*" (1995), following Elaine Scarry's *The Body in Pain* (1985), argues that in *Beloved* "Suffering ... *unmakes* the self and calls violent attention to the practice of making and unmaking selves" (105). Within an anti-essentialist, social constructionist perspective, there is no core self. Baby Suggs, "advocate of self-reliance, learns the futility and slipperiness of such notions ... The violence of slavery ... has unmade her fiction of autonomous selfhood" (111). Paul D similarly finds out that the core self is a fiction: his tin-can heart "opens, finally to release not a self but merely a scattering of dry tobacco leaves" (113). He discovers that his identity is "located in the perceptions and definitions" of others (112). We are "ontologically ... contingent" on others (115). The pain inflicted on *Beloved*'s characters calls attention to "the violent and necessary process whereby self is constructed by other" (115). Against both Romanticism and the blues where pain is ennobling and transfigurative, *Beloved* questions the idea of "humanizing pain" (119). Beloved is exemplary of the fictionality, instability and ghostliness of all subjectivities. She "can exist only as long as her audience chooses to acknowledge her" and disappears when she "loses her desirability" (114). Selves "exist at the pleasure of other selves" (115).

A Marxist reading

K. Sumana's *The Novels of Toni Morrison* (1998) argues that *Beloved* is Morrison's "most [politically] conscious novel" (121); the novel advances "collective class struggle against capitalism as the only viable solution" (114). In this regard Sumana highlights the collective chain-gang escape in Alfred, Georgia; the solidarity between Amy Denver, European indentured servant, and Sethe; and the solidarity between African Americans and Native Americans, who provide shelter to runaway slaves.

Jazz

AFRICANIST AND AFRICAN-AMERICANIST READINGS

Eusebio Rodrigues, in "Experiencing *Jazz*" (1993), argues that *Jazz* aspires to the condition of music: "language tr[ies] to become music as it tries to capture the flow of human time" (167). The novel is a jazz composition and, unlike the "clearly demarcated movements of a symphony", has a "fluid non-Aristotelian experimental form": Morrison "produces a textual continuum by using transitional slurs and glides across sections" (155). The first pages, "like a twelve-bar jazz 'tune'", tell the story quickly; then follow "amplifications ... improvisations, variations and solo statements" (156). Another jazz element is that the characters are "cross-connected" but the "story strands do not assume a plot pattern. Nor do they build to a climax" (156). Instead we are offered "rapid and vivid glimpses" (158); stories are "incomplete" (157); chronology is broken up and "We move back and forth" (160). The narrator is neither consistently extradiegetic nor consistently intradiegetic but switches from one position to the other (164); he/she shares the telling of the story with many voices in flux that "blend and change ... switch ... and slide" (160).

The novel "jazzifies the history of a people" (158). It voices suffering in a distanced and unsentimental manner, like a Louis Armstrong jazz piece. As in jazz, Rodrigues contends, Morrison's aim is not to define past suffering or offer future solutions. As with Louis Armstrong's "West End Blues" (1928), the novel closes with an "ensemble of interludes and breaks and brief solos" (166).

Barbara Williams Lewis's "The Function of Jazz in Toni Morrison's *Jazz*" (2000) argues that *Jazz* is a jazz novel as were Morrison's *Beloved* and *Sula*. The inaugural text in this genre is Ann Petry's novel *The Street* (1946). Some of the jazz elements she identifies are also discussed by Rodrigues, though she does not acknowledge his work. *Jazz*'s first paragraph tells the story and the novel is "derived from 'repetition of the basic material'" (273); and yet, by the end, we are "left with the impression that the story is unfinished" (271). Each one of the main characters "takes a turn telling the story" (272). There is emphasis on repetition both intratextual and intertextual within Morrison's *oeuvre*. There is emphasis on variation such as the seven "variations" in Joe Trace's identity (275). The novel "moves back and forth in time" (273).

Morrison pursues several meanings and connotations of the word "jazz" beyond music, such as sex and "especially gossip … which is precisely what our narrator does" (277). Additionally Morrison makes use of a jazz-related vocabulary, using words such as "slide" (274).

John N. Duvall's *The Identifying Fictions of Toni Morrison* (2000) argues that *Jazz* intertextually engages with Morrison's earlier novels. While in the first three novels the possibility for black authenticity lies in poor agrarian communities, in *Jazz* the Traces are urban and upwardly mobile. *Jazz* also questions the "psychic determinism" (133) of early novels: in *The Bluest Eye* Cholly repeats his early experience of rape; in *Sula* Sula repeats her mother's betrayal of her in her relations to Nel and Ajax. In *Jazz*, on the other hand, the triangle Joe–Violet–Felice is not a repetition of the triangle of Joe–Violet–Dorcas, contrary to the narrator's initial assertion, which proves to be wrong. Finally, while in *Beloved* Baby Suggs is the "empowered artist figure" (133), in *Jazz* Morrison rejects the narrator's position of authority in relation to their work and their characters. Instead the ostensibly extradiegetic narrator of *Jazz* imagines that she or he is embraced and authorized by Wild (*Jazz*, 221). This is a postmodern meeting of two distinct ontological planes: the mimetic or plane of the characters and the diegetic or plane of the narrator (135). In the novel's closing lines the reader's holding of the book in the act of reading is imagined as the reader's amorous embrace of the narrator, as if they belong to the same order of reality.

Linden Peach's *Toni Morrison* (2000) discusses a well-known intertext for the novel, Van Der Zee's *The Harlem Book of the Dead*, particularly Van Der Zee's photo of the dead girl and caption, including his comment: "She was just trying to give him a chance to get away" (Van Der Zee quot. Peach 2000, 131). Another intertext for *Jazz* is the American city novel, as Morrison herself pointed out in interview with Salman Rushdie (*The Late Show*, BBC 2, 21 Oct. 1992). Particularly relevant are the African American city novel of the 1920s – whose central themes are the transition from slavery to industrial production, and ambition and disillusionment – and the African American feminist city novel of the 1980s. Blues and jazz lyrics are also intertexts for *Jazz*. The theme particularly important to Morrison is love: black people reclaiming their emotional and sexual life and choosing whom to love after the effective ban on love during slavery. A final intertext for *Jazz* is Southern romance and its staple themes, such as miscegenation, and staple characters, such as the black mammy. The Southern sections of *Jazz* are a parody of

Southern romance, in contrast with the realism of the Northern urban sections.

Therese E. Higgins, in *Religiosity, Cosmology and Folklore* (2001), explores Morrison's use of African cosmologies. In relation to *Jazz*, Morrison's own emphasis on the use of "ancestors" in her novels is significant (Morrison 1984a). Most characters in this novel are orphans, and *Jazz* demonstrates the devastating effects of the absence or unavailability of the ancestor figure.

Stephen Knadler's "Domestic Violence in the Harlem Renaissance" (2004) reads *Jazz* in the context of the weekly black New York press of the 1920s, particularly the *Amsterdam News* and the *New York Age*, both mentioned in *Jazz*. They have contrasting political orientations: the *New York Age* is conservative, supporting Booker T.Washington and his advocacy of self-reliance, and is dropping in circulation; the *Amsterdam News* endorses political activism and is rising in circulation. However, they share a common taste for sensational headlines and front-page stories with a particular liking for tales of violence among lovers and, in the language of *Jazz*, jealous "Women with knives" (*Jazz*, 81). The two publications contribute to a front-page black discourse constructing the black woman as obsessed with her man, uncontrollably jealous, "lov[ing] her man too much" (106) and showing a "violent self-denial" (107). In surreal contrast the inside pages – for example, the women's section of the *Amsterdam News* – train black women in almost unattainable ideals of middle-class married respectability.

New York in the 1920s was a black woman's city in that it offered quite a variety of jobs for them, while black men were trapped in low-paid industrial jobs. There were 25 per cent more women than men in New York; black women owned property and the number of black female-headed households was rising. Unlike white women large numbers of black women worked after marriage and "60 per cent of black women ... still acted as a principal wage earner" (104). As a result gender roles were in great flux in Harlem. In this context of social change and opportunity for black women, the front-page stories of "jealous, out-of-control women reaffirmed a woman's dependence on her man" (101). The black tabloid press played a conservative role in disciplining women and defining "'natural' ... female behavior" (102). It constructed a false dilemma between two scenarios of black femininity: the narrow and limiting scenario of middle-class respectability versus the non-conventional but also unlivable scenario of the jealous and potentially violent lover.

The texts of the Harlem Renaissance engaged with this local black discourse. Knadler argues that Claude McKay's *Home to Harlem* (1928) misogynistically and uncritically plugs into this tabloid discourse.

McKay alleviates his male protagonist Jake's, and his own, anxieties about the new status of black women as "a 'dominant force' in the Harlem community" (107) by populating the novel with women who live for their men – women such as his Felice. In *Jazz* the narrator expects another shooting because this is what the readers of the weekly black press would expect, but this proves false. Morrison's Felice is a counterpoint to McKay's Felice in that her priority is a job, not a man, and in that she cares for the community. Dorcas's wildness is not defined and circumscribed – as the tabloid "jealous woman" – but instead invites an excess of different interpretations. Like Wild she is "'uncapturable' even by the master hunter" (115). Dorcas's final statement is ambiguous: Felice and Joe arguably understand it very differently and their dialogue and shared storytelling about Dorcas is an open negotiation of gender roles that promises to avoid a repetition of Joe's shooting and Violet's knife attack against Dorcas. The dialogue between the middle-class Alice and the violent and knife-yielding Violet is also a potentially different scenario for black femininity: what they "learn together is that they can make and unmake their lives" (115).

Andrew Scheiber, in "*Jazz* and the Future Blues" (2006), situates *Jazz* in relation to the Black Aesthetic Movement otherwise known as the Black Arts Movement (1965–75) and reads it as a critique of aspects of this movement. Blues and jazz tend to be "contrastive terms" in the discourse of Black Aestheticians (476), as part of a greater contrast between an unfree Southern agrarian past represented by the blues and a free present and future represented by jazz. This discourse contrasts, on the one hand, the idea of a return to a free African past, political radicalism, modernism and the stylistic innovations of Free Jazz figures such as John Coltrane; and, on the other hand, the "resignation" of the blues that "keep us in the past" of slavery (Ron Karenga quot. Scheiber 2006, 473).

In *Jazz* Morrison ostensibly only engages with the discourse of the 1920s modernism of the Harlem Renaissance but her account of it shows that the two discourses – of the Harlem Renaissance and the Black Arts – share a "consciously assumed disjunction" between rural Southern past and urban present (476): "Here comes the new ... There goes the sad stuff. The bad stuff" (*Jazz*, 7). In *Jazz* Morrison undoes this disjunction in a variety of ways. Rather than projecting the "bad stuff" onto the past, she shows the doubleness of 1920s Harlem: the coexistence of old and new, promising and harmful. She also shows the doubleness of the past. The figure of Wild mixes both blues and jazz references. She resembles the Africanist iconography of New Jazz albums, while her name points to the blues. She also shares in the power the male urban heroes of Free

Jazz claim for themselves: "the destruction of the white thing" (Larry Neal quot. Scheiber 2006, 484). Golden Gray disappears without a trace after meeting her, argues Scheiber. *Jazz* therefore contributes to the contemporary rehabilitation of the blues and, while acknowledging the newness of jazz, argues the strong continuity of blues and jazz.

Scheiber points out the "masculinist individualism" (483) underlying the discourse of the "new" shared by the Harlem Renaissance and the Black Aestheticians. Community ties and ties with the past are unwittingly and damagingly sacrificed or repressed in the rejection of the agrarian Southern past. Nevertheless community ties are embedded in the formal "principle of antiphony" (491) which is the deep structure of the blues and which is inherited by jazz. Antiphony is given a healing role in the novel, for example in the conversations of Violet and Alice, which allow Violet to integrate her two selves. Morrison suggests that "black Americans brought with them to the city what they needed eventually to negotiate this perilous transition" to the urban North (489).

FEMINIST READINGS

Elizabeth M. Cannon's "Following the Traces of Female Desire in Toni Morrison's *Jazz*" (1997) stages a dialogue between Morrison, Teresa de Lauretis, Jessica Benjamin and bell hooks. The triangle of Joe, Violet and Dorcas enacts de Lauretis's claim that "narrative demands sadism" (quot. Cannon 1997, 239): a "violent male desire ... drives every narrative" (239). This first triangle literally kills Dorcas but also "*figuratively* kills" the subjectivity of Dorcas and Violet and, ironically, of Joe himself after Dorcas's death (240): "the male subject created by this desire is dependent on having an object, and if the object is removed, the subject, figuratively, dies" (241).

Violet and Dorcas have internalized the dominant patriarchal desire for women as objects. Violet initially desires to be white and young again and, straightening black-women's hair by profession, takes part in the whitening of black femininity. To use the language of bell hooks, she has internalized the "practices of the colonizer" (hooks quot. Cannon 1997, 244). Her desire for a child is yet another internalized patriarchal desire. Dorcas is uncomfortable with her power over Joe and chooses Acton who treats her like an object.

However, Violet gradually distances herself from patriarchal desire. Her cracks and "renegade tongue" (*Jazz*, 24) are points of emergence of a female desire beyond "dominant ideology" (243): a desire for subjectivity and intersubjectivity. For Jessica Benjamin subjectivity involves the recognition of intersubjectivity: one's "agency" but also "receptivity toward the world" and recognition of others as subjects

(Benjamin quot. Cannon 1997, 243). bell hooks discusses the resistant affirmation of the other's subjectivity among African Americans against the racist denial of African American subjectivity. What is specific to *Jazz* is that for Morrison female subjectivity involves the recognition of intersubjectivity among black women, as performed in the relation between Violet and Alice.

The second triangle turns out to be different because it is driven by black female desire. But what is specific to Morrison, controversially in the context of feminist scholarship, is that the pursuit of (black) female subjectivity involves an element of violence; female desire is both creative and destructive – destructive in the sense of resisting one's oppression. Alice senses inside her "a violence to do something to this world that so obstructs her" (236). Female violence is directed against dominant desire and against one's own internalization of this desire: "Violet must kill parts of herself before she can create herself" (241). First she desired a white and young Violet; then she "Killed her" (*Jazz*, 208–09). In this context, Morrison redefines Joe's male subjectivity as the "ability to recognize women as subjects" (239). Morrison closes *Jazz* with Violet, Joe and Felice, a new triangle of "people exploring the power of subjectivity" and its "resulting possibilities for love" (245).

Andrea O'Reilly's *Toni Morrison and Motherhood* (2004) argues that since slavery African Americans relied on other-mothering and community mothering to survive. Morrison's novels warn of the dangers involved in abandoning the resources offered by traditional black femininity. *Jazz* is "about the wounding and healing of the unmothered children" (154). Violet experiences cracks and then a split into two selves, Violet and *that* Violet. Behind Violet's damaging identification with Golden Gray is her loss of her mother, for whom he is a "substitute" (156). Alice, a seamstress, repairs Violet by other-mothering her (159). Violet has a synchronic experience of her fragmentation into two selves; Joe experiences his fragmentation into seven selves diachronically. They "both carry the wounds of unmothered children" (161). For Joe, Wild rather than Dorcas is "the woman shot and it is her death that Joe mourns" (163).

O'Reilly describes other-mothering as a valuable form of black "motherwork" and yet describes Violet and Joe as unmothered. However, it should be pointed out that Joe is other-mothered by Rhoda and Frank Williams and by Hunter's Hunter; and Violet is other-mothered by True Belle after her mother's suicide.

PSYCHOANALYTIC READINGS

Jill Matus's *Toni Morrison* (1998) argues that *Jazz* is about "traumatic re-enactment" (123) and the freedom to escape it. While Joe insists that he is a New Negro and that he has made himself anew many times, he is still in the throes of repetition compulsion in his tracking and killing of Dorcas. Harlem Renaissance texts such as Alain Locke's "The New Negro" (1925) and James Weldon Johnson's *Black Manhattan* (1930) were over-optimistic in announcing a break with the racist past. Morrison points out continuing internalized racism and colour prejudice in Harlem; Wild's and True Belle's fascination with Golden Gray is continued both in Violet's fascination with him and in the whitening beauty products sold in Harlem.

Morrison poses the question of the ethics of fiction presenting historical trauma: "I am unease now. Feeling a bit false. What, I wonder, what would I be without a few brilliant spots of blood to ponder" (*Jazz*, 219). Matus criticizes *Jazz*'s ethics, particularly Dorcas's "marginalization" and "the tendency to blame her for her death" (143).

Gurleen Grewal, in *Circles of Sorrow, Lines of Struggle* (1998), argues that the historical traumas of *Jazz* date back to the post-Reconstruction period: "one of the most repressive periods of white–black race relations, a period of social, political and economic terrorism carried out against freedmen and -women ... It was the period of the Great Migration" (126). Morrison is attentive to the traumatic experience of dispossession underlying the African American migration North. Unlike "the New Negro as envisioned by the leaders of the Harlem Renaissance", Morrison focuses not on the cosmopolitan elite of the Jazz Age but on the urban working class and on the dispossessed (Joe, Violet, Dorcas) who, while living the modern, the urban and the new, are nevertheless compelled to repeat the past (121–24 throughout). In the triangle of Joe, Violet and Dorcas, the motif is "dispossession" (129). All three characters "have lost their mothers to racial violence" (131). Rose Dear, Violet's mother, is broken in spirit by the dispossession from her home when her activist husband has to run for his life. Joe's birthplace, Vienna, and his mother's desertion of him cannot be translated into "the universal Oedipal story of Freud's Vienna" (132). Having unsuccessfully trailed his mother, Wild, Joe now trails Dorcas "by transference"; Wild and Dorcas are also textually connected by common words such as "sugar" and "bush" (134). Dorcas, whose parents were victims of racist violence, "embodies the traumatized survivor's secret impulse to die" (132). Dorcas's death is the repetition of the traumatic past.

However, *Jazz* also promises the healing of historical traumas. The novel "submit[s] to a repetition compulsion in order to heal the collective body stricken by memory that hasn't been worked through" (119). As a result the new trio of Joe, Violet and Felice is a "healing threesome" (133). The narrator, who is in touch both with Wild and the reader, facilitates this process (135). Even though the present is "hunted" or "tracked by the past", in getting it wrong in his or her expectations about the new trio the narrator reveals the space for improvisation (133). The self-consciously unreliable narrator "makes space for narrative reparation" (136) and for the reader's agency and responsibility (137).

J. Brooks Bouson's *Quiet as It's Kept* (2000) argues that *Jazz* explores the "newfound sense of pride" felt by African Americans migrating from the rural South to the urban North (163); but also their "shame- and trauma-ridden pasts" (165), as they catch up with them. Rose Dear's humiliation and suicide and Golden Gray, the golden-haired child adored by her grandmother, haunt Violet. Joe, despite claiming that he is a New Negro, "remains a mother- and shame-haunted person" (171).

Morrison explores racist stereotypes. In presenting Joe's and Violet's violent acts against Dorcas and Dorcas's life as blues-inspired, as unconsciously following a blues script, *Jazz* ambiguously mobilizes racist representations of the blues and of lower-class black people as dangerous. The encounter of Wild and Golden Gray plays on shameful racist stereotypes, in that Wild is animal-like; but it also counter-shames whites, in that Wild is terrified of whiteness. This encounter rewrites nineteenth-century American literature: against its plotlines, the black-fathered Golden Gray is attracted to Wild (177). But this "reparative fantasy" (178) is undercut by Joe's killing of Dorcas. *Jazz* is ambivalent about Dorcas, her "bluesy" sexuality both seemingly endorsed and punished (179–80). Indeed the presentation of her killing arguably silences her, the victim, and "side[s] with the victimizer" (181). Morrison partly redeems her characters by shaming the narrator as an unreliable source of malicious constructions. For example, Felice's relation to Joe and Violet is healing and daughterly rather than scandalous, as initially thought by the narrator.

SELECTED OTHER CRITICISM

A Marxist reading

Doreatha D. Mbalia's "Women Who Run with Wild" (1993) argues that black women's oppressive material conditions – "nearly 70%" of African American families headed by women "living in poverty" (642) – make them wild and suggests that African American women must become aware of this. There are elements of Wild in Violet, Dorcas, Alice and the narrator herself. Morrison "investigat[es] various solutions" (623). Alice comes to recognize the wildness inside her, with Violet's help. Sisterhood is crucial. African Americans migrating North "lost the value of collectivism" (628), and Violet is initially "more concerned with possessions than with love and communication" (629). But she lets out the Wild in her and befriends Alice and Felice, who learn from her.

A reading using Victor Turner's work

Denise Heinze's theoretical starting point in *The Dilemma of "Double-Consciousness"* (1993) is Victor Turner's distinction between *communitas* and structure, in favour of the former (see **pp. 170–1**). Morrison's "fictional communities do not always effect *communitas*, but ... there is evidence of an antistructural component that challenges social stasis" (105). Morrison's project of "fictionalizing the obstacles to *communitas*, ... creates the conditions for its very existence" (148). In *Jazz* Violet does effect *communitas*: she learns to love Dorcas and connects with Alice, Joe and Felice. There are other elements of *communitas* in this novel: its artificial families; and the cooperation of narrator and reader. First, in *Jazz* "families" are artificial and actively chosen rather than natural and connected by blood ties; Joe choses to return, though Heinze objects that Violet and Joe, problematically, "survive under the covers in a self-imposed cave" for two (93). Against Heinze's criticism, it can be argued that Violet and Joe's newfound intimacy is made possible by the new artificial family of Violet, Joe and Felice. Secondly, *Jazz* has a strong metafictional element, and its narrator questions his/her authority and appeals to the reader "in a conspiratorial process of determining meaning" (182). This is "a remarkable admission of the inadequacy of a single vision" (185).

A Derridean reading

Philip Page's *Dangerous Freedom* (1995) argues that *Jazz* can be read as a Derridean undoing of binary oppositions and the affirmation of "play": "readers are encouraged to abandon the old either/or logic and ... encompass the both/and, the neither/nor, *and* the either/or" (34). *Jazz* undoes the binary opposition of self and other. Joe initially overemphasizes the self as determining his life: remaking himself seven times and choosing Dorcas. Violet is initially overshadowed by the other, particularly her mother's suicide. Both develop towards "a healthier location within the play of oppositions" (159). *Jazz* also undoes the distinction between third-person external narrator, character and reader. The narrator progresses from a judgmental, over-confident, monological perspective to the admission of unreliability and "an open embrace of characters as well as readers" (160). The narrator "straddles the conventional dichotomy between third-person (external) narrators and first-person (internal) narrators" (167), while characters "share the narrator's role" (171) in narrating beyond their experience. The gap between narrator and reader is equally "called into question" (173) through the narrator's "references to the reader throughout" (175) and the narrator's final appeal to a physical and emotional proximity with the reader as if they belong to the same order of reality. The novel opens itself to the absence/presence of Wild, acknowledging traces, crevices and cracks with their ambiguous "double-edged quality" (165). The novel finally undoes the opposition between the oral and the written by mixing in an oral element – from the opening "Sth", a sound of "disapproval of someone's behavior" (175), to the use of colloquial language, to treating the reader as if he or she is physically present.

A Kristevan reading

Angela Burton's "Signifyin(g) Abjection" (1998) argues for the "central significance of the theme of miscegenation and of the mixed-race figure" in *Jazz* (177). Many jazz musicians were "mixed race or black Creoles" and the work of "jazz 'greats' indicates the influence of Creole culture" (176). Jazz is a "'mixed race' aesthetic ... It ... has origins in black Creole *and* in wholly white culture" (175).

Jazz addresses "racial hybridity and inter-racial ... love" (176) in order to confront the pariah status of the mixed-race figure: the "mulatto" has been, for both black and white communities, "a trope of cultural anxiety" (174). In 1845 Frederick Douglass pointed out that mixed-race people like himself were "perceived of as a different *class*"; he "did not share the dominant cultural anxieties" and saw this group as a "force for change that would ultimately end racism in America" (175). *Jazz* mobilizes two very different mixed-race figures, Dorcas and Golden Gray. Dorcas represents the stereotypical figure of the tragic mulatto; her "sugar-flawed" skin suggests the well-known scenario of slave-owners raping their female slaves in sugar plantations; and she has the expected flawed character and tragic life (177). Golden Gray, on the other hand, is a revisionist counterpoint, beginning with his name, "Golden", which has positive connotations. Burton uses Julia Kristeva's concept of "abjection" to illuminate his role in the novel.

The mixed-race figure of Golden Gray is a "trope of abjection" (170). We constitute our self through imagined opposition to a non-I and distinguish between objects assimilable to the self and wholly "Other" objects. Kristeva's "abject" is *imagined* as *absolutely* 'Other' "to ourselves" but is "only *relatively* (or *provisionally*) 'Other' to us" (172). If we introject an unassimilable "abject" object we feel that our purity is being polluted or dirtied (this is the language of abjection), we "experience psychological abjection, and suffer a breakdown of identity" (171). Morrison reconfigures the mixed-race figure by offering a study of Golden Gray's "identity collapse ... effected by racism and reformulated in abjection" (181). He is initially negrophobic in his encounter with Wild and uses the language of abjection: Wild is dirty and he feels nausea at the thought of touching her. But it is his father, Lestory, who precipitates in him the experience of abjection. Golden Gray is initially an Oedipus figure. Like Oedipus he is raised away from his father and is blind to his origins. When he finds out his father is a black man he wants to kill him. His particular form of blindness is negrophobia, "his belief that his father has ... 'polluted' his identity as a 'white' man" (178). Golden Gray initially can neither assimilate his father nor expel him as "Other" and he "feels his body coming apart" (181). He becomes a split subject: in this state of abjection he comes to experience "ambivalence" in the form of both "revulsion and desire" for the heavily pregnant Wild; her pregnancy by an unknown man "forces Gray to confront what he seeks to deny, the facts of his own birth" (182). However, the recognition that he is of mixed race is "strangely empowering to him"; it undoes "the false (or imaginary) binary" of racial difference and provides the "resolution of his abjection" (183). Morrison reconfigures the politics of the mixed-race figure so that he is no longer negrophobic; the text suggests that he chooses to remain with Wild and "give up white ideology" (187). Morrison "uses the anomalous, mixed-race figure to deconstruct the authority of racism" (175).

Morrison's intervention also revises the "myth of origin" of the mixed-race figure (173). Against the stereotype, it is "black, and not white, male desire" that fathers Golden Gray and his father, Lestory, is desired by his white mother (179). As a result, the "foundations by which people of mixed race have historically been accorded pariah status in black communities are removed" (179). The name Lestory points to an already hybridized past: Lestory "means 'the story' in Anglo-French ... the language spoken in Creole cultures such as that of New Orleans"; it is a "creolized" or "hybridized" name which points to Storyville, the New Orleans district where jazz emerged (180). Louis Armstrong was a native of New Orleans before migrating North. What also contributes to the reconfiguration of the mixed-race figure and the resolution of his abjection is Lestory's rudimentary recognition of his son. Initially neither white Baltimore nor black Vienna recognized Golden Gray as one of them. Readers are invited to reconfigure their own understanding of hybridity. The narrator's "improvisational solo" that keeps revising his/her view of Golden Gray borrows from jazz aesthetics in order to invite us to "see our own complicity in generating the abjection of the figure of mixed origins" and revise our own views (185). Also, Morrison's narrator addresses the reader directly, making us additionally alive to our responsibility for the way in which we see Golden Gray.

What Kristeva calls abjection Morrison and Fanon call racism. In *Jazz* Morrison uses "the trope of disfigurement or amputation" to illustrate the price of racism (184). Fanon also uses the language of "amputation ... excision ... hemorrhage" to describe the psychic effects of racism (185). However, in addition to signifying the abjection of racism, in *Jazz* Morrison is also oppositionally "Signifyin(g)" – as defined by Henry Louis Gates – on abjection "by showing it as a space of disenfranchisement ... but *also* as a potential space of empowerment" (184), under the conditions of a reconfigured hybridity.

A Bakhtinian reading

For **Justine Tally**'s "The Morrison Trilogy" (2007b) Morrison "narrativize[s] Bakhtinian theory" (85). *Jazz* is "an *enactment*" of Bakhtin's concepts of "heteroglossia" and the "carnivalesque" (81). The "carnivalesque" is egalitarian and questions official truth. "Heteroglossia" stresses the multiplicity of languages and interpretations available to writer and reader alike. Morrison mixes a multiplicity of languages, from song lyrics to newspaper headlines to folk sayings, and stresses "the dialogic nature of language": *Jazz* examines the way in which "stories are told again and again, each time with additional meanings or interpretations" (89). However, Morrison also points to "Something rogue" (*Jazz*, 208), such as Violet's cracks and slips of the tongue, beyond Bakhtinian dialogism.

Paradise

AFRICANIST AND AFRICAN-AMERICANIST READINGS

Therese E. Higgins's discussion of the African cosmology of "ancestors", in *Religiosity, Cosmology and Folklore* (2001), is useful in reading the supernatural reappearance of the Convent women (see **p. 209**). Higgins also points out that in *Paradise* communities can be seen to be organized along African tribal communitarian lines of wealth redistribution (77).

Candice M. Jenkins's "Pure Black" (2009) argues that, while some critics have read *Paradise* as an allegory of white America, the novel can best be read as a critique of "black American nationalism" (274). The novel is an engagement with 1990s African-American intraracial politics and events such as Louis Farrakhan's Million Man March of 1995. Black U.S. nationalism has been defined by Wahneema

Lubiano as involving "racial solidarity, cultural specificity, religious, economic, and political separatism" (quoted in 274). Morrison's novel explores the "contradictions" of black U.S. nationalism (276) and, importantly, the "unacknowledged multiraciality of the 'black' body in the U.S." (289). Slavery in the U.S. systematically produced mixed-race black bodies through the institutionally embedded exploitation of female slaves by white slave owners and through the "one-drop rule" (even one drop of black blood would classify a person as black and therefore potentially a slave) – but there has also been extensive unforced contact of African Americans with Natives Americans and others.

Ruby's leaders view light-skinned women such as Delia and Billie Delia as "fast" (*Paradise*, 59, 278), in misrecognition and blindness to this history. They project their own mixed-race origins into the alleged promiscuity of light-skinned women. The ostensibly racially pure "Blackhorse" family fails to acknowledge the mixed-race, African and Native American, origin suggested by their name and their straight hair. In her treatment of Ruby's reverse colourism, Morrison "implicitly critiques the very notion of racial authenticity" (277) in black U.S. nationalism. The Morgan twins' idealized memory of 19 "creamy" black ladies (*Paradise*, 109–10) – "suggesting that the nineteen ladies, like Delia, may even be light enough to pass for white" (283) – exposes the contradictions of black U.S. nationalism, particularly the coexistence of contradictory separatist and assimilationist desires. Revealing their assimilationism, the meaning of light skin changes, for Ruby's leaders, according to a woman's class and position in the patriarchal order. Their "distaste" (284) for the Convent women is related to their poverty and existence outside the protection of men, not their skin colour.

Latin American and Caribbean models of blackness have been better able to acknowledge the multiracial black body and its cultural creolization in the Americas. The Brazilian Consolata, and her multiracial blackness, confronts black U.S. nationalism with a different model of blackness. In the relation of Consolata and Deek Morgan, she recognizes that they are the same, while he excludes her from his "nation-building" (287). In *Paradise* Morrison shows "purity's literal impossibility in the Americas, given the reach and complexity of cross-racial contact" (285) and embraces the African diaspora not in relation to an unreal ideal of an authentic African identity but as "cultural creolization" (290).

PSYCHOANALYTIC READINGS

Jill Matus's *Toni Morrison* (1998) outlines current trauma theory – (see **pp. 204–5**) – and argues that both Ruby and the Convent are havens from trauma. Matus compares the two and argues that the Convent is more successful in healing trauma. Through Consolata's ritual the Convent women share each other's traumatic re-enactments and "externalize" the past rather than being haunted by it (164). In Ruby the excessive fidelity to the past displayed by the Morgan twins and other Ruby patriarchs can be read as an "excess of commemoration" that is a "symptom of enduring trauma" (154). Forms of apartheid put in place by Ruby's patriarchs – such as their rigid distinction between Ruby women and Convent women as well as Coffee Morgan's repudiation of Tea Morgan – are impediments to overcoming trauma. The way forward is to embrace difference and dissent, as Deek Morgan finally begins to do in relation to his brother Steward (162).

J. Brooks Bouson's *Quiet as It's Kept* (2000) reads Morrison's novels in the context of recent psychoanalytic and psychiatric work on trauma and shame. (See **pp. 205–6**.) *Paradise* reveals the shameful secrets and humiliations hidden under the excessive and "reactive pride" of Ruby (195–96). Coffee/Zechariah projected his traumatic shaming onto Tea; Ruby projected its shame first onto the light-skinned and then onto the Convent; Arnette and Sweetie projected their shame onto the Convent women who helped them (199–203). Shamed by Ruby, the Convent is rehabilitated by Morrison to such an extent that the Convent women discover their true selves. Consolata discovers her true self in her supernatural male visitor; and the Convent women performing Consolata's ritual are ideally open to each other's stories. At the same time, the treatment of the Convent women is deeply ambiguous: their killing "acts out a contempt-disappear scenario", whilst their supernatural return is a magical rescue and glorification of them; the text's "divided perceptions" have divided the critics (213).

FEMINIST READINGS

Magali Cornier Michael's "Re-Imagining Agency" (2002) argues that *Paradise* re-imagines agency through a new feminist model of coalition. This new model goes beyond coalition as theorized and practised within the Civil Rights Movement and the New Left, in that both movements "retained hierarchy" and a "centred, stable subject that was male and gained dominance through processes of othering" (643). It also goes beyond the individualism of early feminist consciousness-raising.

Through the Convent *Paradise* outlines reconceptualized forms of agency, community and justice based on affinity rather than identity; difference and diversity rather than similarity; communitarianism rather than individualism; empathy and care rather than self-interest;

openness rather than exclusionary separatism; non-hierarchical relations; critical distance; recognition of the body; recognition of the contingent, temporary, constructed and dynamic nature of community and agency. Morrison's novel resonates with a number of feminist thinkers articulating a critique of identity politics and outlining anti-essentialist perspectives, such as bell hooks and Chantal Mouffe, amongst others.

Andrea O'Reilly's *Toni Morrison and Motherhood* (2004) argues that Morrison views motherhood as a "site of power" for black women, and views its aim as the "empowerment of children" (1) in a racist world. This distinctively black model of motherhood as "social activism" (7) and "site of resistance" (10) explains why black women have experienced motherhood as liberating rather than oppressing. In Morrison "the term *ancient properties* ... signifies the ways of traditional black womanhood, the term *funk* signals traditional black values" (24). Morrison's novels can be read as "sociological exposés" (85) of the dangers involved in abandoning the resources offered by traditional black femininity. For example, there has been an African American "tradition of egalitarian marriages" which is jeopardized by black emulation of the white patriarchal nuclear family (25).

Ruby fails, as a community, to connect to the ancient properties and nurture its members. It valorizes "patriarchal values of power, status, ownership, and control" (140) because of "the town's identification with the values of the dominant culture" (178). In this context, motherhood is not fulfilling for Ruby women. The Convent, on the other hand, through Consolata, heals "maternal loss" (140) and "affirms the communal values of the funk that the town has outlawed" (142). The womb-like kitchen of the Convent contrasts with the hard and polished Oven of the town. The five eggs Anna discovers in the Convent henhouse after the killing of the Convent women suggest that the legacy of the Convent women will survive: "the sustaining values of the funk have prevailed" (169).

In Morrison "resistance against patriarchal motherhood" can be "conveyed either as 'deviant' maternal nurturance ... or as failed maternal nurturance" (34, 118). Mavis may be read as having unconsciously allowed her twins to suffocate as an act of "resistance ... against her oppression as a battered wife and disempowered mother" (146).

My main criticism of O'Reilly is of her uncritically politically correct or over-optimistic assumption that traditional black femininity comprises a body of traditions all of which are accessible and available, all helpful and relevant today, all enabling and resisting. Unlike Morrison's comments in interviews, O'Reilly doesn't appear to acknowledge that one has to distinguish between helpful and unhelpful, liberating and oppressive African American traditions; or that there is an element of invention and innovation in one's relation to traditions.

METAFICTIONAL READINGS

John N. Duvall's *The Identifying Fictions of Toni Morrison* (2000) argues that Morrison is metafictionally exploring the role of the artist in the two contrasting artist figures, Patricia/Pat and Consolata/ Connie. Patricia has a critical and analytical intelligence: she decodes the Christmas play, the secret disallowing of two out of the nine original families of Ruby due to their mixing of their 8-R blood, and the town's control of women as a means of controlling the purity of the community's blood. However, Morrison fears – as expressed in the novel – that Patricia's work "may only be able to diagnose the disease of American racialized discourse" (151). Morrison opts for Consolata, the visionary, in the hope that her art will heal.

Philip Page, in "Furrowing All the Brows" (2001), argues that *Paradise* is a novel metafictionally addressing interpretation and, in the last four chapters, "construct[ing] an elaborate model of reading and interpretation" (643). Patricia's interpretations are based on "logical deductions" (644) and painstaking notes and charts, but such "methods ... will not suffice" (647); Lone's and Connie's interpretations are based on intuition – leaps of the imagination – and empathy. *Paradise* is an "inscrutable" book with "many versions and endless interpretative possibilities" (649). It invites the readers to "avoid the mistakes of the men of Ruby" and acknowledge "multiple responses" (649).

Lucille P. Fultz's *Playing with Difference* (2003) sets outs to explore Morrison's "narrative techniques" and "aesthetic intention" (9) as they relate to Morrison's "ethics of responsibility" (110). Fultz's reading of *Paradise* focuses on textual strategies designed to enhance the reader's active participation. The novel's opening sends the reader on a thwarted inquiry into the Convent women's race; the reader is invited "to craft race narratives" and then "deconstruct them" (22). Patricia is a figure for the author *and* the reader, and metafictionally comments on their roles. Patricia, both insider (on the dark-skinned father's side) and outsider (on the light-skinned mother's), is "a figuration of the reader, meant to aid in the telling, understanding, and interpretation of the novel as a whole" (80). Patricia also mirrors the author in her interest in telling women's stories. Her narrative is "clearly a textual strategy mobilized to engage readers intimately in the narrative process" (78). The reader, to an extent, is asked to focalize events through Patricia's perspective; however, she is also held up for the reader's scrutiny. Patricia's views and her conformism are questioned in her conversations with Misner. After these critically revealing conversations have taken place, there is a "shift in the reader's focalization" and an "appositional and complementary reading of Patricia as a character": she is "no longer directing the reader's focus; she is now the object of the reader's theories" (89). Patricia's reflections on herself show that she, like the reader, is not necessarily reliable and objective. Patricia's name points to her links with "patriarchy" and "patrician".

Anna's eye-witness account of the Convent after the raid – examining the scene "as closely as her lamp permitted" (*Paradise*, 303) – prevents us from siding with any one version and calls upon us to stay alert and self-aware in our interpretive activity. The scene of the women trying to interpret each other's drawings shows the difficulty of the task and the attentive listening required. It also puts the reader in the position of going beyond both Patricia's and Anna's interpretations: "Ultimately, the writing and interpretive processes are thrust upon us as readers" (98).

INTERTEXTUAL/NEW HISTORICIST READINGS

Justine Tally, in *Toni Morrison's (Hi)stories and Truths* (1999), explores the intertextuality of *Paradise*. The attack on the Convent parodies and subverts the literary, film and TV genre of the Western; the Convent women are fighting back and, according to the conventions of this genre, we expect at least some of them to escape, but they don't. Nor are the men who kill them punished, rather they are "'exonerated' ... by virtue ... of the ghost story" (68). The return of the Convent women as revenants (spirits of those violently killed who return to the living) after the massacre is a ghost story element that is in keeping with African beliefs. Morrison also engages with the discourse of the Nation of Islam: the many and obvious allusions to the Old and New Testament in *Paradise* can be read as a critique of the way in which the Nation of Islam has "adapted the mythology of the Christian Bible ... and a 'strict' interpretation of the texts of the Qur'an" (71). Ruby parallels the isolationism of the Nation of Islam (27), which in the 1990s had a more significant middle-class membership than previously, paralleling the middle-class inhabitants of Ruby (30). Morrison also mobilizes and endorses a feminist narrative: she exposes patriarchy and its fear of women; she presents the Convent women as erotic and sensuous (for example, their love of food). Their retreat to the Convent basement is a return to the womb to heal themselves. Yet another narrative competing for the construction of *Paradise* is a black essentialist narrative, and according to

Tally Morrison proposes its rejection: first, for Morrison blackness is "a question of style, and not of skin colour, something intimately linked with African American culture ... something the patriarchs of Ruby have irrevocably lost by concentrating on the wrong signifier" (86); secondly, in relation to the closing lines of the novel, while "black as firewood" Piedade stands for "Mother Africa", her light-skinned daughter amounts to "a rejection of the essentialist argument" (92).

Tally suggests two further discourses against which to read *Paradise*. The struggles over the Oven's motto "can be interpreted in light of the [U.S.] debate over 'the canon' versus 'multiculturalism'" (53). Morrison has supported the idea of an open canon, strongly objecting to the idea of canonicity, which freezes the canon and sanctifies and monumentalizes certain texts (52–53). Finally Tally suggests the Recovered Memory Movement in the U.S. and subsequent criticism of "recovered memories" as evidence (38).

Paradise explores the dangers of "manipulative and monolithic" historiography (36) and the silencing it involves. Ruby women are silenced; Mavis is silenced by the female journalist writing her story after the death of her twins; the Convent women are initially unable to tell their stories. The numerous discourses and stories *Paradise* burgeons with foreground its constructedness and force the reader to stay active, reminding them of their role in the creation of meaning.

Linden Peach's *Toni Morrison* (2000) suggests reading Morrison's novels "within a Euro-American, New Historicist framework" (26). New Historicism situates texts intertextually, within a web of contemporaneous discourses; Peach explores several intertextual connections in *Paradise*. There are numerous allusions to vampire narratives such as Bram Stoker's *Dracula* in the presentation of Connie: she sleeps in the cellar; has night vision; bites Deacon's lip and draws blood; longs for death. Morrison makes use of the vampire narrative in order to explore the male fear of female sexuality and to reverse conventional sexual roles. Aspects of the narratives of Mavis and Gigi engage with the open-road genre and "post-1970 feminist revisions of it" (163). *Paradise* draws on the small-town novel, community fiction and the family/dynasty chronicle; it is especially "indebted" to William Faulkner's Yoknapatawpha novels: family chronicles concerned with historical forces, historiography, official/public history and occluded histories (167). In *Paradise* "stock motifs are employed to suggest how what may be valuable in the past is occluded by generic historical narratives" (168). The novel also contrasts the Western Frontier of U.S. mythology with the terrifying "Out There" (*Paradise*, 16) of black mythology. This terrifying "Out There" is both what the Convent women have suffered and, ironically, what Ruby visits upon them.

THEOLOGICAL READINGS

Jennifer Terry's "A New World Religion?" (2006) compares three religions: Pulliam's Old Testament African American version of Christianity, Misner's New Testament African American version of Christianity (193) and the Brazilian Consolata's syncretic religion reminiscent of Candomblé (a Brazilian religion mixing Catholicism with African and Native cosmologies), in favour of the third.

Consolata's critique of the separation of body and soul is an aspect of her religion shared by African American versions of Christianity: historically, through the separation of body and soul, "slave owners could promise heavenly fulfilment after death" for their slaves and therefore "African American theologies are thought to have evolved in resistance to such divisions" (201). Terry's criticism of Misner's vision is that his "ideal of the originary time and space of an African home" – like the Morgans' "separatist and essentialist notion of community" – "consecrate[s] permanence" and "negate[s] contact" (205). Consolata's theology, on the other hand, like Candomblé, embraces what Édouard Glissant has called "creolization" (*creolité*): "To assert people are creolized, that creolization has value, is to deconstruct in this way the category of 'creolized' that is considered as halfway between two 'pure' extremes" (Glissant quoted in Terry 2006, 205).

Terry shows the proximity of Consolata's theology to Candomblé and argues that it allows Morrison to "formulate a positive vision of New World creolization" (192). Consolata's supernatural Visitor is "evocative of Eshu Elegbara, one of the orisha gods of Candomblé" (199). Also, the "Convent women's enchantment specifically recalls the initiation rites of Candomblé" (202). Consolata's reference to "gods and goddesses [who] sat in the pews with the congregation" (*Paradise*, 263–64) evokes "the orishas of Candomblé, who join believers during ritual" (202). Piedade is a black Madonna but also displays several characteristics of "Yemanjà, another orisha god of Candomblé" (204).

The historical misfortune of the prolongation of slavery in Brazil until 1888 and the "prolonged direct African influence ... including many Yorubas" on Brazilian culture is thought to have contributed to the development of Candomblé and its striking "intellectual integration of the Yoruba orixás [gods] ... with the deified saints of the Catholic church" (Voeks quoted 204). Glissant and then Paul Gilroy in *The Black Atlantic* (1993) embrace a "positive model of creolization", and Toni Morrison "enacts" it in her depiction of the Convent (204).

Shirley A. Stave's "The Master's Tools" (2006b) argues that Morrison uses her novels "strategically to destabilize Christian theology and to contest its vision" (215). The Oven points to "the Ark of the Covenant that featured significantly in the biblical Israelites' sense of identity as God's chosen people" (218). The Ark was controlled by the priesthood, and the Oven is controlled by a patriarchy excluding women. Ruby represents the "Symbolic Order" as theorized by Jacques Lacan: a world of symbolic differentiations. Like the Lacanian Symbolic, it is "predicated upon the death of the mother" – Ruby, the Morgan twins' sister and K.D.'s mother, dies at the time of the town's founding and gives the town its name (219). Julia Kristeva distinguishes between the Symbolic and what she calls the Semiotic (a world of proximity to the mother) in favour of the latter, and the Convent "embod[ies]" the Semiotic and "ruptures" the Symbolic (ibid.). Relations of mothering abound in the Convent, including Mavis's mothering of her dead children. In that the Semiotic is beyond language and its differentiations and binary oppositions, the Convent women neither define themselves "in opposition to men" nor distinguish between "black" and "white" (220). Piedade, who "never speaks" (228), is also an embodiment of the Semiotic.

Stave identifies further instances of rupture with the Symbolic Order and with Christianity in the novel. Dovey's Friend "speaks without language" and is "antithetical to the Symbolic Order" (222), but just as her criticisms of her husband mount, she loses her nerve and denies the Friend (223). Consolata gives up Christ in favour of a Visitor who is a version of her own self. The window Misner sees after the massacre cannot be "reconciled with his previous beliefs" and is "not sanctioned by mainstream Christian theology" (227). The closing lines, outlining a paradise where both "lost and saved" arrive (*Paradise*, 318), break with Christianity.

AMERICANIST READINGS

Peter Widdowson, in "The American Dream Refashioned" (2001), argues that *Paradise* can be read both as "a black history of the USA" (316) and as a "fictional intervention in contemporary American historiography" (318) – both as a microcosm of African America and as an allegory of America. The novel engages with the Pilgrim Fathers and the Founding Fathers, in the form of Ruby's Old Fathers and New Fathers. It suggests that the Declaration of Independence (1776) is still unfulfilled – especially from an African American perspective – in that the attack on the Convent in July 1976 coincides with the Bicentenary. It examines the participation of the black Exoduster movement in the problematic ideology of "unassigned land" (*Paradise*, 6) or the American dream of a continual movement West in search of freedom. It comments on the Civil Rights Movement (the so-called Second Reconstruction), whose decline the historian Manning Marable locates in 1976. Morrison investigates and "makes an intervention in what [Eric] Foner has called 'America's Unfinished Revolution'" (321).

Paradise is also a feminist novel that imagines a Third Reconstruction brought about by women. The novel offers a realist and a magical version: the magical version of the supernatural return of the Convent women; and the realist version of Billie Delia's appropriation of the legacy of the Convent women. Widdowson claims, unconvincingly in my view, that Morrison considers "the new women's movements" as "the way forward to a transformed future society" (334). His failure to elaborate on "the new women's movements" beyond this vague reference contributes to the weakness of his claim.

Katrine Dalsgård's "'The one all-black town worth the pain'" (2001) influentially reads *Paradise* as a critique of American exceptionalism. One of the dominant narratives in American history has been the European American narrative of a Chosen People and a Promised Land, initiated by the Puritans and inspired by the Bible. The discrepancies between this white utopia and the harsh realities of life in the New World arguably led to the Puritan witchcraft trials of Salem, Massachusetts, in 1692–93 and the execution of 19 people for witchcraft. The attack of Ruby's leaders against the Convent refers to those trials and suggests that Morrison "discerns an exceptionalist strain in African American discourse", problematically adopted from white American ideology (235). Morrison's critique suggests that African American as well as white American exceptionalism "is inevitably entwined with a violent marginalization of its non-exceptionalist other" (237). Morrison's argument is that the American "nation's ideal desire to build a perfect community necessarily implies a violent repression of what it constitutes as its imperfect other", as an integral and ineradicable aspect of exceptionalism (241). Morrison rejects African American exceptionalist nationalism.

The Convent women's healing ritual affirms Morrison's belief in paradise as earthly, temporal and "temporary salvation" (245) and as "personal, non-national inner experience of bliss and solace" (244) that is "independent of African American national aspirations" (245). At the same time, the novel's last chapter and Misner's decision to stay in Ruby reaffirm – outside black exceptionalism – "the possibility of the African American community's salvation as well" (245). In spite of the positive portrayal of the Convent, Morrison chooses Ruby and "African America as her focus of identification" for non-exceptionalist reasons (245): "not because it is perfect or superior to other communities, but because it is the community she has come to know and love" (236).

SELECTED OTHER CRITICISM

A Marxist reading

For **Doreatha D. Mbalia**'s *Toni Morrison's Developing Class Consciousness* (2004) *Paradise* is Toni Morrison's "most class-conscious novel to date" (125). At the centre of Mbalia's reading is Misner's comment on the nine Ruby men who attacked the Convent – "They think they have outfoxed the whiteman when in fact they imitate him" (*Paradise*, 306) – which Mbalia interprets expansively. Ruby's separatism doesn't work because Ruby's men have lost the collectivism and egalitarianism that allowed African Americans to survive slavery, and have blindly adopted capitalism. Ruby is led by the "men who own and control ... major resources" (129) and thereby "imitate their original ... oppressors" (132). Though the novel dwells especially on "gender oppression", it views capitalism, Mbalia argues, as the cause of patriarchy (139). After his transformation, Deek Morgan "understands the necessity of waging class struggle" and "commit[s] class suicide" (163), in the sense of no longer identifying himself as middle-class.

Bizarrely replicating the attitude of Ruby's patriarchs, Mbalia rejects Morrison's valorizations of light-skinned characters such as Consolata as "indices of her own oppression" and refuses to recognize Consolata and her Visitor as black (152–53).

A postcolonial reading

Holly Flint's "Toni Morrison's *Paradise*" (2006) offers a postcolonial reading of *Paradise* combining the methodologies of the "New Western" historians and the new "Americanists". Against the canonical narrative of the American West, "New Western" historians such as Patricia Nelson Limerick view the West as "a land of conquest" (589). They argue that the continuous American expansion westward was in actuality "settler colonialism" (585) – a manifestation of U.S. imperialism. *Paradise* is a New Western narrative from an African American perspective: it "represents homesteading and the black exodus of the 1870s as forms of American settler colonialism" (590).

While the New Western historians take a regional perspective, new "Americanists" such as Amy Kaplan insist on the importance of a global perspective and a global context within which to understand American culture. This global context is imperialism. Morrison's novel suggests the interconnection of regional, national and global contexts; and in particular the interconnection between "the settlement of the West" and "U.S. imperialism both before and since westward expansion" (593). *Paradise* "takes up the concerns of postcolonial studies" (593) and boldly explores African American "participation in U.S. imperialism" (593). The global context of American imperialism illuminates Ruby's official story of the Disallowing. Ruby's participation in imperial designs is masked by the town's adoption of (white) American exceptionalist rhetoric but exposed by the novel. After World War II and the Morgan twins' participation in a "global conflict that had established the United States as the major world power", they react to their continuing national disenfranchisement by reaffirming their exceptionalism, and this leads to isolationism and violence (599). In the public conflict between Ruby's patriarchs and its young men over the Oven's motto, the patriarchs reject national and global contexts and insist on their exceptionalism. The young men's insistence on such national and global contexts alludes to the Black Panther Party, their internationalism and their "fighting against imperialism" (Huey Newton, Black Panther Party leader, quoted 602).

The exceptionalism and isolationism of Ruby's patriarchs, instead of cutting Ruby off from the "imperial landscape from which it had once drawn benefits as a colonial settlement" (602), actually "accommodates" American "imperial projects" (604). Morrison's alternative is a new cultural citizenship that involves enhanced engagement with the world outside Ruby. The perception of a new window or door by Misner and Anna suggests that "a new politics of intercultural coalitions seems possible" (605). The return of the Convent women in a variety of national and international locations allows the women's new type of cultural citizenship to extend beyond the Convent into a global context.

Love

Scholarly criticism on *Love* is still relatively scarce in 2010.

FEMINIST READINGS

Andrea O'Reilly's *Toni Morrison and Motherhood* (2004) argues that Morrison "demonstrates the importance" of black mothering and other-mothering "by describing the devastation ... that arises when children are not ... nurtured, or do not receive cultural bearing" (176). The most striking aspect of *Love* is the "absence of mothers and mothering" (175). May, the only fully described mother in the novel, was a motherless child and is unable to mother her own daughter, Christine. O'Reilly claims that Heed and Junior were also unmothered. The failure of mothering leads the women in *Love* to fixate on Bill Cosey. "[W]ithout the self-love and selfhood that mothering affords", the women make themselves willing participants in patriarchy, complicit in their own oppression: their "search for a Big Daddy is ... motivated and sustained by the absence of maternal love in their lives" (179).

O'Reilly fails to take account of instances of other-mothering in *Love*, involving both women and men: L other-mothers Christine and Heed; Sandler other-mothers Romen; and in the novel's conclusion it is hinted that Christine might other-mother Junior. Against O'Reilly one might argue that these instances of other-mothering are relatively successful and promise to interrupt the cycle of failed mothering.

Mar Gallego's "*Love* and the Survival of the Black Community" (2007) focuses on gender politics "within the black community" (93): Morrison "continues her critique of black patriarchy" (94). Gallego's reading is dominated by her denunciation of the figure of Bill Cosey. Cosey "miserably fails to foster a sense of family and to guide and protect its members" (94). Gallego argues that Cosey raised his son badly and exploited May; points out his "pedophilic inclinations" in his relation to Heed (97); suggests, unconvincingly, "an incestuous relationship" between Cosey and his granddaughter, Christine (95); detects Cosey's "possible affairs" with L and Vida (98); and surmises Cosey's "envy" of the early friendship of Heed and Christine and "his willingness to corrupt and annihilate" it (98). Cosey partly marries the underclass Heed in response to his father's betrayal of the black community; but even this counts against Cosey in Gallego's reading. She concludes that Cosey "was only interested in satisfying his sexual drives and justifying himself by expiating his father's misdeeds" (99). Gallego reads Cosey as a monster and consequently argues that, in the final chapter, Heed and Christine "are finally able to blame" him rather than each other (97).

Gallego argues with some cogency that patriarchal values pose a threat to the black community. But her reading of *Love*, focused so narrowly on Bill Cosey, strangely – one is tempted to say "symptomatically" – repeats the women's obsession with Cosey. This obsession blinds *Love*'s women as well as Gallego to the women's complicity with patriarchy, which survives Cosey's death by two decades. Christine's and Heed's recognition of their complicity with their own oppression is arguably the breakthrough that the novel offers.

PSYCHOANALYTIC READINGS

J. Brooks Bouson's "Uncovering 'the Beloved' in the Warring and Lawless Women in Toni Morrison's *Love*" (2008) argues that *Love* addresses the increasing class and colour divisions and strife within the African American community in the post-segregation era. The relation between the upper-middle-class light-skinned Christine and the underclass dark-skinned Heed is a metaphor for this "intraracial strife" (359). Morrison offers both an historical analysis and a "magical, and purely artistic, rescue of her characters" (372) or a "hopeful vision" of the power of the "ancestral – and artistic – imagination" (359). L embodies this power: she is a "maternal ancestor spirit" (360); she is also a storyteller and an "authorial presence behind the text" (370). L promises to rescue not only the characters but the reader as well: she embodies "the transformative potential of storytelling on an open and receptive reader who is held in a loving embrace by the author-storyteller" (372).

L's ability to rescue the characters lies in enabling Christine and Heed to find "the 'sweet Cosey child' within: the 'beloved' or authentic part of the self that transcends ... barriers of class and caste" (362). In the novel's terms, this is the unearthing of Christine's and Heed's early friendship. The "catalyst" for this process is Junior (367); she becomes L's instrument of healing by bringing together Christine and Heed. Junior is one of Morrison's lawless females, and in *Love* Morrison "associate[s] the lawless female with the 'beloved' part of the self ... the possibility of an unbounded love that looks beyond the social categories that divide people into 'us' and 'them'" (372).

Jean Wyatt's "*Love*'s Time and the Reader" (2008) offers an interesting feminist psychoanalytic reading of the narrative structure of *Love*. The final, ninth chapter, "Phantom", forces upon the reader a dramatic cognitive realignment: "discovering belatedly the original scene of the young girls' love for each other" forces the reader to drastically reinterpret the preceding text; simultaneously, the earlier knowledge of the devastating effects of this lost love on the lives of Christine and Heed "informs and intensifies the reader's response" to the "'second scene' of the women's revelatory dialogue" (195). The "revolution in the reader's understanding carries with it a revolution of affect" regarding the two women's wasted lives (200). The final chapter shows that the earlier text had "misled the reader" into thinking that Bill Cosey was the centre of the story and "makes the reader reconstruct" the story as the love of two little girls for each other (194). As a result, the "male dominant and male-centered narrative discourse" gives way to an "alternative world of meaning and value" in the final chapter, and the reader's "surprise" provokes a "radical reassessment" (195). Morrison's narrative design has a "pedagogical purpose": "to make the reader aware of the extent of her own mental and emotional subjection to patriarchal systems of meaning and value" (200).

Wyatt outlines the narrative means Morrison uses to construct a first part (up to "Phantom") where patriarchal values dominate. We are taught to trust a third-person extradiegetic narrator as objective but, in the first part, both the third-person extradiegetic narrator and the focalizers are "biased towards the interests of the man [Bill Cosey] and permeated by patriarchal assumptions" (200). Chapter titles also "point to the importance of the patriarchal figure" (201). In the first part, Christine and Heed are "firmly enclosed in the meaning world of patriarchy: there is no space ... for a Love story that predates entry into the heteronormative world" (206). Christine has some understanding of male privilege and the commodification of women's bodies, and yet her "patriarchal habits of thinking and feeling persist" (207). Heed's perspective is especially patriarchal in the first part, as she understands her life "through ... the story of Cinderella", which is "founded on the rivalry among women" for the prince's favour (207). Morrison's aim is one of "luring into the open the reader's preconceptions" (204) and exposing the reader's investment in "compulsory heterosexuality" (201). The exception in the first part is L's narration, but it is eccentric, obscure, marginal and appears unreliable. As a result, the first part "lull[s] the reader into accepting a male-centered heterosexual model of love" (202), according to which little girls and old women are "invalid subjects of a Love story" (207).

In "Phantom" the absence of quotation marks in the dialogue between Christine and Heed signals the removal of the third-person narrator. Cosey's ghost also disappears and the chapter title turns out to refer to L, who is revealed to be a ghost and who takes over as a new kind of omniscient narrator. The association of her name with Love confirms her new narrative authority. Here L's narration and the dialogue between Christine and Heed affirm an alternative understanding of love. Marriage emerges as "slavery ... Cosey bought the pleasures of a slaveowner" (210). Cosey's marriage to Heed conceals his earlier sexual molestation of her, and is a "patriarchal structure erected to ... conceal a brute abuse of power" (212). L blames Cosey for Christine's "theft" (*Love*, 200); appropriates the conventions of romantic love to describe Heed's and Christine's first meeting; and locates "'passion' in the love between the little girls" (212–13). Morrison exposes the "discontinuity at the heart of female development" and the "socially-induced trauma of femininity" (213).

Morrison construes the early interruption of Christine's and Heed's friendship by patriarchy as a trauma whose "deferred action" – *Nachträglichkeit* (belatedness, deferred action or retro-action) – they suffer throughout their lives. Wyatt here follows Jean Laplanche's elaboration of Freud's *Nachträglichkeit*. Trauma is a "temporal disorder" (196) – one "comes to the event either 'too early' or too late" (195) – and Wyatt shows Heed's and Christine's "temporal disfunction" and "cognitive misalignment with events" (196). Because of their lack of "conceptual tools to understand their situation", they are caught in the "too early" phase until the final chapter, when it is "too late" and Heed is dying (197). Their final dialogue is *nachträglich*, belated, in the sense that it is "inappropriate to its moment in time" (197). They are ventriloquized by their childhood selves, voicing their early language and values (197); simultaneously, Heed's and Christine's present old selves allow them to give new meaning to the early interruption of their friendship, which is that "patriarchal heterosexuality ... robbed girlfriend love of value" (198).

SELECTED OTHER CRITICISM

A Marxist reading

For **Doreatha D. Mbalia**, in *Toni Morrison's Developing Class Consciousness* (2004), black women "suffer from a triple oppression" (212): according to class, race and gender. They are "the most exploited and oppressed ... human beings on earth" (212). The women in *Love* have not understood this and, instead, blame each other. Another aspect of their lack of true consciousness is that the "women/girls of *Love* all love Cosey, or think they do" (213). However, "[t]his 'love' for Cosey breaks up the *true* love girls have for one another" (213). Morrison "focuses on the friendship of Heed and Christine to examine this idea of true love" (214). Friendship among black women "saves them" because it "cushions the blows of oppression" (212).

Mbalia's reading fails to address the class, money, colour and education divisions among the novel's black women.

An African-Americanist reading

Anissa Janine Wardi's "A Laying on of Hands" (2005) explores Morrison's use of hands as a "leitmotif" in this novel and argues that it "foregrounds the action" and "materiality of love" (202). Wardi interprets the use of healing hands in Morrison's *oeuvre* within the African American context of the "laying on of hands ritual" in black Christian churches (203).

In *Love* "hands ... bespeak characters" (208). Christine's hands, covered with 12 diamond rings, show her "desperate desire to prove that she is the sole inheritor of Cosey's power and capital" (208–09).

Heed's deformed hands are a "testament to her disempowerment"; and the hands of Faye, the gang-rape victim, "epitomize her help-lessness" (209). Romen's hands, against his will, untie Faye. The friendship of Christine and Heed is figured as holding hands and embracing.

In the historical context of the African American experience of hunger, both pre- and post-emancipation, healing and nurturance are connected, and Morrison explores this connection in L's actions that "pair food with healing" (206). For example, when Heed sets Chris-tine's bed on fire, L smothers the sheets "with a twenty-pound sack of sugar, caramelizing evil" (*Love* 134); she is "cook and its con-comitant roles of healer, savior, and peacemaker" (207). L is the "embodiment of love" in this novel (206) and the action of her hands includes "killing Cosey with foxglove" (215) and forging Cosey's will "to keep the [Cosey] women 'connected'" (212). This works in a physical sense; in spite of their animosity, the Cosey women "nur-tured and cared for one another": Heed tended to May and Christine tended to Heed (212–13).

A Derridean reading

For **Benjamin Burr**'s "Mythopoetic Syncretism in *Paradise* and the Deconstruction of Hospitality in *Love*" (2006) the theme of "hospi-tality [is] at the forefront" of *Love* (168). Morrison's treatment of the theme resonates with Jacques Derrida's work on hospitality. The novel might be read as "a deconstructive re-writing of 1 Corinthians 13" (159): "When I was a child, I spake as a child, I understood as a child, I thought as a child: but when I became a man, I put away childish things ... " (quot. 167). Morrison "locates a space where love can exist, which is the moment of 'a child's first chosen love,' ... a moment of indiscriminate hospitality" (167). Derrida writes: "to be hospitable is to let oneself be overtaken, *to be ready not to be ready*, ... to be surprised, in a fashion almost violent, violated and raped, stolen, precisely where one is not ready to receive" (quot. 168). Christine meets the socially unsuitable Heed, May asks Heed to leave, but Christine asks her to wait. Christine, whose grandfather is in the hospitality business, might be read as "the product of a culture of hospitality" as defined by Derrida; she "lacks the discriminating apparatus that would have prevented her from asking Heed to wait" (169). Unlike Derrida, Morrison explores the predatory violence inherent in Bill Cosey's culture of hospitality, as it impacts on Heed's and Christine's life, when Cosey sexually molests and then effectively buys Heed. *Love* is "about the failure of hospitality" (172) when it is unaccompanied by discrimination. Heed's and Christine's "reconciliation comes after they have negotiated the hospitality of their relationship with discrimination" (173).

One might object to Burr that Cosey's form of hospitality – only accepting up-market guests to his hotel, while molesting and buying the underclass Heed – is too discriminating. Arguably, Christine and Heed renew their friendship only when they shed discrimination in favour of unlimited hospitality; for example, Christine asks Junior to stay, even though Junior is partly responsible for Heed's death.

A reading using Wai Chi Dimock's *Residues of Justice* (1996)

Megan Sweeney's "'Something Rogue'" (2006) argues that the modern Western concept of justice is based on the commensurability of crime and punishment; underlying this commensurability is a logic of quantification and equivalence. Justice is therefore "a derivative concept that arises from commerce" (Dimock quot. 441); essentially it understands human interaction in "economic terms" (442). In *Love* Morrison shows that the logic of justice "replicates the logic of commodification that undergirds slavery" (442). *Love* also supports Dimock's claim that literature "plays havoc with any uniform scale of measurement and brings to every act of judicial weighing the shadow of an unweighable residue" (Dimock quot. 443). *Love* is a "utopian valorization of women as rogue agents who can derail" standard legal equations (446). However, *Love* shows "keen awareness" of both the possibilities and the limitations of this "utopian impulse" (446).

L kills Cosey and forges his will to "rectify an injustice" (446). She is one of several female characters in this novel who critique "dominant disciplinary and legal narratives" (449). *Love* foregrounds the commodification of women as a "legally sanctioned crime" and draws a parallel with the "commodification of women in slavery" (450). Christine's analysis of her encounters with the police shows that both her gender and her race as well as Dr. Rio's race play an unacknowledged role in equations of justice where white counts more than black and male more than female. She recognizes in May "legitimate fears about the fundamental incommensurability that structures whites' punishment of blacks' alleged transgressions" (452–53). This unacknowledged incommensurability is present not only in the "system" (453), but also in Christine's political group in its response to the rape of the volunteer: even in ostensibly "alternative economies of justice", there is an equation in which male counts more than female (452). Junior is punished for her resistance to unacknowledged "systemic excesses": her "rejection of her status as a sexual commodity" marks her as "'criminal' in equations of crime and punishment" (454–55).

L but also Celestial, Heed and Junior break the law and "remain largely unpunished within the novel's economy of justice" (455): Celestial works as a prostitute; Heed blackmails Boss Silk; Junior plays a role in Heed's death and forges the will in her favour. L, in particular, defends her actions as "restorative justice" that reconnects Christine and Heed and offers them the opportunity to "contest" narratives disciplining women (459). L also interprets and celebrates Celestial's humming as a refusal of "the imprisoning narratives that equate women's attempts to claim their voices and sexuality with punishable transgression" (460).

However, Morrison is acutely aware that L's "alternative economy of justice" involves its own exclusions. L's destruction of Cosey's will in favour of Celestial "seal[s] Celestial's disenfranchisement"; L's narrative "obscures the ways in which Celestial does not count in her narrative" (461). Celestial is the unacknowledged residue in L's alternative economy: in casting her as a fully free woman (and as fully outside the system), L "writes her out of the law and locks her out of the house" (462). *Love* recognizes the "limitations of its narrative transgressions"; and checks its own "utopian longings" with an "awareness of ... material realities" (462).

A Kristevan reading

Susan Neal Mayberry's *Can't I Love What I Criticize?* (2007) argues that *Love* offers a Kristevan critique of Lacan. For Julia Kristeva, Jacques Lacan's "symbolic order" is the modern patriarchal class society – she makes a distinction between "the symbolic" and "the semiotic" in favour of the latter. Morrison sides with Kristeva: she "attacks" the Symbolic and privileges "the semiotic, or the play of forces inherent in language" (269). *Love* can be described as "semiotic fiction" (262).

For Lacan language is indistinguishable from "the symbolic order" because it is understood as a self-referential system of arbitrary differences, where signs – for example, man and woman – have meaning only in relation to each other. Kristeva's "semiotic" subverts this system from within. Inspired by Celestial, young Christine and Heed invent their own language in their playhouse, Celestial Palace. This is an instance of Kristeva's "semiotic": "language ... reinvented to resist rather than support a patriarchal status quo" (270).

For Kristeva, Lacan's "Law of the Father" is patriarchal social authority. Its representatives in *Love* are: Chief Baddy Silk and his son, Boss Silk; the massively increased and racist police force Sandler fears; the Administrators Junior encounters; and "Police-heads". Police-heads threaten especially disobedient women and children;

and Morrison questions Lacan's misogyny by "comically converting his patriarchal Law of the Father into … Police-heads" (262). There are black representatives of patriarchal social authority or of capitulation to it: Dark, Bill Cosey's father; Dr. Rio and his imitation of the "white male definition of desire" (262); and Bill Cosey himself. There are also those who are complicit in their own oppression. Cosey's people call on him to "sell out to white law in a way merely different from that of his father", which is to play a "black Big Daddy" (277). Bill Cosey's son, Billy Boy, dies because he is too obedient to his father and, as a result, "cannot breathe" (274). Junior believes Cosey is her Good Man. Female institutions such as Maple Valley (Christine's school) and Manila's whorehouse serve the needs of men. In *Love* African American women who search for Big Daddy "lay down (to) the Law of the Father instead of 'living [their] lives hand in hand'" (261).

Morrison's solutions, in line with the nature of the Kristevan "semiotic", include both women and men: "although the semiotic is attached to the feminine, its language does not exclude men" because it "recognizes no gender distinctions" (269). Celestial, L and Sandler all participate in the resistance against the "Law of the Father". Celestial will not be silenced by Cosey. Sandler does not "give himself over" to him (285) and can therefore tell his grandson: "You not helpless, Romen" (*Love*, 154). L kills Cosey in order to stop him. Mayberry concludes that "black male magic can be made … alongside the tales of black women" (292). Morrison suggests that a semiotic use of language can "save you from the attention of Police-heads" (*Love* 201) and calls upon her readers to "scare them off" with their own semiotic use of language (291).

An Americanist reading

Tessa Roynon's "A New 'Romen' Empire" (2007) focuses on the motif of rape in *Love*: particularly Pretty-Fay's gang-rape and Romen's role in it; and Cosey's relationship to 11-year-old Heed. Roynon reads this motif in the context of American self-definition. American historiography and literature have turned to ancient Rome and Latin literature to build a dominant "narrative of American settlement as a kind of glorious sexual assault" (33). Tarquin's rape of Lucretia and Pluto's rape of Proserpina or Kore in Ovid's *Metamorphoses* have been especially important for American self-definition. Ovid's *Metamorphoses* has been used extensively to "represent the annexation of the Americas as a magical, natural or divinely ordained process" and to "obscure political reality" (40). The use of Ovid contributed a "fake romantic pastoralism" in American representations of the "colonization of the Americas" (39).

Love sets out to destabilize "the way the dominant [American] culture glorifies the notion of American settlement as rape while at the same time insisting that colonization was a guiltless, impersonal process of metamorphosis rather than an outrageous violation" (44). Bill Cosey embodies the American dream and his Florida seafront hotel is an allegory of the creation of America. His hotel is the "creation of an empire" that "invokes the European conquest of that region"; while his relationship to Heed is a "parodic version of the configuration of America as the innocent victim" of a European "all-conquering hero" (33). Morrison's description of Romen on the verge of raping Pretty-Fay alludes to "a classic *conquistador* but also a Tarquin" (37).

Love can be read fruitfully in relation to William Carlos Williams's *In the American Grain* and *Kora in Hell*. In both texts rape is "somehow at once necessary and glorious" (43). Williams's writing "epitomizes the kind of 'male pride' in writing about rape and about the discovery and conquest of America that Morrison sets out to 'sabotage'" (38). According to Roynon, Morrison develops both Romen and Bill Cosey as a "counterpoint" to the "tradition in which Williams writes" (45); Morrison "implies that [Cosey] does not in fact rape Heed" (45). Morrison "sav[es] her protagonists from committing the classic, classically associated crimes" (46). Here Roynon seems unconvincing. Cosey's sexual molestation of Heed before their marriage might not technically amount to rape, but it cannot be construed as a "rescue-job" (46).

A Mercy

At the time of writing in 2010 there is hardly any published scholarly criticism on *A Mercy*. I will therefore necessarily focus on interviews and reviews. The two most helpful interviews are Morrison's early interview with Lynn Neary (Morrison 2008d) and her lengthy and exceptionally suggestive two-part interview with Michael Silverblatt (Morrison 2009a, 2009b). In selecting reviews, fruitful suggestiveness was the quality I was looking for.

MORRISON'S INTERVIEWS ON *A MERCY*

In "Toni Morrison Discusses *A Mercy*" with Lynn Neary (Morrison 2008d) Morrison announces the major theme of all her subsequent interviews: the investigation of the process of the coupling of slavery and racism, in the early days of what was later to become America, as part of Morrison's effort to uncouple them and imagine pre-racist and post-racist societies.

Slavery – understood broadly as "owning the labor of people" – was "a constant in the world". Morrison claims that what was novel about slavery in the New World, "the unusual thing[,] was coupling it with racism". If Morrison wishes to make the unqualified claim that early American history provides the first coupling of racism and slavery, this seems a highly controversial claim. In canonical Western thought, one need only turn to the pages of Aristotle's *Politics* to find the explicit justification of slavery in terms of racial inferiority; non-Hellenes and "Asiatics" are "by nature slaves" (157). (See Aristotle 1942, *Politics*, Book I, Ch. 5 and Book III, Ch. 14.)

The coupling of slavery and racism in the New World did not come about naturally but "had to be constructed, planted, institutionalized and legalized". *A Mercy* is set at a time when racism was not yet (fully) embedded, and therefore allows Morrison to explore "how all of this began" and, importantly, to "separate race from slavery; to see what it's like, what it might have been like, to be a slave but without being raced". She highlights Bacon's Rebellion and its aftermath – addressed in *A Mercy* (8–9) – as a moment in this process of race-ing slavery.

"Whiteness", Morrison continues, is a product of this process. It is "a construction in order to divide particularly poor people – and it has operated pretty much throughout the history of the country". The measures taken after Bacon's Rebellion "protected landed gentry because they could divide and conquer".

In "Toni Morrison, Part I" with Michael Silverblatt (Morrison 2009a) Morrison repeats that the laws put in place after Bacon's Rebellion were designed to bring about "a racial and racist division" between "poor whites and black slaves". Advancing her discussion of "whiteness" in the Neary interview, she explains the process of becoming "white":

> Now the poor whites were not "white" until they were deemed opposite of the slaves. They were Polish people, they were Irish people, they were Brits. So the process of becoming "white" depended completely on the process of solidifying a black population that was understood to have no protection.
>
> (Morrison 2009a)

Morrison also introduces a new theme, that of her literary interlocutors in *A Mercy*, in response to Silverblatt's observation that the novel reads like a Hawthorne allegory. Morrison also names James Fenimore Cooper. Cooper's *The Last of the Mohicans* (1826) takes place in the second half of the seventeenth century, as does Hawthorne's

The Scarlet Letter (1850). Morrison comments on the scarcity and limitedness of fiction set in the seventeenth century in America: "in our minds what we have is precisely that story: Puritans, witchcraft ... So that our history, our narrative of the early part ... of what was later to become the United States is so narrow".

Morrison also addresses the idea of freedom and her effort in *A Mercy* to understand it more expansively. She points approvingly to Florens's "enlightenment, bit, by bit, by bit so that whatever happens to her ... she is an adult". She then comments that Lina is "totally loyal ... Connection, being loyal, never letting anybody down ... that's her liberation as it were". Morrison's idea of freedom therefore encompasses mental freedom – enlightenment – but also commitment to others.

In "Toni Morrison, Part II" with Michael Silverblatt (Morrison 2009b), I would single out as highly suggestive Silverblatt's thoughts on the genre of *A Mercy*. Florens's journey-narrative points Silverblatt intertextually towards the picaresque novel. Resonant aspects of the picaresque novel are that it presents realistically the adventures of a lowly anti-hero who survives by his or her wits in a hostile and corrupt environment. Daniel Defoe's *Moll Flanders* (1722) and Henry Fielding's *The History of Tom Jones, a Foundling* (1749) are notable early examples of the genre in English.

Silverblatt suggests that *A Mercy* very deliberately opts for realism. He comments as follows on the final confrontation between Florens and the blacksmith:

> the blacksmith ... essentially says to her: "Stop mythifying everything. I'm not mythic. I can't save you. Your mother, who abandoned you, she will never be there to save you. You must return to whatever it is you came from and bring reality with you. You will be the principle of the real and all of this insanity must find an adult form of solution rather than the mythic one."
>
> (Morrison 2009b)

This is an interesting (and potentially misleading) comment in the context of Morrison's *oeuvre*, in that most of her novels can be described as finding – on the contrary – mythic solutions. Milkman's leap in *Song of Solomon*, Son's joining of the blind horsemen in *Tar Baby*, the Convent women's reappearance in *Paradise* can be read as mythic or visionary solutions. Furthermore, Morrison's entire *oeuvre* has been asking readers not to see realism and "enchantment" (Morrison's term), reality and imagination, facts and fiction, history and story, as opposed terms.

Florens's writing of her narrative and her plans to run away are arguably both a realistic and a visionary solution, in the sense that they embody imaginative historical potentialities, not in the sense that Florens is likely to be successful. From the point of view of conventional realism and of verisimilitude, Florens is highly likely to be recaptured; but from the point of view of Morrison's enchanted realism Florens's narrative is an untimely ancestor of the abolitionist slave narratives of the beginning of the nineteenth century.

REVIEWS OF A MERCY

While Morrison's comments in interview have focused on historical and philosophical themes, reviewers have focused on formal concerns, such as genre.

For **Tim Adams**, in "Return of the Visionary" (26 Oct. 2008), *A Mercy* works both as historical fiction "that lives powerfully as an invented oral history" and as an open-ended parable whose lesson is not obvious or fixed and whose "meaning ... is constantly undermined or elusive". Adams as Silverblatt invites the reader to make comparison with Nathaniel Hawthorne: Hawthorne "has become her model in some ways; like him, she is capable of creating fictional environments in which everything can come to seem symbolic".

John Updike, a major novelist reviewing another major novelist, thinks about the genre of *A Mercy* in "Dreamy Wilderness" (3 Nov. 2008). Morrison's *oeuvre* is well known for its mix of realism and "enchantment". Updike considers that in this novel the Morrisonian mix has changed in favour of enchantment at the expense of conventional realism. Morrison "moves deeper into a more visionary realism" – a conclusion that Silverblatt implicitly contradicts in his interview (discussed above). Updike echoes Tim Adams's language ("visionary") but makes an altogether different argument. The sections focalized through Rebekka and Sorrow partly convey hallucinations and imaginings at times when they were seriously ill or in a state of extremity (Rebekka's "Middle Passage" and Sorrow's shipwreck). Less obviously Updike also describes Florens's state of mind as "feverish" and comments that Morrison "has invented for her feverish mind a compressed, anti-grammatical diction unlike any recorded patois". Updike also finds that Morrison moves away from realism in a character such as Sorrow who "seems less a participant in the action than a visitor from the Land of Allegory".

Updike connects this decline of realism with a rising pessimism: "as Morrison moves deeper into a more visionary realism, a betranced pessimism saps her plots of the urgency that hope imparts to human adventures". This is a puzzling judgement, in view of Florens's progress and enlightenment in the course of the novel – a progress Morrison points to in a number of interviews. For example, Rustin, in interview, tells Morrison that Florens's story is "terribly sad". She is corrected by Morrison, who hints at Florens's progress: "No, no, no! ... do not give yourself over completely to anybody. At least you know she'll never do that again" (Morrison 2008e). Morrison is more explicit in interview with Michel Martin. She argues that Florens's progress "comes through her ability to tell her story, to glean its meaning, and to become something very close to an adult human being, whatever her fortunes are" (Morrison 2008g).

To return to Updike's review, he concludes that the novel "circles around a vision, both turgid and static, of a new world turning old, and poisoned from the start". Is Updike suggesting that the historical, institutional, legal coupling of slavery and racism that Morrison examines is merely her "vision"? Why does he ignore the dynamism of the itinerary of characters such as Florens, Sorrow and Jane Ealing? One is tempted to suggest that he is reluctant to engage with the historical issues that Morrison raises so urgently and insistently in the novel and in her interviews.

Caroline Moore's Review of *A Mercy* (14 Nov. 2008) echoes earlier reviews. As Updike she comments that Morrison uses a "re-forged language ... [A]t her best, Morrison does create a genuine, dense idiom". Echoing Kakutani (Kakutani 2008) she continues that Morrison "creates a fictional world that is not dead history but living fable". However, Moore claims that Morrison lacks realism: "One thing Morrison does not do is to write convincing historical fiction that resurrects the flavour, linguistic texture and mindset of the past era ... When she attempts historical or cultural ventriloquism, the results can be ludicrous." Moore singles out the dialogue among English female shipmates travelling steerage across the Atlantic, as remembered by Rebekka: "That may be the most unconvincing Cockney sprightliness since Dick Van Dyke in *Mary Poppins*."

La Vinia Delois Jennings's Review of *A Mercy* (2009) shows some evidence of haste. For example, Jennings is wrong to state that Morrison locates "the present action of *A Mercy* in colonial Virginia in May 1690" (646) – present action is set in upstate New York. However, I have selected it because it calls for and begins a potentially very interesting reading of the novel in the context of American legal history, one involving the examination of "early American statutes legislating race" (648). Jennings discusses a decision by the Virginia court of 1640 that established legal precedent. Three indentured servants, a Dutchman, a Scotsman and an African, ran away but were all recaptured. The Dutchman and the Scotsman received a sentence that increased their indenture by a total of four years. The African,

John Punch, on the other hand, received a sentence of "perpetual enslavement" (648). Jennings comments that "No servant of European descent in America ever received such a sentence ... Non-whiteness now determined perpetual servitude" (648). Subsequently one colony after another "passed legislation recognizing slavery as a legal institution": Massachusetts in 1641, Virginia in 1661, Maryland in 1663 (648). In 1662 Virginia passed legislation recognizing inheritable slavery: that "all children born in the colony would be free or bond according to the condition of their mother" (647). In *A Mercy*, the white indentured servant Scully is "finishing his mother's contract" (*A Mercy*, 57) and this situation has a "legal kinship" to inheritable slavery (647). However, the gap between indentured servants and slaves was widening. In 1691 the colonies "passed legislation making it illegal to free an enslaved person of African descent unless that freed person left the colonies" (648).

Selected nonfiction

At the time of writing there is a dearth of criticism on Morrison's nonfiction. What there is mainly focuses on *Playing in the Dark*.

For **Frederick D. Robinson,** in his Review of *Playing in the Dark* (1992), Morrison overstates the originality of *Playing in the Dark*. In Robinson's view her project – understood by him as the examination of black characters in American literature – is derivative; it was first developed by Ralph Ellison in his 1946 essay, "Twentieth-Century Fiction and the Black Mask of Humanity".

Michael Awkward, in his Review of *Playing in the Dark* by Toni Morrison and *In My Father's House: Africa in the Philosophy of Culture* by Kwame Anthony Appiah (1994), argues that "the most glaring weakness" of *Playing* is "its failure to recognize that it has entered a critical universe well prepared for its formulations by recent scholarship motivated by a belief that race constitutes an essential area of investigation" (270). Reviewing *Playing* in conjunction with Appiah's *In My Father's House*, Awkward attempts to bring this critical universe into view.

Morrison limits herself exclusively to white American (and largely negative) stereotypical constructions of blackness that she calls "American Africanism"; she "insists that her knowledge of her culture's complexity renders her incapable of participating in" the construction of black stereotypes (270). Appiah, on the other hand, explores African American Africanisms: positive stereotypical constructions of blackness, particularly of Africa, by African Americans. Alexander Krummell (1819–98), Du Bois and the Harlem Renaissance poet

Countee Cullen (1903–46) can be read as contributing to a tradition of African American Africanism working against the pejorative language of white Africanism. Awkward agrees with Appiah that African American Africanism "offers a means by which … to right many of the wrongs" in Africa today – as long as it doesn't "rely on essentialist or romantic notions of black cultural uniformity and changelessness" (270).

Linda Krumholz, in her wholly positive Review of *Playing in the Dark* (1996), argues that "After reading *Playing in the Dark*, it is difficult to imagine reading American literature without recognizing Africanness as the touchstone for the literary imagination" (244–45).

Jan Furman's *Toni Morrison's Fiction* (1996) discusses *Playing* and goes on to claim that Morrison "has never been tempted to the metaphorical and metaphysical use of race in her fiction" (108) – Morrison "shuns Africanism" (111). However, this seems questionable. An example of Africanism would be the African woman in yellow in *Tar Baby*, a de-individuated cipher of traditional black femininity on whom Jadine projects her fears and desires. Furman also argues that there are silences and "gaps" in *Playing* (111); Morrison "does not account for Indians as a dark presence in the literature of early America" (111).

Hanna Wallinger's "Toni Morrison's Literary Criticism" (2007) treats "Unspeakable Things Unspoken" and *Playing* as Morrison's "contribution to the debate over the revision of the canon that dominated much of the scholarship of the 1980s and 1990s" (116). Wallinger also situates those two texts – and their project of examining the American canon in search of Africanisms – in the context of African American criticism. Morrison's predecessor in her project is Ralph Ellison, particularly his essays: "Twentieth-Century Fiction and the Black Mask of Humanity" and "What America Would Be Like Without Blacks" (1970). Going further back, Morrison's project is inaugurated by a generation of black women writers whose preoccupation was "race literature" (120). Gertrude Bustill Mossell (1855–1948), Anna Julia Cooper (1858–1964), Pauline E. Hopkins (1859–1930), Victoria Earle Matthews (1861–1907) and others set out to explore the unacknowledged use of African Americans in literature, criticizing misrepresentation and generalizations; they also "proclaimed" their own positive contribution to "race literature" (120). Wallinger refers to such examples as Cooper's collection of essays *A Voice from the South* (1892) and Matthews' "The Value of Race Literature" (1895).

Leslie Bow's "*Playing in the Dark* and the Ghosts in the Machine" (2008) interrogates *Playing* on its own critical terms and "process of critical inquiry": "what are the repressed yet constitutive shadows" or the "structuring absences" of *Playing*; and "what service do they perform?" (557–58). The outstanding merit of *Playing* is that Morrison, "the elder statesman of American letters gave worth to the project of reading race" (564). However, relations between European Americans and African Americans are not synonymous or coextensive with race relations. Historically, in an American context, Native Americans also served European Americans as a "dehistoricized signifier for 'darkness' or 'savagery'", but Morrison "uneasily incorporates indigeneity under the rubric of 'Africanism'" (559). More recently, again within an American context, Asian Americans and others occupy a position unacknowledged by *Playing*, that of the "racially interstitial subject" (563).

Bow is very keen to resituate *Playing* beyond Morrison's chosen American context and within a transnational context – particularly the "global context of intellectual inquiry concerned with the ways in which the racialized subaltern has been made serviceable to the causes of nationalism and to the unmarked subjectivity of the colonialist" (559). Edward Said and Gayatri Chakravorty Spivak have made influential contributions in this context, but Morrison does not acknowledge them. In a global context America's hegemonic role in the world has constructed new racial "others": "recently it has been the putative 'unfreedom' of a faceless Chinese, Korean, or Vietnamese peasant brainwashed by Communist ideology and on whose behalf projects of global hegemony were enacted" (562).

In conclusion, Bow is critical of *Playing* both for limiting itself to an American context and for limiting itself to Africanism: "not only does it limit its horizon to the nation precisely at the moment in which theories of transnationalism gestured outward, but it ironically participates in a racial erasure of its own in its determination to locate in race a singular darkness, a single point of origin" (563–64).

Chronology

1931	Toni Morrison born 18 February in Lorain, Ohio.
1949	Graduates from Lorain High School.
1949–53	Attends Howard University.
1953–55	MA at Cornell University.
1955–57	Teaches at Texas Southern University.
1957–64	Teaches at Howard University.
1958–64	Marriage to Harold Morrison and birth of Ford (Dino) and Slade.
1965–68	Editor at L.W. Singer, move to Syracuse.
1968–84	Editor at Random House, move to New York.
1970	Publication of *The Bluest Eye*.
1973	Publication of *Sula*.
1974	Publication of *The Black Book*.
1977	Publication of *Song of Solomon*.
1981	Publication of *Tar Baby*.
1982	Performance of *District Storyville*, Morrison's collaboration with Donald McKayle, at the Michael Bennett Studios on Broadway.
1983	Publication of "Recitatif".
1984–88	Albert Schweitzer Professorship of the Humanities at SUNY-Albany.
1986	*Dreaming Emmett* produced in Albany, NY, on 4 January.
1987	Publication of *Beloved*.
1988–2006	Robert F. Goheen Professorship of the Humanities at Princeton University.
1992	Publication of *Jazz*. Publication of *Playing in the Dark: Whiteness and the Literary Imagination*. Edited *Race-ing Justice, En-Gendering Power: Essays on Anita Hill, Clarence Thomas, and the Construction of Social Reality*.
1993	Nobel Prize for Literature.
1994	Publication of *The Nobel Lecture in Literature, 1993*.
1997	Publication of *The Dancing Mind: Speech Upon Acceptance of the National Book Foundation Medal for Distinguished Contribution to American Letters*. Co-edited *Birth of a Nation'hood: Gaze, Script, and Spectacle in the O.J. Simpson Case* with Claudia Brodsky.

1998	Publication of *Paradise*.
2003	Publication of *Love*.
2004	Publication of *Remember: The Journey to School Integration*.
2005	*Margaret Garner*, for which Morrison wrote the libretto, premiered in May at the Detroit Opera.
2008	Letter to Barack Obama on 28 January. Publication of *A Mercy*.

Bibliography

Note: [] denote original dates of publication.

Adams, Tim. 2008. "Return of the Visionary." *The Observer* 26 Oct. http://www. guardian.co.uk/books/2008/oct/26/mercy-toni-morrison (last accessed 7 July 2010).

Andrews, William L., Frances Smith Foster, Trudier Harris, eds. 1997. *The Oxford Companion to African American Literature*. Foreword Henry Louis Gates, Jr. New York: Oxford UP.

Andrews, William L. and Nellie Y. McKay, eds. 1999. *Toni Morrison's Beloved: A Casebook*. New York and Oxford: Oxford UP.

Aristotle. 1942. *Politics*. Trans. Benjamin Jowett. New York: Random House.

Askeland, Lori. [1992]. "Remodeling the Model Home in *Uncle Tom's Cabin* and *Beloved*." Andrews and McKay 1999. 159–78.

Atwood, Margaret. 1987. "Jaunted By Their Nightmares." *The New York Times* 13 Sept. http:// www.nytimes.com/books/98/01/11/home/8212.html (last accessed 7 July 2010).

Awkward, Michael. [1989]. "'The Evil of Fulfillment': Scapegoating and Narration in *The Bluest Eye*." Gates and Appiah 1993. 175–209.

——. [1990]. "'Unruly and Let Loose': Myth, Ideology and Gender in *Song of Solomon*." Furman 2003a. 67–95.

——. 1994. Review of *Playing in the Dark* by Toni Morrison and *In My Father's House: Africa in the Philosophy of Culture* by Kwame Anthony Appiah. *Modern Philology* 92.2 (Nov.): 267–72.

Baker, Houston A., Jr. [1989]. "When Lindberg Sleeps with Bessie Smith: The Writing of Place in *Sula*." Gates and Appiah 1993. 236–60.

Bakhtin, M.M. 1981. "Discourse in the Novel." Bakhtin. *The Dialogic Imagination*. Ed. Michael Holquist. Trans. Caryl Emerson and Michael Holquist. Austin: U of Texas P. 259–422.

Barnett, Pamela E. [1997]. "Figurations of Rape and the Supernatural in *Beloved*." Plasa 2000. 73–85.

Bassett, P.S. [1856]. "A Visit to the Slave Mother Who Killed Her Child." Plasa 2000. 39–41.

Bettelheim, Bruno. 1991. *The Uses of Enchantment: The Meaning and Importance of Fairy Tales*. London: Penguin.

Bloom, Harold, ed. 1990a. *Toni Morrison*. New York: Chelsea House.

——. 1990b. Introduction. Bloom 1990a. 1–6.

Boudreau, Kristin. [1995]. "Pain and the Unmaking of Self in Toni Morrison's *Beloved*." Plasa 2000. 105–15.

Bouson, J. Brooks. 2000. *Quiet as It's Kept: Shame, Trauma and Race in the Novels of Toni Morrison.* Albany: State U of New York P.

——. 2008. "Uncovering 'the Beloved' in the Warring and Lawless Women in Toni Morrison's *Love.*" *The Midwest Quarterly* 49.4 (summer): 358–73.

Bow, Leslie. 2008. "*Playing in the Dark* and the Ghosts in the Machine." *American Literary History* 20.3 (fall): 556–65.

Bowers, Susan. [1990]. "*Beloved* and the New Apocalypse." Middleton 2000. 209–30.

Brenner, Gerry. [1987]. "*Song of Solomon*: Rejecting Rank's Monomyth and Feminism." Furman 2003a. 95–137.

Butler, Judith. 1990. *Gender Trouble: Feminism and the Subversion of Identity.* New York and London: Routledge.

Burr, Benjamin. 2006. "Mythopoetic Syncretism in *Paradise* and the Deconstruction of Hospitality in *Love.*" Stave 2006a. 158–73.

Burton, Angela. 1998. "Signifyin(g) Abjection: Narrative Strategies in Toni Morrison's *Jazz.*" Peach 1998. 170–93.

Byerman, Keith E. 1993. "Beyond Realism." Gates and Appiah 1993. 100–25.

Cannon, Elizabeth M. 1997. "Following the Traces of Female Desire in Toni Morrison's *Jazz.*" *African American Review* 31.2 (summer): 235–47.

Carmean, Karen. 1993. *Toni Morrison's World of Fiction.* Troy, New York: Whitston.

Charles, Ron. 2003. "Prisoners of One Man's Actions." *Christian Science Monitor* 28 Oct. http://www.csmonitor.com/2003/1028/p15s01-bogn.html (last accessed 7 July 2010).

Christian, Barbara. 1985. *Black Feminist Criticism. Perspectives on Black Women Writers.* New York: Pergamon.

——. [1988]. "The Race for Theory." Leitch 2001. 2257–66.

——. [1993a]. "Layered Rhythms: Virginia Woolf and Toni Morrison." Peterson 1997. 19–36.

——. 1993b. "Fixing Methodologies: *Beloved.*" *Cultural Critique* 24 (spring): 5–15.

Cockayne, Emily. 2007. *Hubbub: Filth, Noise & Stench in England, 1600–1770.* New Haven and London: Yale UP.

Coleman, James. 1986. "The Quest for Wholeness in Toni Morrison's *Tar Baby.*" *Black American Literature Forum* 20.1/2 (spring and summer): 63–73.

Dalsgård, Katrine. 2001. "'The one all-black town worth the pain': (African) American Exceptionalism, Historical Narration, and the Critique of Nationhood in Toni Morrison's *Paradise.*" *African American Review* 35.2 (summer): 233–48.

Defoe, Daniel. [1722]. *Moll Flanders.* Ed. G.A. Starr. World's Classics. Oxford: Oxford UP, 1981.

Denard, Carolyn C., ed. 2008. *Toni Morrison: Conversations.* Jackson: UP of Mississippi.

Douglass, Frederick. [1845]. *Narrative of the Life of Frederick Douglass, an American Slave Written by Himself.* Eds. John W. Blassingame et al. New Haven and London: Yale UP, 1999.

Du Bois, W.E.B. [1899]. *The Philadelphia Negro: A Social Study.* Introduction Elijah Anderson. Philadelphia: U of Pennsylvania P, 1996.

——. [1903]. *The Souls of Black Folk: Authoritative Text, Contexts, Criticism*. Eds. Henry Louis Gates, Jr., Terri Hume Oliver. New York and London: W.W. Norton, 1999.

Duvall, John N. 2000. *The Identifying Fictions of Toni Morrison: Modernist Authenticity and Postmodern Blackness*. New York: Palgrave.

Eliot, T.S. 2003. *The Waste Land and Other Poems*. Ed. Frank Kermode. Penguin Classics. New York: Penguin.

Emberley, Julia V. 1999. "A Historical Transposition: Toni Morrison's *Tar Baby* and Frantz Fanon's Post Enlightenment Phantasms." *Modern Fiction Studies* 45.2 (summer): 403–43.

Equiano, Olaudah. [1789]. *The Interesting Narrative of the Life of Olaudah Equiano, or Gustavus Vassa, the African, Written by Himself*. Ed. Werner Sollors. New York and London: Norton, 2001.

Erickson, Peter B. [1984]. "Images of Nurturance in *Tar Baby*." Gates and Appiah 1993. 293–307.

FitzGerald, Jennifer. [1993]. "Selfhood and Community." Peach 1998. 110–27.

Flint, Holly. 2006. "Toni Morrison's *Paradise*: Black Cultural Citizenship in the American Empire." *American Literature* 78.3 (September): 585–612.

Foucault, Michel. [1971]. "Nietzsche, Genealogy, History." Trans. Donald F. Bouchard and Sherry Simon. *The Foucault Reader*. Ed. Paul Rabinow. Penguin: Harmondsworth, 1984. 76–100.

Franklin, John Hope and Alfred A. Moss, Jr. 2000. *From Slavery to Freedom: A History of African Americans*. 8th edition. Boston: McGraw-Hill.

Fultz, Lucille P. 2003. *Playing with Difference*. Urbana and Chicago: U of Illinois P.

Furman, Jan. 1996. *Toni Morrison's Fiction*. Columbia, SC: U of South Carolina P.

——, ed. 2003a. *Toni Morrison's "Song of Solomon": A Casebook*. New York: Oxford UP.

——. 2003b. Introduction. Furman 2003a. 3–20.

Furst, Lilian R. and Peter N. Skrine. 1971. *Naturalism*. London: Methuen.

Gallego, Mar. 2007. "*Love* and the Survival of the Black Community." Tally 2007a. 92–100.

Gates, Henry Louis, Jr. 1993. Preface. Gates and Appiah 1993. ix–xiii.

Gates, Henry Louis, Jr. and K. A. Appiah, eds. 1993. *Toni Morrison: Critical Perspectives Past and Present*. New York: Amistad.

Gibson, Donald D. 1993. "Text and Countertext in *The Bluest Eye*." Gates and Appiah 1993. 159–74.

Gilroy, Paul. 1993. *The Black Atlantic: Modernity and Double Consciousness*. London: Verso.

Goyal, Yogita. 2006. "The Gender of Diaspora in Toni Morrison's *Tar Baby*." *Modern Fiction Studies* 52.2 (summer): 393–413.

Grewal, Gurleen. 1998. *Circles of Sorrow, Lines of Struggle: The Novels of Toni Morrison*. Baton Rouge: Louisiana State UP.

Guerrero, Ed. [1990]. "Tracking 'The Look' in the Novels of Toni Morrison." Middleton 2000. 27–44.

Harper, Frances Ellen Watkins. [1857]. "The Slave Mother: The Tale of the Ohio." Andrews and McKay 1999. 21–24.

Harris, Trudier. 1991. *Fiction and Folklore: The Novels of Toni Morrison*. Knoxville: U of Tennessee P.

Hawthorne, Nathaniel. [1850]. *The Scarlet Letter*. Ed. Brian Harding. World's Classics. Oxford: Oxford UP, 1990.

Heinze, Denise. 1993. *The Dilemma of "Double-Consciousness": Toni Morrison's Novels*. Athens and London: U of Georgia P.

Henderson, Mae G. [1991]. "Toni Morrison's *Beloved*: Re-membering the Body as Historical Text." Andrews and McKay 1999. 79–106.

Higgins, Therese E. 2001. *Religiosity, Cosmology and Folklore: The African Influence in the Novels of Toni Morrison*. New York; London: Routledge.

Hirsch, Marianne. 1995. "Knowing Their Names: Toni Morrison's *Song of Solomon*." Smith 1995a. 69–92.

Holloway, Karla F.C. and Stephanie A. Demetrakopoulos. 1987. *New Dimensions of Spirituality: A Biracial and Bicultural Reading of the Novels of Toni Morrison*. Westport, Connecticut: Greenwood.

hooks, bell. 1982. *Ain't I a Woman*. London: Pluto.

Horton, James Oliver and Lois E. Horton. 2001. *Hard Road to Freedom: The Story of African America*. New Brunswick: Rutgers UP.

Horvitz, Deborah. [1989]. "Nameless Ghosts: Possession and Dispossession in *Beloved*." Plasa 2000. 59–66.

House, Elizabeth B. 1990. "Toni Morrison's Ghost: The Beloved Who is Not Beloved." *Studies in American Fiction* 18.1 (spring): 17–26.

Irving, John. 1981. "Morrison's Black Fable." *The New York Times* 29 March. http://www.nytimes.com/books/97/06/15/lifetimes/irving-tar.html (last accessed 7 July 2010).

Jacobs, Harriet. [1861]. *Incidents in the Life of a Slave Girl*. New York and Oxford: Oxford UP, 1988.

Jenkins, Candice M. 2009. "Pure Black: Class, Color, and Intraracial Politics in Toni Morrison's *Paradise*." *Modern Fiction Studies* 52.2 (summer): 270–93.

Jennings, La Vinia Delois. 2009. [Untitled] review of *A Mercy*. *Callaloo* 32.2 (spring): 645–49.

Johnson, Barbara. 1993. "'Aesthetic' and 'Rapport' in Toni Morrison's *Sula*." *Textual Practice* 7.2 (summer): 165–72.

Kakutani, Michiko. 2003. "Family Secrets, Feuding Women." *The New York Times* 31 Oct.http://www.nytimes.com/2003/10/31/books/books-of-the-times-family-secrets-feuding- women.html (last accessed 7 July 2010).

——. 2008. "Bonds That Seem Cruel Can Be Kind." *The New York Times* 4 Nov. http://www.nytimes.com/2008/11/04/books/04kaku.html (last accessed 7 July 2010).

Knadler, Stephen. 2004. "Domestic Violence in the Harlem Renaissance: Remaking the Record in Nella Larsen's *Passing* and Toni Morrison's *Jazz*." *African American Review* 38.1 (spring): 99–118.

Kramnick, Isaac, ed. 1995. *The Portable Enlightenment Reader*. New York: Penguin.

Krumholz, Linda. [1992]. "The Ghosts of Slavery: Historical Recovery in Toni Morrison's *Beloved*." Andrews and McKay 1999. 107–25.

——. [1993]. "Dead Teachers: Rituals of Manhood and Rituals of Reading in *Song of Solomon*." Furman 2003a. 201–32.

——. 1996. Review of *Playing in the Dark*. *Signs* 22.1 (autumn): 243–45.

——. 2008. "Blackness and Art in Toni Morrison's *Tar Baby*." *Contemporary Literature* 49.2 (summer): 263–92.

Lee, Catherine Carr. [1998]. "The South in Toni Morrison's *Song of Solomon*: Initiation, Healing, and Home." Furman 2003a. 43–64.

Leitch, Vincent B. et al., eds. 2001. *The Norton Anthology of Theory and Criticism*. New York and London: Norton.

Lewis, Barbara Williams. 2000. "The Function of Jazz in Toni Morrison's *Jazz*." Middleton 2000. 271–81.

Lidinsky, April. [1994]. "Prophesying Bodies: Calling for a Politics of Collectivity in Toni Morrison's *Beloved*." Plasa 2000. 100–04.

Lubiano, Wahneema. 1995. "The Postmodernist Rag: Political Identity and the Vernacular in *Song of Solomon*." Smith 1995a. 93–116.

Lyotard, Jean-François. [1982]. "Answering the Question: What is Postmodernism?" Lyotard. *The Postmodern Condition*. Trans. Geoff Bennington and Brian Massumi. Manchester: Manchester UP, 1986. 71–82.

MacKethan, Lucinda H. [1986]. "Names to Bear Witness: The Theme and Tradition of Naming in Toni Morrison's *Song of Solomon*." Furman 2003a. 185–200.

Magness, Patricia. 1989. "The Knight and the Princess: The Structure of Courtly Love in Toni Morrison's *Tar Baby*." *South Atlantic Review* 54.4 (Nov.): 85–100.

Marks, Kathleen. 2003. *Toni Morrison's* Beloved *and the Apotropaic Imagination*. Columbia and London: U of Missouri P.

Matus, Jill. 1998. *Toni Morrison*. Manchester: Manchester UP.

May, Samuel J. [1856]. "Margaret Garner *and seven others*." Andrews and McKay 1999. 25–36.

Mayberry, Susan Neal. 2007. *Can't I Love What I Criticize?: The Masculine and Morrison*. Athens and London: U of Georgia P.

Mbalia, Doreatha Drummond. 1993. "Women Who Run with Wild: The Need for Sisterhoods in *Jazz*." *Modern Fiction Studies* 39.3 & 4 (fall/winter): 623–46.

Mbalia, Doreatha D. 2004. *Toni Morrison's Developing Class Consciousness*. 2nd edition. Selinsgrove, Pa.: Susquehanna UP; Cranbury, N.J.: Associated UPs.

McDowell, Deborah E. [1988]. "'The Self and the Other': Reading Toni Morrison's *Sula* and the Black Female Text." Bloom 1990a. 149–64.

McKay, Nellie Y. 1999. Introduction. Andrews and McKay 1999. 3–20.

Michael, Magali Cornier. 2002. "Re-Imagining Agency: Toni Morrison's *Paradise*." *African American Review* 36.4 (winter): 643–61.

Middleton, David L., ed. 2000. *Toni Morrison's Fiction: Contemporary Criticism*. New York: Garland.

Middleton, Joyce Irene. 1995. "From Orality to Literacy: Oral Memory in Toni Morrison's *Song of Solomon*." Valerie Smith 1995a. 19–40.

Miller, Laura. 2003. "*Love*: Extreme Emotions and Unthinkable Deeds." *The New York Times* 2 Nov. http://www.nytimes.com/2003/11/02/books/review/02LAURAT. html (last accessed 7 July 2010).

Milton, John. [1674] *Paradise Lost*. Ed. and introduction John Leonard. Penguin Classics. London: Penguin, 2003.

Miner, Madonne M. [1985]. "Lady no Longer Sings the Blues: Rape, Madness, and Silence in *The Bluest Eye*." Bloom 1990a. 85–100.

Mobley, Marilyn Sanders. [1984]. "Narrative Dilemma: Jadine as Cultural Orphan in *Tar Baby*." Gates and Appiah 1993. 284–92.

——. [1990]. "A Different Remembering: Memory, History and Meaning in Toni Morrison's *Beloved*." Plasa 2000. 48–56.

——. 1995. "Call and Response: Voice, Community, and Dialogic Structures in Toni Morrison's *Song of Solomon*." Smith 1995a. 41–68.

Moore, Caroline. 2008. Untitled review of *A Mercy*. *Telegraph* 14 Nov. http://www.telegraph.co.uk/culture/books/fictionreviews/3563259/A-Mercy-by-Toni-Morrison-review.html (last accessed 7 July 2010).

Morrison, Toni. [1970]. *The Bluest Eye*. London: Vintage, 1999.

——. 1971a. Review of *Amistad 2, New African Literature and the Arts* and *The Black Aesthetic*. *The New York Times* 28 Feb. BR5, BR34.

——. 1971b. "What the Black Woman Thinks About Women's Lib" [22 Aug.]. Morrison 2008b. 18–30.

——. 1972. Review of *Who Is Angela Davis? The Biography of a Revolutionary*. By Regina Nadelson. *The New York Times* 29 Oct. BR48. http://select.nytimes.com/gst/abstract.html?res=F5071FF73C59107A93CBAB178B D95F468785F9 (last accessed 7 July 2010).

——. [1973]. *Sula*. London: Picador, 1991.

——. [1974a]. "Rediscovering Black History" [11 Aug.]. Morrison 2008b. 39–55.

——. [1974b]. "Conversation with Alice Childress and Toni Morrison." Taylor-Guthrie 1994. 3–9.

——. [1976a]. "Intimate Things in Place: A Conversation with Toni Morrison." With Robert Stepto. Taylor-Guthrie 1994. 10–29.

——. [1976b]. "A Slow Walk of Trees (as Grandmother Would Say), Hopeless (as Grandfather Would Say)" [4 July]. Morrison 2008b. 3–14.

——. [1977]. *Song of Solomon*. London: Picador, 1989.

——. [1978]. "The Seams Can't Show: An Interview with Toni Morrison." With Jane Bakerman. Taylor-Guthrie 1994. 30–42.

——. [1979]. "The Song of Toni Morrison." With Colette Dowling. Taylor-Guthrie 1994. 48–59.

——. [1980]. "The One Out of Sequence." With Anne Koenen. Taylor-Guthrie 1994. 67–83.

——. [1981a]. *Tar Baby*. London: Picador, 1991.

——. [1981b]. "'The Language Must Not Sweat': A Conversation with Toni Morrison." With Thomas LeClair. Taylor-Guthrie 1994. 119–28.

——. [1981c]. "A Conversation with Toni Morrison." With Judith Wilson. Taylor-Guthrie 1994. 129–37.

——. [1981d]. "Toni Morrison." With Charles Ruas. Taylor-Guthrie 1994. 93–118.

——. [1981e]. "Toni Morrison's Black Magic." With Jean Strouse. *Newsweek* (30 Mar., U.S. Edition). http://www.lexisnexis.com/uk/nexis/results/docview/docview.do?docLinkInd=true&risb=21_T9686131814&format=GNBFI&sort=BOOLEAN&startDocNo=1&resultsUrlKey=29_T9686131818&cisb=22_T9686131817&treeMax=true&treeWidth=0&csi=5774&docNo=2 (last accessed 6 July 2010).

——. [1983a]. "Toni Morrison." With Claudia Tate. Taylor-Guthrie 1994. 156–70.

——. [1983b]. "An Interview with Toni Morrison." With Nellie McKay. Taylor-Guthrie 1994. 138–55.

——. 1984a. "Rootedness: The Ancestor as Foundation." Mari Evans, ed. *Black Women Writers (1950–1980): A Critical Evaluation*. Garden City, N.Y.: Anchor Press/Doubleday. 339–45.

——. 1984b. "Memory, Creation, and Writing." *Thought: A Review of Culture and Ideas* 59 (Dec.): 385–90.

———. [1985a]. "A Conversation: Gloria Naylor and Toni Morrison." Taylor-Guthrie 1994. 188–217.

———. [1985b]. "An Interview with Toni Morrison." With Bessie W. Jones and Audrey Vinson. Taylor-Guthrie 1994. 171–87.l

———. [1986]. "An Interview with Toni Morrison." With Christina Davis. Taylor-Guthrie 1994. 223–33.

———. [1987a]. *Beloved*. London: Picador, 1988.

———. [1987b]. "Author Toni Morrison Discusses Her Latest Novel *Beloved*." With Gail Caldwell. Taylor-Guthrie 1994. 239–45.

———. 1987c. "The Site of Memory." William Zinsser, ed. *Inventing the Truth: The Art and Craft of Memoir*. Boston: Houghton Mifflin. 101–24.

———. [1987d]. "Talk with Toni Morrison." With Elsie B. Washington. Taylor-Guthrie 1994. 234–38.

———. [1988]. "In the Realm of Responsibility: A Conversation with Toni Morrison." With Marsha Darling. Taylor-Guthrie 1994. 246–54.

———. [1989a]. "Unspeakable Things Unspoken: The Afro-American Presence in American Literature." *The Black Feminist Reader*. Eds. Joy James and T. Denean Sharpley-Whiting. Oxford: Blackwell, 2000. 24–56.

———. [1989b]. "The Pain of Being Black: An Interview with Toni Morrison" [22 May]. With Bonnie Angelo. Taylor-Guthrie 1994. 255–61.

———. [1989c]. "A Conversation with Toni Morrison." With Bill Moyers. Taylor-Guthrie 1994. 262–73.

———. [1992a]. *Jazz*. London: Picador, 1993.

———. 1992b. *Playing in the Dark: Whiteness and the Literary Imagination*. Cambridge, Mass.: Harvard UP.

———, ed. [1992c]. *Race-ing Justice, En-gendering Power: Essays on Anita Hill, Clarence Thomas, and the Construction of Social Reality*. London: Chatto & Windus, 1993.

———. 1992d. "Introduction: Friday on the Potomac." Morrison 1992c. vii–xxx.

———. [1993a]. *The Nobel Lecture in Literature, 1993*. Morrison 2008b. 198–207.

———. [1993b]. "The Art of Fiction." With Claudia Brodsky Lacour and Elissa Schappell. Furman 2003a. 233–66.

———. 1997a. *The Dancing Mind: Speech Upon Acceptance of the National Book Foundation Medal for Distinguished Contribution to American Letters on the Sixth of November, Nineteen Hundred and Ninety-Six*. New York: Knopf.

———. 1997b. "The Official Story: Dead Man Golfing." Morrison and Brodsky Lacour 1997. vii–xxviii.

———. 1998a. *Paradise*. London: Chatto & Windus.

———. 1998b. "This Side of Paradise." With James Marcus. Amazon.com. http://www.amazon.com/gp/feature.html?ie=UTF8&docId=7651 (last accessed 7 July 2010).

———. 2003a. *Love*. London: Chatto & Windus.

———. [2003b]. "The Nature of Love: An Interview with Toni Morrison." With Diane McKinney-Whetstone. Denard 2008. 214–15.

———. 2003c. "Toni Morrison: Love at the Last Resort." With John Freeman. *The Independent* 21 Nov. http://www.independent.co.uk/arts-entertainment/books/features/toni-morrison-love-at-the-last-resort-736490.html (last accessed 7 July 2010).

———. [2004]. "'I Want to Write Like a Good Jazz Musician': Interview with Toni Morrison." With Michael Saur. Denard 2008. 224–27.

——. [2005]. "Pam Houston Talks with Toni Morrison." Denard 2008. 228–59.

——. 2008a. *A Mercy*. New York: Knopf.

——. 2008b. *What Moves at the Margin: Selected Nonfiction*. Ed. and introduction Carolyn C. Denard. Jackson, Miss.: UP of Mississippi.

——. 2008c. Letter to Barack Obama. [28 January.] http://www.observer.com/2008/toni-morrisons-letter-barack-obama (last accessed 7 July 2010).

——. 2008d. "Toni Morrison Discusses *A Mercy*." With Lynn Neary. NPR, 29 Oct. http://www.npr.org/templates/story/story.php?storyId=95961382 (last accessed 7 July 2010).

——. 2008e. "Predicting the Past." With Susanna Rustin. *Guardian* 1 Nov. http://www.guardian.co.uk/books/2008/nov/01/toni-morrison (last accessed 7 July 2010).

——. 2008f. "Back Talk: Toni Morrison." With Christine Smallwood. *The Nation* 19 Nov. http://live.thenation.com/doc/20081208/smallwood2 (last accessed 7 July 2010).

——. 2008g. "Toni Morrison on Human Bondage and a Post-Racial Age." With Michel Martin. NPR, 26 Dec. http://www.highbeam.com/doc/1P1–159437350.html (last accessed 7 July 2010).

——. 2009a. "Toni Morrison, Part I." With Michael Silverblatt on Bookworm. KCRW, 22 Jan. http://www.kcrw.com/etc/programs/bw/bw090122toni_morrison_part_i (last accessed 7 July 2010).

——. 2009b. "Toni Morrison, Part II." With Michael Silverblatt on Bookworm. KCRW, 29 Jan. http://www.kcrw.com/etc/programs/bw/bw090129toni_morrison_part_i (last accessed 7 July 2010).

Morrison, Toni and Claudia Brodsky Lacour, eds. 1997. *Birth of a Nation'hood: Gaze, Script, and Spectacle in the O.J. Simpson Case*. London: Vintage.

Nicholls, Peter. [1996]. "The Belated Postmodern: History, Phantoms, and Toni Morrison." Plasa 2000. 134–42.

Nietzsche, Friedrich. [1888]. *Ecce Homo*. Trans. R.J. Hollingdale. London: Penguin, 1992.

O'Reilly, Andrea. 2004. *Toni Morrison and Motherhood*. New York: State U of New York P.

Otten, Terry. 1986. "The Crime of Innocence in Toni Morrison's *Tar Baby*." *Studies in American Fiction* 14.2 (autumn): 153–64.

——. 1989. *The Crime of Innocence in the Fiction of Toni Morrison*. Columbia, Missouri: U of Missouri P.

Page, Philip. 1995. *Dangerous Freedom: Fusion and Fragmentation in Toni Morrison's Novels*. Jackson: UP of Mississippi.

——. 2001. "Furrowing All the Brows: Interpretation and the Transcendent in Toni Morrison's *Paradise*." *African American Review* 35.4 (winter): 637–51.

Paine, Thomas. 1995. *Rights of Man, Common Sense and Other Political Writings*. Ed. Mark Philp. World's Classics. Oxford: Oxford UP.

Pater, Walter. [1873]. *The Renaissance: Studies in Art and Poetry*. Oxford, Oxford UP, 1986.

Peach, Linden, ed. 1998. *Toni Morrison: Contemporary Critical Essays*. Basingstoke and London: Macmillan.

——. 2000. *Toni Morrison*. 2nd edition. Houndmills and London: Macmillan.

Pérez-Torres, Rafael. 1999. "Between Presence and Absence: *Beloved*, Postmodernism, and Blackness." Andrews and McKay 1999. 179–201.

Peterson, Nancy J. 1997. *Toni Morrison: Critical and Theoretical Approaches*. Baltimore: Johns Hopkins UP.

Plato. 1998. *Republic*. Trans. Robin Waterfield. World's Classics. Oxford: Oxford UP.

Plasa, Carl, ed. 2000. *Toni Morrison*: Beloved. *A Reader's Guide to Essential Criticism*. Cambridge: Icon.

Propp, Vladimir. 1968. *Morphology of the Folktale*. Trans. Lawrence Scott, revised by Louis A. Wagner. Revised (second) edition. Austin: U of Texas P.

Robinson, Frederick D. 1992. Review of *Playing in the Dark*. *Black Enterprise* (Oct.): 14.

Rodrigues, Eusebio. [1993]. "Experiencing *Jazz*." Peach 1998. 154–69.

Roynon, Tessa. 2007. "A New 'Romen' Empire: Toni Morrison's *Love* and the Classics." *Journal of American Studies* 41.1 (spring): 31–47.

Rushdy, Ashraf H.A. [1992]. "Daughters Signifyin(g) History: The Example of Toni Morrison's *Beloved*." Andrews and McKay 1999. 37–66.

Ryan, Judylyn S. 1993. "Contested Visions/Double-Vision in *Tar Baby*." *Modern Fiction Studies* 39.3/4 (fall/winter): 597–621.

Said, Edward W. [1978]. *Orientalism*. London: Penguin, 2003.

——. 1993. *Culture and Imperialism*. London: Chatto & Windus.

Sale, Maggie. 1992. "Call and Response as Critical Method: African-American Oral Traditions and *Beloved*." *African American Review* 26.1 (spring): 41–50.

Savannah Unit, Georgia Writers' Project. 1940. *Drums and Shadows: Survival Studies Among the Georgia Coastal Negroes*. Athens: U of Georgia P.

Scheiber, Andrew. 2006. "*Jazz* and the Future Blues: Toni Morrison's Urban Folk Zone." *Modern Fiction Studies* 52.2 (summer): 470–94.

Scott, Joyce Hope. 2007. "*Song of Solomon* and *Tar Baby*: The Subversive Role of Language and the Carnivalesque." Tally 2007a. 26–42.

Shklovsky, Victor. 1998. "Art as Technique." *Literary Theory: An Anthology*. Rev. edition. Ed. Julie Rivkin and Michael Ryan. Oxford: Blackwell. 17–23.

Showalter, Elaine. 2003. "A Tangled Web." *Guardian* 29 Nov. http://www.guardian.co.uk/books/2003/nov/29/fiction.tonimorrison (last accessed 7 July 2010).

Sitter, Deborah Ayer. 1992. "The Making of a Man: Dialogic Meaning in *Beloved*." *African American Review* 26.1 (spring): 17–29.

Smith, Barbara. [1977]. "Toward a Black Feminist Criticism." Leitch 2001. 2302–15.

Smith, Valerie. [1985]. "*Song of Solomon*: Continuities of Community." Gates and Appiah 1993. 274–83.

——, ed. 1995a. *New Essays on Song of Solomon*. Cambridge and New York: Cambridge UP.

——. 1995b. Introduction. Smith 1995a. 1–18.

Spillers, Hortense J. [1983]. "A Hateful Passion, a Lost Love." Gates and Appiah 1993. 210–35.

——. [1987]. "Mama's Baby, Papa's Maybe: An American Grammar Book." *Literary Theory: An Anthology*. Rev. edition. Ed. Julie Rivkin and Michael Ryan. Oxford: Blackwell, 1998. 656–72.

Stave, Shirley A., ed. 2006a. *Toni Morrison and the Bible: Contested Intertextualities*. New York and Oxford: Peter Lang.

——. 2006b. "The Master's Tools: Morrison's *Paradise* and the Problem of Christianity." Stave 2006a. 215–30.

——. 2007. "*Jazz* and *Paradise*: Pivotal Moments in Black History." Tally 2007a. 59–74.

Stuart, Andrew. 2008. "*A Mercy*, By Toni Morrison." *The Independent* 7 Nov. http:// www.independent.co.uk/arts-entertainment/books/reviews/a-mercy-by-toni-morrison-997070. html (last accessed 7 July 2010).

Sumana, K. 1998. *The Novels of Toni Morrison: A Study in Race, Gender and Class*. London: Sangam.

Sweeney, Megan. 2006. "'Something Rogue': Commensurability, Commodification, Crime, and Justice in Toni Morrison's Later Fiction." *Modern Fiction Studies* 52.2 (summer): 440–69.

Tally, Justine. 1999. *Toni Morrison's (Hi)stories and Truths*. Hamburg: LIT.

——, ed. 2007a. *The Cambridge Companion to Toni Morrison*. Cambridge: Cambridge UP.

——. 2007b. "The Morrison Trilogy." Tally 2007a. 75–91.

——. 2009. *Toni Morrison's* Beloved: *Origins*. New York and Abingdon, Oxon: Routledge.

Taylor-Guthrie, Danille, ed. 1994. *Conversations with Toni Morrison*. Jackson, MS: UP of Mississippi.

Terry, Jennifer. 2006. "A New World Religion? Creolization and Candomblé in Toni Morrison's *Paradise*." Stave 2006a. 192–230.

Tirrell, Lynne. [1990]. "Storytelling and Moral Agency." Middleton 2000. 3–26.

Truth, Sojourner. [1850]. *Narrative of Sojourner Truth*. http://digital.library.upenn. edu/women/truth/1850/1850.html (last accessed 7 July 2010).

Turner-Sadler, Joanne. 2006. *African American History: An Introduction*. New York: Peter Lang.

Updike, John. 2008. "Dreamy Wilderness." *The New Yorker* 3 Nov. http://www.new yorker.com/arts/critics/books/2008/11/03/081103crbo_books_updike (last accessed 7 July 2010).

Walker, Alice. 1982. "If the Present Looks Like the Past, What Does the Future Look Like?" Walker. *In Search of Our Mothers' Gardens*. London: Phoenix, 2005. 290–312.

Wallinger, Hanna. 2007. "Toni Morrison's Literary Criticism." Tally 2007a. 115–24.

Walpole, Horace. [1764]. *The Castle of Otranto*. Ed. Michael Gamer. London: Penguin, 2001.

Wardi, Anissa Janine. 2005. "A Laying on of Hands: Toni Morrison and the Materiality of *Love*." *MELUS* 30.3 (fall): 201–18.

Wegs, Joyce M. [1982]. "Toni Morrison's *Song of Solomon*: A Blues Song." Furman 2003a. 165–84.

Whitman, Walt. [1855]. *Leaves of Grass. The First (1855) Edition*. Ed. Malcolm Cowley. Penguin Classics. New York: Penguin, 1986.

Widdowson, Peter. 2001. "The American Dream Refashioned: History, Politics and Gender in Toni Morrison's *Paradise*." *Journal of American Studies* 35.2 (summer): 313–35.

Wilde, Oscar. 1891. "The Critic as Artist: With Some Remarks upon the Importance of Doing Nothing." Ed. and introduction Richard Ellmann. *Oscar Wilde: Selected Writings*. Oxford: Oxford UP, 1961.

Wilentz, Gay. [1992]. "Civilizations Underneath: African Heritage as Cultural Discourse in Toni Morrison's *Song of Solomon*." Furman 2003a. 137–64.

Williams, Tennessee. 1970. *Five Plays*. London: Secker & Warburg.

Woolf, Virginia. 2004. *A Room of One's Own*. London: Penguin.

Wordsworth, William. [1802]. Preface to *Lyrical Ballads*. Leitch 2001. 648–68.

Wyatt, Jean. 1993. "Giving Body to the Word: The Maternal Symbolic in Toni Morrison's *Beloved*." *PMLA* 108.3 (May): 474–88.

——. 2008. "*Love*'s Time and the Reader: Ethical Effects of *Nachträglichkeit* in Toni Morrison's *Love*." *Narrative* 16.2 (May): 193–21.

Index

(TM) indicates work by Toni Morrison